Context-based Modeling of Activity in Real-World Projects

Context-based Modeling of Activity in Real-World Projects

Patrick Brézillon

iSTE

WILEY

First published 2026 in Great Britain and the United States by ISTE Ltd and John Wiley & Sons, Inc.

ISTE Ltd
27-37 St George's Road
London SW19 4EU
UK

www.iste.co.uk

John Wiley & Sons, Inc.
111 River Street
Hoboken, NJ 07030
USA

www.wiley.com

British Library Cataloguing-in-Publication Data
A CIP record for this book is available from the British Library
ISBN 978-1-83669-095-5

The manufacturer's authorized representative according to the EU General Product Safety Regulation is Wiley-VCH GmbH, Boschstr. 12, 69469 Weinheim, Germany, e-mail: Product_Safety@wiley.com.

Contents

Preface ix

Acronyms xiii

Introduction xv

Chapter 1. Theoretical and Pragmatic Basis of Our Context Modeling 1

1.1. Introduction 1
1.2. Theoretical basis 2
1.2.1. Model and representation 2
1.2.2. Concepts used 11
1.2.3. The proposed scientific approach 22
1.3. Projects and applications 28
1.3.1. Introduction 28
1.3.2. The SEPT project (1986–1995) 29
1.3.3. The SART project (1996–2002) 31
1.3.4. The FlexMIm project (2012–2015) 34
1.3.5. The TACTIC project (2013–2015) 35
1.3.6. The ACA project (2005–2009) 38
1.3.7. "Contextualizing scientific workflows" project (2009–2011) 40
1.3.8. The MICO project (2011–2014) 43
1.3.9. The winemaking project (1997–1999) 44
1.3.10. The OSSMOSE project (2009–2011) 46
1.3.11. "Computer-mediated collaborative work" project (1997–1999) 48
1.4. Review of the chapter 50

Chapter 2. Context Modeling for Actor Activity (CxG_1.0) 53

2.1. Introduction 53
2.2. Conceptual level 55
2.2.1. Contextual knowledge and external knowledge 55
2.2.2. Conceptual elements used in the research 57
2.3. Operational level 63
2.3.1. Operational knowledge and context 63
2.3.2. Contextual elements 68
2.3.3. Mental models and mental representations 69
2.4. Implementation level 71
2.4.1. The CxG_1.0 formalism 71
2.4.2. Modeling tools 72
2.4.3. Exploitation tools 79
2.4.4. Review on the CxG_1.0 formalism 88
2.5. Environment level 89
2.6. Variants of the context modeling 91
2.6.1. Introduction 91
2.6.2. The COM 92
2.6.3. Parallel with BPEL for workflows 95
2.6.4. Comparison with two other context-based formalisms 98
2.7. Review of the chapter 103

Chapter 3. Context Modeling for Group Activity (CxG_2.0) 109

3.1. Introduction 109
3.2. Conceptual level 110
3.2.1. Introduction 110
3.2.2. Concept of activity for a group 111
3.2.3. The shared context 113
3.2.4. The turn 117
3.2.5. CxG-based simulation 118
3.3. Operational level 121
3.3.1. Introduction 121
3.3.2. The notions of group activity and interaction 121
3.3.3. The CxG_2.0 formalism 123
3.4. Implementation level 124
3.4.1. Introduction 124
3.4.2. From actor activity to group activity 124
3.4.3. Reserved contextual elements 125
3.4.4. Mechanisms of the CxG-based simulation 128
3.5. Environment level 136

3.6. Two examples 137
3.6.1. "Submission management" example 137
3.6.2. The TACTIC project 146
3.7. Review of the chapter 152

Chapter 4. The Two Versions of the CxG Formalism 157

4.1. Introduction 157
4.2. The key points of the research 158
4.2.1. Discussion on key concepts of the approach 158
4.2.2. Definition of the context of an activity 166
4.2.3. Contextual reasoning 167
4.2.4. Global and local contexts. 175
4.3. The "Internship-offer analysis" example 186
4.3.1. The actors 186
4.3.2. Conditions of the experiment 187
4.3.3. Development of the experiment 188
4.3.4. Interpretation of the results. 192
4.3.5. Comparison with the "DVD-reader diagnosis" task 199
4.4. CxG formalism for CIAS Design. 204
4.5. Review of the chapter 214

Chapter 5. Use of the CxG Formalism in Different Modeling 221

5.1. Introduction 221
5.2. Breast cancer diagnosis 223
5.3. Hierarchical task analysis (HTA). 229
5.4. The ACA project. 237
5.4.1. Introduction 237
5.4.2. The ACA method 237
5.4.3. Application in road safety 240
5.5. Workflow modeling in an ACP Department 249
5.5.1. The initial work 249
5.5.2. Contextual modeling of the workflow 252
5.5.3. Discussion on context-based modeling of workflow. 257
5.6. Context modeling and semiotics 258
5.7. Review of the chapter 266

Conclusion 271

References. 285

Index. 297

Preface

Everyone knows the word "context", hears it several times a day, and uses it for making decisions from the choice of a drink to rent for vacations or to move from one place to another. Context is an intrinsic part of our life, objectives, reasoning and actions, of the situation we are in and the local environment where we require resources. We are so steeped in this notion that context seems obvious to us, and we leave it implicit. However, everyone uses a personal definition of what context is, and even different definitions from one day to the next. We all have different (eventually contradictory) views on context. This situation mostly comes from the lack of operational use of context, except in a few domains like Natural Language Processing.

During our research on modeling context, we collected 271 definitions. It is a weakness for communication, especially interdisciplinary communication. The collection of definitions comes from approximately 30 domains. We organized a series of biannual international and interdisciplinary conferences on modeling and using context from CONTEXT-97 (Rio de Janeiro, Brazil) to CONTEXT-19 (Trento, Italy) for an interdisciplinary community of researchers wishing to share their views on context in order to develop a unified definition of context.

The research, which was led using AI on a wide range of applications, was beneficial for attacking modeling and the use of context because each application only puts an emphasis on some specific aspects of context, but results of the context modeling in a particular application may be directly applicable in other applications, often leading to highlighting in these applications some aspects of the domain initially not considered. At a more conceptual level, this research on context modeling intersects with most theoretical approaches to contextual reasoning, decision making, diagnosis and problem-solving and also cognitive approaches such as activity, mental models and mental representations that do not always arrive at an operational expression. For example, in decision-making, the result is not the most important aspect, rather it is the process leading to this result, a process that is context-dependent.

This book presents the sum of 25 years of research on modeling, and using context in real-world applications, these applications coming from a very large spectrum of domains, such as Power Systems, Control and Command Systems, Psychology and Medicine. Ten of these applications are presented in this book for illustrating the aspects of context that are put center stage. Our approach covers conceptual, operational and implementation aspects as far as a software is implemented and used in all the applications presented (except the first application for Electricité de France, which served as a trigger initiating this research). Thus, the research was not limited to a sketch of what a model of context could be but to an operational and implemented model.

The research presents several original findings. Clearly, one cannot speak of context in an abstract way. This point explains the excessive number of definitions of context: most of these definitions are given without concern about real-world applications. The givers of definitions consider that it is sufficient to have a definition, even though the definition has nothing to do with the subject of their paper (like a justification for their claims). However, context cannot be modeled disconnected from the actors' focus of attention, the activity, the situation in which the actor has to accomplish the activity, and the environment where the required means for that are. This does not mean that a model of context is specific to each application.

Indeed, context is understood through its relationships with knowledge and reasoning in real-world applications; that is, context, knowledge and reasoning must be modeled in a uniform representation formalism based on a bottom-up approach. It is fascinating to see that the resulting pieces of software, the Contextual-Graphs (CxG) formalism, rely on a handful of items, which makes the software very easy to use (training of 15 min) by students in domains far from computer science and AI (e.g. psychology, medicine, lawyer). The 25 key points of the research identified throughout the presentation are summarized and discussed for a coherent view of the research as a whole. These key milestones rely on the framework with four levels for modeling an activity with the CxG formalism.

The second successful challenge is the extension of the CxG formalism from one actor realizing a task to a group of actors realizing an activity. The transition from one actor to N actors necessitates considering the mental representation of one actor (based on mental models) in a group mental representation (based on independent subtasks of actors). The solution proposed is the modeling of actors' activities in the group activity in terms of independent subtasks. Thus, group-activity development could be represented as the assembling of a sequence of subtask execution, that is, a dynamic building of a group mental model from the mental representation constituted of independent subtasks of the actors. The evolution from a task realization (for one actor) to an activity (for N actors) is possible with the building of a shared context during group activity development to represent the exchanges of contextual information between actors developing the activity. In a kind of reverse engineering, the notion of activity has been used as a unifying concept in all the books.

Such an evolution of the conceptual approach is not a bifurcation point because – as a return on investment – the actor's activity has benefited from a deep change in its modeling from an internal viewpoint (the task model) to an external viewpoint (a set of independent subtasks) in the group activity. This change at the conceptual level has left the CxG formalism unchanged on the implementation aspect. However, this transition enriches the modeling of the task realization/activity by making context management explicit in group-activity development, leading to deep simplifications in the modeling of artificial or living systems because the resulting framework covers the strong connections between context and group activity. At the conceptual level, context is a general, non-formalized concept, that is organized and structured at the operational level and is fully implemented for confrontation with the real world at the environment level where the application is. The concept of contextual element shows how a fuzzy concept like "contextual knowledge" becomes formally "pairs of contextual and recombination nodes". The CxG formalism has a version CxG_1.0 for actor activity and a version CxG_2.0 for group activity of the CxG software.

The CxG formalism allows context-based modeling of activity in AI systems that rely on human-experience bases represented by contextual graphs. The bottom-up approach does not lead to discovery as deep learning, but a possibility would be to use the sum of the bases of experiences developed for different activities in a domain as a support for a *glocal* (global and local) learning in the domain that, indeed, would be a context-based learning. Some elements are identified in the book for designing and implementing context-based intelligent assistant systems. Beyond applications used during the modeling and use of context, the CxG software (and thus, all our research) has been validated by other researchers on their applications, either using context at least implicitly or not while clearly it was possible. Our validation concerned applications in breast cancer diagnosis, Hierarchical Task Analysis, self-evaluation of drivers, and a context-based workflow in an ACP Department and in semiotics.

Last but not least is my expression of gratitude to the numerous people (about 150) that participated in this successful adventure. In particular I would like to thank two special people, Juliette and Céline, who have been enthusiastic and active supporters with their participation in the organization of two CONTEXT conferences, on the use of the CxG formalism, one in their Master's dissertation (for modeling the revocation of the Edict of Nantes as a contextual graph) and the other in their PhD thesis (see the ACA project for a context-based intelligent tutorial system for the self-evaluation of drivers' behavior). Finally, I consider this book, paradoxically, as a new starting point from which this exciting adventure may be continued. I hope to collaborate with researchers in order to transmit this research to the community interested in the modeling and use of context and particularly the CxG software.

Patrick BRÉZILLON
Paris, France
November 2025

Acronyms

The list does not contain acronyms corresponding to applications used in this document, those acronyms only having local interest and definition.

ACA	Adequate Category Learning
ACP	Anatomical and Cytology Pathology
AI	Artificial Intelligence
BPEL	Business Process Execution Language
CBR	Case-Based Reasoning
CDR	Contextualization-Decontextualization-Recontextualization
CIAS	Context-based Intelligent Assistant System
CMB	Context-Mediated Behavior
COM	Context Oriented Model
CxBR	Context Based Reasoning
CxG	Contextual Graphs
CxG_1.0 version	Version for an activity realized by a unique actor
CxG_2.0 version	Version for an activity realized by a group of actors

DES	Discrete-Event Simulation
EHV	Extra High Voltage
ESIA	Executive Structure of Independent Activities
FlexMIm	French acronym for "Platform for processing and sharing medical images in a cloud environment"
GADGET	Guarding Automobile Drivers through Guidance Education and Technology
GNU	"*GNU's Not UNIX*"
HTA	Hierarchical Task Analysis
IBD	Inflammatory Bowel Disease
KBS	Knowledge-Based System
ODE	Ordinary Differential Equations
OSSMOSE	Open Source Software for Medium Organization Enterprises
SART	French acronym for support systems of traffic regulation
SEPT	French acronym for Monitoring of equipment in extra high voltage substation
SWF	Scientific Workflow
TACTIC	French acronym for "Contextualized support on a tablet for the transmission of command information"
XML	eXtensible Markup Language

Introduction

This book is a summary of 25 years of research on the modeling of context and its use in about 20 real-world projects and applications[1]. The topic "Modeling and using context" is found in a number of disciplines either directly (i.e. as context) or indirectly (i.e. such as situations, constraints, etc.), but we do not present a thorough study of the literature in all the disciplines. Most of the references cited in this book come from Artificial Intelligence (AI) and Computer Science, and from some related disciplines. We made (and continue) a collection of definitions of context (271 in 2024 found in about 30 different domains). The success of our research comes from the challenges arising from the "real-world" projects and applications upon which we have worked and that obliged us to avoid arbitrary simplification. In this book, we present 10 of these projects and applications that have been selected to show that our modeling and use of context cover conceptual aspects, operational aspects and implementation aspects, thanks to the role of environment inactivity modeling being made explicit.

The research was led using AI, from the modeling of task realization, decision-making and problem-solving that we consider now as "activity" to the operational concepts "mental model" and "mental representation" coming from Cognitive Sciences. There are two reasons developed hereafter. First, the activity performed by an actor is closer to the actor's experience than the "focus of attention" that only concerns the current point of the activity development. Second, the activity is larger than the realization of a task by including other elements such as the actor and the environment, far from a task model itself.

1. The list of the publications (and PDFs for most of them) for most of the projects and applications (including the software) can be obtained from the author (Facebook, LinkedIn, email).

Our interest in developing an AI system in decision-making led us first to establish an operational definition of context and then design and implement a model of context in concrete terms for actors with whom we collaborated in very different domains. The research presented in this book has been the object of numerous papers published in different journals, reviews and conferences; thus, we will not enter into all the details of the results obtained. We limit here the research presentation to what is necessary for a coherent view of the research progression on modeling and use of context and the main lessons learned in our research. Our objective is to propose a formalization for approaching the fuzzy concept of "context" from an AI viewpoint – as was done with the concepts of mass, length, speed, etc. in Physics and Biology – for modeling how an actor and a group of actors have an activity in real-world projects or applications. Modeling context for a given activity is supposed to clearly establish its close relationships with human knowledge and reasoning such as in real-world applications. The midterm goal of our context modeling is to establish a pragmatic approach to design, develop and implement context-based AI systems that rely on operational knowledge used by humans in relationships with their activities. Making context explicit makes it possible to use human experience that encompasses the nature of the task, the situation in which the activity must be accomplished, and the available means within the environment that are necessary for that. Human, task, situation and environment are strongly intertwined, and context emerges as the expression of the whole.

A preliminary step for modeling the concept of "context" is to clarify the starting point of our research and provide the readers, before starting the first chapter, with a shared context for the benefit of the lessons learned and provided in this book. We thus want to begin by giving our understanding of different common questions about context such as What is context? Which definition of context? And why do we need context?

To become informed about a topic we generally use a search engine. The first observation is that the information provided depends on the search engine. In 1996, we found about 1,000 links by Yahoo! and 650,000 by Google (Brézillon 1999). Our annual count of the number of webpages containing the word "context" showed an exponential increase over 10 years from 650,000 in 1996 to 325,000,000 webpages in 2006 (after 2006, Google filtered unused webpages). About 90% of the pages were not relevant for our purpose of modeling context (e.g. containing ". . . in this context, we think that . . ."). Nevertheless, the number of relevant pages increased by 500 during this interval of 10 years. In 1999, we made an interdisciplinary survey of the literature (e.g. for our collection of 271 definitions), but it rapidly became clear that such a survey was only possible at the level of each discipline. The situation was aggravated by the move of bibliographic references from printed paper to digital ones. The consequence was that references had to "be on the Web or they do not exist" in most of the disciplines, and the corollary is a lack of accessibility to old papers judged as "THE" references in some disciplines (especially books). With respect to our research, the bibliography we made is mainly on what was accessible on the Web (and updated frequently) and not on what is only printed paper, especially in other disciplines.

The second important point was finally to ask for the definition given by each author because one discovers that each definition was (almost systematically) criticized for its lack of generality. A look at our collection of definitions shows the accuracy of this criticism. One surprise was to discover that the notion of context plays a role in a number of very different disciplines, although this role may be an excuse to simplify discipline problems. For example, three definitions are: in AI, "a context is a *collection of relevant conditions* and surrounding influences that make a situation unique and comprehensible"; in philosophy, context is "a *body of information* available to participants in the speech situation"; in economy, context is compared to "the *fibers of a rope* for describing the conditions of a system." The italics words in the definitions correspond to the actor's focus of attention that is concerned by the context in the definition. Some immediate observations can be made: (1) there seem to exist as many definitions as authors (and sometimes several definitions per author), (2) few definitions make it possible to formalize context to make it operational, (3) definitions are given in terms of the discipline (i.e. highly contextualized) and (4) even if definitions are "author-dependent", some generic features emerge, linking context to activity.

The third challenge is to address the need for context that appears as soon as humans and their activities intervene (Why do we need context?). We consider activities with an operational purpose (especially modeling and simulation). When humans realize a task, make a decision, solve a problem in the real world, they adapt methods, tools, etc., during the process for integrating the constraints of the task, the situation, the environment and also their preferences, emotions, etc., that is context. Our question then is how an AI system can effectively use context for exploiting the human's knowledge and reasoning put into the machine without enumerating all the contextual variants. This supposes, on the one hand, a coherent view on knowledge, reasoning and context in a uniform representation, and, on the other hand, an efficient software for modeling human focus of attention in context. In all our projects and applications for large (and small) enterprises, the human that we considered is an actor that faces an activity.

The book addresses the previous questions in five chapters covering all the aspects of modeling and use context in real-world projects and applications. Note that the important points of our research from Chapter 2 to Chapter 3 are called "key points" (KPs) in the text and are summed up and discussed in Chapter 4.

Chapter 1 presents the scientific foundation of our research based on the distinction between model and representation in mathematics and the concepts of interest such as activity, mental model and mental representation. Section 1.2 is dedicated to our scientific approach, and the framework with its four modeling levels, which is used for activity modeling. Section 1.3 introduces the main real-world projects and applications that rely on these 25 years of research in a large spectrum of domains.

A model is an abstraction of the reality that is used in a large number of disciplines. A model can be formalized in numerous formalisms of representation. If you do not have the right representation formalism for what you are looking for, you may miss some relevant observations in reality and/or obtain a model that is not relevant for testing your assumptions about reality. We illustrate the situation with two examples: the autocatalytic model in Biochemistry and a formal model of the calcium metabolism in Physiology. In these disciplines, a mathematician and a biologist interacted on a given model in two different representation formalisms, ordinary differential equations for the mathematician and a compartmental formalism for the biologist. This is the origin of our four modeling levels.

The role played by context has been identified by leading an approach as scientific as possible, such as in Biology for modeling calcium metabolism (Brézillon 1983). In brief, the idea is to identify the concepts of interest for activity modeling, that are refined and organized in a mental model that the actor has in mind when accomplishing the activity. The next step is to find an efficient implementation of the mental model confronting it with the observable phenomena that happens in the environment of the activity.

The spectrum of domains concerned by our research is large, from formal to less formal. The retained projects aim to illustrate the aspects of context put center stage in the projects: SEPT (1986–1995), SART (1996–2002), FlexMIm (2012–2015), TACTIC (2013–2015), ACA (2005–2009), "Contextualizing scientific workflows" (2009–2011), MICO (2011–2014), "Prediction of the stuck of wine fermentations" (1997–1999), the OSSMOSE project (2009–2011) and the project "Computer-mediated collaborative work" (1997–1999). The 10 projects and applications are introduced in a unique frame of presentation in three parts: domain overview, contribution to the project (or application) and lessons learned for our research on context modeling and use. Additional information is given in the following chapters.

The SEPT project highlighted that context modeling cannot be replaced by ad hoc tools or artifacts. The SEPT expert system was designed from technical reports corresponding to a "theoretical model", and it appeared rapidly that a knowledge configurator was mandatory to play the role of a "contextualizator". The SART project (for the subway company in Paris) was the beginning of modeling context bridging a conceptual framework, an operational framework and an implementation framework, the latter containing the CxG_1.0 version of the Contextual-Graphs formalism. Procedures and practices show how context intervenes in reasoning. The FlexMim project in Medicine was the opportunity to develop new concepts in group activity like a voting system for representing reasoning in a domain where science is more of an art than a science: experts generally reach the same conclusion by different interpretations of criteria or different combinations of criteria for diagnosing and glocalization for identifying cancer by first looking for global zones of interest on a slide and zooming-in on "spots" at the cell level for a local search. The TACTIC project was the opportunity to study the interaction of an operator, a simulator (cognitive interaction) and an interface (physical interaction). The consideration of the simulator with a similar status to the operator leads to the modeling of group activity in the CxG_2.0 version of the CxG formalism. In the ACA project, an experience base corresponds to all drivers' practices developed for situation solving in different contexts. An experience base includes good and bad practices executed by novices, bad drivers or drivers under drug influence. Driver's context awareness is sensible to any change of instantiation of contextual elements. Thus, actors' behavior can be studied and compared by simulation of their activities to determine, say, those that develop safe or risky practices (and also for statistics). The objective of Scientific-Workflows (SWFs) is to use context for obtaining flexible SWFs. The use of the Contextualization–Decontextualization–Recontextualization (CDR) approach leads to the identification of the SWF model (decontextualization) and specifies how the SWF model is instantiated (recontextualization). It allowed the scientist's activity to be extended in a contextual graph that guides the scientist in search of a variant of the initial SWF to solve their specific problem. The MICO project highlighted the interest of the tree representation that offers a "cognitive measure" of the diagnosis. More precisely, a mental tree representation offers fast decision-making by identifying mental models as context and situations are presented. Tree representation is an important component of the CxG formalism. The "Wine making" project is based on the onion metaphor for a temporal ordering of contextual elements around a focus. The alcoholic fermentation, being too complex for modeling, is considered a black box by enologists, but a relevant contextual element that can be found far from the focus of attention. The OSSMOSE project concerns the design and configuration of a contextualized platform for a given enterprise, taking into account the advice of the actors, the consultant and the customer, who have different expertise on tools to assemble on the platform. The customer's expertise concerns the selection and configuration of tools to assemble on the contextualized platform to be used. Consultant's expertise concerns experience base development and the way to assemble tools. The "Collaborative work" project shows the role of context in the cooperative building of an answer to a given question. Participants first gather contextual information for establishing the shared context and second for building the proceduralized context and preparing the answer.

Chapter 2 shows the initial concepts retained and those used for context modeling in actor activity to reach an operational implementation of the context-based representation formalism in CxG_1.0 version. Context modeling is presented in the framework with four levels, namely conceptual, operational, implementation and environment levels, as presented in Chapter 1.

The conceptual aspects concern the relationships of context with knowledge and reasoning. The notion of "contextual element" gives practical consistency to the concept of "context" as being constituted of objective elements (but possible subjective instantiations of them). Upstream, activity allows for the discrimination of context into contextual knowledge and external knowledge. Downstream, the activity concerns a specific actor that realizes a task in a given situation with the available resources of the local environment.

The selected concepts at the conceptual level are transposed in terms of the mental model at the operational level, showing the coherence between operational knowledge (knowledge effectively used in reasoning) and contextual knowledge in the framework of the CxG formalism (related to the activity) that leads to the importance of contextual reasoning. The implementation level helps to design and develop a contextual graph as a piece of software expressing mental models in projects and applications. The CxG-1.0 version of the CxG formalism is based on four functions but allows the representation of complex models by the combination and recursivity of the functions. In section 2.6, variants of the context modeling proposed here are presented, such as the context-oriented model attempting a programming approach, a parallel with BPEL used for workflow development, and a comparison with the two other context-based formalisms, CBR and CXBR.

Chapter 3 presents the first extension of the results presented in Chapter 2 for adapting the context-based modeling of an actor to an implementation for group activity. The presentation of four-modeling levels (conceptual, operational, implementation and environment) is used in the spirit of the previous chapter. The extensions include the notion of group activity and new notions such as independent subtasks, shared context, turn, CxG-based simulation and the CxG_2.0 version of the CxG formalism. Otherwise, the changes required for modeling, implementing and using context are an accommodation of the context-based modeling levels leading to the CxG representation formalism. Shared context is associated with group-activity development by elaboration from contextual elements of individual working contexts. Group activity is an assembling of independent subtasks realized by different actors. Reserved contextual elements make it possible to represent role and subtask management in a group activity. The notion of turn is introduced naturally as the realization of a subtask by a given actor by crossing the contextual graph and also includes the management of the turn transition and of the next actor (and its subtask). The CxG-based simulation of a sequence of turns requires a cyclic use of the contextual graph as long as the shared context is modified during the turn. The tree view of mental models is an alternative to the contextual graph to get directly to the decision to be made. Three examples chosen in our projects and applications illustrate the mechanisms implemented.

Chapter 4 presents the CxG_1.0 and CxG_2.0 versions of the CxG formalism. Section 4.2 discusses the KPs identified in Chapters 2 and 3, and a new definition (a dynamic one) of context. The role of contextual reasoning is naturally linked to activity accomplishment. An activity is considered on two levels, the operational level with the mental representation and mental-model development and the implementation level with the instantiation of the contextual elements and the deduction of the proceduralized context. Section 4.3, considers the findings of the "Internship-offer analysis" application. The mission was to model the activity as a contextual graph in the CxG_1.0 version; students had the same objective but personal goals. The same activity was later modeled in the CxG_2.0 version. The results are contrasted with those obtained on the modeling of "DVD-reader diagnosis" activity (also modeled by students). The explicit consideration of context in the modeling of an activity as a contextual graph leads to context-based intelligent assistant systems (CIASs) for reuse and an extension of the human experience in the spirit of Generative AI. CxG formalism provides powerful experience bases that can be served as a basis for deep learning in order to complete the known practices.

Chapter 5 presents a discussion on the use of the CxG formalism in five relatively experimental real-world applications where context was implicitly considered, namely breast cancer diagnosis, hierarchical task analysis (HTA), context-based training system for car drivers, workflow modeling in ACP Department and semiotics. The first example concerns a high-level summary about all that was known in the 1990s about breast cancer diagnosis. A context-based model is proposed in the CxG_1.0 formalism. The second example concerns HTA for conducting a task analysis. The idea was to breakdown the overall goal into the next level of subgoals triggered under plans introduced for a flexible approach. Experience was a complex combination of (contextual) elements for flexibility in plans. "Plans", initially judged as comments, become integrated into activities and their nesting. The third example presents the ACA (Adequate Category Learning) project, which concerns the long-term objective to improve bad drivers' abilities to detect a pre-critical situation and assess the potential risk of having an accident. The fourth example presents a contextualization of the Anatomical and Cytology Pathology (ACP) workflow for analyzing non-conformity during the reception and registration steps of the department. Non-conformity may be prejudicial to the patient. The semiotic approach concerned the transfer of the Walt Disney Company made at internationalization with the same international strategy. We revisited this study in terms of context-based approaches of the sociocultural environments of the source (USA) and the targets (Japan and France) and finally replaced this study in the CDR paradigm. A parallel is drawn between the concepts of *sign, signifier* and *signified* (in semiotics) and contextual elements and instantiations in the CxG formalism.

We want to point out right now for Chapters 1 and 2 that context is defined as a set of contextual elements. The real definition is introduced more formally in Chapter 3; the operational definition and the consequences are detailed in the last Chapters 4 and 5. Finally, we propose an extended evolutive definition of context that is valid for any activity and also at any step of the development of an activity.

1

Theoretical and Pragmatic Basis of Our Context Modeling

1.1. Introduction

Section 1.2 pinpoints the theoretical basis of our approach. First, we return to the conceptual difference between a model and representation. On the one hand, a model is an abstraction of the reality with the power of prediction; and, on the other hand, a model has as many different expressions as representation formalisms. Moreover, the concept "model" has different meanings in different disciplines. We also describe the concepts of activity, mental model and mental representation in Cognitive Sciences in light of the Contextual-Graphs (CxG) formalism for contextual reasoning and conversely, the contribution of the mental-model concept to the CxG formalism. We end this section with the proposed scientific approach and an overview of the origin of the four-modeling level framework.

Section 1.3 briefly presents several real-world applications over a period of 25 years in a very large spectrum of domains: Power Systems, Subway Exploitation, Enology with winemaking, Computer Security, collaborative understanding, car driver support, website analysis, self-training of car drivers, medical image access, contextualization of platforms of interoperable open-source tools for enterprises, database administration, a strategic infrastructure project in transportation, a cognition-driven explorer for histopathology in breast cancer grading, process and sharing of medical images, and contextualized support on a tablet for a Control & Command system for the French military. The ten retained projects used in this book for showing the aspects of context put center stage are: SEPT (1986–1995), SART (1996–2002), FlexMIm (2012–2015), TACTIC (2013–2015), ACA (2005–2009), "Contextualizing scientific workflows" (2009–2011), MICO (2011–2014), "Prediction of stuck wine fermentations" (1997–1999), the OSSMOSE project

(2009–2011) and the project "Computer-mediated collaborative work" (1997–1999). All the projects have a common presentation: domain, our contribution to the project, and the lessons learned for our research on context modeling and use.

Section 1.4 sums up the main points covered in this chapter.

1.2. Theoretical basis

The concept of "model" often has different meanings from one discipline to another. After a presentation of our view on models, we point out that a model can have different representations, and their difference must be made explicit. We illustrate our points using the theoretical example of the autocatalytic model and a formal modeling of calcium metabolism with important findings in the scientific approach we followed to illustrate the richness of such an approach in the elaboration of our representation formalism.

1.2.1. *Model and representation*

Consider a general idea and several examples that illustrate the idea *(MUSTIL Team 1996)*. There are two opposed viewpoints:

– In the first viewpoint, the general idea is a model of the examples. It is the viewpoint in applied mathematics (Physics, Economy, Biology, etc.) where the mathematical model is an abstract representation of a tangible reality to provide a better understanding of some aspects of the reality or to better enable action on it. The main use of the mathematical model is the simulation of a real process or system.

– In the second viewpoint, examples are models of the general idea. This is the viewpoint in Logics. Models are concrete objects that illustrate or interpret abstracted ideas generally expressed as logical formulas or axioms. Abstracted ideas constitute a theory, and a model (an example) makes a transition from the abstract to the real.

To sum up, a model in applied mathematics is a tool to act on the reality, whereas a theory in logic is a tool to study abstract properties independently of the real objects that can satisfy this theory.

A model is either a model of decision-making or a model of simulation. In decision-making, a model represents a part of reality within the framework of a given theory, and its sensitivity is studied on datasets (Lévine and Pomerol 1995). In biology, the model is a tool for confronting our ideas and assumptions with reality.

It has qualitative aspects expressed as a statement and quantitative aspects represented by the specifications associated with the statement (Brézillon 1983).

Our research is ascribed in the first viewpoint. A model is a simplified version of the "real world" containing only the characteristics judged important by an observer. The model is expressed in a representation formalism that plays a crucial role of "concept revealer" between the model and reality. If we do not have the right representation formalism, we may miss some observations in the reality and/or have a model that is not relevant for testing our assumptions about the reality. For instance, in biology, a decay curve of a radioactive element given by discrete measures (observations) is supposed to be representable by the sum of exponentials as a representation formalism (another representation formalism is a set of ordinary differential equations (ODEs)), supposing that differences between the curve and the experimental data could be explainable by measurement accuracy and biological variability. For example, the concept of homeostasis expresses the paradigm of the "constance du milieu intérieur" of Claude Bernard (1865). As a result, a metabolism, like calcium metabolism, was assimilated to a linear system. However, Perault-Staub et al. (1975) highlighted the existence of circadian rhythms that could not be explained by a linear model and required a representation of the calcium metabolism as a nonlinear self-oscillating model. A new set of assumptions was necessary at the level of calcium-hydroxyapatite crystal formation in bone (observations) that could be explained by the role of dissipative structures pointed out in Chemistry (Goldbetter and Lefever 1972). Then, the choice of a nonlinear representation formalism was natural.

A model allows interpolation and extrapolation of a possible evolution of the real-world system beyond the observed behavior, thanks to the predictive power of the model in the limits of the chosen representation formalism (oscillations will never appear in a linear formalism like the sum of exponentials). A model can be expressed in different representation formalisms, each formalism allowing the model to exhibit (or not) targeted behaviors. Thus, the observer must define clearly which characteristics of the model are relevant for the study. However, it is possible to jointly use two different formalisms, like ODEs for a mathematician and a compartmental formalism for a physiologist (Jacquez 1972). The "Paper submission" example (see section 3.6.1) shows that the example has been used for several formalisms of representation: production rules, UML, Bayesian networks, Petri nets, fluence graphs, etc. A model has some properties that are important for a nonlinear model: the steady state – $dQ/dt = 0$ – and its stability or instability. A nonlinear model may present several steady states, and the choice of the initial conditions is thus important because there are several distinct stability zones. Usually the stability of a steady state is computed by the discriminant of the Jacobian matrix, which is composed of parameters in the model (transfer constants $\mathbf{K}_{ji}$ from compartment **i** to compartment **j** below) and of the values of the variables at the steady state. Note that when the steady state is unstable, the stability zone generally corresponds to a limit cycle (in natural systems with positive masses there is always a stability zone). There are other subtasks related to parameters and initial conditions such as identifiability, identification and sensibility. However, nonlinear models often have no theoretical solution, only numerical ones, and thus, the solution is obtained by numerical simulation.

Figure 1.1 presents the example of the autocatalytic model (Goldbetter and Lefever 1972) that has the following expression in (a) a nonlinear differential equation representation formalism and (b) the compartmental representation formalism (Jacquez 1972).

$$\frac{dQ_1}{dt} = -(K_{01}+K_{21})*Q_1 + k_{12}*Q_1^2*Q_2 + K_{10}$$

$$\frac{dQ_2}{dt} = -k_{12}*Q_1^2*Q_2 + K_{21}*Q_1$$

(a)

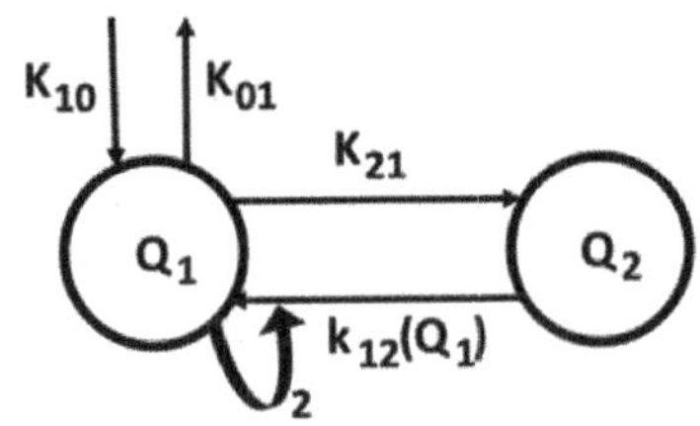

(b)

Figure 1.1. *Representations of the autocatalytic model by (a) differential equations and (b) compartmental formalism*

The steady state is:

$$Q_{10} = K_{10} / K_{01}$$

$$Q_{20} = K_{21} / k_{12}*Q_{10}$$

The conditions of stability of the steady state in the example are given by:

$$K_{12} < K_{01} + k_{12}*Q_{10} \quad \text{stable}$$

$$K_{12} > K_{01} + k_{12}*Q_{10} \quad \text{unstable}$$

When the steady state is unstable, the stable trajectory is a limit cycle in the state space (Figure 1.2a) and variables present oscillations as a function of time (Figure 1.2b).

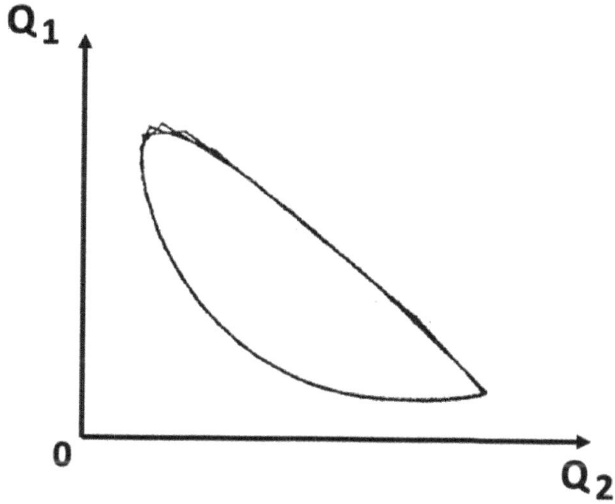

a

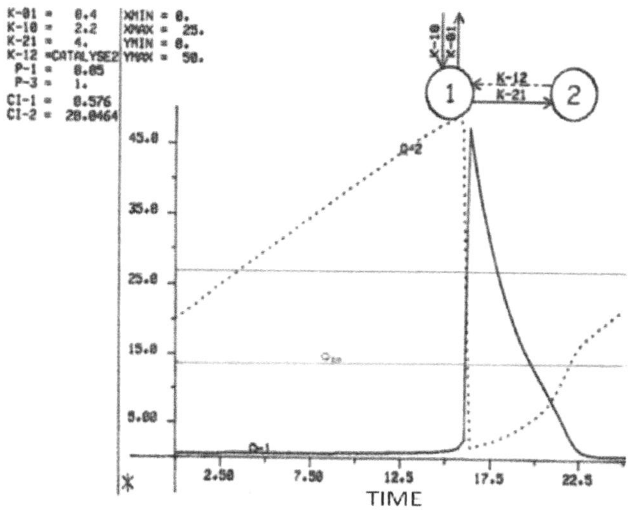

b

Figure 1.2. *Limit cycle in the phase plane (a) and oscillations in a temporal representation (b)*

We used this approach in the modeling of the calcium metabolism (Brézillon 1983). The concept of homeostasis of the calcium metabolism was considered as a statement relative to the state of a variable y (the calcemia). The concept of homeostasis conventionally corresponds to maintaining the variable y at a constant value y_0 ($dy/dt = 0$). It is built on concepts such as mass, time, error, stationarity, etc., and principles such as regulation and small variations.

In the SART project, we have changed the representation, initially for pragmatic reasons of scarcity. We started from the notion of a decision tree (Pomerol et al. 2002) and its development in the SART project as summed up in (Pasquier 2002). In a decision tree, each event at an event node carries on a part of the uncertainty of the situation. There are no probabilities for the events, but there are several contexts in which a decision has to be made. For example, in Figure 1.3, which represents the incident "lack of train power" in the SART project, the branch with $\{C_{12}, C_{21}, C_{32}\}$ describes a context in which there is no immediate repair possible but still enough power and a steep incline in view. For this reason, we replaced the event nodes used in decision-making with *context nodes*, and *states of nature* are replaced by *contexts*. There is no interest in the probability of, say, *C12* versus *C11*, because, first, these instantiations are exclusive, and, second, our representation intends to be used for any incident, whatever the probabilities are. In this sense, the *Ci* are not random variables unlikely in influence diagrams. When an incident occurs, the probability of occurrence no longer matters; what matters is the chaining of troubleshooting actions.

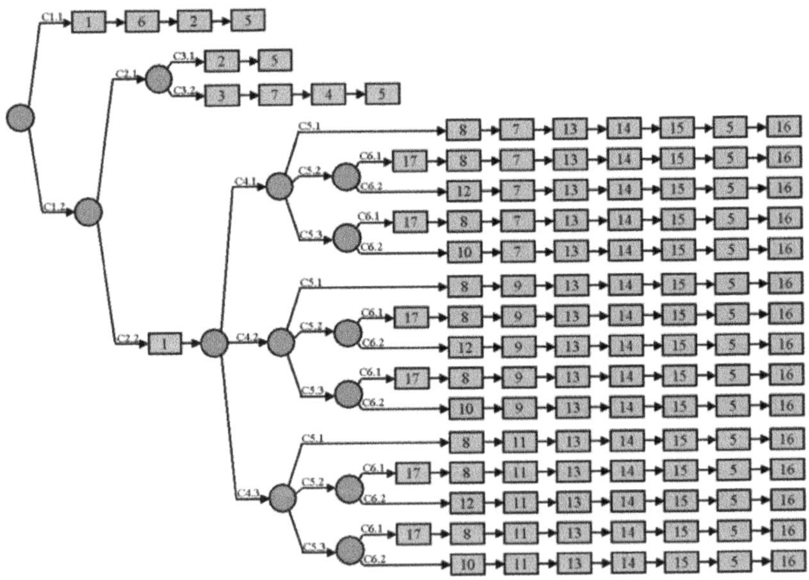

Figure 1.3. *Decision tree of the procedure for "lack of train power" incident. For a color version of this figure, see www.iste.co.uk/brezillon/contextbasedmodeling.zip*

The postponement of actions to the leaves observed in Figures 1.3 amounts to relating each decision to a state of nature, here, the context described in the branch. Note that a branch corresponds to a contextual node that is instantiated to a given value. For example, the branches C_{11} and C_{12} are more important than the contextual node C_1 that will play a central role in our CxG formalism. Thus, our representation tends to stick to operators' behavior. This means that when operators undertake an action in the tree, they consider that, due to the contextual information they got, the state of nature between the root and the action undertaken is the true state of nature.

The tree representation was made of two types of elements: actions and contextual nodes, which select a branch depending on the knowledge about the current context. Figure 1.3 shows the decision-tree representation of the procedure for "train lack of power" solving (the meaning of the boxes is not important here but can be found in Pasquier (2002)). In summary, our representation is inspired by decision trees but mainly differs on two points: (1) our trees have no chance nodes but have contextual nodes and (2) there are no probabilities.

This representation shows several important characteristics that have some consequences on the size and structure of a tree:

– Operators use many contextual elements to perform their choice. This leads to a large number of pragmatic strategies, even for the same incident, and multiplies the number of branches and the tree size grows rapidly.

– Operators prefer to gather a maximum of information before making their decision. This behavior postpones most of actions to the end of tree branches. It is an observation similar to Watson and Perera's observation (1998) that a hierarchical case representation holds more general contextual features at its top and specific building elements in its leaves.

– Operators privilege actions allowing us to reach common intermediary situations. Thus, they can reuse common strategies to clear the incident. Graphically, the tip sequence of actions is often repeated from one branch to another.

– Several action sequences are executed in the same order in different situations (paths).

– Two actions could be done in any order but must precede a given third one. For example, before linking two trains, both have to be emptied, but the order in which they are emptied does not matter (partial order on the actions as in the onion metaphor).

The large expansion of the tree structure does not easily make it possible to represent highly contextual decision-making in complex applications. We now explain the modification we have done, based on the characteristics discussed above, to obtain a manageable structure for representing operational knowledge on incident solving for subway lines.

The first operation was to reduce the number of objects in the structure by replacing repeated sub-sequences of actions with a single object called *macro-action*. The choice made for defining the different macro-actions is based on common sub-procedures known by the operators, such as "linking trains" and "return to end-station without travelers". The principle of replacing is explained in Figure 1.4.

Figure 1.4. *From a sequence of actions to a macro-action. For a color version of this figure, see www.iste.co.uk/brezillon/contextbasedmodeling.zip*

This replacement simplifies the lecture of the tree but does not reduce structural expansion of the tree. The second operation was to merge tree branches as soon as the sequence leading to the end of the incident are similar, as shown in Figure 1.5.

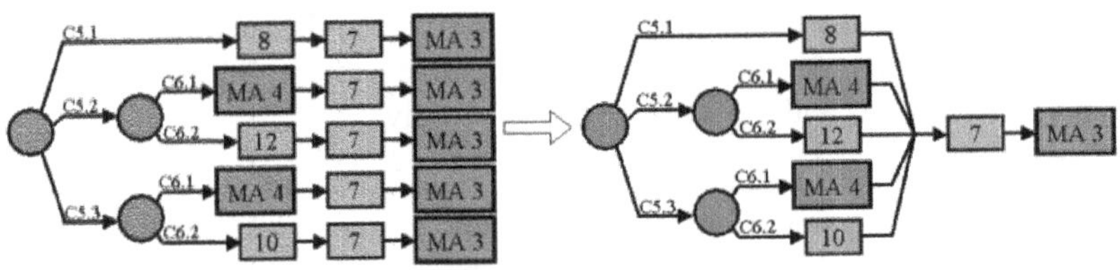

Figure 1.5. *From tree to graph. For a color version of this figure, see www.iste.co.uk/brezillon/contextbasedmodeling.zip*

Cognitively speaking, all of this to use a scarcity principle leads operators to reuse well-known procedures as soon as possible. This operation has several consequences on the representation structure and the model meaning:

– We no longer face a tree but an acyclic and directed graph with exactly one root and one goal, and branches express only different strategies, depending on context, to achieve this goal.

– Structure size is now under control, and consideration of a new contextual element will add some elements in the graph but will not drastically increase its size.

– Structure change introduces a life duration of the instantiation of contextual nodes. When two branches are merged at a recombination node, the contextual node is initially proceduralized, and their instantiations do not matter anymore.

Even in part of a subgraph, it may happen that actions are only partially ordered. In Figure 1.6, all the branches join together in one node, according to an implementation simplification rule (the blue arrows now correspond to an Executive Structure of Independent Activities (ESIA)). As a result, the C1.1 branch of Figure 1.6 is connected directly to the branch C3.1, not at the final node because it connects to the macro-action MA1 for avoiding a duplicate. We observe a similar situation at the level of the contextual element 6. As a result, arriving at the final node, the trace of the development is lost. The same problem appears for mental models through the macro-action MA4. The representation respects syntax but not semantics: the macro-action MA1 exists in two different contexts (C1.1 and C3.1).

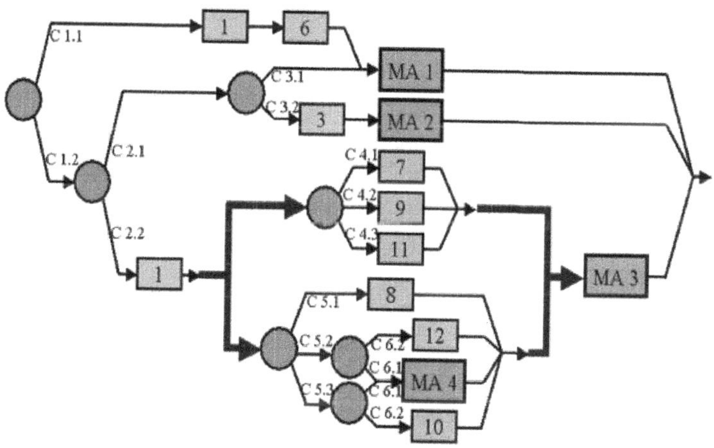

Figure 1.6. *The contextual graph for "lack of train power" incident in Figure 1.3. For a color version of this figure, see www.iste.co.uk/brezillon/contextbasedmodeling.zip*

Thus, a simplification at the implementation level for avoiding double occurrences implies an inconsistency at the conceptual level. Coherence between conceptual and operational levels is lost. Moreover, updating the knowledge representation (conceptual level) is difficult because knowledge organization is at the implementation level. At the time of expert systems, screening clauses for representing procedural knowledge in a declarative formalism had the same effect.

Changes introduced in the CxG formalism take into consideration the identified weaknesses:

– A distinction between contextual node and instantiation and an association of similar concepts at the operational and the implementation levels of modeling (mental representation and contextual graph, mental-model development and path in the contextual graph).

– A contextual element is a pair of contextual and recombination nodes with as many exclusive branches between nodes and values. A contextual node must be associated with a unique recombination node.

– Branches between a contextual node and a recombination node represent variants of the reasoning step that is the contextual element, and there are as many variants as branches that differ only on a defined part.

– An action or a macro-action can occur in different contexts (like MA1).

– If a contextual node C2 is on a branch of a contextual element C1, the recombination node of C2 must be before the recombination node of C1. As a result, the contextual element C2 is embedded on a branch of the contextual element C1. Thus, a contextual element includes another contextual element, as with Russian dolls. There is no partial overlapping.

Figure 1.7 is the rewriting of Figure 1.6 in the CxG_1.0 version (explained later). The blue circles represent the pairs of contextual and recombination nodes, green square boxes represent the actions, the violet boxes represent the macro-actions and the two red bars the ESIA.

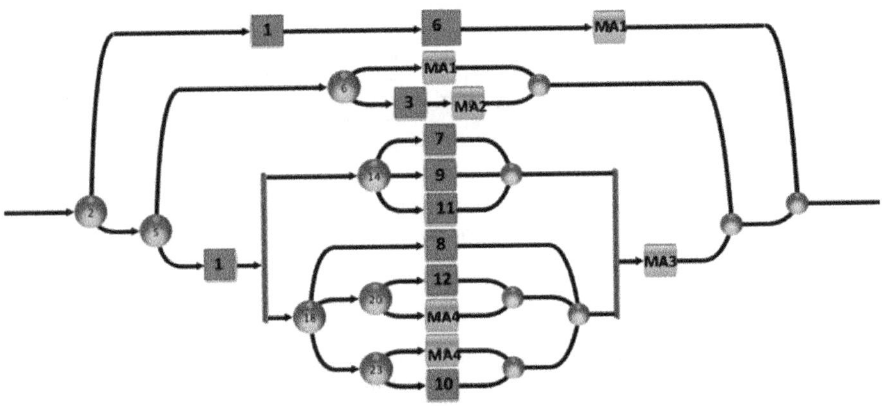

Figure 1.7. *CxG version of the diagnosis of "lack of train power" incident. For a color version of this figure, see www.iste.co.uk/brezillon/contextbasedmodeling.zip*

With coherence of conceptual and implementation levels ensured, changes can now be managed automatically in the contextual graph. The simplicity is at the level of the whole: A unique mental representation implemented as a contextual graph plays the role of a base of experiences. A mental model is a path in this contextual graph, and following the path (i.e. developing the mental model) consists of just having the instantiation of the next contextual elements encountered on the path when needed.

1.2.2. *Concepts used*

The goal of this section is to present the literature on activity, reasoning, mental model, mental representation and situation models and how a "context-based interpretation" of the strengths and weaknesses of these notions could help benefit the strengths of these concepts and to suggest solutions for their weaknesses. Thus, it is not a deep survey of the literature that is beyond the scope of this book on modeling context for its use in real-world projects. However, we only limit our presentations of concepts with respect to the context modeling that is our purpose.

We adhere to the definition of Sarrazin et al. (1996): "an *activity* is the (physical and mental) behavior that an actor exhibits for realizing a task". The notion of activity encompasses those of "task realization" and the actor that realizes the task. Companies often provide actors with procedures, but actors prefer to optimize procedures as practices in activities that are in specific contexts in which procedures cannot be applied as such. Activity depends strongly on their context, which then cannot be defined in an abstract way (Brézillon 2005). Modeling an activity involves modeling reasoning to explain the move from one step to the next. There are five phases in the interaction between actor and activity: (1) an external view that relates to the life cycle of the activity at an abstract level (e.g. the actor accomplishes the activity), (2) preparation of the activity (e.g. the actor plans the activity), (3) initiation of the activity (e.g. the actor launches the activity), (4) development of the activity (e.g. the actor performs the activity) and (5) finalizing the activity (e.g. the actor closes the activity). As a result, an actor comprehends an activity like a mental model, including development, combining steps based on reasoning on evolution and decisions made at each move between steps. At the end of each activity step, the next step is chosen by either deductive (i.e. sequential) reasoning or contextual knowledge if there are alternatives. Thus, the common thread is the reasoning.

Wyer (2007) observed that *human reasoning* draws no clear distinction between deduction, induction and abduction, because it tends to exploit what we know, and its representation is typically constructed in the course of a goal-directed processing. As such, "reasoning is more a simulation of the world fleshed out with all our relevant knowledge than a formal manipulation of the logical skeletons of sentences" (Johnson-Laird 2010). This definition implies a contextual nature to reasoning. Reasoning held by an actor during activity development must appear in the modeling of the activity. However, each domain has a personal view on reasoning: a mental activity of relating propositions or ideas logically to produce valid conclusions (Philosophy); a mental process of drawing conclusions or solving problems using available information (Psychology); algorithms defined to manipulate represented knowledge (formal logic, expert systems) in AI; the process by which an individual, or a group, evaluates options and anticipates consequences to maximize a given goal (decision-making). Disciplines from the human sciences to the exact sciences define reasoning along different priorities: formal exploration of logical rules, psychological mechanisms or practical applications. Decision-making being central in most activities, reasoning consists of starting from collecting, assembling and structuring knowledge and information justifying a valid decision that maximizes a given goal. Reasoning is a cognitive process that underlies and guides the activity, a mental framework that helps actors to decide how to perform an activity, make choices during the activity and assess outcomes once the activity is completed. As a result, the actor is part of the context-based modeling loop. Reasoning is based on the actor's experience and the actor's information and knowledge on the accomplishment of the activity. For Johnson-Laird (2010), "reasoning depends on envisaging the possibilities consistent with the starting point – a perception of the world, a set of assertions, a memory, or some mixture of them, then we construct mental models of each distinct possibility and derive a conclusion from them".

We propose (1) expressing humans' experience in long-term memory as a *mental representation* providing a homogeneous view on the mental models developed by an actor and that will be implemented (and sharable) in a contextual-graph representation; (2) articulating mental models like practices, and mental representations as close as possible to procedures in contextual graphs and (3) associating mental-model development with the successive instantiations of contextual elements on the path followed in the contextual graph.

In the framework of the CxG approach, mental models may have two different diverging meanings:

– In long-term memory, a mental model is an "internal representation" (a knowledge structure) that is contextualized in the context of a focus; the corollary being an accumulation of contextualized internal representations (the elaborated mental models) in long-term memory, knowing that any contextualized internal representation cannot be reused in another context directly.

– In working memory, a mental model is an internal representation from long-term memory that must be contextualized for fitting actor's context awareness and sent to long-term memory in the case of success, but it is not said if it is as a new internal representation or not.

Actors attempted to first clearly understand the situation they faced and the dynamics of events, and then proceeded to formulate courses of action and other decision-making activities in the specific situation. What we pay attention to, is very much determined by what we expect to see, that is, how our mental model is linked to our focus of attention. Andonovski (2022) argues that episodic system constructs mental models for simulating events by retrieving and flexibly recombining previously stored episodic elements. Endsley (2000), Nersessian (2002) and Jones et al. (2011) and consider long-term memory contain knowledge structures that called upon mental models formed in working memory, instantiated from situation awareness and used to support reasoning in activity. We extend this view by making context explicit for (1) integrating the actor's role, activity (task realization, decision-making or problem-solving), the situation in which the actor addresses an activity and local environment where resources are needed for addressing mental models; (2) making explicit the contextualization process of mental-model development in the working context and (3) organizing (contextualized) mental models in mental representation in long-term memory.

The human approach considers the notions of mental model, mental representation and situation model but with diverging viewpoints of literature; mainly a situation model is supposed to contextualize mental models during activity evolution. Craik (1943) suggested that the mind constructs "small-scale models" of reality to anticipate events, to reason and to generate explanations. Alternately, Johnson-Laird (1983) considered a mental model a reasoning mechanism that exists in a person's working memory (Endsley 2000; Jones et al. 2011). Such mental models are formed through analogical thinking that allows people to "create new mental models that they can then run to explain the current state of the mental model and generate predictions about what should happen in various situations in the real world" (Collins and Gentner 1987). The literature shows a discrepancy in the location of mental models in the mind: working memory (Johnson-Laird 1983), long-term memory (Craik 1943) or both as Nersessian (2002) considers mental models in long-term memory as knowledge structures called upon to support the mental models, which are formed in working memory to support reasoning and problem-solving. Thus, a knowledge structure in long-term memory is decontextualized and reused directly in another context, while the mental model in working memory is contextualized to support reasoning for the given step of the activity. As a result, long-term memory would contain a collection of contextualized mental models not necessarily in a uniform representation. Jones et al. (2011) propose a global solution. First, humans construct and exploit mental models in their working memory for reasoning. Second, once the specific problem is solved, the mental model just built is stored in long-term memory. The set of internal representations in long-term memory can be reused, based on personal life experiences, perceptions and an understanding of the world.

Mental models of physical and organizational systems concern objects (e.g., a house) or procedures (e.g., how to change a tire) according to the types of knowledge one acquires. The locality of mental models allows reasoners to explore the structure of a target domain without worrying about its "global" connections. Sensory information only serves to supplement, evoke or actualize these skeletons. Generally, mental models represent what is true at the expense of what is false (Johnson-Laird and Savary 1999). As a counter-example, consider the experiment of "inattentional blindness" (Most et al. 2005) in which subjects have to focus on an external object or event (a mental model) and fail to notice the unattended stimulus. The video shows a scene where two teams, one with white clothes and the other with black clothes, are each exchanging a ball between themselves and moving on the scene mixed with the members of the other team. Subjects are required to concentrate on counting the exchanges of the ball inside the "white" team (their mental model to develop). During the sequence, an actor with a black-gorilla suit walks through the scene. This strong signal (black gorilla crossing the scene) is unconsciously put on the side and becomes a kind of weak signal (external to the task realization) for subjects when seeing the video (inattentional blindness). Adoption of a specific *attentional set* (mental model) makes us ready to receive specific information participating in the mental model but overrides the capturing power of external information. The unclear points are (1) the relationships between the mental models and mental (internal) representation(s), (2) the way in which successful mental models are archived in long-term memory and (3) the contextualization process of internal representations in long-term memory based on personal life experience, perceptions and understandings of the world, showing that mental models result more from context than situation awareness.

Mental representation is an expression often used instead of mental model as a synonymous term, or a set of common features, or a formalism for representing mental models. However, a model has a power of prediction (extrapolation), while a representation only allows an interpolation of situations. Mental models are contextualization of knowledge structures for a specific focus in a given context, and a mental representation expresses all mental models in a uniform representation. In the spirit of the CxG formalism, a mental representation is the accumulation of all the mental models obtained for an activity in different contexts. Mental models are built from a mental representation, which behaves as the operators' experience. It is important to know that any formalism of representation puts some features of mental models center stage that are supposed to be essential for addressing them, while other features are not considered.

Indeed, Cognitive Science presents a mental model as a contextualization resulting from a *situation model*. However, our approach by contextual elements and instantiations supposes four sources of context that are not considered in cognitive science, the actor, the activity, the situation and the local environment. For Zwaan and Radvansky (1998), a situation model is a particular mental model that concerns events or states of affairs that are situationally and temporarily constrained (Endsley 2000). A situation model is "a person's mental model of the world around them at a particular time and place". The situation model incorporates the values of system parameters and also includes an understanding of the dynamics of the system developed from the changes in the situation model over time. It represents human's knowledge and understanding of the present state of the system. Figure 1.8 represents Endsley's view on the relationship between mental model and situation awareness.

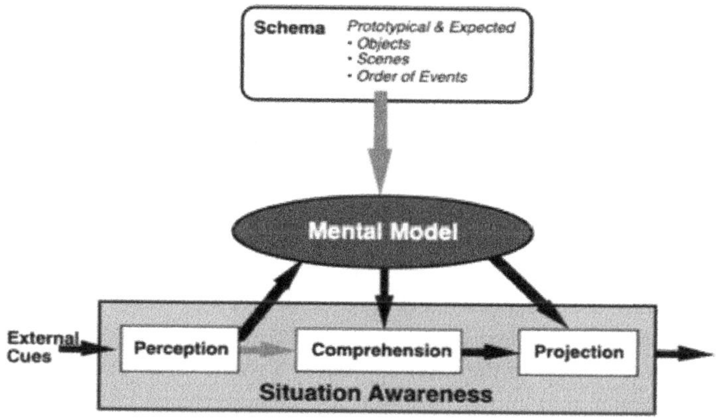

Figure 1.8. *Relationship between mental model and situation model*

Endsley and Jones (1997) elaborate a mental model from many "snapshots" of the situation model across a wide range of circumstances. A mental model is obtained by simulation of the actors' activity (the snapshots) during the situation. The simulation of mental-model development is stopped at various random times, and people are asked what their situation awareness is at this particular point in time. A snapshot is supposed to catch operators' representation of the situation with their decisions as well as the correct action for that situation. A mental model is built from the mining of the "snapshot base", but context (circumstances) is not made explicit in the situation model. In the CxG approach, the situation model corresponds to sources of context (the user, the task model and the local environment). For example, a mechanic has a mental representation of how an engine works, and the sources of context concern how this particular engine is functioning right now, the state of its components (new, worn, dirty) and its exact capabilities and features (model, horsepower, etc.).

During the mental-model development, actors may not notice irrelevant features despite their effects on the mental model they consider, especially if weak signals come from external knowledge with respect to the activity at hand. For example, if drivers are attending to their driving (e.g. the car in front of them, road signs, etc.), and if they do not expect pedestrians to step in front of the car, they are unlikely to see them (Simons 2000). The importance of a signal depends on the actor that memorizes and constructs meaning from the signs they perceive according to their mood, intentions, their project, their interpretation of the organization, the environment, their memory and experiences. The exploitation of *weak signals* is an activity of construction of meaning (i.e. an interpretation) to compose and structure one's environment, which requires attention processes specific to weak signals, the goal being to build a meaningful situation model (Ansoff 1975). It is a process specific to each actor that intervenes in the first essential step of processing contextual information (Weick 1995). Weak signals are uncertain, imprecise and fragmentary, of little significance taken individually, they only enrich themselves when cross-checked and arranged in relation to each other. Moreover, they are weak because (1) they are drowned and scattered in a multitude of noisy information; (2) they are unexpected, unfamiliar and not very repetitive and therefore likely to go unnoticed; (3) they are of apparently low utility for the focus where the consequences of the event evoked do not impose themselves; and finally, (4) they are difficult to comprehend. This shows the necessity of a context-based building of mental models recalled from the mental representation of the actor. In the CxG approach, a weak signal comes from external knowledge, not contextual knowledge used for the activity, and thus not represented in the contextual graph either. The event that is the cause of the weak signal is not considered as important or cannot be linked to the activity evolution. In some way, the mental model does not allow the actor to detect this weak signal.

The process of improving action through better knowledge and understanding is integrally connected to *sense making* (Koenig 1996). Literally, sensemaking means making sense of things. It is a cognitive construction of a hypothetical mental model of the current situation and how it might evolve over time, what threats and opportunities for each action are likely to emerge from this evolution, what potential actions can be taken in response, what the projected outcomes of those responses are, and what values drive the choice of future action (Klein et al. 2006). Such a hypothetical mental model is considered when actors make sense instead of decisions because they do not know what the "appropriate action" is until they take some action (in a kind of look-ahead), guided by preconceptions and see what happens (Weick 1995). Generally, sensemaking is an examination of past mental models in order to learn/unlearn things about the current context. It offers a larger perspective than the rationalistic and mechanistic characteristics of decision-making (Boland 2008). Instead of developing a comprehensive mental model for a complex, open system, most people rely on fragments of local cause–effect connections, rules of thumb, patterns of cues and other linkages and relationships between cues and information to guide the sensemaking process and other high-level cognitive processes (Sieck et al. 2007). In the CxG approach, sensemaking is based on elements of mental models existing in the mental representation. Context plays an important role in sensemaking with the identification of relevant contextual elements from their instantiations. Sensemaking includes both explicit and implicit mental processes of scanning, framing, interpreting and constructing a conception of the situation at hand (situation awareness).

Mental models allow actors to filter out most signals, so they can concentrate on the few that truly make a difference. Most et al. (2005) pointed out that, what we become aware of, depends on what we are looking for. To sum up, mental representations (and thus mental models) are personal to each actor who is accomplishing an activity based on an operational mental model in the context at hand. Sensemaking is a way, for actors to legitimate their mental models with respect to their mental representation. Hereafter, we propose an implementation of a mental representation in the CxG software as a contextual graph where paths from the input to the output correspond to mental models. The working context, which is associated with the contextual graph, is used by the instantiation process of the contextual elements.

Our conclusion is that mental models and mental representations are two different concepts that are not interchangeable in the CxG formalism. Two examples illustrate this conclusion, the first one from the TACTIC project and the other from a public platform. In the TACTIC project (Kabil et al. 2015; Brézillon 2022), the experience of 12 experts in the domain of battlefield was visualized as a tree of contextual elements with the Freemind software. This mind map visualizes the mental representation that contains each actor's experience with a given activity in different contexts, that is, leading to a set of different mental models. A scenario then was proposed for letting each actor develop their mental model that addresses the activity given in the scenario (i.e. chosen position and goal of the enemy on the battlefield). The contextual elements effectively used by the actor during the scenario defined the mental model developed by the actor for the specific context at hand. Figure 1.9 represents the mental representation of one actor on "Give a reconnoitering order" (find out what the enemy is doing). The mental representation corresponds to a tree of contextual elements (a mind map). The successors of a contextual element (e.g. green items after the blue items in Figure 1.9) can also be considered as (qualitative) instantiations of the contextual element (the ancestor). The mental model is the not shaded part of the mental representation where contextual elements are used by the actor during the simulation. The mental model evolution is expressed as a "contextual element centered visualization", in which the reasoning partially appears as arrows linking two or more contextual elements on different branches (e.g. ephemeris and perception in Figure 1.9). The tree visualization of contextual elements does not include reasoning, which is "action-directed", and cannot be specified beforehand (the moderator had introduced different unforeseen events during the simulation).

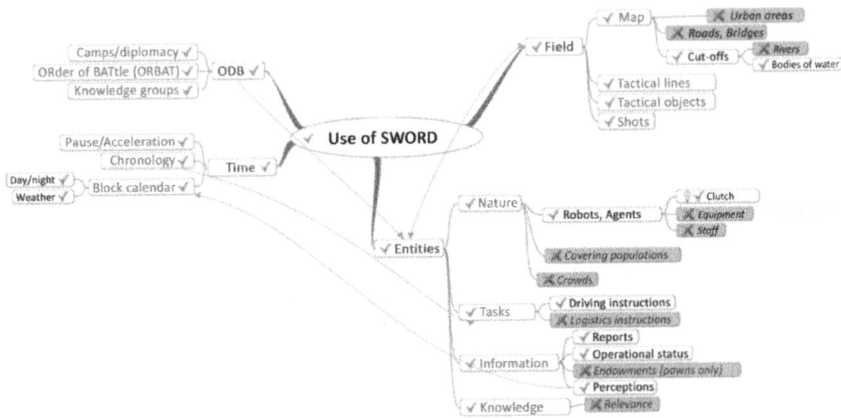

Figure 1.9. *Example of mental representation and mental model in the TACTIC project. For a color version of this figure, see www.iste.co.uk/brezillon/contextbasedmodeling.zip*

The second example provides another view on the differences between the mental model and mental representation on the public platform myfitnesspal.com. The platform proposes a weight management program that proposes keeping a food diary and/or an activity log. The actor's activity is "Tracking food intake to weight loss", as shown in Figure 1.10. Figure 1.10-A presents the window for filling daily meals (breakfast, lunch dinner and snacks). Each meal is the object of a mental model of what the actor plans to eat today. The first one, "Breakfast", is already filled (and was an automatic copy-and-paste of the previous day). Each item of this "mental model" is considered an instantiated contextual element that is provided by the user with a name (e.g. milk) and a quantity (10 ml) as instantiation. Calories, carbohydrates, etc. are (contextual) information coming from the database of the platform that proposes a list of all items chosen the previous days by actors (the list corresponding to "Add checked"), but a new item can be introduced in the empty window in Figure 1.10-B. The list of the proposed items corresponds to the mental representation (all the elements already used previously) from which the mental model will be built.

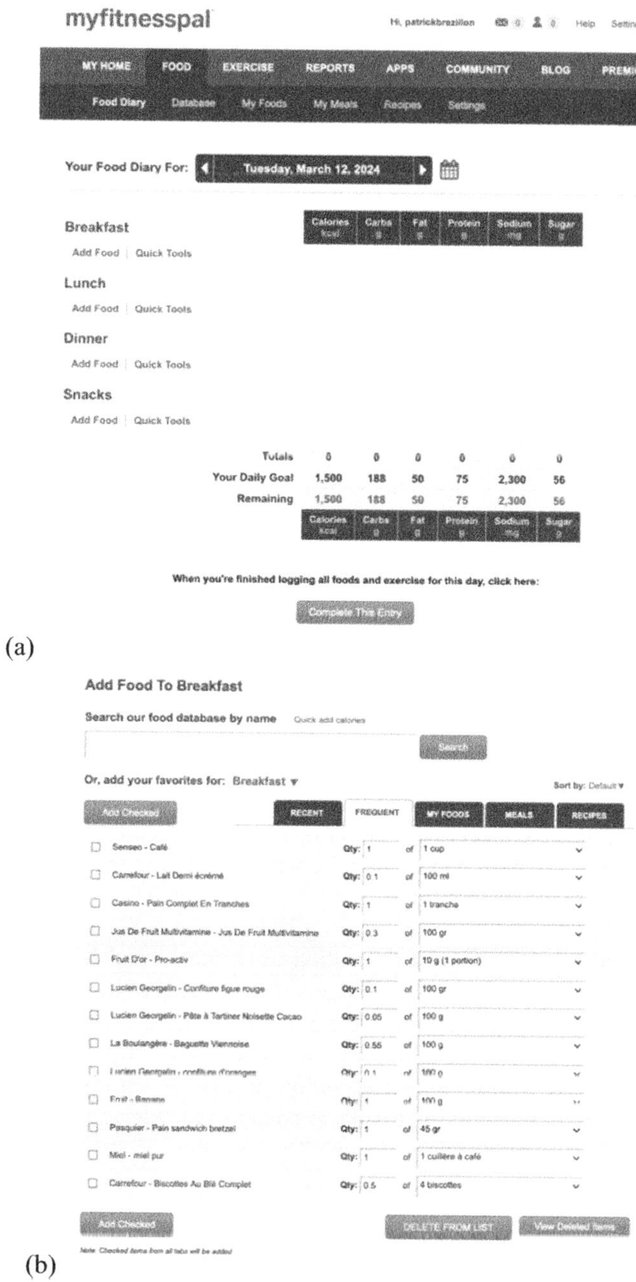

Figure 1.10. *Two screenshots from Myfitnesspal (https://www.myfitnesspal.com). For a color version of this figure, see www.iste.co.uk/brezillon/contextbasedmodeling.zip*

These two examples illustrate the difference between the mental model and mental representation, a difference that depends on the degree of formalization of the domain (e.g. as many mental representations as actors in the TACTIC project and a unique shared mental representation in the second example). The more a mental model corresponds to a formal model, the closer the meaning of the mental model and mental representation are because the effects of context are small, generally as values and initial conditions to fit experimental data.

Conversely, if a mental model concerns the realization of the task more than the task itself, then context plays a more visible role mainly at the realization level, and the context becomes essential in the definition of the mental model and generates differentiation with the mental representation. Therefore, the mental model and mental representation are situated in long-term memory, and working memory is the place for instantiating contextual elements during mental-model development and its execution.

In the CxG approach, the modeling of an activity is concerned with the way an actor realizes a task (not only the result of the task), makes a decision (not only obtains the final result) or solves a problem (not obtains the solution only). As any with any decision-maker, the actor first collects the maximum contextual information related to the focus and surroundings, second establishes a plan (optimal for the identified context) and thirdly executes the plan. Thus, a mental model and its development are personal to an actor that accumulates them in the mental representation. A direct conclusion is that we cannot speak of a mental model out of the actor. The actor is not the unique source of contextual information needed to better understand mental models. As in the CxG approach, the context of interest for developing mental models also comes from other sources of contextual information: the activity itself, the situation and the local environment. It is the reason we prefer the term "context awareness" instead of "situation awareness" for mental models.

The lack of real formalization of the notion of mental model leads to relatively unformal definitions, for instance, knowledge structures cannot be really formalized without making the nature of the structure explicit for actions. We have shown that in the CxG approach, the development of a mental model in the mental representation is linked with a contextualization process of contextual elements in the local environment of the activity, thanks to context awareness. Successful mental models are stored in mental representation. The question is, "How can a mental model, which is contextualized, be reused with another contextualization?" The CxG approach proposes a concrete explanation by saying that a mental representation is the accumulation of mental models in a uniform mental representation based on contextual elements at the implementation level.

In the mental-model approach, several meanings are given to "mental representation": (1) synonymous with mental model, (2) a set of common features of mental models and (3) formalism for expressing mental models.

The problem with the first meaning is found equally in mathematics with the terms of "model" and "representation" (see section 1.2.1), the two terms being as different as prediction and interpolation in mathematics because a model has (or must have) a prediction power while a representation only gives a global coherent picture of what is known (e.g. as the actor's experience for the mental representation).

The second meaning, representation as a set of common features of mental models, is similar to contextual elements and their instantiations in the CxG approach; to know, a mental representation contains mental models in a unified (and reusable) way of all the possible contextual variants. A specific mental model is obtained by identifying the relevant contextual elements first and the instantiations given by situation awareness second. Indeed, the CxG approach relies on a mental representation concretized as a contextual graph in which all the (contextualized) mental models are merged in a uniform representation. A specific mental model is retrieved as a path in the contextual graph by the known instantiations of the contextual elements.

The contribution of the CxG approach to the mental-model approach can be summarized to the following points. First, it is important to consider explicitly that a mental model is contextualized from the sources of context in the environment of the activity and uploaded at upper levels. Second, the actor's experience is the accumulation of mental models concerning an activity in different contexts, that is, a mental representation in which mental models are expressed in a global and uniform view.

Third, a mental representation can be implemented as a contextual graph, and a mental model corresponds to a path from the input to the output of the contextual graph. The development of a mental model is associated with an instantiation process leading to a proceduralized context, that is, the process of contextualization of a mental model from "context awareness". Therefore, mental model and mental representation are not interchangeable in the CxG formalism. The notions of mental model and mental representation allow the extension of the CxG formalism to a fully actor-centered formalism.

If lessons have been learned for the use of mental models and mental representation, thanks to the CxG approach, we have found, conversely, lessons from the mental-model approach for the CxG approach. We will use now in the CxG approach the terms of mental representation in correspondence with the contextual graph, and mental model as path in the contextual graph because these terms are more generic than procedure and practice that are limited to task realization and do not cover decision-making and problem-solving.

Finally, the last transformation in our discourse concerns the fact that the development of a mental model corresponds to the simulation of contextual reasoning, this reasoning covering any human activity such as task realization, decision-making and problem-solving.

1.2.3. *The proposed scientific approach*

This section presents the origins of the proposed scientific approach for context-based modeling of an activity in AI, starting from the approach developed in biology, which is illustrated by a previous work on the modeling of the calcium metabolism. Then, we develop the foundation of the scientific approach for AI as we used it in more than 20 applications. From this basis, we present the four-modeling level framework for an activity realized by an actor (Chapter 2) and, after, by a group of actors (Chapter 3).

The scientific approach in life sciences relies on the development of formal models of real systems with an explanatory value (Brézillon 1983). For ensuring the relevance of the explanatory value, the model behavior is compared to the behavior of an observed real system in order to make the logical link explicit between the description and explanation in a deductive approach, from the notion of concept to the notion of observable phenomena. The explanatory value depends on (1) a rigorous approach for ensuring consistency between elaboration and use of the model; (2) an operational formalism for representing the model (Ziegler 1976) and (3) the potential of the model, such as theoretical experiments, prediction of not yet observable phenomena, and the possibility of model refutation and revision in an inductive approach based on hypothesis on discrepancy between model prediction and observed phenomena.

The confrontation of conceptual ideas to observable phenomena first supposes the operationalization of ideas, that is, expressing them in a statement capable of confronting the behavior of the real system. The initial idea relies on two types of concepts, non-formalized concepts and fully formalized ones. For example, mass, time, concentration and speed are formalized concepts, while homeostasis proposed by Claude Bernard in 1855 (Corvol 2013) is a non-formalized concept that can be explained in terms of formalized concepts (see Figure 1.11).

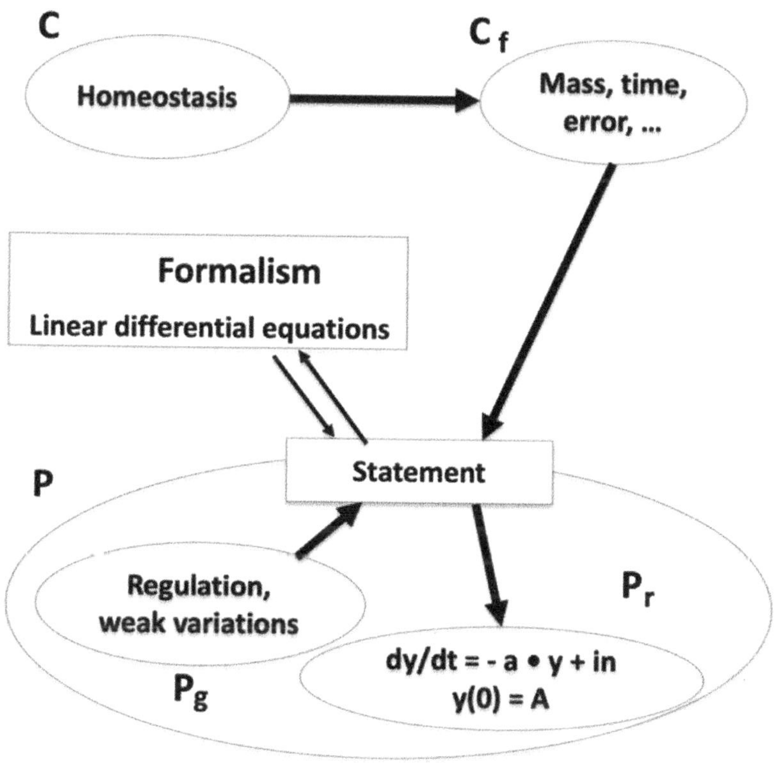

Figure 1.11. *First steps of the scientific approach for Homeostasis modeling*

Operationalization also implies the assembling of concepts based on general principles P_g such as mass conservation, regulation and thermodynamics. The statement, which emerges from assembling through a relevant formalism, corresponds to a resulting principle p_r that is a model of the initial non-formalized concept, like homeostasis in Figure 1.11. The model thus has a formal expression "dy/dt = -a * y + in = 0" in the formalism of linear differential equations in which the variable y (e.g. serum calcium) has the constant value "y_0 =in/a" at the steady state by measures from any weak variation y(0) = A and structural parameters (a, in). The model is identified by its structural parameters on a subset of observable phenomena and must have a power of prediction for a larger set of observable phenomena to validate its explanatory nature. The modeling approach aims to verify the rational coherence between observable phenomena and theoretical phenomena obtained by the model (often by theoretical simulation).

Figure 1.12 presents the framework of the scientific approach used in biology that introduces four levels of interest, namely conceptual and operational levels for the theoretical part of the model and implementation and phenomena levels for the quantification part of the model based on its use (elaboration, validation, exploitation and refutation) for theoretical experiments instead of the real system for comparison to observable phenomena.

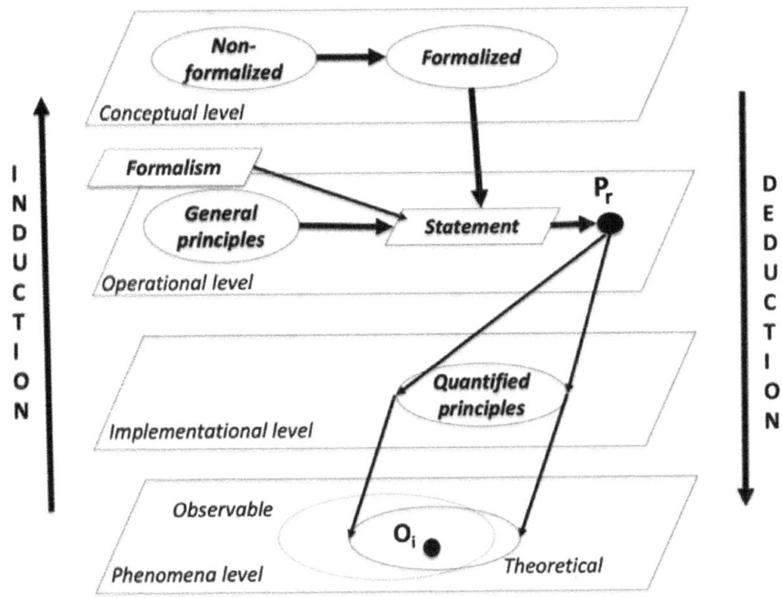

Figure 1.12. *Modeling levels of our scientific approach in living sciences*

The introduction of the phenomena level makes it possible to compare theoretical phenomena generated by a model to observable phenomena. The confrontation is obtained by comparing a theoretical simulation of the model of the minimal set O_i of observed phenomena of the real system. For example, the validation of our model of the calcium metabolism in rats was based on set O_i containing serum calcium and its radioactive tracer ^{45}Ca, other observable phenomena being kept for posteriori validation (weight and growth of rats, role of hormones in serum-calcium regulation, etc.). The intersection of sets of theoretical and observable phenomena in Figure 1.12 is not limited to the initial set O_i chosen. We distinguish case A, observable phenomena that are explained by theoretical phenomena; case B, observable phenomena that are not explained by the model; and case C, theoretical phenomena that do not correspond to phenomena already observed.

The exploitation of the model is led at the phenomena level (see Figure 1.12): Case A (phenomena that are observed and simulated) validates the model; Case B shows that the model is valid but cannot explain some observable phenomena, and thus, the model must be extended to reinforce its explanation of the real system and Case C predicts experiments to obtain new observable phenomena and new knowledge on the real system. Cases B and C may lead to refutation of the model, and a new model must be elaborated by induction from assumptions of the discrepancy between observable and theoretical phenomena. The induction must allow the extraction of relevant concepts or refinement of used concepts, can be reintroduced at the level of the statement of the resulting principle, and the deductive process can start again.

Perault-Staub et al. (1975) highlighted daily fluctuations of serum calcium that were assimilated to circadian rhythms. The explanation proposed was that the first process forming a nucleus is followed by crystallization processes leading to the growth in size of the nucleus, and the multiplication of the number of nuclei formed. The crystal formation rate of this secondary nucleation is autocatalytic, that is, the crystal already formed controls its own rate of formation. The order of this auto-catalysis has been set at 2 for the formation of calcium oxalate (Robertson 1982). In other words, this autocatalytic process (where the order must be greater than one) involves the transformation of amorphous and unstable forms of calcium phosphates into crystals of calcium hydroxyapatite:

Ca^{++}, HPO_4^{--} → $CaHPO_4 . 2H_2O$ → amorphous salts → $Ca_5 (PO_4)3OH$

Solution of CA x P Brushite Crystal of hydroxyapatite of Calcium

The modeling of the calcium metabolism leads to the following compartmental model (Figure 1.13):

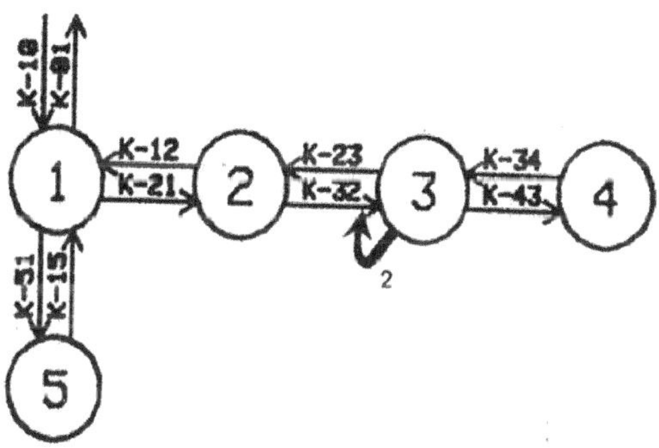

Figure 1.13. *Compartmental model of the calcium metabolism with circadian rhythms*

The model has five compartments, 10 variables (the observations concerned the calcium and a tracer, ^{45}Ca, in compartment 1), 8 parameters and 10 initial conditions.

The physiologists analyzed the model of the calcium metabolism in the rat and noted a clear similarity between the theoretical data and observed data (not all observations were initially used) on the following:

– the daily balance sheet (weight gain per day) and physiological variations in the calcium balance of the rat during its development;

– the different calcium masses in rats (plasma calcium, extracellular calcium, calcium from calcified tissues);

– the daily calcium growth;

– the extrapolated calcium mass in young rats to adulthood;

– daily loss of calcium by the kidneys;

– positioning of the autocatalytic nonlinearity in bone.

Beyond data, evolution of the calcium metabolism is similar to the fasting rat simulation and includes the expression of hormones PTH and CT in the regulation of the calcium metabolism. The compartmental model allowed physiologists to study the mathematical model instead of the real systems (the rats) for developing new assumptions. For example, a new role of hormones as synchronizers of the oscillations of the calcium in plasma was considered. Thus, the model made it possible to study complex and strongly interacting mechanisms and led to guide future bench-top experiments to easily observable points.

The formal model is close to the task model or procedure, except that the lack of a theoretical solution of a nonlinear model would mean that there is no explicit task model or procedure. Hereafter, we speak of nonlinear behaviors that can be observed only by simulation, as discussed for model-based and CxG-based simulations for describing nonlinear reasoning. We also met this situation with scientific workflows (SWFs) for which researchers contextualize, decontextualize and recontextualize in order to establish a proceduralized task model specific to the context at hand.

The scientific approach in living sciences concerns the theoretical modeling of a real system by adjustments of the model behavior established from concepts supposed to explain system behavior when confronting observable phenomena. Although the behavior of the real system is as normal as possible, an experiment is realized with maximum constant parameters (temperature, food, etc.) to isolate the real system from the variations of its environment and thus make the experiment repeatable by any researcher. Thus, the experiment is independent of the actor, the situation and the local environment. Indeed, without context, the model must be able to behave in the environment like the real system (strict identical behavior) not the opposite, that is, the environment indicating how the model is to behave (what are the instantiation of the contextual elements). The main reason is that the real system is context-independent.

In AI, the real system is not an object like calcium metabolism, but rather an activity executed by the object, for instance, like the role of the calcium metabolism in bone formation (the autocatalytic process). As a result, the scientific approach in living systems cannot be applied directly in AI, where context plays a key role through the actor, the activity, the situation and the local environment. A mental model only needs to know the instantiation of contextual elements (the parameters) to choose itself the path to follow. Thus, the four modeling levels of the framework presented in Figure 1.12 must be revised for outing center stage the actor and context in the approach. The formal model must be replaced by a mental model, which acts as a tool for monitoring the real system from an external viewpoint.

We adapt this scientific approach for modeling how an actor manages an activity. An activity relies on a known model, but its modeling concerns its realization by the actor in a given situation with a local environment and the resources required for the realization. All these conditions constitute the context of the activity. Thus, an operational model of an activity is context-based. Here, we call context "what surrounds the activity". It is in the spirit of our initial definition of context (Brézillon and Pomerol 1999): "Context is what constrains the focus of attention of an actor without intervening in it explicitly." Other important differences with the initial scientific approach are: the effective role played by the actor, the identification of the context at hand and the correction of failures in the activity model. This supposes that the actor has tools built on an efficient context-based formalism.

Our approach is based on a modeling of the actor's activity in four modeling levels, namely, conceptual, operational, implementation and environment levels. The activity carried out by a group of actors is shown in Chapter 3 as an extension of the framework established for one actor. Interaction between the activity and its environment is context-dependent. An important difference with the scientific approach for living systems, where the theoretical phenomena have to be as close as observed phenomena, in AI, the observed phenomena (provided by the sources of context) are used by the instantiation process for guiding the mental model development. The four sources of context contain the specificities of the context at hand for instantiating contextual elements during the mental-model development and feed the implemented model with the information, knowledge and reasoning of the actor(s) for activity exploitation. Thus, a context-based formalism of representation plays the important role of "concept revealer" in the activity model at different levels from concepts to an operational model and then to implementation to be confronted with context sources in the activity environment. Such a four-level referential shows that a full understanding of an activity realized by an actor is supposed to globally model the activity in the four modeling levels.

We are aware that concepts such as context, activity, reasoning, mental model and mental representation are not totally formalized and thus have various meanings in different domains at the conceptual level. Moreover, we use the concept "activity" with two meanings, one given in cognitive science, and the other close to subprogram in computer science (the differences are pointed out in the text when needed). Reasoning is defined in various disciplines (more or less formal) along different priorities: formal exploration of logical rules, psychological mechanisms or even practical applications. Decision-making being central in activities, we consider that reasoning consists of starting from collecting, assembling and structuring contextual knowledge and information for making a valid decision that maximizes the means to use for a given goal.

Chapter 2 presents our approach for modeling an actor activity at four levels, from the more abstract to the more concrete, starting from concepts used in our modeling with refinement of concepts at the other levels. Chapter 3 describes group-activity modeling as an extension of the actor-activity infrastructure.

1.3. Projects and applications

1.3.1. *Introduction*

We present in this section 10 projects and applications undertaken between 1986 and 2015 that lead to significant findings on the context-based modeling of an activity. However, the scope of these findings is not limited to the area where they were made, and the use of the CxG formalism on all the projects and applications (and by numerous students at the master with a course on context management) was a way to reinforce its "universality". The first project was the SEPT project that triggered all this research by proving that a real modeling of context was mandatory, the solution retained was ad hoc with a piece of software for configuring knowledge to a particular context, a manual solution ad hoc. The real start of our research on context (and the first version of the CxG formalism) was in the SART project. The other projects are the opportunity for more specific points on context modeling. Note that, at that time, we spoke of task not of activity because AI was more concerned by the formalization of the AI approaches to center research on the realization of the task than on a task model. Moving the focus on task realization was a means to indirectly introduce into the loop the actor that realized the task and the context in which the task was realized. The transition then to the notion of activity was natural (but made explicitly later).

1.3.2. *The SEPT project (1986–1995)*

The SEPT project ("Surveillance d'Equipements dans les Poste à très haute Tension") concerned equipment monitoring in Extra High Voltage (EHV, 400 000 volts) substations of Electricité de France (EDF; Bau and Brézillon 1992). An automated control system monitors a system and automatically eliminates faults, but such control systems are themselves subject to failures. When a fault appears on the network, a whole set of control systems "see" the fault and react. It results in an avalanche of signals arriving at the status logger for a very short period of time (usually 1–2 seconds), with problems such as telescoping of signals (simultaneity of two signals, which results in only one being recorded on the status logger). Normally, only the control systems, which directly supervise the element of the network supporting the fault, must open.

The diagnosis of equipment failures (or inconsistency between the operation of two devices) is carried out by analyzing the operation of the equipment during fault elimination (controllers can emit 100 signal events). The diagnosis is realized by comparing the logical sequence of events and the real sequence of events that have occurred: at the level of each device, at the level of the devices in a control system and at the level of the EHV substation. The offline diagnosis of automated control systems has two special features:

– Reasoning concerns the overall system (both the controlled system and the control system).

– Many redundant observations must be analyzed to identify an abnormal behavior in the control system.

The SEPT project was a nine-year experiment. SEPT has been in operation since September 1990. It was able to cover several power substations, each comprising 15 power lines, four busbar sections and two transformers. However, three expert systems finally have been developed: a diagnostician (the SEPT expert system), a simulator and a knowledge configurator. SEPT was written in a production rules formalism based on the logic of first-order predicates using an expert systems generator initially developed at EDF. It was coupled with a simulator for an exhaustive theoretical validation of SEPT because incidents on the power system are rare and of very short duration (and corrections must be made rapidly). The diagnostician and simulator were initially designed from technical manuals. Without altering the knowledge base, the diagnostic tool successfully resolved the whole set of incidents that occurred in EHV substations of different topologies.

After the theoretical validation by the simulator, EDF carried out a pragmatic validation on site in an EHV substation in the north of the Paris region. The version of SEPT installed in this workstation was running in parallel with the usual human operations in the EHV substation (SEPT was supplied directly by the data found on the status logger, and the workstation topology at the time of the problem was provided by another software). The operators of this EHV substation then checked the diagnosis of SEPT in relation to their own diagnosis. After one year, it was possible to correct some minor errors in SEPT. The first real-size validation in an EHV substation was a success (the expert system also diagnosed equipment failures not detected by operators).

On the strength of these two validations, EDF then decided to begin a gradual installation of the expert system in all EHV substations in France, starting with a substation in the Alps, which had very different characteristics from the substation in the Paris region. Rapidly, it became obvious that it was not a question of porting SEPT without modifications so far-reaching that a rewrite of SEPT appeared mandatory. Indeed, although domain knowledge is the same in all EHV substations, the contexts in which this knowledge was used were very different. For example, in the mountains it is not possible to space the equipment as in the plains. This had consequences on the way in which the information was repatriated to the status logger (e.g. the "fallout" of information was not recorded while part of the diagnosis of SEPT essentially depended on this information). Other reasons also existed, like only official equipment was recorded, and certain equipment not approved by the company was used (and the expertise was not in SEPT), etc.

As a result, a third step of the research concerned a knowledge configurator for tailoring the SEPT expert system to the specificity of each EHV substation. (In terms used nowadays, the knowledge configurator would be called "contextualizator".) The knowledge configurator KA7 ("Knowledge Acquisition for SEPT") system aims to develop specific clones of SEPT for each EHV substation, which are adapted to specific environments (topologies, equipment on the site, adaptation of "EDF rules" to the current context, etc.), because if all EHV substations are supposed to perform the same task, they are in different contexts, one by the sea, the other in high mountains. Thus, it was important to contextualize the clones of SEPT. Such a configurator was also an idea for managing a set of contextual elements called a generic frame in the head of the consultant and a subset of contextual elements that are relevant for tailoring a platform for a given organization in order to develop a context-based configuration to adapting the tool to users and not users to the tool (OSSMOSE project, section 1.3.10).

However, the SEPT representation possessed other weaknesses, the main one being an artificial structuring of knowledge (mainly the topology of the electrical network) based on screening clauses to handle procedural knowledge in a declarative language. The initial rule-based formalism of production has been modified, first to support explicitly the structure of domain knowledge in the form of independent rule packets for equipment pieces, and, second, the possibility of simulating the behavior of the diagnostician in different contexts to get explanations at different levels of detail. An explanation provides contextual information that is not necessary for the diagnosis but makes this diagnosis explicit. There is other contextual information that was kept more deeply implicit (because it was obvious for experts) such as the fact that equipment pieces work only as long as the fault is seen on the network (control equipment stops functioning when the fault disappears).

The SEPT project highlighted that a real modeling of context was missing. First, the lack of possibility to represent quantitative domain knowledge with the qualitative nature of rule-based representation, obliged us to introduce screening clauses and rule-packet management instead of a real modeling of context. Second, because the SEPT expert system was established for a "decontextualized" EHV substation (a theoretical model or task model as said in the following), a knowledge configurator was implemented for "contextualizing" the SEPT expert system for each particular EHV substation. If the SEPT project would be revisited, we will put context at the core of the knowledge (instead of screening clauses and rule packets) and reasoning (instead of control knowledge in the inference engine) representation. This has been done in the SART project for the subway in Paris (France) and Rio de Janeiro (Brazil).

1.3.3. *The SART project (1996–2002)*

The SART project (1996–2002; SART stands for "Système d'Aide à la Régulation du Trafic", French acronym of support system for traffic control, Brézillon et al. 2000) aimed at developing an intelligent decision support system to help operators who control a subway line to react to incidents that occur on the line. Incident management on a subway line is a difficult task mainly for two reasons. First, the global strategy of the company is to rapidly return to a normal operating mode, and this strategy concerns any incident solving. Second, when an incident occurs, numerous parameters intervene from several heterogeneous sources. All operators monitor their lines in a unique control room, and each has just a few minutes (or seconds) when an incident occurs to analyze the situation, collect contextual information, identify the context in which the incident occurred and make a decision.

One of the main characteristics of a subway line is its large transport capacity (e.g. about 60,000 travelers per hour in the Parisian subway) combined with a regular transport supply. For the sake of security and incident-solving standardization, the company head established secure procedures for each type of incident. For example, the procedure for the incident "ill traveler on a train" instructs the driver to stop at the next station because it is easier to assure the security of passengers at a station rather than in a tunnel. A procedure is a safe action sequence that is supposed to solve a type of incident in any situation or context and mainly relies on the natural structure of the domain knowledge. This decontextualization by abstraction leads to robust procedures that cover a large range of similar incident-solving procedures but, as a counter effect, often resulting in sub-optimal solutions.

As a result, operators adapt procedures as useful guidelines (more or less officially) for each new incident (Brézillon 2003) because (a) the standard procedure is rarely well-adapted to the situation at hand and could lead to improper actions or sub-optimal incident-solving strategies; and (b) a standard procedure may cause the operator to miss important information or lead them to notice too late to adequately solve the incident. Thus, many operators develop practices based on a use-oriented organization of domain knowledge and of their experience. For example, a procedure may preconize to stop the train at a station, but if the station is a connection with another subway line, there is a danger of a massive influx of travelers wanting to get on the train at the station. This is generally built up case by case and complemented with "makeshift repairs" that allow operators to reach the required efficiency. It is a way to achieve the result no matter the path followed. However, this part of the operational knowledge is not captured in procedures.

Operators give a great importance to contextual knowledge (e.g. it is rush hour) for monitoring subway lines. An operator told us, "when I am informed of an incident on my line, I first look to the current state of the whole line to gather contextual information" and then make the decision accordingly. Landauer and Bellman (1993) similarly conclude that the process of problem-solving presents three major steps: "find_context", "pose_problem" and "study_problem". Context includes information and knowledge on the situation that do not intervene directly in the incident solving (e.g. it is rush hour) but constrain the way in which the operator will choose a strategy (e.g. choose the faster way) at each step of the incident solving. To identify a situation's specificity, operators elaborate a scenario (a sequence of actions intertwined with events that do not depend on operators but constrain their actions) based on contextual knowledge and postpone actions in order to quickly make a decision after first collecting and analyzing a maximum of contextual information. Built scenarios enable access to common intermediary situations, as they can reuse common strategies to solve the incident. Consequently, some common action sequences exist in different practices. Operators contextualize their operational knowledge and store it in an adapted computational structure, which will be easily understood by other operators and efficiently used by computer systems.

The contribution is presented in detail throughout this book, and we will be brief in this subsection. The SART system was designed and implemented for helping operators and train drivers facing an incident to rapidly find the right procedure to apply. We first develop a rule-based system for representing official procedures. However, this representation was rejected by operators because it was illegible (too much redundancy) and the representation did not consider the contextual variants of the procedures (Pasquier et al. 2000). We then translated the rule-based representation into a decision-tree representation. There was a better acceptance of the representation by operators, but we (designer and developer) faced a representation too difficult to manage, especially when the addition of a new practice led to doubling the number of branches of the decision tree. A new transformation of the tree into a graph representation finally was the right solution for controlling the development of the graph and for introducing *contextual nodes* instead of "chance nodes". The contextual graph representation formalism was born and used in practically all our projects and applications.

In the SART project, we had to model highly contextual reasoning. We use the contextual graph to take into account temporal and context-based reasoning. This model relies on observed reasoning modes in which the context and its dynamics are essential. The analysis of operators' behavior during incident solving has shown that context takes three different forms, namely external knowledge, contextual knowledge and proceduralized context, with a dynamic of the exchanges between these three kinds of context. The operational definition of context established in this project, but applicable to other projects too, bridges a coherent conceptual framework and an operational framework, the Contextual-Graphs formalism and a piece of software used later in numerous applications. Our research was the topic of a course "Context Management" in the Innovation Master of Sorbonne University for more than 10 years. Pointing out the difference between procedures developed from an engineering viewpoint and practices of end-users that tailor what the tactician says to stick to the problem more deeply and respecting the policy of the company. Something that exists in a number of domains. For example, we see that in the domain of bank loans, where employees secretly use a magical notebook of the (non-official) practices they developed to satisfy clients but staying in the policy of the company, even without respecting the tactical rules.

There is an opposition between engineering and cognitive viewpoints that is only superficial because these viewpoints do not consider context at the same level: one is at the level of the knowledge representation and the other at the level of the interaction between two agents (Brézillon and Abu-Hakima 1995). The incident manager of this project is a decision support system based on the contextual analysis of events that arise at the time of the incident. It uses a context-based representation of incidents and applies, thus, a context-based reasoning.

1.3.4. *The FlexMIm project (2012–2015)*

The FlexMIm project (French acronym for "Platform for processing and sharing medical images in a cloud environment: adaptation to anatomo-pathology") concerns the formalization of medical practices in chronic inflammatory bowel disease (IBD) diagnosis. The consortium comprised two large enterprises, four research laboratories and 27 experts, anatomo-cyto-pathologists (ACPs). Anatomical pathology aims to examine macroscopically, and also microscopically, patients' tissue samples and cells in order to establish not only the diagnosis but also the factors of severity of the tumor, contributing thus to therapeutic decisions. For that, the ACP physicians have procedures that include a gross examination (visual examination of diseased tissues), dissection and sampling of surgical specimens according to well-defined protocols and then a microscopic examination of stained tissue sections. The ACP's diagnosis uses several techniques such as immuno-histochemistry, cytogenetic and molecular biology to identify molecular abnormalities in cells or tissues. Beyond this large spectrum of data, information and knowledge about the problem, there are the interventions of external elements like the type of task to accomplish, the actor realizing the task, the situation in which the task is realized and the available resources in the immediate environment.

The FlexMIm project aimed to provide ACPs a platform for their collaborative work (initial diagnosis, tele-expertise, remote learning) based on the technology of "digital slides" (the images viewed in a microscope are scanned in 30-Go files and used instead of the "real slides" on the microscope). Digital slides have the advantage of allowing relocation of reading and collaborative work, but their processing is yet to establish. Our work concerned the modeling of ACPs' reasoning during IBD diagnosis as a contextual graph to identify a consensual methodology (Brézillon et al. 2014). The main goals of the FlexMIm project are: (1) to facilitate consultation of digital slides, ensuring the quality of the scanned slides and pre-annotation of the regions of interest that can then be downloaded and/or pre-analyzed in priority; (2) to develop and implement a cognitive approach that will be integrated into hospital workflows between patients, pathological reports and image archiving system; (3) to identify regions of interest on digital slides and (4) to record manual annotations of ACPs for completing the automatic annotations. Twenty-seven experts participated in the project to evaluate and validate the effectiveness of cooperative work processes and collaboration provided by the project centered on pathological imaging, leading to its ownership in its scale and spread after drafting a trade repository. The knowledge-acquisition phase and expertise modeling were organized around three workshops about the choice of diseases to study, the observation of how pathologists worked, the identification of similarity in pathologists' works and the proposal of a unified view. The "knowledge manager" for our modeling was a physician (a medical intern) knowing the expert knowledge used by ACPs but not having their expertise. Patient's data are collected during complex diagnostic decision-making and long-term treatment in oncology. They do not simply form a chronology of events, but they build up a network of various relationships between numerous information pieces. In the domain of cancer therapy, a single laboratory value, for example, is useless without knowing the previous values and the particular temporal context (e.g. chemotherapy or radiotherapy administered before or at the same time).

Our model of the IBD expertise, as represented in the contextual graph, is original under several aspects. First, the contextual graph contains the different ways to diagnose dysplasia by different ACPs in a domain that is not formalized. Its validation by the 27 ACPs means that each ACP agrees on the representation of their expertise and accepts the expertise of the other ACPs. This validation was the opportunity for ACPs to establish a shared glossary. Thus, the mental representation and the glossary constitute a shared experience base. Second, glocalization of the analysis of a digital slide of a biopsy is mandatory in this project because cancer identification relies on fuzzy "spots" at the cell level. Thus, the exploration of the slide (global level) aims to find a "zone of interest" where zoom is realized for a local search. The modeling of the glocal search is an important process of decision-making for them that associates a global search of zones of interest on an image and a local search in each zone of interest (Brézillon et al. 2014). Third, the voting system is an alternative to formal approaches in decision-making because the vote process can be tailored to each ACP. Fourth, experience sharing – knowledge as glossary and reasoning as in the contextual graph – offers a new platform for efficient collaborative decision-making. A voting system is a particularly useful concept for group activity, especially when group members are all experts in a domain where science is more an art than a science, that is, where the expert's experience is the main tool. We observed that experts reach the same result for each slide analyzed, but in different ways due to different criteria, different weights given to criteria, different interpretations of criteria, consideration of different combinations of criteria, that is, on the method to apply for the diagnosis.

1.3.5. *The TACTIC project (2013–2015)*

The objective of the TACTIC project (French acronym for "Contextualized support on a tablet for the transmission of command information", Kabil et al. 2015) was the development of a man–machine interface on touchpad for a software of Command & Control (C2) for military, easy to use, that helps operators to manage the complexity of the commands and information at their disposal. Responses to a crisis on the battlefield require systematical gathering, analyzing and fusion of a large amount of heterogeneous data and information of varying significance and accuracy, which is often redundant, unreliable or contradictory. The operator has to face three interrelated challenges:

– Collecting the data from three sources. It is the problem of identifying what the problem is and extracting the relevant data for handling the problem.

– Translating data and information into knowledge. It is the problem of situation and impact assessment that infers, approximates and predicts the critical characteristics of the environment to produce a contextual understanding of the events and behaviors of interest in relation to particular goals, capabilities and policies of the decision-makers.

– Using that knowledge wisely. It is the problem of crisis management, a collection of methods and tools aimed at helping decision makers control dynamic situations and act effectively to prevent and/or mitigate crises.

The three sources of information provided by a C2 system are presented in Figure 1.14 as the operators see them.

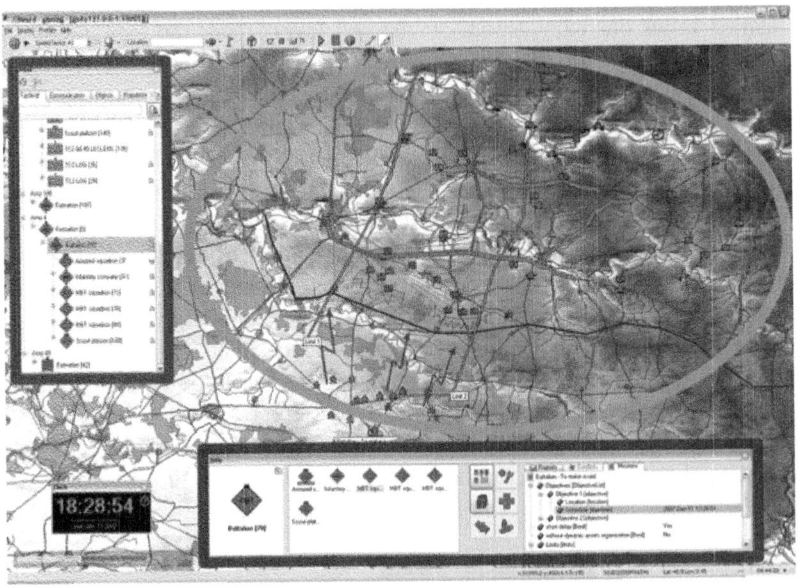

Figure 1.14. *The three sources of information in a C2 system. For a color version of this figure, see www.iste.co.uk/brezillon/contextbasedmodeling.zip*

Information and communication systems, as shown in Figure 1.14, give operators a view of the operational situation, typically with a map overlaid with symbols that represent (military) units. A C2 system gathers information from several sources and lets the actor communicate and give orders directly. Such systems also are used, or on the way to being used, by first responders or large operators in the private sector. Military C2 systems that are used on the field generally have a tactile interface of small size to address the requirements of mobility and simplicity of use in difficult situations. Up to now, interfaces were complex to use and required training. There are three zones on the interface. First, a geographical map as a representation of the global situation for following events; second, the ORder of BATtle (ORBAT) as the representation of the units and their activities and, third, the event chronology as the representation of the scenario and the actions responsible for the events.

The result of the TACTIC project was a mockup of an intelligent interface on a tablet for a C2 system to handle commands. This interface takes advantage of all the possibilities of gestural touch interfaces to effectively provide information that applies to a broad spectrum of orders and to develop a cognitive man–machine interface that includes the context and history of use to enable actors to manage the complexity of the system. The project proposed (1) using the range of possibilities offered by tactile interfaces (multi-touch control, gestures) for an easy and efficient interface to use and (2) presenting interface behavior at any time with shortcuts and intelligent assistance in order to help it understand the complexity of the system. The interface was integrated in a C2 system and a simulator that receives the order of the C2 system and sends reports on a realistic simulated operational situation that evolves depending on the messages coming from the operator, as a test and validation tool for the interface. The smart touch interface model explicitly incorporates the notion of context as contextual elements to present the actor with the most relevant commands and information at any time.

Our actors were nine experts of the company developing the battle simulator SWORD. Only one was a military scientific consultant (considered as a strategy expert) and the civil experts had an expertise very close to that of the military experts. The two main classes of actors were tactical experts (project development manager, pre-sales project managers) and operational experts (modelers, quality manager), with thus two distinct concerns for interacting with the simulator SWORD in real conditions. An interesting point of the TACTIC project was the modeling of mental representations of experts. A domain model was adjusted to the use of the simulator by experts, and finally, only 105 contextual elements were selected for constituting a kind of generic mental representation (Hoffman 1997). This provides experts with a starting point for describing their personal mental representations as mental mind[1]. After, experts were put in real conditions for working with the simulator on a given scenario (reconnaissance of a situation). At the end of the session, experts were required to suppress the contextual elements of their mental representation they did not use during the session and thus establish their mental model corresponding to the scenario development, the decisions made and the actions taken. The mental representation corresponds to the partially

1. Mental minds were built by experts with the software Freemind.

structured knowledge that experts used at least once during their work. This mental representation can move away from the domain model by a total reorganization of the elements that correspond the best to the experts' reasoning during task realization. Each mental representation is personal to an expert, while experts realize the same task in different ways from the same domain representation. Variants of the procedures appear as soon as there exists freedom of degrees in the way to realize the task, including the use of tools. The interface is a communication medium similar to a shared context through which the operator and the simulator interact via interface actions (currently, mapping, tabs, zooming, window management, etc.). Changing the interface (or using several ones) then obliges us to ensure the conversion of domain actions performed by the operator into those performed by the simulator, and reciprocally. This approach opens the way to new graphic and gestural concepts for a new medium like the tablet. The interface between the actor and the simulator is "physical" and also "cognitive". It is an active intermediary for translating messages (information, order to execute) from human to the simulator and vice versa.

There are three lessons learned from the TACTIC project (Brézillon 2017). The first lesson, at the physical interaction level, concerns action differentiation of the operator and those of the simulator for the control of the simulation, and finally the identification of the actions that are related to the interface. As a result, the operator associates the control of the simulation with actions on the interface that are supposed to play the role of the simulator for the operator. Operator-simulator interaction (cognitive interaction) is considered secondary to interaction with the interface (physical interaction). Indeed, operators in our experiment said to "interact with the simulation" not with the simulator because the simulation was the visible part of the combined work of the interface and the simulator. The second lesson is to make compatible, at the cognitive–interaction level, the operator's mental representation and the three sources of information of the simulator, say the "simulator's mental representation" (i.e. the geographical map, the ORBAT and the event chronology). The third lesson is the importance of considering the interface as a full group member in a computer-mediated group activity (but not modeled in this study) with the operator and the simulator.

1.3.6. *The ACA project (2005–2009)*

Car driving is a complex set of activities that needs practical experiments to be safe. Initial training for obtaining a driving license is not sufficient because the apprentice does not know how to contextualize learned procedures in effective practices. The main factor of novice drivers' errors is an inadequate mental representation of the driving situation. Indeed, a driver's decision-making is not based on the objective state of the world but on a crude mental model of the driving context they developed in real-time. This "circumstantial representation" (Richard 1990) is built from perceptive information extracted in the road scene and from permanent knowledge stored in long-term memory. Bailly et al. (2003) illustrate the potential effect of inexperience at different levels of situation awareness.

The long-term objective of the ACA (Adequate Category Learning) project was a training simulation tool to detect a pre-critical situation and assess the potential risk of accident. The human self-training support system was based on two measures of similarity: the similarity of belonging, which is defined as a numerical "distance" between an apprentice and one of the given categories in a defined typology. The second measure of similarity is the similarity of transformation, which is the distance between the category where the apprentice can be placed initially (starting category) and the category goal targeted by the learning. The ACA project is about human learning based on these similarities (Brézillon et al. 2009; Brézillon 2010). This training method involves three steps: (1) positioning the apprentice in a starting category, (2) establishing the sequence of transformations that are necessary to bring the apprentice from their starting category to the appropriate category and (3) validation of the category of arrival. The ACA method requires two things: first, a preliminary definition of a typology of categories based on behaviors specific to the problem studied, where links between all the categories represent how to move from one category to another and, second, the establishment of an analysis situation, in which the apprentice can interact and show their behavior when confronted with the studied problem. In each analysis situation, all the potential behaviors of the learner are determined and instantiable in the typology of categories.

This method has been applied in the field of road safety. The typology of driver behaviors was established from a questionnaire based on 420 answers from Internet users. Eleven scenarios (sequences of driving situations that can end in a critical situation where an accident can occur) have been created to test driving errors of attendees. The experiment involved 45 participants, 39 of them improved their behaviors, going into a category closer to an adequate category than the initial category. The driver modeling relies on two complementary representations that provide an efficient tool to improving drivers' context awareness: one for situations (an objective representation by a lattice) and the other for driver's behaviors (a subjective representation by a contextual graph), both being related through scenarios.

The driver's behavior is modeled simultaneously at the four decisional levels of GADGET (an acronym for "Guarding Automobile Drivers through Guidance Education and Technology"), a European project on road safety (Hatakka et al. 2002). The GADGET variables for describing car-driving activity were enriched with contextual variables concerning the driver (age, gender, motivation, etc.), the environment (e.g. climatic conditions), the driving environment (e.g. animal on the road) and the car (e.g. if the driver takes care of their car). The typology was established based on driving errors. The links between the different categories have been created to establish the path of an apprentice who must reach the category goal. The ACA method offers a progressive learning for the apprentice that is adapted since the training is established from the starting category of the apprentice. This method has been applied to road safety to improve driver behavior by improving their situational awareness. It was tested during an experiment that took place on a driving simulator.

Using good and bad practices for the training of human actors constitutes a relevant base of experiences (Brézillon et al. 2006). Concretely, training is based on scenarios with critical driving situation learned from bad drivers, and it interacts with the driver to help them to avoid the critical situation by identifying it before in pre-critical situations, thanks to context made explicit. A pre-critical situation occurs when the driver identifies a change in the situation or in its context, or a change in their behavior and has to make a decision between alternatives (i.e. to modify the initial driving plan) when the driver still has the option to retrieve a normal situation. The Goals for Driver Education (GDE) matrix shows that any decision-making must be considered globally at the four decision levels (policy, strategy, tactic, operation), with roots in upper levels and consequences at lower ones. Scenarios aim to model a driver's behavior in a space of behaviors and a space of situations.

1.3.7. *"Contextualizing scientific workflows" project (2009–2011)*

Searching for a specific SWF in a repository is as difficult as finding a specific entity in a collection. As a result, it is difficult to establish direct relationships between SWF models and thus difficult to organize them for a reuse purpose. Thus, SWF systems are not able to provide reasons for selecting a particular SWF model because the context of the SWF exploitation (e.g., user's preference, common knowledge and their behaviors) is not shared, while this context guides the translation of the routine in the new exploitation context (Fan et al. 2011).

SWF technology has merged over the last decade to automate the composition and execution of complex computational and data analysis tasks in the science domain (Buyya et al. 2009). It is not possible to design an SWF in advance. Unfortunately, research attempts seem to be interested solely in addressing technical challenges, such as specification, execution and computing resources, while overlook the human dimension, such as user–system interaction, collaboration patterns and intelligent decision support. For example, routine workflow realizations blow up in a huge number of variants with similar functionality but different quality; thus, their differences largely rely on various contexts and the situations at hand (Fan et al. 2011). In data-centered scientific research, hypotheses are increasingly generated by combining and mining the pool of data already available. However, current SWF systems fail to address such challenges for the following main relevant reason:

– *Lack of "Context"*. Current SWF systems are not capable of making the "context" of the case accessible to scientists that could not shift to a specific practice to address their focus at hand.

– *Inflexible decomposition of workflow representation*. Scientists need to carry out their work at a "fine-grained" level, such as "changing the parameters whenever needed in real-time".

– *Push-oriented perspective*. Most SWF systems impose inflexible practices on scientists and block the decision-making process.

– *Insufficient sharing of SWF representation*. No smart automatic rerun of SWF is available to scientists to deliver new outcomes when fresh data become available in a new context.

The approach has been confronted with the application "Virtual screening research on avian influenza H5N1 virus" as a case study. Virtual screening is about selecting in silico the best candidate drugs acting on a given target by docking millions of small molecules separately on the target. The principle is to dock all the ligands presented in a database into the binding pocket of the selected target and evaluate the fit between the molecules. The quality of the fit is then used to rank the small molecules. To perform virtual screening computation, many tools are usually needed: target structure prediction, structural analysis, compound collections, target preparation, definition of ligand binding site (selection of targets) and in silico docking and scoring methods. In silico virtual screening requires intensive computing, in order to reduce the number of molecules requiring in vitro and then in vivo testing from a few millions to a few hundred. Access to very large computing resources has resulted in successful high-throughput virtual screening.

The identification of H5N1 crystallized structure marked an important milestone in global efforts to address the threat of H5N1 virus. The challenges for scientists were (1) to determine the parameters by performing virtual screening research on the complex of H5N1 and (2) to dock millions of molecules separately to select candidate drugs to struggle with the disease. The main problems in the docking preparation scenario are:

– A lack of guidance and notification for scientists to make contexts explicit during the SWF designing phase because scientists do not know the contextual reason behind each choice and the consequent actions to be taken after.

– The previous prototype could only validate the constraints and parameters after the SWF execution, but the scientist may not be aware of the source of a mistake and cannot trace the fault.

– The SWF repository did not contain the representation of scientist reasoning. Specifically, there are no links between an SWF abstract model and its corresponding concrete model, and other scientists may find it difficult to reuse this model when searching.

The objective of the work was to enable making contexts explicit in SWF to provide decision supports and practice learning assistances for scientists by implementing a context-oriented methodology to figure out which kinds of contextual information behind the choices of scientists are missing. Flexibility is an important challenge for scientists because scientific discovery is, by nature, explorative and an adaptive process. Thus, several methods could be used alternatively for the same experimental goal. The lack of flexibility is an inhibitor in the use of SWF systems to transform hypotheses into scientific discoveries. The challenges for a flexible SWF are: (1) the SWF representation is not necessarily rigidly structured, i.e. portions of SWF can often be redone several times while other parts can be skipped; (2) a number of tools, resources and services are not available in advance of the SWF execution and (3) the SWF execution depends heavily on professional knowledge. The positive point is a certain degree of flexibility due to the separation of process logic from the actual execution. However, the negative point is that current approaches are mainly targeted at the implementation and programmatic level; thus, they overlook the human-aspect flexibility at the global viewpoint, which is very important for scientists because a certain number of possible execution paths are unknown before execution. The use of the Contextualization–Decontextualization–Recontextualization (CDR) approach leads to identification of the SWF model (result of the decontextualization) and precisely how the SWF model is instantiated (recontextualization). Thus, it was possible to extend the scientist's activity in a contextual graph that guides the scientist in the search for a variant of the initial SWF for solving their specific problem.

Fan et al. (2011) applied the CDR process in the search for an SWF in the virtual screening of the H5N1 virus: A researcher extracts a successful SWF from a repository that is considered close to the object of the study (phase of contextualization), extracts the corresponding SWF model (phase of decontextualization) and then instantiates the SWF model in the working context at hand (phase of recontextualization). Then, a workflow engine ensures the execution phase in which input data is consumed according to the instantiated SWF and output data are produced as results. If it is a success, the new SWF is put in the repository for other scientists. Otherwise, a new iteration is needed by reconsidering either the phase of decontextualization for finding a new model or by trying a different recontextualization of a new SWF.

1.3.8. *The MICO project (2011–2014)*

The Cognitive Microscope project (MICO) aims at developing a cognition-driven visual explorer for histopathology (Brézillon 2012). MICO proposes a radical change in medical practice by proposing a cognition-driven medical imaging environment enabling safer decision-making for histopathology. MICO system integrates dynamic capture, representation and use of specific visual medical knowledge, in order to setup the bases of a cognition-driven medical imaging, able to address pervasive adaptation and physical–virtual confluence challenges for histopathology. Apart from the use for safe and robust decision support, the huge amount of available medical information captured and represented by MICO constitutes a source of new knowledge for pathologists and medical researchers. Thus, the improvement of the pathology-prognosis accuracy comes from integrating history, contextual information, earlier stage diagnostic results (physical examination, previous radiologic exam results, etc.) as well as a cognitive driven prognosis support (such as retrieval of similar cases and similar virtual slides, prognosis expert procedures and methods, etc.).

In image analysis, the objects to which the diagnosis applies play an important role for the expert because there is no frame or prototype for analyzing images. Thus, the same diagnosis may apply to objects for different reasons. As a result, different experts may conclude differently on the same object and thus decision-making often results from a negotiation between experts. Indeed, experts collect images resulting from the same diagnosis and constitute a “wall of images” to compare several objects in order to confirm their diagnosis.

For helping the organization of image walls, Figure 1.15 shows a tree representation (see section 2.4.3) of the contextual graph representing the diagnosis in order to follow more carefully the organization of the images on the wall. A path in the tree (and the corresponding contextual graph) represents the mental model leading to a diagnosis on a digital slide (mitosis, no mitosis, uncertain mitosis). Then, the mental model becomes the explanation of the decision-making, and when two mental models lead to the same diagnosis, it is in two different contexts that can be analyzed.

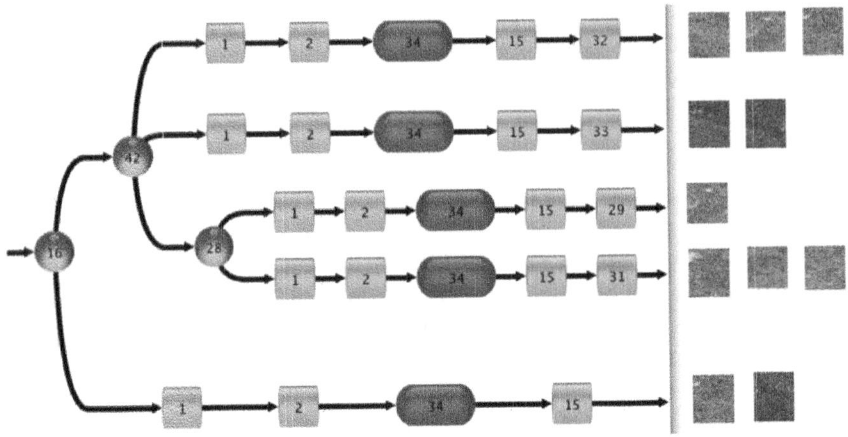

Figure 1.15. *Tree representation of the "mitosis diagnosis" for a wall of images. For a color version of this figure, see www.iste.co.uk/brezillon/contextbasedmodeling.zip*

The tree representation shows clearly the two steps of the decision-making process: (1) collecting and instantiating contextual elements for building the proceduralized context; and (2) making the decision. A possible extension would be to use this approach by replacing digital slides with, say, the results of a mental model (e.g. accept, refuse, wait for additional information), the situation to analyze, etc. The tree representation also offers the possibility to define a "cognitive measure" on two points. First, on the objects of the diagnosis either corresponding to a given mental model that will not be possible otherwise (very important for digital slides that are very heterogeneous) or on objects classified by two different practices. Second, a contextual distance can be applied to mental models to improve or re-organize the contextual model. The tree representation also presents an interest for improving coordination and collaboration between different experts or for optimizing a team work (or a sport team). The mental-model tree representation that is associated with the contextual graph offers to end-users the possibility to make their decision rapidly by identifying what is the situation (given by the proceduralized context) and then what must be done.

1.3.9. *The winemaking project (1997–1999)*

The fermentation step of the winemaking process is strongly correlated with events that occur at previous steps. The winegrowing is not directly related to alcoholic fermentation, even though knowledge of the former step is used by the wine maker in the latter step. We call such knowledge contextual knowledge, and our goal is to design and implement a contextual-knowledge-based system. The problem to solve (fermentation stops) is the heart, and contextual knowledge is organized in layers around the heart in an order that relies on a qualitative distance. In the most frequent cases of blended fermentations, the good fermentative qualities of one wine variety can compensate for the faults of another. The consequences are lost money, full vats, critical time deadlines not respected and possible noxious effects (Agabra et al. 1997). Several actors intervene all along the process, the main ones being vine-grower, cellar master, enologist, the microbiologist and a laboratory. Each actor has their own working context different from that of others but shared some knowledge with them. Our modeling of the problem had to account for all the types of knowledge, the ones concerning directly the fermentation as well as those as far away as the weather during vine-growing, for example.

In this project, we addressed the critical problem of stops in alcoholic fermentation and the difficulties that may rise in its achievement. Winemaking is a domain where formalization is very difficult (or even impossible), mainly because we have to deal with heterogeneous knowledge that comes into play at different steps of the winemaking process. Whatever the causes are, the consequence of a stop in alcoholic fermentation is the same: the fermentation process, in which sugar is transformed into alcohol, slows down (sometimes very much) or even stops completely, leaving too much sugar in the wine. These events are respectively called sluggish and stuck fermentations. They can result in wine spoilage because there is a severe control on wine quality (e.g. for quality reasons, the final sugar concentration in the wine must be lower than 2 g/l, except for sweet wines). Our contribution aimed to help winemakers to predict stops in the normal fermentation process as soon as possible. Several approaches already existed (e.g. neural networks, knowledge-based systems). However, these attempts failed to give a satisfactory solution mainly because they had a too partial view of the problem.

From the expert knowledge gathered from interviews, a model of the domain (deep knowledge) and a set of rules (shallow knowledge) have been implemented. A simulation based on the model provides an evaluation of the risk of stuck fermentation of a particular must. Before the simulation, we have a set of data that leads to a description of a must at the beginning of the fermentation phase or during it. We use all the available information about previous phases (measured chemical parameters, actions already done, etc.). Unfortunately, it is not always possible (and almost never in the fermentation case) to derive an explicit path between contextual knowledge and the focus, mainly due to lack of information that can correspond to a lack of communication between experts or by a too complex deep knowledge for being organized correctly. To overcome the problem, we first used contextual knowledge as shallow knowledge. The incomplete path is replaced by a global link between known pieces of knowledge and the focus in the spirit of subgoaling in SOAR (Laird et al. 1987). For example, some enologists use the following rule: if a vat's temperature is higher than 30°C (for red wines), and if there is no frequent airing, this will be damageable to yeast. Contextual knowledge thus becomes contextualized knowledge for the solving of a weaker problem. Our contextual-knowledge-based system was working with a neural-network representation of the wine fermentation step (the deep knowledge).

This project shows that the onion metaphor was relevant for the ordering of contextual elements around a focus. However, in this application, alcoholic fermentation was too complex to be modeled, and enologists preferred to consider this step as a black box. The work then was to (1) model contextual elements along the onion metaphor and (2) model enologists' expertise in an expert system coupled to a neural network. Another observation of interest is that a relevant contextual element, which explains the result, can be far from the focus of attention. This is a justification of our view of context as constituted of contextual knowledge and external knowledge with exchanges of contextual elements between them.

1.3.10. *The OSSMOSE project (2009–2011)*

The OSSMOSE project (open source software for medium enterprises and small organization) offers entrepreneurs and companies a contextualized platform of interoperable open source tools to allow the enterprise to manage its various steering business processes and supports integrating the possible evolution of the platform. The context-based configuration of a platform for an organization showed the need to adapt the tool to users and not users to the tool. It is the case of a platform for an organization of real size and also contextual information on enterprise growth. The solution is based on the context-based modeling of an experience base managed by the consultant through a "contextualizator" and a configurator used by the customer to build its contextualized solution that can easily be updated. This configuration consists of the development of a solution by setting (instantiating) contextual elements according to the specifics of its business. The customer then can easily "play" a number of situations, especially depending on their enterprise's growth prospects, and have a platform not only adapted to current needs but also anticipated its future prospects.

The experience base with the consultant's expertise is modeled as a contextual graph where each path represents the effective realization for a given entrepreneur of a professional platform that results from the contextualization of a configuration file generated and implemented as a configurator output. The customer can therefore control the extent to which a solution used by another entrepreneur can apply to their business, and which specific changes are needed to adapt the solution to its specificities. The customer then has the opportunity to ask a consultant for making the decision whether to add this new component and record the underlying reasons for this choice (the contextual elements). The "actor-task-situation-environment" set (i.e. the sources of context) is considered to be capable of being described by a set of contextual elements representing a generic frame, that is, coming from the professional platform generated for addressing the specificities of the customer. In the OSSMOSE project, this generic framework brings together all the contextual elements that were used by a consultant applying their experience when helping various entrepreneurs in the construction of a portal.

This approach makes it possible to go beyond the usual simple personalization, to go as far as a real contextualization that considers the entrepreneur, their core business, their company, their situation, the local environment where the entrepreneur works and the potential evolution of the enterprise. This generic frame is enriched incrementally during its use in two ways: on the one hand, upstream by the technological watch carried out by the consultant to introduce new tools on the market (such as free software) and, on the other hand, from original requests of contractors that the consultant may deem relevant and usable for other contractors. Figure 1.16 summarizes how the generic frame is managed in the OSSMOSE project. The generic framework corresponds to contextual knowledge in the consultant's experience.

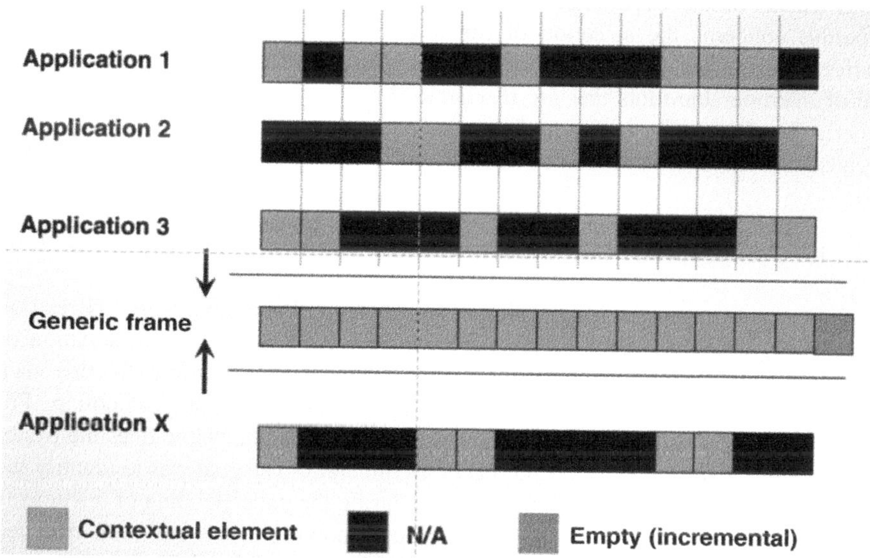

Figure 1.16. *Management of the generic framework in OSSMOSE. For a color version of this figure, see www.iste.co.uk/brezillon/contextbasedmodeling.zip*

Based on their experience in the realization of portals for entrepreneurs (Applications 1, 2 and 3 in Figure 1.16), the consultant is able to identify the most important contextual elements in the realization of each application. Some contextual elements appear in the realization of several applications; others, on the contrary, are specific to an application. All these contextual elements are accumulated in order to allow a new entrepreneur to benefit from these past experiences for the assembly of their portal. This portal is said to be contextualized and not personalized because, on the one hand, contextual elements come from past experiences, and, on the other hand, the portal corresponds to the explicit expression of the entrepreneur's needs and not to a model of the entrepreneur that the consultant could have. This approach is clearly not a statistical approach but an entrepreneur-oriented approach, which leads to an enrichment of the generic framework by an accumulation of individual experiences and not by averaging the accumulated data. Any use of the system leads to the enrichment of its experience base (therefore at a higher level than the historical knowledge bases).

The activity to model concerns the building of a contextualized platform for a given enterprise (i.e. a path in the contextual graph, but at an upper level than in the other applications). The actors, the consultant and the customer have different expertise on tools to assemble on the platform. Consultant's expertise concerns the development of the experience base and the way to assemble tools. Customer's expertise concerns the selection of the tools to assemble on the contextualized platform to be used. The shared context concerns knowledge on the selection and use of interoperable tools that are reachable in the contextual graph. Note that the generic frame is quite different from the onion metaphor in the SART project because the "distance" between contextual elements is not the most important point.

1.3.11. *"Computer-mediated collaborative work" project (1997–1999)*

The research project called "computer-mediated collaborative work" (Brézillon et al. 2006) described cognitive and contextual aspects involved in a situation of collaborative understanding when two or more subjects interact with each other via a computer network to achieve a joint goal and to understand a new notion. For example, subjects had to co-build an answer to questions like "How does the oyster make pearls?" and "How does water becomes mineral?" The goal was to identify the nature of mental models built by the subjects during the understanding of documents and mechanisms underlying this understanding, knowing that it has been enriched by a preliminary and dynamic phase of collaboration mediated by the computer. Several types of cognitive indicators are used: descriptors of verbal interaction during collaboration, analysis of eye movements during reading and error rate to assess comprehension. A mapping of all these indicators provided a holistic view of the collaborative understanding process. Our contribution was a modeling of verbal interaction during the collaboration based on contextual graphs.

The experiment setup was in two phases: a phase of collaboration (a constant duration of 1 min 30 sec) and then the reading/comprehension phase by analysis of eye movements and answers to questions. We only discuss the first phase in this book. Subjects followed naturally a dialog model in four phases, namely reformulate the question, find an example, gather domain knowledge and build the answer either by looking for characteristics or by assembling explanation elements (for an integration). The collaboration model concerned four paths: none of the subjects had knowledge about the answer, subjects had some elements of explanation but were not able to build the answer; the two subjects co-built the answer, each bringing elements to share with the other; and when one subject knew the answer, she spent the 1 min 30 sec imposed to explain the other subject the elements of the answer (often developing explanation based on contextual knowledge). The collaborative process of answer building started with a phase of building understanding of the shared context of the question. Each subject introduces a contextual element from their individual working context. The other subject may agree, or ask for explanation, and eventually negotiate with the first subject. Thus, subjects agree on their shared context, satisfying both of them. In the second phase, the subjects organize, assemble and structure the contextual elements of the shared context to generate a proceduralized context that will be integrated into the answer building. Eleven pairs of participants had to address 16 questions (176 MP3 files of 1 min 30 sec correspond to answers). The experiment setup was in two phases: a phase of collaboration (1 min 30 sec) and then a reading/comprehension phase, including analysis of eye movements and answers to questions. Participants were shown the following four-step process, namely, reformulate the question for reinforcing their understanding, find an example for validating their understanding, then gather domain knowledge and elements of their working context based on this understanding and build the answer either by looking for characteristics or by assembling explanation elements (for an integration).

Several observations could be made about the role of context in this project. First, subjects can know the answer as a whole but not the elements of the answer. As a result, they try to exploit their shared context to express an external and superficial viewpoint on a possible answer. Second, subjects begin by repeating aloud the question to be sure they correctly understand the question (with a possible correction by the other subject), i.e. to activate their mental representations for developing a joint mental model that could address the question. Three, subjects can give an answer at different granularities according to the shared context constituted from their respective working contexts and understanding of the question (e.g. say "gas" instead of "CO_2" for sparkling water). Four, subjects first gather contextual information for establishing shared context about their understanding of the question and second for building a proceduralized context for the answer. Hereafter we mainly use the modeling of the shared-context building about this application.

1.4. Review of the chapter

A model has predictive power that a representation does not because it is limited to observation smoothing. A model can be expressed in different representation formalisms, with more or less expressiveness, although each formalism has strengths, weaknesses and limits. As a result, the choice of a formalism of representation is crucial for a good modeling because it must play the role of revealer of concepts.

Our consideration that a model has predictive power to exploit (Brézillon 1983) explains the crucial choice of the representation formalism. For example, a formalism of linear representation is not adapted for modeling self-oscillations in a nonlinear system. By putting context center stage, we obtain a uniform representation of knowledge, information, reasoning and context coming from different sources. We thus have been able to model activities in very different domains (subway, army, different types of cancer in medicine and workflows), thanks to the Contextual-Graphs formalism that is very simple to use by actors such as physicians, engineers, and students in Psychology. Moreover, the experience bases obtained in the CxG formalism could serve as the foundation for deep learning and for AI generation to achieve known practices and develop new practices when facing new contexts.

We show it is not possible to assimilate a mental representation to a mental model. A reason is a difference of level; mental-model development and mental representation are at the operational level, and mental-model building and the instantiation process of contextual elements are at the implementation level. Mental representation corresponds to actor's experience by the accumulation of mental models developed by the actor in different contexts. In cognitive science, the notion of "chunk" plays a role similar to mental model. A chunk is a collection of basic units (like a "meta basic unit") that are strongly associated with one another (i.e. contextualized), and grouped together and stored in a person's memory (Miller 1956; Schank 1982). These chunks can be retrieved easily due to their coherent grouping like mental models. The CxG formalism is effective for modeling an activity, not for visualizing its evolution. A tree representation supports a simple visualization of contextual reasoning (and all its known variants) in the CxG formalism. The mental-model tree view shows the actors the relevant contextual elements as a proceduralized context and postpones actions to quickly make decisions. A tree representation corresponds to a mental representation, and its branches are the mental models already developed in different contexts, the contextualized contexts in the tree representation.

Our research benefits from this realm of thoughts but needs to implement operational Contextual Intelligent Assistant Systems in real-world applications. Our scientific approach applied over 25 years of research on how to model and use context in real-world applications on a spectrum from technology-centered to human-centered applications, that is, from well-defined domains to not formal ones, but all having the goal to model an activity. Modeling actors' experience was central to our research and led to the identification of four levels: conceptual, operational, implementation and environment levels that are described in the next chapter. The model of an activity has two sides, operation, used as a mental model drawn from their mental representation, and implementation, that can be used and transmitted as a contextual graph. This explicit integration of context in the representation follows the human style of actors' activity (collecting and structuring information, making decisions and acting). Mental model and mental representation of Cognitive Science are treated as two different concepts that have been integrated in the CxG formalism.

We started our research on context in the technological domain in which formal models of equipment exist to monitor. Globally, even though domain knowledge is accessible such as reports or rules, some external elements have to be considered concerning how to use domain knowledge with respect to the actor, the task the actor must realize, the situation in which the task is realized and the local environment where there are resources available for the task. All these external elements may constrain the normal functioning of the task. Actor, activity, situation and environment are sources of contextual knowledge that matter for task realization. We discovered rapidly that modeling context supposes the actor considers task realization, not a model of the task only. The unique consideration of a formal model is insufficient for developing a competent computer software: it is also important to consider the context in which the activity is realized by an actor. Actors interpret the task model (e.g. procedures of the company that are declared as mandatory) according to the contextual information collected to determine how to address the activity in the specific context, whatever this way is if policy and strategic decisional levels of the company are respected (e.g. prioritizing a fast solution to avoid a degraded situation in the SEPT project and traveler security and traffic regularity in the SART project). Again, actors use contextual knowledge from sources such as the activity, the situation and the local environment. As a result, context is strongly related to operational knowledge and reasoning, both in models and in the actors' heads.

The 10 projects and applications presented in section 1.3 of this chapter are the foundation of our progress in the modeling and use of context. Each project concerns some contextual elements that are specific to the project and also contextual elements specific to other projects. The other projects or applications, which are not cited, concerned just the exploitation of the results of our research without new findings for it.

Chapter 2 introduces a general approach to formalize the notion of context modeling when the activity to model is under the responsibility of a unique actor.

2

Context Modeling for Actor Activity (CxG_1.0)

2.1. Introduction

This chapter proposes a refinement of the concepts initially considered in Chapter 1 for the effective modeling and use of context in projects and applications. The evolution of our approach is followed at four levels. First, the conceptual level leads to identifying relevant concepts and their organization. For example, the concepts of context, knowledge and reasoning are chosen, and relationships between them are identified, for instance context divides knowledge into contextual knowledge and external knowledge with respect to an activity. Second, the operational level discusses three important notions: mental model, mental representation and contextual element, the latter being central in our context modeling. Third, the implementation level presents the Contextual-Graphs (CxG) formalism from its design to the piece of software (CxG_1.0 version), with the keystone that downstream is the implementation of contextual elements as pairs {contextual node, recombination node}, and upstream explains context from contextual knowledge to contextual elements. Fourth, the environment level allows the explicitation of the interaction between the activity and its local environment under two aspects: one is the four sources of context (the actor, the activity, the situation, the environment) and the second is the instantiation mechanism of the contextual elements encountered on the path of the contextual graph during the mental-model development.

The general framework of our approach for modeling actor activity is presented in Figure 2.1. The four modeling levels are (1) the conceptual level where ideas are stated on the basis of the concepts of interest for modeling an activity in context, (2) the operational level where ideas are organized in a mental model, thanks to a relevant context-based formalism of representation, (3) the implementation level where the actor's mental representation is programmed as a contextual graph from which a mental model is developed and (4) the environment level, first, where the model interacts with the activity environment (with mainly the actor as the source of context) through software, and, second, where contextual elements are instantiated when needed from the four sources of contextual elements at hand.

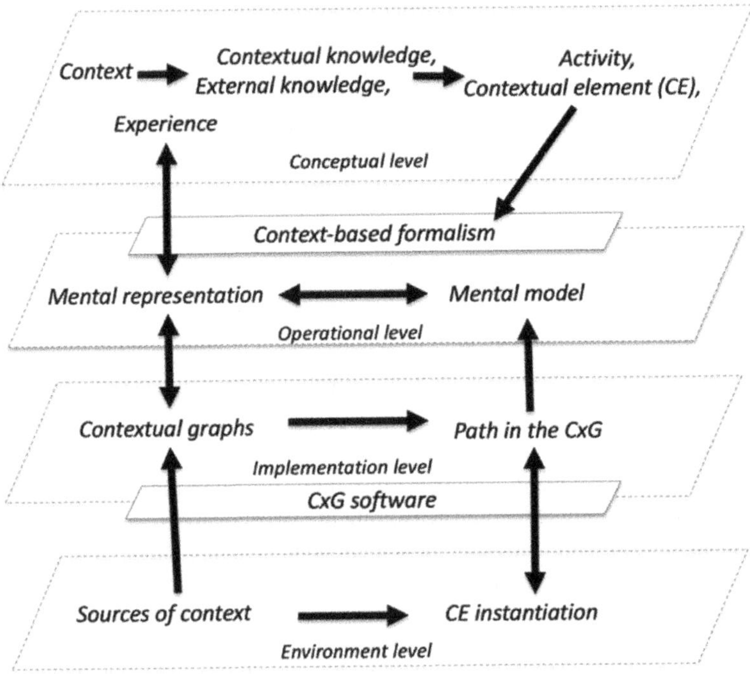

Figure 2.1. *Actor activity at four modeling levels*

The actor plays a central role in the four modeling levels when interacting with the activity. For example, actor's understanding of the activity at the operational level relies on a mental model, while, at the implementation level, the actor's understanding of the activity development corresponds to a path in a contextual graph that is developed by exchanges with the environment, the fourth level where the activity is put in context. The operational and implementation levels represent two views of the actor's experience (as mental representation and as contextual graph), the development of the mental model being considered as extracted from the mental representation. The concepts represented in Figure 2.1 are defined in the text when they appear in italics.

The important points of our research from this chapter and the following Chapter 3 are represented in a cartridge-shaped like:

KP0	Definition of the key point noted KP0

2.2. Conceptual level

2.2.1. *Contextual knowledge and external knowledge*

The conceptual level concerns the concepts “activity”, “reasoning”, “context”, “contextual element” and “experience”, these concepts of interest being not (at least totally) formalized. Our goal is to propose a formalization of “context” in order to have an efficient formalism for modeling the other concepts of interest, mainly that of activity. *Context* allows us to distinguish contextual knowledge and external knowledge concerning activity development. *Contextual knowledge* is the set of elements related in a flat way to activity development at the current actor’s focus, while *external knowledge* concerns elements of the context that are not important for the actor’s focus at hand. Context evolving during activity development, the frontier between the two types of knowledge is porous. An element of contextual knowledge can become external if it is of no more interest at the following step of the reasoning, and, conversely, an element of external knowledge can become contextual because it is considered for the development of the activity.

For Brézillon and Pomerol (2001), context is the framework that reveals *know how*. In other words, knowledge is the information that (1) results from the actor’s interpretation of data and (2) is integrated and understood in the mind of the actor as knowledge. The first key point is the focus of attention (identified later as activity).

KP1	The focus of attention of the actor divides context into contextual knowledge and external knowledge.

The focus of attention is on a step of activity development, where activities considered in our projects concern decision-making, task realization and problem solving.

Contextual knowledge constitutes a set of elements more or less related to the activity in a flat way. *External knowledge* concerns elements that are not important for the activity at the moment the actor considers it. The distinction between contextual knowledge and external knowledge is personal to an actor and is evoked by situations and events. It is something that is stored in long-term memory and recalled as a whole at some step of the activity. The distinction between contextual knowledge and external knowledge avoids the problem of the infinite dimension (McCarthy 1993) that is linked to external knowledge. As said in the presentation of the TACTIC project, actors rely on mental representations (see section 3.5.3) from which they extract a mental model depending on the activity at its current step, the situation in which the task is being realized and the local environment in which resources are available. The mental representation of actor's experience represents the personal working context in which the actor will extract a mental model that will guide the focus. The personal working context of the actor is an important facet of knowledge that is not captured in traditional knowledge measures, such as its operational and dynamical organizations, especially because knowledge organization is different from one actor to another.

Consider an exercise of mathematics in a college. To reach the goal of the exercise, the teacher (normally) decomposes the problem into several questions acting as successive steps for students' reasoning (the activity is problem solving). When the focus reaches the step in question 2, elements used for solving question 1 leave contextual knowledge for external knowledge, but the answer to question 1 (and new elements) enters contextual knowledge related to the focus on question 2. The selection of the contextual knowledge related to the new focus is a kind of first instantiation of contextual knowledge, or background context, that needs some specification to perfectly fit the activity step. The precision and differentiation brought to contextual knowledge is obtained by a process of proceduralization. *Knowing how* is "instantiating in doing", and contextual knowledge obeys a dynamic of instantiation and proceduralization during action. The proceduralization process compiles a part of contextual knowledge into a proceduralized context.

The links established between an activity and context lead to considering context as composed of contextual knowledge and external knowledge, contextual knowledge being conceptually more or less related to the activity. The next step, for reaching an operational level, is to relate contextual knowledge to four sources of context that are of interest in our research, namely, the actor, the activity, the situation in which the actor oversees the activity and the environment where there are available means for the realization of the activity. These four sources of context being highly heterogeneous, we will consider that contextual knowledge is available as contextual elements coming from the four sources of contextual elements without specifying semantically what a contextual element represents.

KP2	Contextual knowledge is assimilated to contextual elements that come from four sources, namely, the actor, the activity, the situation and the environment.

The *proceduralized context* is quite similar, in spirit at least, to a chunk of knowledge (Miller 1956; Schank 1982), and, in its creation, to Clancey's (2002) view of diagnosis as the construction of a situation-specific model.

KP3	The proceduralized context is the expression of the operational knowledge in contextual knowledge that is used in the focus of attention at the current step.

The proceduralized context is built all along the activity development (e.g. the development of a mental model). It is activated and structured to satisfy the accomplishment of the activity (Pomerol and Brézillon 1999). If contextual knowledge is background knowledge, the proceduralized context is foreground, that is, immediately useful at the given step of the reasoning. Hereafter, we discuss the implementation of the proceduralized context from contextual elements after making links with contextual knowledge. It is possible to explain how the proceduralized context was built, the reasons behind choices (contextual elements considered and their instantiations), the alternatives abandoned (actions corresponding to the values of the contextual elements not retained), etc.

2.2.2. *Conceptual elements used in the research*

Complementary to the engineering approach, the cognitive approach provides a computational support for effectively representing, analyzing and simulating activities in real-world applications. This computational support relies on the Contextual-Graphs formalism that provides a uniform representation of elements of knowledge, reasoning and contexts that intervene in a task realization (Brézillon 2005). The approach allows the determination of how contextual elements are taken into consideration by actors during task realization, not on the task model itself that is generally a decontextualized model (Brézillon 2007). In the "Contextualizing Scientific Workflows" project (see section 1.7), the study shows how the use of Contextual-Graphs formalism enriches scientific workflows in virtual screening, demonstrating that it is possible to model actors' behavior with complex task only based on its realization because the task itself is not always well defined (Fan et al. 2011). A similar conclusion in road safety is given in (Brézillon et al. 2014).

Brézillon and Pomerol (1999) proposed a working definition of context as "what constrains the focus without intervening in it explicitly". In our applications, the activities concerned decision-making, problem solving and task realization (that we will sum up later by mental models). KP1 shows that context as contextual knowledge depends on the focus (the activity at hand); KP4 points out that the dependence is biunivocal.

KP4	We cannot speak of context in an abstract way: context and focus of attention are interdependent.

KP4 means that context makes focus explicit, and focus defines contextual elements that are relevant at each step. The next key point, KP5, defines that interaction between context and an activity (actor's focus of attention) leads to considering the concepts as processes, not as objects.

KP5	The means and methods to accomplish an activity are as important as the activity itself.

Concretely, a procedure often is built from a decontextualization process of a large set of practices to extract what is common to a maximum of practices. In the SART project, procedures are established and used in a kind of Contextualization-Decontextualization-Recontextualization, CDR (see section 1.3.7), process by analyzing incident-solving reports (identification of the Contextualization in the practices) that are formalized by merging all reports on a given incident in a procedure supposed to be applicable to the largest class possible of incident-solving (Decontextualization). However, train drivers prefer to recontextualize procedures when needed because procedures are exceptionally directly applicable to "real-world" incidents. In their daily work, actors have to apply procedure in specific contexts that require its adaptation (i.e. Recontextualization). As a result, the actor uses operational knowledge and experience (as mental representation at the operational level) to develop practices that (re)contextualize the procedure during their task realization (activity) in the specific context.

Formally, a practical unit of reasoning can be expressed as "IF P1, P2, … THEN C1". In logical and theoretical reasoning (e.g. a procedure), the action leads to the conclusion C1 that is added alone to the knowledge base. In practical reasoning (e.g. a practice), the premises P1, P2, … stay attached to the conclusion, that is, C1 has a meaning coming from the premises. An element like C1 is defined in a context of use (P1, P2, … are true) that is lost in the procedure, which aims to be applicable to a large class of similar problems, whereas a practice is a contextualized procedure in a specific context, and a mental model is a contextualization of the mental representation as discussed later in the chapter.

KP6	A mental model is the contextualization of a mental representation in a specific context.

Such a practice generally is the "best practice" in that specific context, and there are as many best practices as encountered contexts. In the following, we replace in AI the term "practices" (in Engineering) with the more generic term "mental model" (in Cognitive Science), but procedure and mental representation are of a different nature: procedure is contextualized to become a practice, while a mental representation corresponds to the sum of all the mental models performed in different contexts (and thus already contextualized) in a uniform representation.

If a procedure could be compared to a task model, then modeling practices occur in as many contexts as applications. Because mental models differ from each other by a few elements, the mental representation has a unique global representation of all mental models (Brézillon 2005). The CxG representation formalism (presented in the next section) allows a unified modeling of all the practices developed by actors in a unique contextual graph with the important side effect of making the *distance* between practices explicit.

KP7	The contextual graph is a unified implementation of the mental representation representing all mental models developed.

McCarthy (1993) shows that context has an infinite dimension: each contextual element recursively is embedded in a context that makes it possible to specialize each contextual element. Thus, modeling may reach an excessive degree of refinement due to a concern for precision based on this specialization. In the example of coffee preparation, we use "coffee" without precision if it is coffee beans or ground, in a sachet or pod, a special trademark, etc. The degree of granularity depends on the goal of the model. As a result, the more we refine mental models, the more there are details, and the more we enter into details, the more the mental representation becomes complex, difficult to instantiate and time-consuming for the actor. Thus, it is important to find the right granularity for modeling an activity. In the "Computer-mediated collaborative work" project (see section 1.11) participants built their answer shortly and developed, in the lack of answer, an explanation with rich elaborations. Indeed, entering into a too detailed modeling often leads to mixing different levels of description. It is a usual situation in medicine where, for example, the "cancer diagnosis" activity requires, say, a mammography and biopsy analysis that are at a lower granularity.

The concept of "contextual element" gives practical consistency to the concept of context as objective elements (but possible subjective instantiations). Some applications are based on a limited set of contextual elements like a kind of data interpretation of an actor, and other applications use different contextual elements coming from a group of actors with different roles (Rosa et al. 2006). Context-aware applications integrate context in engineering as data coming from a limited set of sensors that measure the state of the environment such as location and temperature (Arnaboldi et al. 2014; Perera et al. 2014). However, all these approaches strongly reduce the scanning of context to a few contextual elements collected from sensors, disregarding the infinite dimension of context (McCarthy 1993). The *sources of context* are the actor, the activity, the situation and the immediate environment where the resources needed for the activity are (Brézillon 2005).

Our model of the contextual element results from a long maturation process. In a general decisions tree, each event is represented by an event node that carries on a part of the uncertainty of the situation. There are no probabilities on events, but decision can be made in different contexts (with generally different results). This was the reason for the series of changes we introduced. The first change was to replace event nodes with context nodes. The postponement of actions to leaves in a decision tree amounts to relating each decision to a state of nature. Such a representation tends to stick to actors' behavior because actors consider that, due to the contextual information they got, the state of nature between the root and the actions undertaken is the true state of nature. The decision-tree representation then is made of two types of element: actions and contextual nodes that select a branch depending on the knowledge about the current context. Thus, the representation evolved to make context more explicit with knowledge and reasoning during the SART project. The simplicity is at the level of the whole representation of all mental models in a contextual graph (mental representation), the latter playing the role of a base of experiences. The ordering of instantiated contextual elements led to some interesting uses like the onion metaphor (SART project), the role of distant contextual element in the focus (Enology project) and the definition of a metric like the "contextual distance" in psychology (Ganet 2006). The contextual distance makes it possible to identify an intruder in a group of objects from a tree representation (the intruder is the object that is the farthest of all the others).

The organization of the contextual elements proposed by the onion metaphor in the SART project is also used in the application concerning wine fermentation. The focus of attention is the onion heart, and contextual elements can be organized in layers around the heart. Figure 2.2 shows the onion metaphor in the solving of the incident "Sick traveler in a train" in the SART project. The reasoning step "Stop at the next station" is the onion heart, and ovals around it represent the successive layers of contextual elements. For instance, the contextual element "Procedures" is in the first layer and "Past experience" in the second one. It is the explanation given for using procedure, etc.

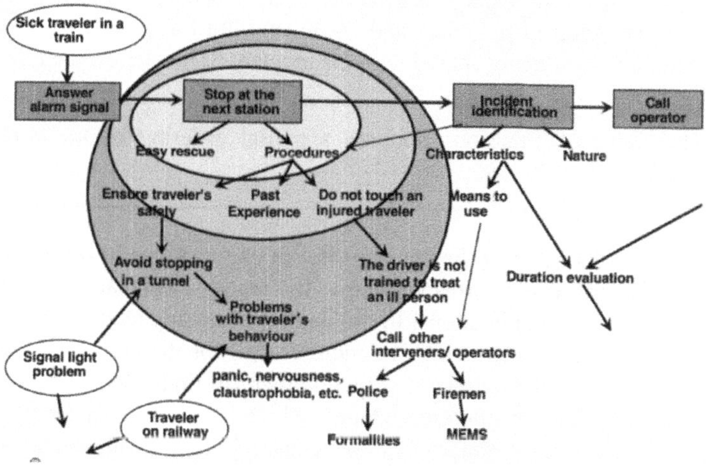

Figure 2.2. *Contextual organization in the incident "Ill traveler in a train". For a color version of this figure, see www.iste.co.uk/brezillon/contextbasedmodeling.zip*

The onion metaphor offers several interesting points for our modeling of context for real-world applications:

– A reasoning step has a meaning within a context, even though contextual knowledge does not intervene explicitly at this reasoning step.

– A contextual element itself has meaning within a context. For example, the contextual element "Procedures" in Figure 2.2 has its own context containing contextual elements such as "Past experience" and "Do not touch an injured traveler". This observation corresponds to McCarthy's definition of any context in an outer context, but note also that such contextual elements are instantiated.

– Layers imply a partial ordering of contextual elements with respect to the reasoning step. For example, "Procedures" (layer 1) < "Don't touch an injured traveler" (layer 2) < "Driver are not trained to treat ill persons" (layer 3) < etc. The partial ordering implies a dependency between the use of contextual elements, a contextual element being of interest for a reasoning because another contextual element just before has been instantiated to a given value.

– Ordering of contextual elements in a graph allows the consideration of different possibilities for contextual-element management like proceduralized context but also the possibility to introduce a kind of contextual distance on a set of contextual elements in a domain for discriminating a weak signal.

– Incidents may be linked to each other through a sequence of ordered contextual elements. For example, "Ill traveler in a train" is linked to the incident "Traveler on the railway" through contextual elements such as "procedure", "ensure traveler's safety", "avoid stopping in a tunnel" and "problem with traveler's behaviors", this latter contextual element being shared with the incident "Traveler on the railway".

KP8	The focus of attention supposes a partial ordering of the contextual elements.

The onion metaphor allows the development of explanations of different natures and in different detail levels corresponding to the layers. Explanation generation is useful in many different applications. In the wine-making application (Agabra et al. 1997), "far" contextual elements may be more crucial for the activity development than some close ones. For example, it is well known (in France) that the contextual element "weather" a few days before vintage – which is qualitatively far from "wine fermentation" – plays a central role in winemaking. It is particularly important because, unlike the technical domain, often a task model may be too difficult to model formally. For example, enologists consider the step of wine fermentation as a black box due to numerous and complex chemical reactions occurring (often in parallel) during the process. The onion metaphor shows a representation of contextual elements that allows us to remember that contextual elements are connected, and even a distant contextual element can be more important than a close one. Conversely, fisheye views (Furnas 1986; Pook et al. 2000) also are one way of integrating context and activity into a single view on local details and global context simultaneously. However, the global context cannot be exploited as local details.

In contrast to previous knowledge bases built from procedures (or equivalent), an experience base meets the use of mental models in different contexts. The SART project presents the "Ill traveler in a train" example in which this problem solving is considered in connection with another incident solving, "Traveler on the railway", by a network of contextual elements (see Figure 2.2). A consequence is the possible sharing of some activities in the same domain. More globally, this approach opens a path for research on the grouping of contextual graphs (experience bases) associated with different activities in a given domain and may favor context-based intelligent assistant systems able to tackle several activities simultaneously and learn lessons from a holistic integrated view on the domain. There are two types of learning, the actor learns from the system and, conversely, the system learns from the actor. In the former situation, with mechanisms such as explanation, generation and simulation, the system plays the role of a trainer for novices not familiar with practices developed by other actors. During this learning by the actor, the experience base is exploited in a kind of mental model-based learning. The second type of learning occurs when the actor stops the system to specify a new mental model that does not exist yet in the experience base (often because a contextual element was not considered up to now because it keeps the same instantiation during the entire activity). Thus, the system plays the role of a learner that will have to modify its experience base. In the CxG formalism, such a variant occurs generally when a contextual element was not considered up to now (e.g. it kept the same value during all the progress of the activity development), but in that specific context, the instantiation is different and the actor decides to execute a different action. The system thus will enrich incrementally the experience base in a kind of learning.

A system using "experience bases" would be able to explain, show alternatives, anticipate by simulation, complete incrementally its experience base by refinement of existing mental models when failing and alert about the variants abandoned for simulated activity development in a specific context. In our approach, the consideration of activity in different contexts can easily be learned by incremental acquisition of knowledge within its new context as an explanation of the different simulations. An experience-based system then can become increasingly "intelligent" because it can benefit from the situation to incrementally acquire new knowledge and learn a new mental model when it fails. In that sense, the new generation of AI systems being developed is context-based intelligent assistant systems working on a local base of experiences. Conversely, an experience base developed for an activity can be used for the training of future (human) experts to behave in the different contexts to make a decision according to the variants of the working context (Tahir and Brézillon 2013). Moreover, storing "bad" practices in an experience base also can be an important asset in training and self-training for human experts (see the example for car driving in the ACA project, section 1.3.6).

2.3. Operational level

2.3.1. *Operational knowledge and context*

In a real-world application, experts use their experience with an activity based on their *operational knowledge* as well as domain knowledge. With respect to our first distinction between contextual knowledge and external knowledge, operational knowledge is the part of contextual knowledge that intervenes in the activity.

In the TACTIC project, experts were asked to build mental maps as a semi-structured expression of their experience (this was done in another project in medicine too, Brézillon et al. 2014). Although working on the same domain knowledge, experts' mental maps show depth- and breadth first strategies for modeling how they address an activity. Usually, reasoning is between a "depth-first" strategy and a "breadth-first" strategy. The "depth-first" strategy goes to the finest possible granularity on a line of reasoning in order to anticipate, as much as possible, the course of events from a maximum of instantiated contextual elements. This strategy assumes that we are able to contextualize what we have to do and how to get there quickly. It also allows the study of technical feasibility of an approach as well as the needs in terms of resources before, in a second step, to gradually expand the approach the activity is put in context. Conversely, the "breadth-first" strategy is applied when it is necessary to consider first all possible options (potential lines of reasoning) before choosing a line for making a decision. Mental representations in a breadth-first strategy allow experts to keep an "open mind", for example, detecting weak signals. Such experts reason at a strategic decisional level and do not consider low-level details of contextualization of the activity. Conversely, expert maps made by experts in a depth-first strategy can be used to decide rapidly at the operational decisional level. The breadth-first strategy is observed in expert maps where represented contextual knowledge is not limited to the object of the activity. For example, "environment" was considered by an expert in the TACTIC project only as a part of "situation", even though, by itself, environment is an important source of context on the battlefield map. The reason is that experts consider environment through what soldiers on the ground really need to know for realizing their task. For example, it is only when there is contact with the enemy that experts zoom on the exact location of the enemy (e.g. in a city or in landscape). Experts thus are more interested in an external event through its effect on the activity rather than by the origin of this event.

In the context-aware community, we distinguish two types of context: the "local" context (contextual knowledge) that is close of the focus and highly detailed, and the "distant" context (external knowledge) that is general. In the spirit of Sowa's (2000) conceptual graphs, all the concepts can be expanded in the local context and aggregated in the distant context. Local details are needed for expressing local interactions with a structure. Global context is needed to tell the actor which other interesting parts of the structure exist and where they are. Global information is important even in the simple interpretation of local details. The two types of reasoning (depth-first strategy and breadth-first strategy) are shown in Figures 2.3 and 2.4 respectively (only the general form of the two maps obtained by the Freemind software are of interest here). The activity to model was "Give a reconnoitering order" (find out what the enemy is doing). It has been elaborated by knowledge acquisition techniques from a panel of ten experts that routinely used the battlefield simulator for different purposes. Each expert expressed in a mind map (a tree representation of contextual elements) the knowledge they generally used for realizing the task (starting from their mental representation) and simplified the corresponding map for the specific scenario proposed (i.e. the development of their mental model of the mission in the specific context of the scenario). Gray items in both figures correspond to contextual elements of mental representation that are not used in the mental model that is developed for the specific scenario on which experts had to work.

Figure 2.3 shows the knowledge organization of a tactical expert (a simulator trainer) in a breadth-first way, an organization that is very close to that of the operator interacting with the simulator (the end-user). The main point is on the position of the mission in the context of the battlefield, with the other problems staying at the periphery of their mental representation. The expert also introduces links between leaves in the mind map to express their strong compilation of the contextual elements in their mental representation. For example, the item "perceptions" (the bottom-right in Figure 2.3) is linked to the item "Ephemeride" (the middle-left in Figure 2.3) because the useful information on weather and day/night only addresses the question of the soldier's vision around them.

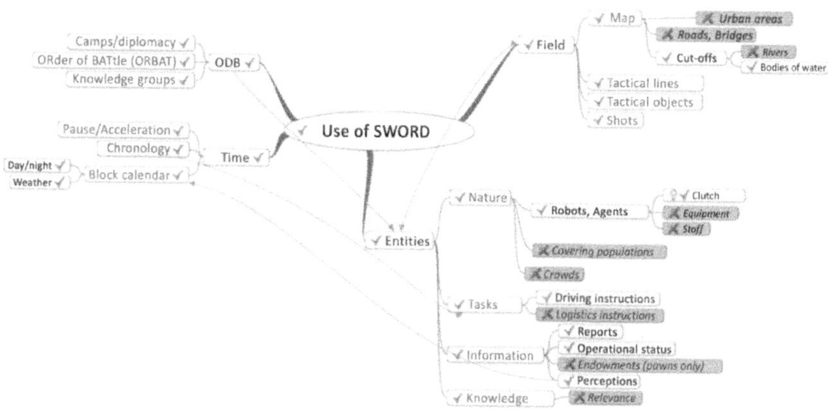

Figure 2.3. *Knowledge organization in a tactical viewpoint (Brézillon 2018). For a color version of this figure, see www.iste.co.uk/brezillon/contextbasedmodeling.zip*

Figure 2.4 shows how an operational expert (a developer) organizes their knowledge in a depth-first way, more for analyzing what action execution on the simulator is than what the action is on the battlefield (i.e. in the simulation).

Figure 2.4. *Knowledge organization in an operational viewpoint (Brézillon 2018). For a color version of this figure, see www.iste.co.uk/brezillon/contextbasedmodeling.zip*[1]

The qualitative comparison of Figures 2.3 and 2.4 (called F1 and F2 in this paragraph) shows several interesting points. First, F1 is a representation of a local reasoning with a detailed organization (depth of eight levels) on the ground with specific items such as "agent", "situation", "information" exchanged, while F2 represents a more global reasoning with an organization at a general level (depth of four levels) with general items such as "ground", "entities", "ODB" and "time chronology". F1 and F2 show different contextual-knowledge organizations that appear at the contextual-element level with more than 100 elements in F1 (60% retained in the mental model), while F2 contains 38 elements (but 85% retained in the mental model), the consequence being the development of different proceduralized contexts that exhibit different types of reasoning. It appears clearly that mental models of tactical experts are close to their mental representation, while operational experts develop specialized mental models from mental representations developed from different scenarios.

1. The data contained in this figure is irrelevant. Its purpose is to provide a structural comparison of knowledge organization with Figure 2.3.

There are five lessons learned on operational knowledge and mental representations in this example.

First, tactical experts tend to develop mental representations (visible on their mental maps) with a predominant parallel structure (breadth-first strategy), while operational experts are more prone to model specific problems by developing detailed mental representations with a predominant series structure (depth-first strategy). Such a detailed mental representation in a series structure is close to a mental model. The two experts have mental representations of different types but can reach the same conclusion.

Second, the quality of a mental model depends directly on the expert's knowledge about the activity, the situation and the local environment. Operational experts concentrate on the precise understanding of the problem at hand, while tactical experts see the problem at hand as a problem among other problems for finding a solution. The main difference between experts' mental representations is in the methods for using contextual knowledge during the activity rather than the consideration of the task model only.

Three, a tactical expert thinks in an organized and structured way, avoids assumptions leading to unrealistic scenarios and identifies actions that can be performed in parallel. An operational expert executes actions sequentially without paying particular attention to the logic of the task. The latter eventually may add subtasks or change the order of the subtasks (i.e. developing a practice), while a tactical expert applies the general scenario of collecting contextual information and, after, of selecting the better strategy to apply, with respect to the proceduralized context.

Four, the tactical expert has a holistic view of the activity development and identifies relevant contextual elements in a kind of "cognitive simulation" to look ahead in the mental model. The operational expert has a context-centered view of the task realization and, thus, reasons reactively (in a pure proceduralization process), discovering the task during its realization, sometimes missing some details, considering irrelevant aspects or establishing no links between the different steps.

Five, expert maps (such as shown in Figures 2.3 and 2.4) show working contexts, with contextual elements, their instantiations and their organization. A whole expert map corresponds to a mental representation, and the clear part of expert map is the "mental model" used by experts for decision-making during the scenario. The simple observation of such actor maps shows there is no unique mental model (and mental representation) because the working context of one actor is different from that of another actor.

The organization of contextual knowledge, which gives the structure of an actor's representation, depends on the actor's experience with an activity. These observations lead to the conclusion that, at the operational level, there are different sources of context.

KP9	There are four sources of contextual elements: the actor, the activity, the situation and the environment.

2.3.2. *Contextual elements*

The keystone of the CxG formalism is the particular model of *contextual elements* that has been chosen. Initially, the CxG formalism was elaborated for modeling decision-making in a large-scale problem in a decision-tree representation with initially arbitrary duplication of the same (very large) units on branches (Pomerol et al. 2002). The first operation was to assimilate decision nodes of the tree to contextual nodes (Pasquier et al. 2000). The second operation was to reduce the number of objects in the structure by replacing repeated sub-sequences of actions by a single object called a "macro-action". A scarcity principle leads actors to reuse such well-known procedures as soon as possible; thus, the third operation was to merge decision-tree branches as recombination nodes in a graph representation as soon as the final sequence was the same on all the branches. Indeed, a last change was necessary in the representation formalism. It is explained at the implementation level.

An interesting point is that, conversely to other representation formalisms, the distinction between a contextual element and its instantiation is mandatory.

KP10	The contextual element and its instantiation must be processed separately.

The explicit introduction of contextual elements for representing contextual knowledge and the distinction of the contextual elements with their instantiations offer new perspectives: the acquisition of a new practice corresponds to the addition of either a new contextual element (learning by accommodation) or a new value for an existing contextual element (learning by assimilation), the latter case leading to simply a refinement of the practice.

The type of values of a contextual element can be either qualitative or quantitative. For example, the contextual element "Temperature?" may have qualitative values such as "warm" or "cold" but, according to the activity, quantitative values such as "24.5°C" are possible instead of "warm". During activity progress, the instantiation of contextual elements may be altered by either an external or internal event. The external event corresponds to an unpredicted event (e.g. the power supply being cut off) and thus is not represented in the activity. An internal event occurs as the result of action execution. For example, a fuse becomes too hot and blows. The change of instantiation of a contextual element modifies the working context because it may lead either to a change of task to realize if the initial hypothesis is abandoned for the development of a new practice in another activity or to a modification of the conclusion of the activity considered.

The notion of contextual element links conceptual and operational views, which ensures a direct implementation of a conceptual model of context. Figure 2.5 summarizes our approach up to now from conceptual view to operational view into the context-based formalism in the four modeling levels (see Figure 2.1). This double viewpoint (conceptual and operational levels) constitutes the foundation of all our (successful) research in real-world applications.

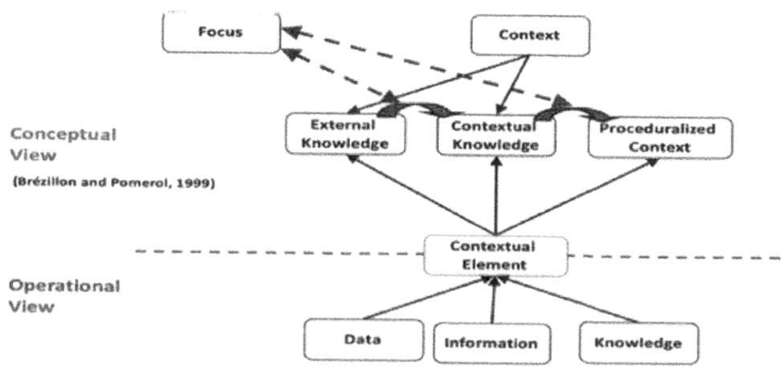

Figure 2.5. *Conceptual and operational views on contextual elements. For a color version of this figure, see www.iste.co.uk/brezillon/contextbasedmodeling.zip*

2.3.3. *Mental models and mental representations*

The concepts chosen at the conceptual level acquire a more efficient expression at the operational level, thanks to general principles, through a context-based formalism. The notion of activity coming from Cognitive Sciences, we also retained in the same domain the notions of *mental representation and mental models*, but with a different interpretation of their relationships. An activity is more than a task model, because it integrates how the task is realized and the actor's reasoning. Activity depends on context, and context comes from contextual knowledge on the activity. We consider that an actor has a mental representation of *experience* that brings together all the realizations of the activity made in different contexts. Such a formalism makes context explicit in activity modeling because contextual elements play a key role in what happens during activity development. Reasoning influences decisions and the overall approach to activity and ensures that actions are aligned with goals or desired outcomes. Decision-making, as an operational expression of reasoning, often is described as the process of collecting, assembling and structuring the relevant knowledge and information for contextualizing the decision for action.

A *mental model* is a comprehensive representation of an activity accomplished by an actor in a given context. It contains the reasoning of the actor that performs an activity in a specific context. It is a static structure that needs an external processing to be "personified" or "tokenized". Craik (1943) spoke of internal representation of external reality that suggested that the actor constructs "small-scale models" of reality that are used to anticipate events. For Johnson-Laird and Byrne (1991), reasoning depends, not on logical form, but on such mental models. Practices are modeled as mental models at the operational level that are proceduralized at the implementation level. Practices are paths from input to output of the contextual graph, and often a practice differs from other practices (i.e. other paths) generally on small parts, for example, by different instantiations of a contextual element.

KP11	*Mental models* are at the operational level, while their development in specific contexts corresponds to a *path in the contextual graph* at the implementation level.

Conversely to several authors (e.g. see Endsley 2000), we consider that the "mental representation" is not synonymous of the "mental model" because, for us, the *mental representation* results from the accumulation of mental models developed within their specific contexts, where each mental model corresponds to an explanation of the activity. In our applications, actors were experts in their domain on their activities such as task realization, decision-making and problem solving. In CxG formalism, such activities are addressed from mental representations developed by experts as a result of their experience.

KP12	The mental representation is like a local experience base containing all the known mental models for a given activity in different contexts.

A mental representation results in a kind of local experience base (Brézillon 2013) associated more with the activity development than the activity itself. An activity is developed from experience by identifying progressively contextual elements that are relevant in the activity context (first step of decision-making) and looking for their instantiations from context sources (second step of decision-making). An actor, facing a familiar activity, does not seek to have a global picture of the activity but wants to follow step-by-step the reasoning to detect if all elementary decisions were justified in the context at hand or how to change a reasoning step (for another one or a new one). In the "Paper submission" example (see section 3.6.1), the author may use a cover letter to provide the editor contextual elements (e.g. the paper is a summary of 25 years of research on modeling and using context) regarding the submission.

2.4. Implementation level

2.4.1. *The CxG_1.0 formalism*

After the qualitative phase of modeling at the operational level, the activity model must be implemented to be confronted with the environment (and instantiations gathered). The operational definition of context and the in-depth study of different aspects of context have allowed the design and implementation of the context-based representation formalism called Contextual-Graphs (CxG). CxG formalism has been used with success in all the applications cited in section 2.1 (except the SEPT application). This section is centered on the CxG_1.0 version of the context-based formalism for an actor facing an activity in a real-world application. We give the features of the formalism and software needed to understand the lessons learned about context and its role in applications. If conceptual and operational frameworks allowed the implementation and use of CxG formalism, reciprocally, findings at the CxG formalism level led to reinforcement of conceptual and operational modeling of context.

We have implemented the CxG formalism in a piece of software called Contextual-Graphs (CxG). The preliminary version, CxG_1.0, was in the major part the object of Pasquier' Ph. Dissertation (2002), other references are Brézillon et al. (1997, 2000). Since 2002, the CxG software has been corrected, adapted and enriched by a number of students that I want to warmly thank. The CxG formalism represents knowledge, reasoning and context in a uniform way called a contextual graph. A contextual graph is a collection of knowledge and experience that experts accumulate by performing an activity in different contexts. It is a "contextual" model of all the known mental models for solving a problem or making a decision in these different contexts. As such, a contextual graph is a kind of experience based more on the way to solve a problem than on the problem itself (the goal of a knowledge base). In contrast to previous knowledge bases built from procedures (or equivalent), a contextual graph concerns practices, that is, the use of a procedure integrating context specificity. The double process, mental-model development and instantiation management, is an efficient translation of good decision-making in the CxG formalism: gathering contextual information for identifying the context at hand, instantiating contextual elements concerned with building the proceduralized context, making a decision corresponding to the identified context and executing the actions associated with this context.

The *CxG software*[2] is written in Java under GNU Public License, and contextual graphs are stored in XML for reuse in other applications (Brézillon 2011). The CxG software proposes an interface to actors wishing to edit a contextual graph, reading activities for selecting the best one, browsing alternatives of an activity, exploring a contextual graph at a different granularity (e.g. unfolding of a system activity in the contextual graph) and analyzing contextual information attached to each item (date of creation, comments, etc.). The mechanisms of aggregation and expansion of activities, similar to those of conceptual graphs (Sowa 2000), allow the observation of one part of the contextual graph or another one according to the actor's focus and also with the possibility of hiding some parts of the graph. Software design and development was user-centered for an intuitive use by non-specialists in computer science and mathematics. It is possible to link an item to an external document (Word, PDF, Web page, etc.), to run an external application (e.g. weather report, exchange rate, etc.), to track activity development as a roadmap for an employee, etc. Note that the functioning of the CxG platform itself can be modeled recursively with the CxG formalism and used in context-based intelligent assistant systems for controlling their activities (Brézillon 2014). A contextual graph integrates mental models because two mental models generally differ by only a few different instantiations of an existing contextual element that do not affect the structure of the contextual graph, or by an additional contextual element in one mental model by simple accommodation. A simple view of the path in the contextual graph is sufficient for the actor to follow mental-model development.

2.4.2. *Modeling tools*

This subsection presents the tools developed to implement the idea of CxG formalism. The main tools are the contextual graph and its four functions (action, activity, contextual element, Executive Structure of Independent Activity (ESIA)).

A *contextual graph* corresponds to a mental representation (at the operational level), mental-model development being identified as a *path* from input to exit of the contextual graph. Contextual graphs are directed, acyclic and series–parallel structure with exactly one root and one exit. A contextual graph has a unique input, a unique output and an organization of nodes connected by edges, in which each node can be an action, an activity, an ESIA, a contextual node or a recombination node. A contextual graph takes a series–parallel structure from sets of elements placed one after the other in series, and the contextual elements bring the parallel

2. The software is available freely from the author on simple request.

dimension. Series–parallel graphs are used in the literature in a wide range of applications, the most common being electrical circuits (Eppstein 1992) and scheduling problems (Finta et al. 1996). In these domains, flows follow all the branches simultaneously, while, in a contextual graph, only one path at a time is followed because an instantiation activates a unique path in the contextual element. Moreover, each path in the graph (from the input to the output) corresponds to a unique mental model developed in a specific context. A contextual graph has a parallel structure for a tactical expert who wants to "keep an open mind" and has a series structure for an operational expert who prefers to consider first the details of the activity at hand without a holistic view (see examples in the project TACTIC, section 1.3.1). The idea is not new. For example, Microsoft uses The Parallel Actions[3] shape that provides a mechanism by which two or more different actions can take place concurrently but independently. For example, if we are waiting to receive three messages and do not care in which order they arrive, we can place a "Receive" shape in three different branches of Parallel Actions shape, and whichever branch receives a message first can operate on it without having to wait for the other branches to complete their actions. All branches come together at the end of the Parallel Actions shape, and processing does not continue until all have completed.

Contextual elements give contextual graphs a formal structure that is a directed acyclic and series–parallel graph for expressing different strategies, depending on context, to achieve a goal.

KP13	A contextual graph is a directed, acyclic, series–parallel graph with exactly one root and one exit.

The lessons learned on the use of *contextual graphs* are:

– A contextual graph is an "experience base" that contains successful solutions (but may also contain failures, say, for training purpose). There is a compromise to find between the level of details on the activity and complexity of the representation.

A contextual graph implements a mental representation (and mental models).

– A path in a contextual graph represents the development of a mental model by progressive instantiation of the contextual elements on the path.

– An actor develops a new mental model as a variant of an existing one (such as the addition of an instantiation or a contextual element) by incremental knowledge acquisition and learning of the new mental model in context.

3. See: https://msdn.microsoft.com/en-us/library/ee253584(v=bts.10).aspx.

Figure 2.6 shows the four components of contextual graphs: action, contextual element, activity and ESIA. The CxG software shows all the figures representing a contextual graph (Brézillon 2003).

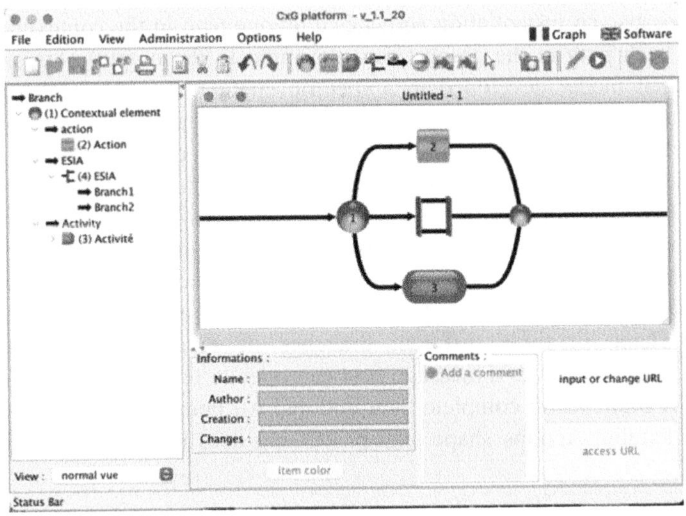

Figure 2.6. *Components of CxG formalism in the CxG software. For a color version of this figure, see www.iste.co.uk/brezillon/contextbasedmodeling.zip*

An *action* is the building block of the model at the chosen granularity of the representation. An action must be understood as a unit that provides an output for its input in a way that does not matter at the chosen granularity (e.g. for the example coffee preparation, I use coffee but I do not need to say the trademark of the coffee parcel for my purpose). Actions are represented in green square boxes.

The operational aspects of *contextual elements* are described in section 2.3.2. The problem of scarcity evoked in the previous section occurs when, for example, two branches are connected to the same macro-action (macro-action MA1 in Figure 1.6), as initially proposed for limiting redundancy, instead of their respective recombination nodes. As a result, after arriving at the final node of the contextual graph, it is not possible to explain which path (i.e. branch) was followed. The merging of two branches means that the undertaken macro-actions in different contexts led to the same macro-action in a shared context after this recombination node. Branches at a diverging node (contextual node) correspond to different instantiations of the contextual node that do not matter after the recombination node, branches being merged to continue on a common branch. Initially, recombination nodes aimed at simplifying implementation by limiting the duplication of macro-actions in the whole graph. Each contextual node then was associated with a unique recombination node, and the pair of contextual and recombination nodes was identified as a contextual element with the realization of an activity step on one of the exclusives branches between contextual and recombination nodes at a given time.

In the CxG formalism, it is more the final realization of the sub activity that matters than its duration. The change of representation finally leads to a context-based modeling of activities and to their development. The lesson learned is that a simplification at the implementation level led to an inconsistency at the conceptual and operational levels. Optimization at one level may have negative effects at the other levels. Moreover, updating knowledge representation (conceptual level) is difficult because the unique organization of knowledge is at the implementation level. This representation respects the syntax but not the semantic, especially concerning recombination nodes.

Suppression of implementation simplifications required the revision of our modeling of a contextual element in the CxG formalism in the following way:

– The instantiation of a contextual element corresponds to the execution of a reasoning step, and, thus, makes sense up to a recombination node that will be specific to that contextual node, not a global recombination node.

– Between a contextual node and a recombination node, there are as many branches as known instantiations of the contextual element corresponding to variants of a mental model that differ at the contextual element by the reasoning step considered because branches are exclusive. There are no limits on either the number of instantiations or their quantitative or qualitative natures, and an instantiation can be another contextual element too. As a result, a mental representation is constituted of all the known mental models with their interdependencies.

– Contextual elements are nested, one in the other, without partial overlapping. If a contextual node C2 is on one branch of a contextual element C1, the recombination node of C2 is before the recombination node of C1 (the actions associated with C2 must be executed before returning to the C1 branch where C2 is). As a result, the contextual element C2 is nested in the contextual element C1 and the contextual graph has a series–parallel structure.

The main points concerning contextual elements are that:

– There are as many exclusive branches between a pair of nodes as known values for the contextual element, and the assimilation of a contextual element to an activity step locally corresponds to the retained reasoning step on the selected branch. The consequences are that a contextual element is a unit of decision-making and reasoning contextual at the operational level.

– An instantiation is the value that corresponds to the selection of a branch between the two nodes of a contextual element, and thus, all branches are exclusive as long as an instantiation stays present (the reasoning rests on the branch). Instantiation is provided by an actor from their working context (as a source of context at the environment level).

– Each branch is a unit of contextual reasoning because the choice of an instantiation is based on the modeled activity context. The instantiation corresponds to the execution of a reasoning step and, thus, makes sense up to a recombination node that will be specific to that contextual node.

– Two contextual elements are either independent or one is on a branch of the other, ensuring recursion in the representation and no partial overlapping. More formally, this gives a series–parallel structure to contextual graphs, although only one branch is followed in the contextual graph.

– Contextual elements give the directed, acyclic and series–parallel structure to contextual graphs, and their instantiations constitute the variable part, that is, the path in the contextual graph corresponding to the four sources of contextual elements (actor, task, situation and environment).

A contextual element is represented by a pair of a contextual node (blue circle with a number) and a recombination node (blue circle without a number) where, in Figure 2.6, the three exclusive paths come from the contextual node. Contextual elements provide a parallel structure to a graph since they lead to several different alternatives for completing a reasoning step. The contextual node has one input and N outputs (exclusive branches) corresponding to N known values of the contextual element. The recombination node is a [N, 1] relationship that represents the moment at which the instantiation of the contextual element does not matter anymore.

KP14	A contextual element is implemented as a pair {contextual node, recombination node} with as many exclusive branches as known instantiations of the contextual element.

The key point KP14 is an essential contribution in the development of the CxG formalism by ensuring the link from the conceptual level (contextual knowledge) to the implementation level (pair of contextual and recombination nodes) through the operational level (contextual element), thanks to the distinction between the contextual element and instantiation that is treated at the implementation level. The coherence between operational and implementation levels being ensured, it is easy to update the contextual graph because changes now can be managed automatically. Note that the change of instantiation of a contextual element also corresponds to a type of nonlinearity of the reasoning (change of mental models).

From the key point KP9 contextual elements come from four heterogeneous sources (actor, activity, situation, environment). A contextual node corresponds to a question (e.g. "Temperature?") about its instantiation at that time. A (quantitative or qualitative) value of the contextual element corresponds to a branch between the two nodes with an action or an activity or an ESIA specific to the decision-making for this particular instantiation of the contextual element (e.g. the instantiation "warm" of the contextual element "Temperature" may lead to the action "choose a T-shirt"). The reasoning step in this contextual element will be different on branch 1 or branch 2. This implies that the global reasoning at the level of the contextual graph is contextual and nonlinear.

An *activity* is a (sub-)activity that is independent of the whole activity (in the cognitive psychology sense) that we try to model with the CxG formalism. It is an extension of the notion of macro-action used initially. In the Engineering sense, an activity is implemented as a complex action (a contextual subgraph) that may appear several times in the global contextual graph or be introduced by the actor for different types of knowledge.

It is a work unit, not necessarily of the same nature as that in the main contextual graph. This notion allows the compatibility of different viewpoints because a simple activity for one actor can result in a complex activity for another actor. For example, an operator and a train driver in the SART project have the same objective but two different ways of achieving it. For the operator responsible for the subway line, the activity is an action (the request "Make your train empty of travelers", while it is a complex procedure (the subgraph of the activity) for the train driver. Thus, the mechanism of aggregation and expansion of an activity leads to different detailed views on the contextual graph at different granularities. The work unit also can appear in several places in the contextual graph or contain different types of knowledge (e.g. ductography analysis in the breast cancer diagnosis example in section 5.2). In the latter case, the actor can define a subgraph (i.e. an activity) in a contextual graph, and the system then offers the possibility to aggregate it in a node in the contextual graph. All the characteristics of the CxG software thus make it possible to study parts of reasoning and all the variants. This is particularly interesting for understanding variants between two practices, the role played by a contextual element in the choice of one action instead of another, etc.

An *ESIA* avoids the introduction of an artificial complexity into the representation for a local goal (e.g. a task is given in parallel to several actors). In the editor's activity contextual graph, the ESIA shows that all reviewers must send their reviews before the editor makes a decision on the submission (see section 3.6.1). The order for executing independent activities does not matter (activities can be executed in parallel too), but both independent activities must be executed before continuing the crossing of the contextual graph. An ESIA is considered as a building unit of the

CxG formalism, such as an action or an activity (an important use is for managing votes on different independent criteria like in the FlexMim project in section 1.3.4).

An ESIA is represented by two vertical red bars with independent actions and/or activities between them. These independent activities (i.e. a decision made on one branch of the ESIA does not influence decision-making on the other branches of the ESIA) can be treated in any order (or in parallel), but all must be executed before resuming the traversal of the main graph. The executive structure (considered as a unit) represents an internal management of the independent activities. If a contextual element is comparable to an exclusive OR (contextual-element instantiation leads to a unique branch and eliminates the others), an ESIA is similar to an inclusive OR (all the branches will be crossed regardless of the order, like the use of a series–parallel structure for water or power). The ESIA supposes a local reasoning, while the CxG demands a global reasoning. In an example extracted from the MICI application (see FlexMim project in section 1.3.3), experts build their diagnosis based on a series of criteria that they use in one order or another. Their decision is only based on the consideration of all the criteria (represented by a voting system). Figure 2.7 shows the case of two criteria (of the 12 criteria in the application).

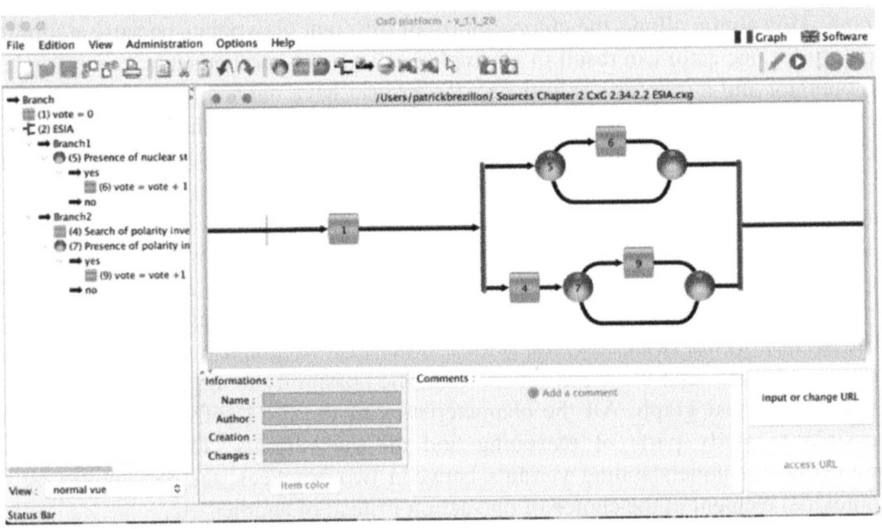

Figure 2.7. *Example of an ESIA inspired by the MICI application. For a color version of this figure, see www.iste.co.uk/brezillon/contextbasedmodeling.zip*

There are two types of information in the ESIA, an internal information like the contextual element "nuclear stratification" (action 2 in the figure) whose instantiation matters for vote computation but not for the final diagnosis, and an external information; here, the result of the vote relies on diagnosis to conclude on the presence, uncertainty or absence of a sign, not on the way in which nuclear stratification is identified (see section 2.4.3 for details).

2.4.3. *Exploitation tools*

This subsection presents the cognitive and designed tools for the full exploitation of the CxG formalism, namely the CxG elaboration, working context, proceduralized context, voting system and the tree representation.

Figure 2.8 shows the evolution of a contextual graph at three steps of its elaboration in the "modeling coffee preparation" example:

Step (a) The modeling of the action 1 "Take water" is a part of the procedure for coffee preparation. Implicitly, we consider filling the tank of the coffee machine with running water.

Step (b) The contextual element "Are you in a hurry?" (CE1) with value (CE1)-1= "no" (with action 1 "use cold water") and value (CE1)-2= "yes" (with the action 2 "Take hot water") because an actor decides to take hot water to have their coffee more rapidly, the actor being in a hurry.

Step (c) The contextual element "Type of water?" (CE2) with value (CE2)-1= "running water" as previously and value (CE2)-2= "mineral water" for an actor that uses mineral water and thus does not need hot water.

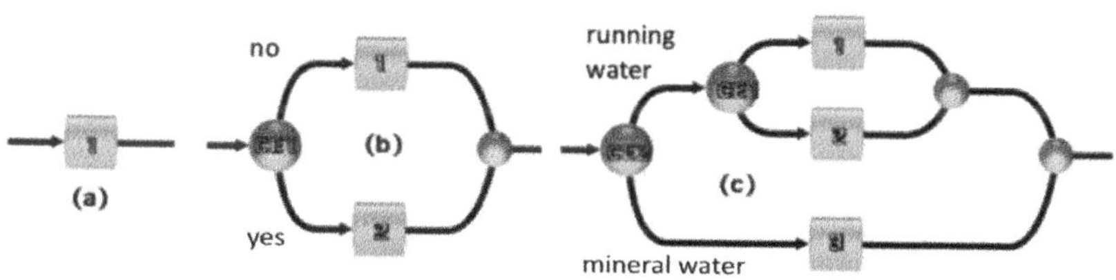

Figure 2.8. *Evolution of a contextual graph in example "coffee preparation". For a color version of this figure, see www.iste.co.uk/brezillon/contextbasedmodeling.zip*

This example shows how a contextual graph is enriched by the progressive introduction of changes (introduced generally from right to left) in the initial mental model corresponding to different contexts and increasingly finer granularity (the three branches in Figure 2.8). The contextual graph represents the experience of actors with the task realization "coffee preparation" (the mental representation), and the three branches represent different mental models. For example, the third mental model is composed of the contextual element CE2 with the instantiation

Value(CE2)-2 and the action 3. Note that the contextual element CE2 belongs to the mental representation and the instantiation Value(CE2)-2 is given when the reasoning is on CE2. In the example, there are two types of learning for an AI system using such an experience base. In the first learning, the AI system learns by assimilation of a new practice (refinement of an existing practice like choice between cold and hot water). It is a mental model-based learning. In the second learning, the structure of the experience base is modified for integrating a new method for coffee preparation (i.e. use of mineral water instead of running water). It is a mental representation-based learning, and the AI system then learns by accommodation. The evolution of the contextual graph corresponds to a refinement of the model of "coffee preparation". It is important to find the right compromise between refinement and complexity of the model.

The notions of contextual knowledge and proceduralized context being introduced, we now can discuss a *working context*. The visible part of a working context contains contextual elements that an actor associates with an activity, all the known values of each contextual element and the chosen instantiation. Arriving at a contextual element, the instantiation of that contextual element is necessary for the progress of the activity development and leads to a partial proceduralization of working context (proceduralized context evoked previously) and the action to execute (see also Grimshaw et al. 1997). The instantiations can be known prior to the activity either from the actor when (and if) needed or the system in the local environment. The instantiation of contextual elements corresponds to a proceduralization process of the contextual elements. The working context is for an actor what the shared context is for a group of actors having an activity. After the crossing of the graph, working context may be modified (generally by a change of the instantiation of a contextual element by an action during practice development). Working context plays a central role in the modeling of collaborative work, after an extension of the CxG formalism for managing iterative use of a contextual graph (see CxG-based simulation in Chapter 3). The problem is that, if the mental model development can be considered in the "visible part" of the working context, the mental representation "actor's experience" stays in the mind of the actor.

The development of a mental model relies on identification of the relevant contextual elements and the recovery of their instantiations in the context at hand. Identification and instantiation of contextual elements are part of reasoning from one step to the next one. This step-by-step evolution of the activity produces an ordered sequence of instantiated contextual elements that we call the *proceduralized context*, that is, a kind of contextual signature ("fingerprint") of the activity in the specific context. Proceduralized-context building, the first part of decision-making, concerns the gathering, assembling and structuring of instantiated contextual elements. Based on proceduralized context, the actor may interpret how reasoning contextualizes a mental model during its development. Reasoning, mental-model development and proceduralized context are expressions of the same concept in the first three modeling levels (conceptual, operational and implementation). The modeling of contextual elements offers a context management in CxG formalism, and thus, mental-model development has a trace that is kept as the proceduralized context.

KP15	The proceduralized context is the ordered sequence of contextual elements that are instantiated during the crossing of the contextual graph.

Contextual elements are organized in a contextual graph in the spirit of "Russian dolls" (matriochka) and are always defined (embedded) with respect to another contextual element (McCarthy 1993). As a result, there is never partial overlapping of contextual elements and any contextual element is itself in a context. It is interesting to note that the contextualization process (the proceduralized-context building) is part of mental-model development.

KP16	The building of the proceduralized context is part of the mental-model development.

Contextual elements in a proceduralized context may be at different granularities depending on the path followed (entering in all the activities encountered) during an activity development.

Figure 2.9 shows an ESIA for applying two independent criteria for diagnosing in an MICI application (section 1.3.4). Beyond the simple realization of a set of independent tests in an examination, an ESIA may help when several experts use the same set of criteria differently to make their diagnosis. Experts can weight each criterion by a *voting system* where a reserved contextual element "vote" is incremented by +1 (by the action "vote = vote + 1", and with the possibility of a digit other than 1) if the criterion that is present on a branch of the ESIA is verified. At the output of the ESIA, the contextual element "vote?" leads to the best option for decision-making. This explains why different experts may reach the same conclusion based on different appreciations (different votes) of the criteria. Figure 2.9 presents a simple transformation of the ESIA in a mental-model tree with all the eight combinations of mental models that conclude on three results only (absence of disease, uncertain answer, presence).

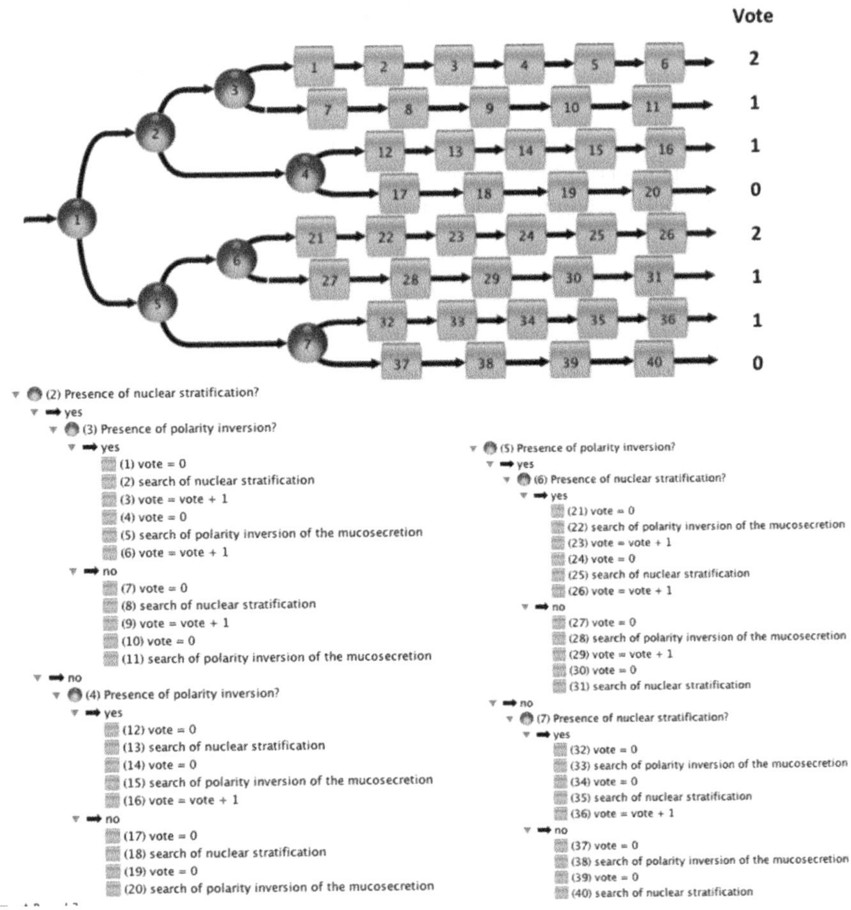

Figure 2.9. *Tree representation of the ESIA in Figure 2.7. For a color version of this figure, see www.iste.co.uk/brezillon/contextbasedmodeling.zip*

The comparison of Figures 2.9 (the tree) and 2.7 (the contextual graph) shows the simplification coming from an ESIA structure on the representation because the number of conclusions is reduced, thanks to the independency of activities in an ESIA. However, the legends have a lot of redundancy due to the multiplication of some macro-actions. This means that the working context associated with the contextual graph is not concerned by those specific contextual elements (they constitute the particular working context of the ESIA).

This example shows the concept of voting system for criteria appraisal. The 12 customizable criteria in the FlexMim project were put on 12 branches of an ESIA, that is, accessible in any order and different weightings of the criteria. The evaluation of criteria is obtained directly by observation or may require an additional analysis. For example, the criterion concerning "pseudo-stratification or nuclear pseudo-stratification" needs contextual information on the "presence" or "absence" of pseudo-stratification. It is this result that is used to modify the (reserved) contextual element "vote" that may be incremented ("vote = vote + 1") in an action if the expert judges that the criterion is verified. Finally, once all the branches of the ESIA are checked, the final value of the contextual element "vote" is used to make the decision after the ESIA. We had a similar situation in the SART project (section 1.3.3) in the example in the SART project where two trains must be moved one after the other, whatever the order is.

A lesson learned on the use of the CxG formalism in real-world applications is that a contextual graph is mainly a tool for modeling activities, but the richness of the context-based representation is not compatible for an efficient exploitation of the contextual graph. The main reason is that unfolding a contextual graph relies on a "contextual-element centered" approach (internal description of the activity in different intertwined contexts) not a "mental-model centered" approach (external description of the activity in different distinct mental models) that is closer to the actor's view. The retained solution is a "tree representation" that makes it possible to interpret mental models of decision-making extracted from the contextual graph more easily than the "graph representation" (Garcia and Brézillon 2018). The solution was identified after interviewing operators in a control room of the subway company in Paris (indeed like other decision-makers), the first thing is to gather a maximum of contextual elements for guiding their decision-making of the local incident. In the terms defined previously, the tree corresponds to the mental representation, and each branch of the tree corresponds to a mental model in a specific context given by its proceduralized context.

Thus, mental models present two parts: diagnosis and action. The diagnosis part contains the proceduralized context, and the action part contains the "macro-action" that appears as a proceduralization of an activity, corresponding to this specific context. The tree representation supports the actor for having a global apprehension of mental models by exhibiting separately the proceduralized contexts and the action sequences to execute. Note that we speak of a mental-model tree not of a decision tree.

We thus propose two mental representations of the same model of the process to get directly to the decision (the mental model). The tree view allows actors to: (a) visualize each individual mental model that can be followed to complete a task, (b) quickly identify contextual information needed for that (the proceduralized context) and (c) immediately visualize the output as the resulting mental model. The mental representation view tree is based on the properties of general series–parallel structures (Valdes et al. 1979) that can be applied to contextual graphs and then lead to develop an algorithm for creating a tree view of a contextual graph. Identification and treatment of nodes in a series–parallel graph received special attention to extrapolate composition/decomposition methods to CxG formalism without loss of the semantics and expressivity that they provide. Series–parallel graphs are used in a wide range of applications, the most well-known being electrical circuits and scheduling problems. Thus, CxG formalism belongs to a series–parallel graph category. Their structure combines series of actions and activities (i.e. vertices) that can be realized successively, and contextual elements give the parallel structure by providing multiple paths to follow. However, in contrast with other series–parallel applications with no semantics, contextual elements represent exclusive branches, the path to follow (i.e. mental-model development) is determined by a unique value (the instantiation) given to a contextual element. The important consequence is that only one path is followed in a contextual graph, while in other series–parallel structures in electricity and scheduling, all the parallel paths are simultaneously followed.

According to the definition of a series–parallel graph, it is possible to create a decomposition tree of a graph by performing series and parallel compositions. Each tree branch represents a path from source to sink of the complete contextual graph. However, the type of vertex in the CxG representation of practices makes it possible to gather all contextual elements on the left side of the tree ("in" side of the graph) and actions and activities on the right side of the tree ("out" side of the graph). It is obtained by several scans of the graph. When a contextual element (representing a parallel structure) is found, the elements on each branch of the contextual element are left as they are (the series structure); however, the elements that succeed the contextual element (i.e. after the recombination node) are duplicated at the end of each branch of the contextual element, and the corresponding recombination node is deleted. In the same spirit, non-contextual elements that precede a contextual element (before the contextual node) are duplicated at the beginning of each branch of the current contextual element. Figure 2.10 shows the transformation process on a contextual graph in one step.

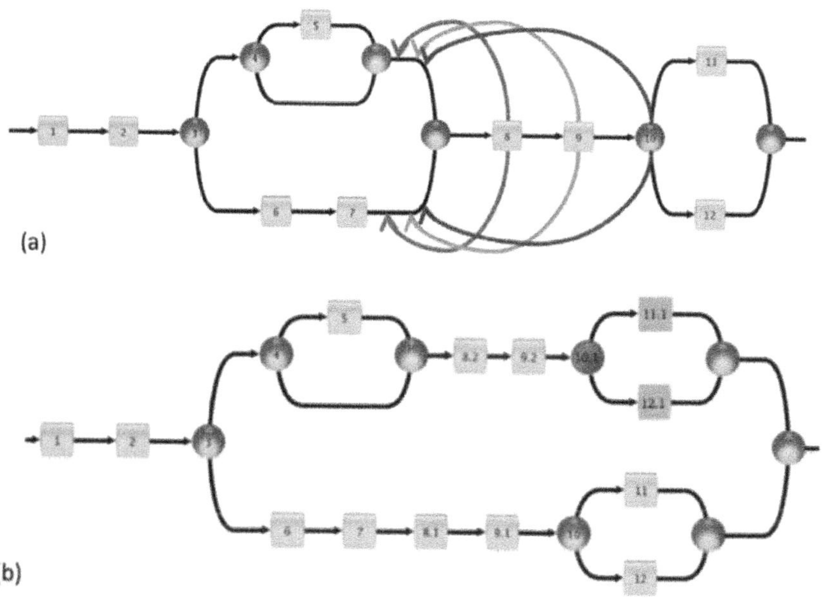

Figure 2.10. *Tree-view building (Garcia and Brézillon 2018). For a color version of this figure, see www.iste.co.uk/brezillon/contextbasedmodeling.zip*

The tree representation is obtained by successive scans of the contextual graph with a "permutation rule" between nodes and items. Figure 2.10 shows the implementation of the "permutation rule" at one step of the transformation process on recombination nodes from right to left. For example, action 8 (corresponding to the first red arrows) is moved on the two branches of the previous contextual element before the recombination node. The activity being performed, it is no longer necessary to keep the last recombination node that can be suppressed (i.e. contextual elements become contextual nodes). The equivalent transformation process from left to right at contextual nodes is applied too. Note that the proposed tree representation is not a decision-tree representation that would concern only the application of the permutation rule on recombination nodes (from right to left like in Figure 2.10).

The complexity of a tree representation depends on the predominance of the series structure on the parallel one in the organization of contextual elements (and the number of branches inside each element). The tree view is a part of the CxG software. Actors can identify the observed proceduralized context at the beginning of a branch to follow and visualize the output that the corresponding mental model produces. In complex contextual graphs mixing series and parallel structures, the number of mental models may increase exponentially due to duplication of elements, especially in series structures. This makes a mental representation tree view difficult to analyze without the support of the software allowing us to switch on the graphical window between the tree organization of the legends and the tree representation of the mental representation (clicking on one item in one side highlights the item on the other representation).

However, Brézillon (2023) shows that the experts tend to create mental models with a predominant parallel structure because experts contextualize situations as soon as possible (like for decision-making), while, by lack of experience, novices' reasoning proceeds step-by-step for realizing directly a given mental model of the activity. Thus, novices are in a depth-first strategy and cannot have a more global apprehension of the activity by a breadth-first strategy. In a contextual graph with a predominant series structure, in which the neighbor to the right of a contextual element is another contextual element, the width of the tree view increases proportionally to the number of branches N1 of the current contextual element -1 times the number N2 of branches of its neighbor, that is, (N1-1)*N2. The decision tree for the "lack of power" example of SART (Figure 1.3) is a good example. Conversely, in a predominant parallel structure, contextual elements are nested in other contextual elements (i.e. the parallel structure already exists); thus, the tree width will not increase quickly. Therefore, the mental representation tree view of a contextual graph is more likely to be manageable if the number of possible mental models (i.e. paths from the starting item to the last one) remains small, meaning the graph has a predominant parallel structure similar to the expert's reasoning. Thus, Garcia and Brézillon (2018) propose a solution to the problem that arises when a contextual graph has a predominant series structure (novices that are procedural).

The mental representation tree view follows the two-steps decision-making (presentation of contextual elements for making a diagnosis of the situation, and actions to perform once the context is proceduralized). Thus, experts easily identify first contextual information to know, second, the mental model to perform (and make the right decision). A contextual graph concerns the way a problem is solved by providing a chronological representation of mental-model development. Meanwhile, a mental representation tree is on the link between the situation (e.g. an image to be categorized) and the conclusion (e.g. a decision) by, first, presenting the rationality of the conclusion (the proceduralized context) obtained in each mental-model, and, second, the actions to realize. It is a question of knowledge organization as explained in section 2.3.1 with the comparison of the "tactical expert" and the "operational expert". The mental representation tree view is now a part of CxG software.

The example given in Figure 2.11 corresponds to mitosis identification in medicine (see section 1.3.7), mitosis being a sign of the possible existence of cancer. Thus, the analysis presented in the contextual graph in Figure 2.11a shows how the expert reach a conclusion like "no mitosis", "mitosis sure", "mitosis likely" by the contextual graph and how the expert classifies the images of mitosis by the tree representation in Figure 2.11b. The two figures represent the same task model (mitosis identification) in two different representations, CxG formalism for modeling and tree view for visualizing. Figure 2.11c presents the common legend of the two representations.

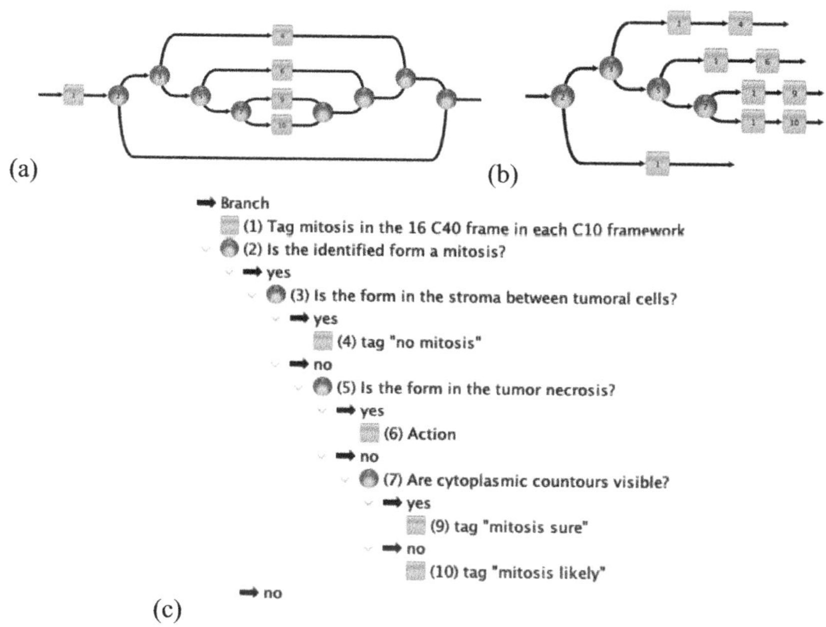

Figure 2.11. *Contextual graph (a) and tree (b) representation with the common legend (c) in the activity mitosis identification (MICO project). For a color version of this figure, see www.iste.co.uk/brezillon/contextbasedmodeling.zip*

The tree view is particularly interesting for anapathologists (our actors) because there is no unique model of a mitosis (see pictures on the right of Figure 2.11-b). Thus, they generally have "magic books" as a "wall of pictures" that allow visual comparison of pictures for reinforcing their diagnosis or to reject an initial diagnosis. Figure 2.12 shows the usual "wall of mitosis slides".

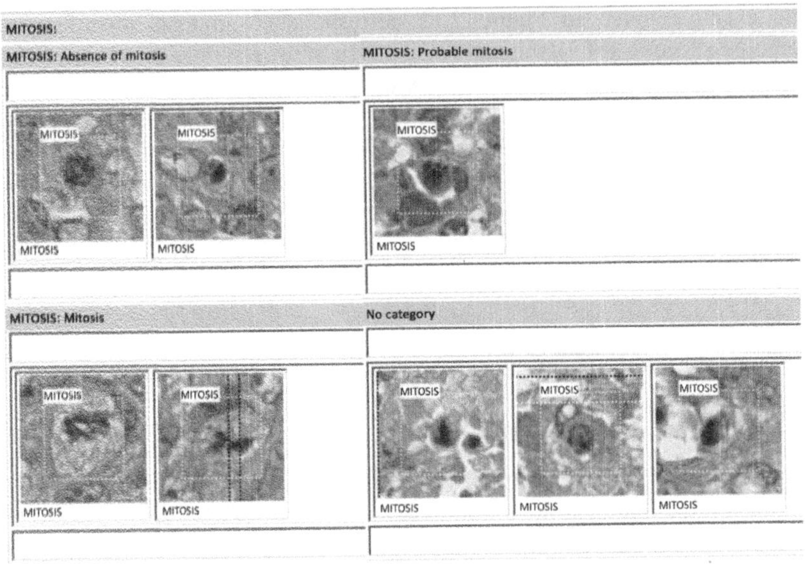

Figure 2.12. *"Wall of mitosis slides" (MICO project). For a color version of this figure, see www.iste.co.uk/brezillon/contextbasedmodeling.zip*

An analysis of the contextual graphs developed by different types of actors in various domains for several years showed that experts tend to create contextual graphs with a predominant parallel structure accounting for contextualization of situations as soon as possible, while novices create preferentially graphs with a series structure because they lack the experience required to tackle contextual elements that impact a situation and prefer a step-by-step approach to realize the task. This observation was made in all our projects because the end-users act as novices of the CxG system that is fed by the experts of operational knowledge. It is a problem when the designer (although expert) of the contextual graph and the end-users both act like novices in the application for DVD-reader diagnosis (see section 4.3.5) that was a different activity for students with a different expertise in another domain (management) and not troubleshooting diagnosis. Moreover, we point out in the TACTIC project diverging approaches among experts that depend on their objectives (in the TACTIC project, an expert develops a mental model based on a detailed analysis of their task realization).

2.4.4. *Review on the CxG_1.0 formalism*

The notions of sense-making and weak signal, which are presented in section 1.2.2, can be discussed in terms of context. Sense-making is a cognitive construction of a hypothetical mental model of the situation at hand for the actor that uses sense instead of decisions in a look-ahead way. Here, the problem is the distance between the hypothetical model and the context at hand. This distance corresponds to a difference between the instantiations of a given contextual element or the decision of adding a contextual element or not. The notion of a weak signal must be considered with respect to the context of a reasoning step. In terms of contextual elements, a weak signal corresponds to a contextual element that is in either the contextual or external knowledge, but it is not a contextual element judged relevant. The contextual element "weak signal" is not considered in the mental model under development, that is, the set of relevant contextual element, the operational knowledge and its detection would require at least to consider all the contextual knowledge. In the CxG formalism, an option is to browse regularly all the contextual elements identified to limit the risk of missing something.

A contextual graph is built on the basis of four functions, namely action, activity, ESIA and the contextual element, and a voting system with an action "vote = vote + n" with n is any integer value associated with a contextual element "vote?", integer values corresponding to the different options identified by the actor, such as "accept", "reject" and "accept with changes" for the "Paper submission" example.

The contextual element is the component that is the most important for modeling context, therefore reasoning. Contextual elements provide the structure of the contextual graph and the instantiation process, which is associated with activity development, at the implementation level, operates in interaction with the sources of context at the environment level.

KP17	Contextual elements structure mental representation at the operational level, and their instantiations are processed dynamically at the environment level.

The proceduralized context is a context-based model of reasoning at the implementation level. It is directly associated with the contextual graph that implements the mental representation from where the mental models come from. Unfolding a proceduralized context allows us to reproduce mental-model development in a specific context by CxG-based simulation of the activity (see section 3.4.2).

2.5. Environment level

The immediate environment of an activity is all that is not in the activity but constrains its development. In the CxG formalism, the environment of an activity is considered as four sources of contextual elements covering contextual and external knowledge on the activity and the instantiation process of contextual elements. The four sources, upstream, come from the actor, the activity, the situation and the available resources needed in the local environment, and, downstream, they provide in routine the instantiations for contextual elements on the path followed in the contextual graph. Indeed, the environment impacts the evolution of an activity in real-time because they evolve in parallel. As a result, the simulation of the reasoning in the activity requires us to know the value of contextual elements when they intervene in the reasoning. The instantiation mechanism plays a distinct role for contextual elements (the fix structure); it is an additional reason to distinguish the contextual element and its instantiation. As a result, the real comparison of a mental model to the observed activity implies a comparison of their evolutions, which also includes the potential effect of an activity on its environment. For efficient decision-making, actors seek first to identify the context at hand to determine the sequence of actions to realize and act rapidly. In the CxG approach, it is possible to know the sequence of contextual elements to instantiate by unfolding the proceduralized context and then to find the relevant value of the contextual element at hand corresponding to the instantiation obtained from the environment.

Actors play a central role because the knowledge involved in a contextual graph (i.e. experience at the conceptual level and mental representation at the operational level) comes from actors. Actors provide directly, or indirectly through the CxG software, the instantiations of contextual elements that are encountered on the trace followed in the contextual graph. In the scientific approach in Biology, deduction leads from concepts to confrontation to observable phenomena and an induction helps to correct the model by determination of the concepts to modify. In the CxG approach, the actor intervenes at the four levels of the activity modeling, directly at the higher (conceptual and operational) levels, and through the implementation of the activity model and instantiation of contextual elements from environment in a bottom-up way, and the actor corrects the activity model directly at the implementation level for finding a compromise between the top-down building of the activity model and the bottom-up instantiation of contextual elements for a specific context.

There are three main reasons for having unexpected situations. First, the mental model is correct, but its context is new for the actor. Thus, the right instantiation in the context at hand does not exist in the contextual graph (and the relevant reasoning step too). For example, in the "paper submission" example (section 3.6.1), the submission is written by a non-native English that confuses US and UK words (two different instantiations) of language (contextual element). For managing such a new author, the contextual element "Language?" is added with two branches with "US" (nothing to do) and "UK" for replacing UK words with US words. Second, a contextual element is missing in the model because it kept the same instantiation in all the previous contexts (the constant instantiation is integrated in the activity before the development). For example, always in the submission example (section 3.6.1), each country routinely uses a paper format (contextual element) and generally the US editor leaves implicit in a call for papers that the paper format is US Letter (instantiation). However, a French author may submit a paper with his usual A4 format (another instantiation). The contextual element "Type of paper?" must be made explicit with two values, "US Letter" (nothing to do) and "A4 format" (with the action "reformat" the text for "US Letter" paper). Third, the activity must be performed in a radically different context that requires an extension of the activity model. The intervention of the actor leads to extending the mental model for integrating the new part of the activity. In the example of the "Submission management" in Figure 5.6, the editor only "asks for review" to from three reviewers, while in Figure 5.7, the model is extended for including conflict management between reviewers' evaluations by proposing three options (editor as additional reviewer, call for an external reviewer and ask reviewers to find a compromise between them). As a result, the contextual graph becomes enriched by this extension of the editor's activity because this new situation has appeared once.

2.6. Variants of the context modeling

2.6.1. *Introduction*

There are very few works in the literature on modeling and using of context in real-world applications. A reason is theoretical attempts to use existing tools like Logics in which context is considered as first-class object. For our purposes, this leads to giving an intrinsic identity to context because we consider that a contextual element is a piece of contextual knowledge. The two main schools were around John McCarthy (with later Buvac), and Fausto Giunchiglia and his team (1997) in Trento (Italy). The main divergence with our research was different grounds for modeling context because their orientation towards logics is not directly concerned with modeling context from real-world applications. Nevertheless, two important findings of McCarthy (1993) resonate with ours:

– A context is always relative to another context with the corollary that context cannot be described completely because it has an infinite dimension.

– When several contexts occur in a discussion, there is a common context above all of them into which all terms and predicates can be lifted.

There are other pragmatic approaches like ours. For example, Salber et al. (1999) and his team have a bottom-up approach of context-aware applications based on the *context toolkit*, not human activity that is more a top-down approach. The popular definition given by Salber et al. is "Context is any information that can be used to characterize the situation of an entity. An entity is a person, place or object that is considered relevant to the interaction between a user and an application, including the user and applications themselves." It is easy to retrieve our four sources of contextual elements, but our concern is not limited by human–machine interaction, although we have modeled operator-simulator interaction with an emphasis on the operator (Kabil et al. 2015).

The Context Toolkit contains a combination of features and abstractions to support context-aware application builders. The approach aims to acquire a certain type of context information (generally through sensors), and it makes that information available to applications in a generic manner, regardless of how it is actually sensed and modeled. Thus, the origin of context for Salber et al. is more from data and information than knowledge and reasoning as in our approach.

Different implementations of context models are presented in this section. There is the context-oriented model (COM) that proposes three layers (generic, domain, specific application) leading to a generic structure instantiable at two sublevels. It is a clone of the CxG_1.0 formalism centered on programming aspects. In scientific workflows, BPEL presents in an ad hoc way 21 patterns with some characteristics of contextual graphs (four items). Concretely, the CxG formalism proposes a kind of contextual reasoning under different forms such as glocalization and the CDR approach. Moreover, accumulation of mental models in a contextual graph leads to developing an experience based on an activity. Potentiality of grouping experience based on the various task models in a given domain. Thanks to incremental knowledge acquisition, mental-model learning opens the possibility of multiform explanations.

2.6.2. *The COM*

A context manager should abstract away domain or application particularities. Vieira et al. (2007) propose the COM approach to deal with context modeling problem through the separation of generic context concepts from domain/application particular concepts. COM is a top-down modeling approach that can generate generic context managers that will be specified further in the lower layer. The COM approach is based on the interest to specify a generic context model for domain-independent approach and a reusable context manager across domains.

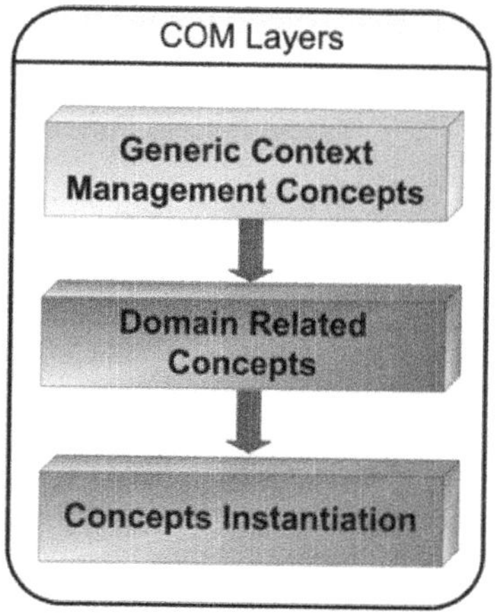

Figure 2.13. *The three layers of the Context-Oriented Model. For a color version of this figure, see www.iste.co.uk/brezillon/contextbasedmodeling.zip*

The COM approach guides a modeling of the activity in three decisional layers (see Figure 2.13) to (i) formalize in a high-level layer the context-related concepts that will orient the context management; (ii) identify in a given domain the contextual elements that should be considered; and (iii) instantiate contextual elements according to an application usage. These three decisional layers are close to the first three levels of our modeling framework (conceptual, operational and implementation). The upper layer characterizes the generic context management-related concepts and can be qualified as a "model" since it is used for creating individual models. The middle layer defines the domain-specific context-related concepts in accordance with the upper layer. The lower layer represents the instantiation of the domain concepts according to a specific application, incrementally acquired during the system usage. The idea behind the separation into these three layers is that if we define the context-specific concepts in a high-level domain-independent layer, these concepts can be managed in a generic manner, without worrying about the domain particularities. Thus, the mechanics of a context manager will be applied over the upper-layer concepts. A compatible context-sensitive system must model application concepts as instantiation of the upper-layer concepts. The COM relies on five main concepts: *Entity, Contextual Element, Focus, Rule* and *Action*, and three derived concepts: *CEF-Set, RF-Set* and *Proceduralized Context*. The main concepts must be specialized by the application/domain analyst, while the derived concepts are built by the context manager based on the main concepts and guided by the focus.

Figure 2.14 shows the instantiation of the main concepts and the interaction between the three layers in Figure 2.13 in the scenario "attend a conference".

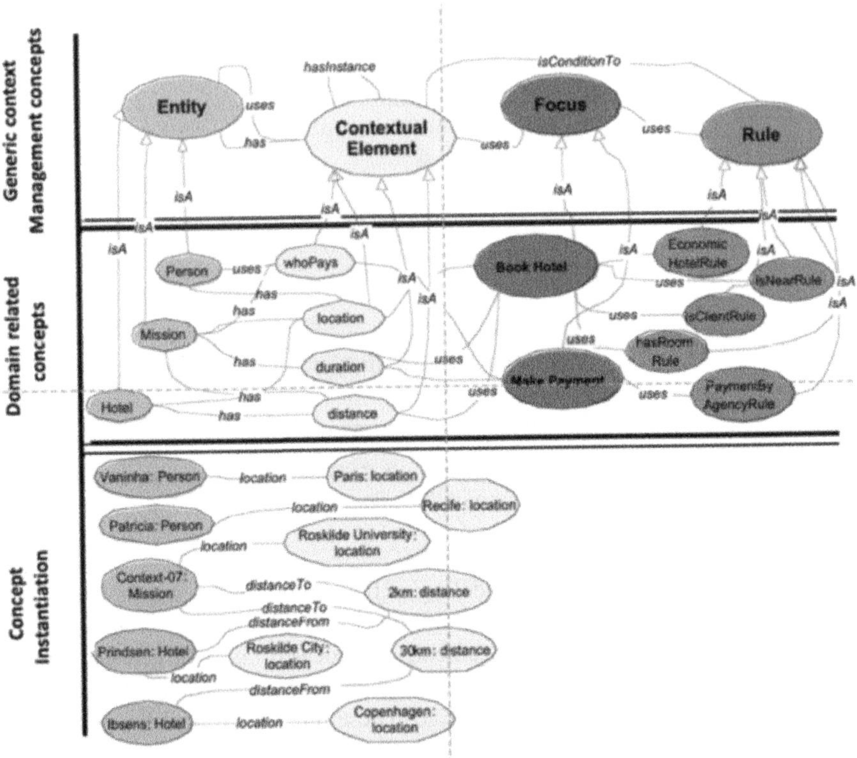

Figure 2.14. *"Academic mission" example in a COM modeling. For a color version of this figure, see www.iste.co.uk/brezillon/contextbasedmodeling.zip*

In the example, three entities were defined: *Person, Misson* and *Hotel.* The entity *Person* has the CE *location* (CE in this paragraph stands for contextual element). The entity *Mission* has the CEs *location*, *duration* and *whoPays* (the entity *Person* indicates that the value for the *whoPays* for a mission will depend on who the missionary is). The entity *Hotel* has CEs *location* and *distance* (who uses the entity *Mission* to indicate that the distance of the Hotel is relative to the mission location). The concept of the generic context management in Figure 2.14 means:

– *Action* is represented by a description and exists as a function of a rule but is modeled separately from the rule to ease modeling of context-dependent actions that could be implemented by the systems.

– *Focus of Attention* is a central concept in the COM, since context is always related to a focus of attention. It is an objective to be achieved, such as a task in problem solving or a step in decision-making.

– *Entity* is anything in the real world that is relevant to describe the domain. An *Entity* is defined through: a name, a type (e.g. an entity *Missionary* is of type *Person*, an entity *Country* is of type *Location*) and a link to an external resource that contains further knowledge. The *Entity* has an association *isCharacterizedBy* with the concept "Contextual Element" (CE), each *Entity* being characterized by one or several contextual elements.

– A contextual element identifies the atomic part of the context of an entity. A contextual element may be composed of one or more entities, meaning that an entity is related to the contextual element. A contextual element may represent contextual data, information or knowledge and is used to characterize entities. Examples of CEs for the entity *Mission* include: *location, initialDate, endDate, duration, whoPays* and *officialReasons*, and for the entity *Hotel* include *location, numberOfStars, category, minimunPrice* and *numberOfRoomsAvailable*. A CE may be associated with one or more other CEs, creating a hierarchical structure of contextual elements. For example, the CE *officialReasons* may have a possible set of values {*presentation, experimentation, meeting*}.

Rule is associated with contextual elements to produce contextual information from contextual data and supports the proceduralized-context building during focus progression. Each rule has one or more conditions and returns one action. Conditions are represented by instances of type *Contextual Element* and returned action is an instance of the class *Action*. *Action* indicates what a context-sensitive system is supposed to trigger when a rule is activated; thus, the rules are specified according to defined actions.

Concepts in the COM are represented by a combination of extended ontology and topic maps based on the model presented in Figure 2.13. Ontology enables knowledge sharing between human and software agents, easy knowledge reuse between systems and can be easily used by inference engines for reasoning. Thus, they are appropriate to represent the hierarchical structure between the contextual elements and its instantiations. Topic maps can be used to organize large sets of information, building a structured semantic link network over existing resources. This representation formalism allows easy and selective navigation to the requested information. An interesting characteristic of topic maps is that topics can have relationships (associations) with each other, and topics can play different roles in different associations.

2.6.3. *Parallel with BPEL for workflows*

Section 1.3.7 introduces the project for contextualizing scientific workflows by implementation of the contextual graphs (version CxG_1.0) in the language Business Process Execution Language (BPEL) largely used in workflow community. Workflow analysis helps managers understand the process leading to task completion. A workflow may be viewed as an optimal (or near-optimal) realization of the mechanisms required for executing the same plan repeatedly. Workflow analysis tells the manager what happens after a project is delegated to a department or work team. The analysis may include a list of which employees complete each task, and when and how tasks are completed. Decision points in a process lead to branch the process in different ways during execution. Thus, a process can contain several possible workflows, and each workflow corresponds to a particular set of values for all relevant branching conditions, that is, an instantiation of the process (Fan 2011).

Workflow is a process of automation where there is real-time decision-making at each phase of the workflow lifecycle, but contextual information is not saved with the workflow. Automation of the BPEL is represented at the operational level and CxG at the implementation level. Immersion of a workflow in a contextual graph is a way to fuse real-time decision-making with workflow application. Russel et al. (2006) provide a formal description of forty-three control-flow patterns. The original 20 control-flow patterns are embodied (in an ad hoc way) in existing offers in response to actual modeling requirements. Any pattern could be interpreted and implemented in several distinct ways, and its operation is described with a Colored Petri-Net model. Table 2.1 (patterns come from Russel et al. 2006) presents the parallel between workflow patterns given by BPEL and CxG to show that the same concepts exist in the two different approaches.

Structural patterns characterize design restrictions on the form of process models that are represented and how these models behave at runtime, such as: (1) the form of cycles or loops that can be represented within the process model and (2) whether the termination of a process instance must be explicitly captured within the process model. In classical programming terms, these processes correspond to the notions of (1) loops based on GOTO statements, which tend to be somewhat unstructured in format with repetition achieved by simply moving the thread of execution to a different part of the process model, possibly repeatedly, (2) more structured forms of repetition based on dedicated programmatic constructs such as *while ... do* and *repeat ... until* statements and (3) repetition based on self-invocation.

We conclude from Table 2.1 that ESIA elements and contextual elements in the CxG formalism correspond to structural activities in BPEL such as <flow> and <if> if they were a unique item. Although BPEL and CxG share common modeling elements, the correspondences are not completely matched. For example, in BPEL, <flow> activity, which is at the programming level, allows dependences between parallel activities, while, in the CxG formalism, ESIA represents independent activities that can be executed in any order or in parallel.

Workflow Patterns (Van der Aalst et al. 2003)	BPEL activities (Arkin et al. 2007)	CxGs elements (Brézillon 2005a)
Pattern 1: Parallel split. 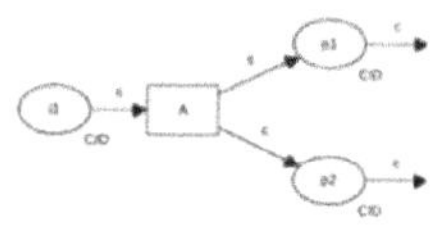 Pattern 2: Synchronization. 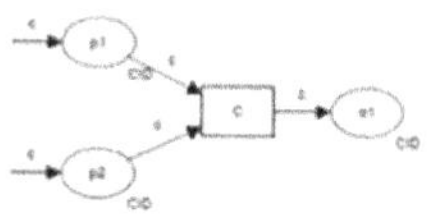	<flow> activity executes all activities inside concurrently. 	GAP allows the execution of actions or activities in any order or in parallel. 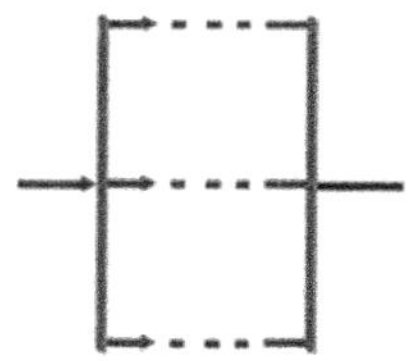
Pattern 3: Exclusive choice. 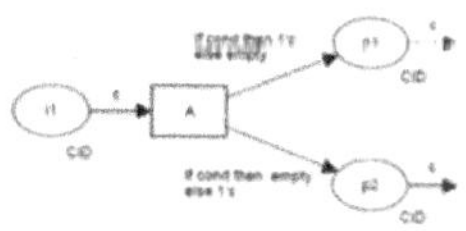 Pattern 4: Simple merge. 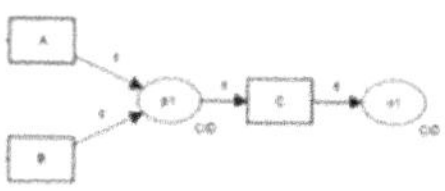	<if> activity performs exclusive execution based on evaluation of a boolean expression 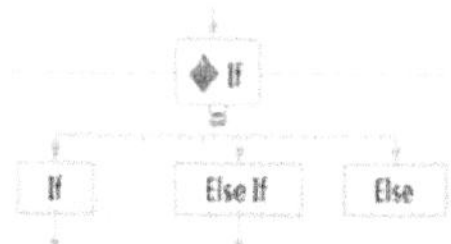	CE enables us to distinguish between several practices corresponding to different Instantiation of the CE 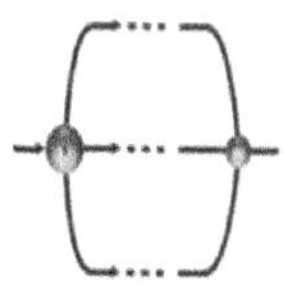

Table 2.1. *Expression of workflow patterns in BPEL and CxG. For a color version of this table, see www.iste.co.uk/brezillon/contextbasedmodeling.zip*

Moreover, BPEL is a programming language in a "logic of functioning", while CxG is developed in a "logic of use", although users often do not make the distinction between BPEL as a programming language or BPEL as a representation formalism. In any case, BPEL is relevant for a technical approach, while CxG addresses a social approach. Merging BPEL and CxG formalism proposes a socio-technical approach for users in workflow orchestration. This leads to express users' knowledge, reasoning and context in a "rich" representation (i.e. the CxG formalism) while automating the composition and execution of complex workflows.

There is disparity between modeling languages and actual product implementation in terms of the number of patterns that they support. Indeed, representation formalisms do not demonstrate how these patterns will actually be realized in practice. They proposed partial mappings between these modeling languages and particular execution tools. Pattern identification in any domain is, by definition, an experiential activity, and thus, it is not possible to guarantee the completeness of any patterns collection. Workflow modeling languages are often used for describing organizational and group levels, while task analysis and task modeling are used for describing and formalizing the individual level. Task analysis and modeling are based on what the user does or should do, not by which means it is done. It is important to separate the act of understanding goal/action structures and the act of designing them for their support. Workflow modeling, on the contrary, aims to provide a user with the necessary tools for performing the required actions. The main difference between task and workflow approaches generally is task ontology's lack of a tool concept like Contextual-Graphs, that is, the software artifact supporting the user when performing tasks.

2.6.4. *Comparison with two other context-based formalisms*

Brézillon and Turner (2022) compare CxG to two other formalisms of representation for context-sensitive reasoning: Context-Based Reasoning (CxBR), comparison which were initiated in Gonzalez and Brézillon (2008), and Context-Mediated Behavior (CMB) in Turner and Brézillon (2022). The initial comparison was based on 10 different criteria, with some indication of which one excels at each particular facet of performance. It discusses the comparison on how each would represent human or agent tactical behavior, either in a simulation or in the real world. CMB was added in the evaluation to support generalizing conclusions about properties and abilities needed for any pragmatic CxBR approaches. The three context-driven approaches were developed in different contexts for addressing initially different objectives. Conceptually, the three context-driven approaches are not on the same decisional level. This could provide an opportunity in the future to combine them synergistically for a more global approach to context-based reasoners. The inclusion of CMB here broadened the range of application of the systems studied, since CxBR concerned specifically human behavior in tactical situations, while CMB was developed for AI agents acting autonomously or in multiagent systems at tactical and strategic levels, and CxG is, on the one hand, at the tactical level with a contextual graph containing all the practices developed for realizing a given task, and, on the other hand, at the operational level for developing specific practices of the contextual graph corresponding to the working context at hand.

The context-based approaches aim to attack the most challenging problems in modeling human and artificial agent behavior through:

– Identifying a context and its relevant features (the classical frame problem is closely related to this issue).

– Deciding what is the most appropriate behavior (actions, practices) for the current context.

– Knowing when a change in context has taken place. Humans know this instinctively. However, it is difficult to generalize rules that dictate when to switch to another context as a result of environmental and/or internal events.

– While these approaches share similarities, they are also quite different in how they model contexts and use contextual knowledge. Therefore, they address the above problems from different perspectives.

CxBR (Gonzalez and Ahlers 1998; Gonzalez and Brézillon 2008) is based on three ideas:

– A *situation* is associated with a set of actions, procedures and expectations that properly address the situation. These sets of actions, procedures and expectations correspond to *contexts*.

– Evolution of the situation requires a new set of actions, procedures and expectations to manage the newly emerging situation. Therefore, the *transition* to a new context must be done successfully.

– A future situation is identified supposing that things in the current situation are limited by the current situation itself. This facilitates *situational awareness*.

CxBR encapsulates into contexts knowledge about appropriate actions, procedures and expectations as well as knowledge about possible new situations. CxBR is based on concepts such as not all inputs are relevant; a situation may evolve towards a finite number of next situations; decisions are made in contexts with a defined set of tools and context changes depend on external events.

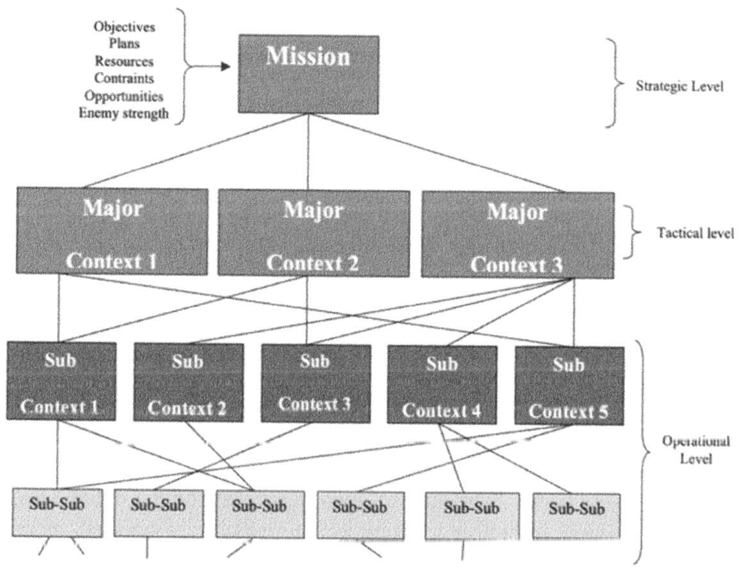

Figure 2.15. *CxBR hierarchical organization for a particular mission. For a color version of this figure, see www.iste.co.uk/brezillon/contextbasedmodeling.zip*

The hierarchical organization of CxBR is shown in Figure 2.15. CxBR contexts are organized as a graph, with each context having possibly multiple parents. The hierarchy consists of three levels, the Mission Context, the Major Contexts and the Minor Contexts. There is only one Mission Context, and it serves to define rather than control the agent. Major Contexts are the main control element, and while there may be several assigned to a particular mission, only one is the active context that controls the agent at any one time. The Minor Contexts play a refinement role, and there can be several levels of minor contexts, starting with the Sub-Contexts.

CMB (Turner 1998, 2022) is a pragmatic approach to using contextual knowledge. Context is defined somewhat differently in CMB compared to other approaches. An agent's *situation* is considered to be comprised of all the features of the world, the agent, the mission, etc., that currently exist. As such, its full extent is in general unknown and non-representable in most realistic domains. In CMB, a *context* is defined as a class of similar situations that have similar implications for the agent's behavior. Thus, a context represents a generalization of these situations and so refers to the *salient* features of the world, agent, problem, etc., that impact how the agent should behave. In this comparison to the two other representation formalism, such situations would be considered as contextualized situations inside finite and representable contexts. Contexts are not necessarily monolithic in this view, but they can often be seen as the merger of other contexts. For example, an autonomous underwater vehicle may find itself on a search mission in a shallow harbor when there is a storm overhead. It may never have encountered this particular kind of situation before, but it may know about contexts such as "in a storm", "in a harbor", "in shallow water" and "on a search mission". Since the current, novel context can be thought of as a combination of these other known contexts, the agent can combine its knowledge about them to create a representation for the novel context.

CMB is part of a reasoning style called *schema-based reasoning* (Turner 1994), in which most knowledge is stored as packets of related knowledge (*schemas*). *Contextual schemas* (c-schemas) represent contextual knowledge, and *procedural schemas* store knowledge about plans, goal decompositions, scripts, rules, etc. A c-schema contains descriptive and prescriptive knowledge about a context. Context assessment is modeled after work on abductive medical diagnostic reasoners (Miller et al. 1982). A dynamic memory watches the evolving situation "evoking" c schemas which it provides to the context manager, which then does differential diagnosis to determine which one(s) best match the situation. These are merged to represent the context. The process repeats as the situation changes. CMB is meant to incorporate learning. When used with a dynamic memory, simple inductive learning is automatically supported, as c-schemas are updated as new cases of problem solving are organized relative to them. Other types of learning can be added to more intelligently modify and create c-schemas, although to date they have not been implemented. CMB does not make a clear distinction, as does CxG, between contextual knowledge and proceduralized contextual knowledge (PC).

CxBR, CxGs and CMB are very similar in some ways, yet still have significant differences. All three approaches generally attempt to emulate human-like intelligence by using context as the basic modeling element. CxG is designed to work with context-based intelligent assistant systems, where the agent needs to work like a human and be understandable to a human. CMB was developed in part to control simulated agents in training simulations, and so it is important that it, too, have behavior that is understandable by and similar to humans. CMB has been mostly used for autonomous systems where human-like behavior is not as important as effectively accomplishing the mission, but it, too, is based on cognitively plausible principles, and in at least two implementations in medicine, it needs human-like behavior.

CxBR and CxGs are both task-based, in sharp contrast to several popular cognitive architectures such as SOAR (Laird et al. 1987). In CxG, goals are implicit in the context being experienced. CxBR introduces its mission goals in the separate, non-controlling Mission Context, of which there is only one. The intermediate goals of the agent in the mission are defined by a plan consisting of a sequence of Major Contexts with the transition criteria defined. However, the control contexts themselves contain the functionality to perform the tasks appropriate to that context. In contrast, CMB is more agnostic on the distinction between being goal- or plan-based; it can be either depending on the agent in which it is embedded. If used with a planner, then it will provide context-appropriate goal information, including how to achieve goals in the context; when used with other reasoners (e.g. a deep-learning system), then it will provide non-goal-based guidance (e.g. appropriate net topology, weights and hyper parameters). The three approaches are compared with respect to 11 criteria chosen for their importance for one or several approaches. As a result, some of them maybe irrelevant for one or another approach because the approaches are at conceptual and implementation levels simultaneously. Thus, for the criterion "task- vs. goal-based", the CxG formalism concerns task realization at the implementation level (need to integrate context with knowledge and reasoning), but the contextual graph, sum of all the context-based realizations of a task, is associated with the operational level.

In terms of formalism, CxBR, CxG or CMB are conceptual modeling approaches where knowledge is organized by context. This gives the developer great flexibility in adapting to the specific needs of the computing environment available. Transition knowledge, while traditionally represented by production rules (i.e. *transition rules*), also has been incorporated through neural networks. The CxG formalism contains four items only (action, activity, contextual element and ESIA) for representing numerous problems in various domains. It is interesting to note that while a contextual graph can be expressed fully in terms of productions, conversely, a set of productions cannot be expressed in a unique way as a contextual graph. CMB's contextual schemas are implemented as frames, semantic networks, description logic, etc. The three approaches differ with respect to the kinds of applications they have been used for.

CxBR has been used for the hierarchical (strategic, tactical, and operation) organization of missions for real and simulated agents. CxG has been used extensively in modeling (human) practice development for real-world CIASs in about 20 disciplines. CMB has been used in the domains of a medical diagnosis assistant, hierarchical organization of missions for autonomous agents, for the organization of multiagent systems, and most recently, in the domain of context-dependent deep learning.

The approaches can be compared with respect to the decisional level of reasoning they control: strategic, tactical or operational. CxG exists primarily at the tactical level (practices in a contextual graph) and operational level (practice development). CxBR is primarily at the tactical level and also extends to the strategic and operational levels. CMB similarly extends across all three levels but makes no hard distinction between contexts existing at different levels. The focus by the three approaches promises what has been done on the strategic and tactical levels to inform future work on those levels and work on the operation level to inform future work on the operation level, which was not a focus of the other two. The difference here can be explained by the fact that the CxG formalism is dedicated to the modeling of human behaviors and does not attempt (now) to learn from other sources because the guide here is to integrate knowledge acquisition and learning from failures in a specific context. The approaches can also be compared based on their treatment of the dynamic nature of contexts. All three take context dynamics seriously, with provision for representing the changing context as the situation or the context evolves. CxBR and CMB treat contexts as discrete and relatively large scale. The context is tracked and represented as a sequence of representations of entire contexts, even though any particular context may be represented by several knowledge structures. In contrast, CxG takes a more continuous approach, with the context changing smoothly as the agent progresses through the graph when a contextual element is instantiated differently.

The three approaches, developed contemporaneously for the particular needs of their applications, resulted in some important differences, but remarkably also many commonalities. In particular, we see that all three approaches developed explicit, rich representations of contexts centered around the salient features of similar problem-solving situations and how to behave appropriately in them. Contexts in each approach are represented as first-class entities about which the system can reason, not just symbols or a collection of axioms. All approaches also explicitly recognize the changing nature of context and have developed different, although potentially compatible or even synergistic, ways to transition from context to context. All three highlight the benefit of organizing knowledge by context for acquiring knowledge from humans. In addition, in their differences, the three approaches still point out potentially important characteristics of pragmatic context-based systems. For example, two of the approaches highlight the importance of the tactical and strategic levels of reasoning, while another shows the importance of context in developing and using operation knowledge at the right tactical level. Two of the approaches highlight the need to acquire context-related knowledge from humans (experts and especially users), while the third shows a route to automatic contextual knowledge acquisition and update via a process borrowed from memory update in case-based reasoning.

Thus, CxBR, CxGs and CMB are very similar in some ways yet still have significant differences (Turner and Brézillon 2022).

2.7. Review of the chapter

The chapter discusses the modeling and use of context for the activity of an actor (next chapter extends the research discussed in this chapter for group activity). Note that the two chapters organize the research presentation in four interdependent levels, namely, the conceptual level, the operational level, the implementation level and the environment level

First, context cannot be discussed in an abstract way. Context finds its origins in four sources, namely the actor, the task that actor realizes, the situation in which the activity occurs and the local environment where resources are required for the activity. A common denominator in the four sources of contextual elements is knowledge that is used to describe what is in the four sources. It is the first link between context and knowledge and consequently reasoning. Context is composed of contextual knowledge and external knowledge. Contextual knowledge is a set of elements more or less related to an activity in a flat way, and external knowledge concerns elements that are not important for the activity at the moment the actor considers it. The actor's focus enables the distinction between the two types of knowledge, and focus evolution, following the progress of the actor's reasoning, provides dynamics to elements of each type of knowledge that can go into the other type, and thus, the frontier between contextual and external knowledge is porous. The selection of contextual elements from one of the four sources is a kind of first instantiation of the contextual knowledge (or background context) that needs some specification (a second instantiation) to be practically used in the actor's reasoning during the current step. Specification results from a proceduralization process that transforms contextual knowledge to operational knowledge, the latter corresponding to the contextual elements that will be instantiated and used in activity development to produce finally the proceduralized context. This first instantiation can bring a solution to the problems of weak signals and of sense-making.

The working definition of context proposed in Brézillon and Pomerol (1999) is: "what constrains the focus without intervening in it explicitly". Context and focus of attention are interdependent; the context makes focus explicit, and focus defines contextual elements in contextual knowledge that are relevant at each step (operational knowledge). The actor uses operational knowledge and experience to develop mental models (activities in a particular context) that (re)contextualize the mental representation in the specific context. Mental models generally differ from each other by a few contextual elements, and the sum of all the mental models can be expressed in a unique global mental representation that covers all the mental models made by an actor in different contexts. The CxG representation formalism proposes a unification of the mental representation at the operational level as well as the contextual graph at the implementation level.

Contextual knowledge is assimilated to a set of contextual elements coming from the four sources (actor, task realization, situation, environment) of context that provides instantiated contextual elements at any given moment. However, reasoning progresses and the instantiation process are dynamic. What is changing are not the contextual elements but their instantiations. For example, the actor can see that the temperature (a contextual element) evolves from normal to critical (two instantiations) that may imply a change in actor activity. Thus, it is important to process different contextual elements and instantiations. Contextual elements offer a conceptual frame (i.e. the stable part of the activity) and instantiations (the dynamic part) from the environment level. As a result, first, context, knowledge and reasoning must be managed jointly and need to be modeled in a unified representation such as in the CxG formalism.

At the implementation level, the CxG formalism uses a representation of contextual elements (operational framework) as pairs {contextual node, recombination node}. The different possible instantiations of the contextual element correspond to exclusive branches between the two nodes, each branch containing a specific step of reasoning held during the corresponding instantiation. Contextual elements are organized in the contextual graph in the spirit of "Russian dolls" (matriochka) and always defined (embedded) with respect to another contextual element: any contextual element is itself in a context. The separation of a contextual element and instantiation presents different interests:

– Contextual elements are nested, one within another, without partial overlapping.

– Working context contains contextual elements associated with an activity, all the known values of each contextual element and the chosen instantiation.

– There is a partial ordering of contextual elements relative to an activity step.

– The implementation as contextual and recombination nodes gives a directed, acyclic and series–parallel structure to a contextual graph (the mental representation).

– The instantiation process defines (1) the selection of a branch in the contextual element (i.e. the model of the reasoning step) and (2) the path in the contextual graph that describes the reasoning held during the task realization.

– The ordered series of instantiated contextual elements corresponds to the proceduralized context that is associated with the practice development.

– A contextual element behaves as a unit of nonlinear reasoning.

Context must be considered for the four modeling levels because the different expressions of contextual elements are interdependent. At the conceptual level, we consider that an activity accomplished by an actor has its development constrained by its environment, that is, context. The processing of an activity relies on the actor's reasoning for exploiting contextual knowledge about the activity and its processing. Making context explicit allows a uniform representation of knowledge, reasoning and context. At the operational level, a part of the contextual knowledge, the operational knowledge, is used to contextualize the activity with instantiated contextual elements coming from the environment of the activity. The actor develops a mental model of this contextualization of the activity process in a specific context, and the repetition of this process in different contexts enriches the actor's experience in the form of a mental representation. At the implementation level, the embedding of instantiated contextual elements with knowledge and reasoning during activity processing requires comparing the mental model to observed phenomena of the activity. Based on the results of the SART project, contextual elements are modeled as pairs of a contextual node and a recombination node with as many exclusive branches between the two nodes as specific contexts in which the activity was treated. Each branch contains the relevant expression of the reasoning step corresponding to a contextual-element instantiation. Contextual elements give a fixed structure to the contextual graph (i.e. the mental representation) and instantiations define the dynamic part corresponding to a path in the contextual graph (i.e. a mental model). Such a reasoning step inside the contextual element is like a nonlinearity in the reasoning at the activity level. At the environment level, the constraints on activity processing concern contextual elements for which the values (instantiations) are required for choosing the path across contextual elements for explaining the activity development. In case of failure, the mental model must be modified. In the first part, instantiation may be automated at least partially, but in the second part, the actor must intervene to identify the reason for the failure (an unknown instantiation with a new expression of the reasoning step in a contextual element, a contextual element missing and a new reasoning step must be introduced in the mental model) to correct the mental model.

Actors use mental representations for extracting a mental model addressing an activity in a specific context. A mental representation is an expression of *operational knowledge* that experts mobilize for addressing the activity in different contexts, that is, mental models that are developed for the specific context at hand. The joint play of mental-model development and instantiation process is a contextual reasoning.

The Contextual-Graphs (CxG) formalism provides a uniform representation of elements of knowledge, reasoning and contexts that intervene in an activity. The formalism calls on four elements (action, contextual element, activity, ESIA) that are sufficient for modeling complex real systems, thanks to the new functionalities that can be unfolded. There is the implementation of contextual elements as pairs {contextual node, recombination node}. When a mental-model development arrives at a contextual node, the contextual element needs to be instantiated at one of its values (known initially or the actor is asked) to select the corresponding branch and progress in the development of the mental model. At the recombination node, the instantiation does not matter anymore, since the corresponding action has been completed. This modeling of contextual elements offers a context management in the CxG formalism, and mental-model development has a trace that can be kept as a proceduralized context. Moreover, there is the concept of the voting system associated with an ESIA. The evaluation of the criteria on branches of the ESIA is obtained either directly by observation or may require an additional analysis on each branch between a pair of contextual and recombination nodes. The results (of the observation or analysis) modify a contextual element "vote" that may be incremented by a reserved action (such as, vote = vote + 1). Finally, once all the branches of the ESIA are checked, the final value of the contextual element "vote" is used to make the decision after the ESIA.

The CxG formalism is an excellent tool for modeling a problem but is not adapted for visualizing simply its solution. Thus, the CxG formalism is associated with a mental-model tree view for end-users. The contextual graph is at the implementation level and represents the mental representation of a problem at the operational level. The conceptual and operational aspects of context modeling have allowed the design and implementation of the Contextual-Graphs (CxG) formalism, which, reciprocally, leads to reinforcing the conceptual modeling of context. However, the modeling in CxG can reach a too high degree of refinement due to a concern for precision based on this specialization. The granularity of a model depends on the goal of the modeling. As a result, the more we refine the mental representation, the more details are introduced, and the more we enter into details, the more the mental representation becomes complex, heavy to instantiate and time-consuming for the actor. Thus, it is important to find the right level of granularity for modeling.

The chapter finishes by considering the positioning of the first version (CxG_1.0) of the CxG formalism at conceptual and operational levels and the translation at the implementation level as the CxG_1.0 formalism. Some variants are also discussed, concerning the COM, an application for scientific workflows, and a comparison with two other context-based formalisms. The CxG formalism is compared to CxBR and CMB. The three context-driven approaches are not at the same decisional level. The CxBR formalism encapsulates into contexts knowledge – what we call reasoning steps – about appropriate actions, procedures and expectations as well as knowledge about possible new situations. The CMB formalism defines a *context* as a class of similar situations with contextual schemas (c-schemas) and procedural schemas. CxBR and CxGs both are task-based, in sharp contrast to several popular cognitive architectures such as SOAR (Laird et al. 1987). CMB is more agnostic on the distinction between being goal- or plan-based. In terms of formalism, CxBR, CxG or CMB are conceptual modeling approaches where knowledge is organized by context.

3

Context Modeling for Group Activity (CxG_2.0)

3.1. Introduction

Chapter 3 naturally extends the context-based modeling of an activity, accomplished by an actor in the previous chapter, applying the results to group activities. The presentation is based on the four levels – conceptual, operational, implementation and environment – the extensions at the conceptual level including the concepts of shared context, turn and the notion of CxG-based simulation.

The extensions at the operational level concern the notion of the turn mechanism and group activity and the new specifications of the CxG formalism. At the implementation level, we introduce the notion of the reserved contextual element and the mechanism of a CxG-based simulation. At the environment level, we show the importance of looking at the interaction between activity development (operational and implementation levels) and its environment. Two examples conclude the chapter to show the exploitation of the CxG formalism for modeling group activity and an interesting side effect of applying back to a one actor activity with the benefits of extending models initially for expressing a "one-shot" activity but possibly with intermediate variants like alternative checking. Task realization for an actor is equivalent to activity for a group of actors.

Figure 3.1 presents the four-modeling level framework as an extension of that of an actor's activity in Figure 2.1.

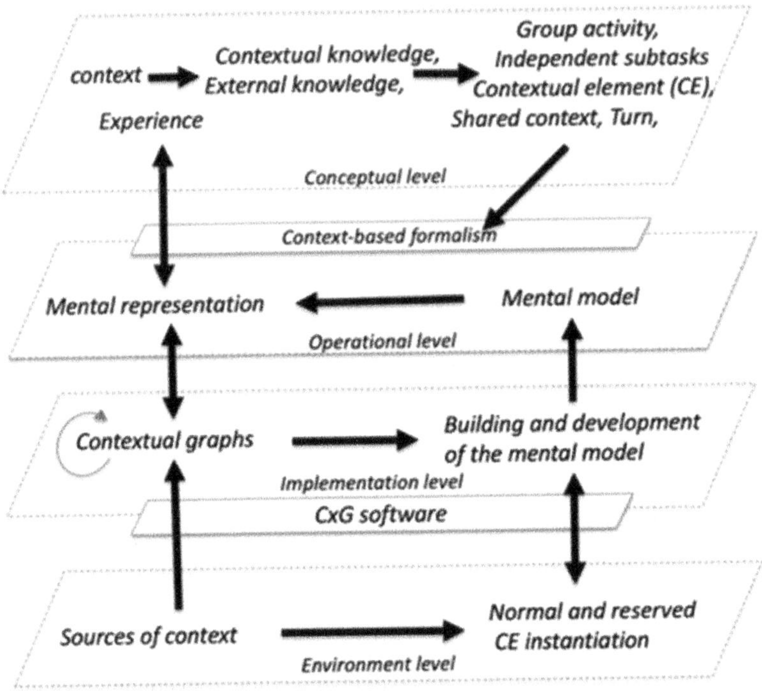

Figure 3.1. *Group activity at the four modeling levels*

The cyclic use of a contextual graph is concretized in Figure 3.1 at the implementation level by the rounded arrow at the head of the word "Contextual graphs". Contrary to the framework for actor activity, the mental model is not developed from the mental representation because it is built by assembling independent subtasks in the contextual graph, the building process being at the implementation level and converted at the operational level as a mental model that may contribute to the group mental representation and thus a collective experience. The assembling of independent subtasks is associated step-by-step with the instantiation of the contextual elements in the last independent subtask that is realized and added.

3.2. Conceptual level

3.2.1. *Introduction*

In organizational settings, groups do not work in the isolation like in a laboratory setting. Groups need to manage their boundaries and adapt to their organizational environment. As a consequence, organization is a context variable influencing group behavior (Gladstein 1984), and the group, another context, is a variable affecting individual reactions (Black 1979). Enterprise organization often is described in terms of roles, each role being associated with different tasks. Here, we consider group activity in the opposite situation, where it is the activity that is associated with different roles, first at the operational level, where group activity is modeled as a sequence of turns between actors, where it is an actor that holds a unit of reasoning. Second, at the implementation level, group activity is represented as a unique contextual graph for actors and their interventions during the group activity with a turn mechanism relying on shared context. As a result, group activity is simultaneously built and developed by associating activity and interaction management. Then, the development of the group activity results in a CxG simulation of a dynamic scenario that describes reasoning evolution in group activity.

This section presents the new concepts needed for our purpose, such as the notions of group, activity of a group, shared context, turn and the previous concepts that need to be revised like "activity" for a group. The shared context (especially its building) is based on our personal experience, first, as one partner in a large project with more than 15 partners from six to seven different domains (thus participating in the building of shared context) and, second, as an observer in an experiment for modeling verbal exchanges between two actors for collaboratively generating answers to questions (Brézillon et al. 2006). The notion of turn allows, on the one hand, the presentation of the cyclic crossing of a directed graph during group-activity development, supposing an activity model with the integration of the notion of turn for actors and, on the other hand, the notion of CxG-based Simulation for unfolding the contextual (and nonlinear) reasoning holds during the group-activity development.

3.2.2. *Concept of activity for a group*

The notions of team and group are commonly used interchangeably to refer to a set of people that are concerned by a given work. However, such notions differ in their characteristics and purposes. Generally, an organization structure relies on the notion of team. A team is a group of employees in a company making a collective effort in the interest of a common cause (Rosa et al. 2006). Team members are selected according to their characteristics and skills in order to accomplish a mission. Before team members start working together, the leader learns about the team members, recognizes their competences and skills and is able to design a precise work plan. Once the process is completed, the team leader is responsible for dividing the work among the team members and for controlling the evolution of the teamwork. Teamwork is a notion relatively well specified.

The term "group" replaces "team" when the completion of some works requires crossing organizational frontiers, enabling the creation of groups involving actors from different organizations (i.e. different hierarchies). Thus, an actor can be spontaneously added (or removed) as a member in a group at any moment. Group actors have the will to act as a whole in order to get something done (Bikson and Eveland 1991). Group work results from the distribution of workload among group actors, and the group lasts up to work completion. As in a team, there is a unique group leader, but each group actor can ask for support directly from other actors. The meaning of group work is less accurate than teamwork because the term "work" is at a too abstract level and is not related to what is done effectively. The "use of task" instead of "work" corrects the problem because there is an emphasis on the way in which the task is done (one speaks of task model, not of work model, except for some particular aspects like performance).

The activity, which extends the "task" (Leplat and Hoc 1983), is the concrete implementation of the task that is realized by an actor in a specific situation. The task is what an actor must do, and the activity is the (physical and mental) behavior that the actor exhibits for realizing the task (Sarrazin et al. 1996). Associated with each activity, there are one or more scripts that describe the ways an activity must be executed. A particular context determines the script to be run for an activity. Thus, activity takes into consideration the result as well as the process leading to the result, i.e. task realization from an external viewpoint. Task has a formal definition, but activity reveals, in addition to its theoretical definition, practical aspects of the realization of the task with planning, launching, performing and finalizing the accomplishment of the activity.

The actors' engagement during group work is often discussed based on three concepts: coordination, cooperation and collaboration. Coordination is the technical organization of the different elements of a collective activity to enable participants to work together effectively according to a plan. The term coordination has a well-accepted definition across disciplines such as cognitive sciences (AI, psychology, etc.) or engineering Computer-supported cooperative work (CSCW, interface design, etc.) (Elmarzouqi et al. 2007; Bedwell et al. 2012; Gulati et al. 2012).

Collaboration and cooperation are ambiguous terms with different meanings across domains and sometimes from one author to another in the same domain. Collaboration is "working together" to reach a negotiated and consensual solution to create something new with a shared vision. Collaboration concerns the realization of the same task by different actors. The unit is not the participant but the group with a global and collective responsibility. There are two types of realization in parallel, a joint realization and individual realizations. Each participant contributes to the action of any other participant of the group to increase the performance, and collaborative interaction is permanent: the coherence of the group achieves the objective. Cooperation means "operate together" with, first, a negotiated division of task realization among participants (a common goal reached by autonomous actions) and, second, a pooling by assembling subtasks realized in a flat way. It is a negotiated division of task realization between participants (a common goal but autonomous actions) and a pooling by assembling task realizations, each participant having to bear a definite part of the shared task realization. Cooperative interaction is limited to organization, coordination and monitoring of task realization. The ambiguity between collaboration and cooperation is related to the nature of actor interaction and, more specifically, (1) the goal of the interaction, (2) the shared objectives of actors; (3) the entities involved (from individuals to enterprises); (4) the context that needs to be shared among actors; (5) the type of interaction (i.e. collocated/remote synchronous/asynchronous); (6) the technologies required to support the different types of interaction and (7) the scope of the joint work regarding actors' individual work. As a result, it is difficult to identify clearly what group work is.

The term group work evolves dynamically along with interaction between two humans (or a human and a machine). What is a simple collaboration at one moment becomes cooperation at the next moment. Indeed, we join McEwan (1997) who presents a continuum for describing group activity from isolation (each group actor works for themselves) to collaboration (sharing a collective goal and acceptance of personal subtasks to realize), through independence (independent work with acceptance of collective rules), coordination (actor work realized in a common framework of rules, calendar, means), collegiality (integration of the actor work with other actor works) and cooperation (integration of actor subtasks in task realization). When working collaboratively, people discuss important topics, observe each other, help each other and learn from each other. There is an associative-type interdependence with a pooling of ideas and sharing of achievements. Collaboration excludes competition as well as indifference.

3.2.3. *The shared context*

The initial notion of working context must be enriched by the notion of shared context. Shared context contains contextual elements that are specific to the interaction between group actors, in addition to contextual elements specific to group-activity development. Thus, shared context can be compared to the medium of communication on the current state of the group-activity development when the development moves from one actor to the following one, with the identification of the next actor with the subtask that this next actor must realize.

Shared context is an extension of the working context of an actor for an activity by a group of actors. Shared context is elaborated from elements of individual working contexts, elements that are shared by all group actors (eventually after explanations or negotiation). Shared context evolves continuously as part of the group-activity development and additions of contextual elements by actors. Shared-context building is the first explicit step of group-activity development. In some sense, shared context is the working context of group activity, except that all the shared context is public, while a part of working contexts is private for actors.

KP18	Shared-context building is the first step of group-activity development.

Group members first gather a maximum of contextual elements without looking for a global picture (in a kind of brainstorming), a member proposes a contextual element supposed to be relevant and other members accept it or ask for explanation. Group members accept the new contextual element if they can integrate it in their personal working contexts. Shared-context building does not concern only contextual knowledge but also external knowledge that the proposal originator can express (e.g. "I had the opportunity to visit a place concerned with this topic a couple of years ago"). Thus, the collective shared-context development allows group actors to keep their mental representations compatible and adjusted to the joint activity (Karsenty and Brézillon 1995).

When group actors reach a consensus on shared-context content, they enter the second phase of the process by organizing, assembling and structuring contextual elements of shared context in a proceduralized context for reaching the group activity.

The "Computer-mediated work" project (section 1.3.10) concerns an experiment for modeling verbal exchanges between two actors for collaborative generation of answers to questions such as "How does the oyster make pearls?" and "How does water become mineral?" (Brézillon et al. 2006). The collaborative process of answer building includes the first phase of shared-context building for collaboration. Each actor proposes elements from their working context. The other actor may agree, or ask for an explanation, and eventually negotiate with the first actor. Finally, actors agree on elements of shared context satisfying both of them.

During the next phase of shared-context exploitation, actors organize, assemble and structure contextual elements of shared context to generate a proceduralized context that will be integrated into answer building.

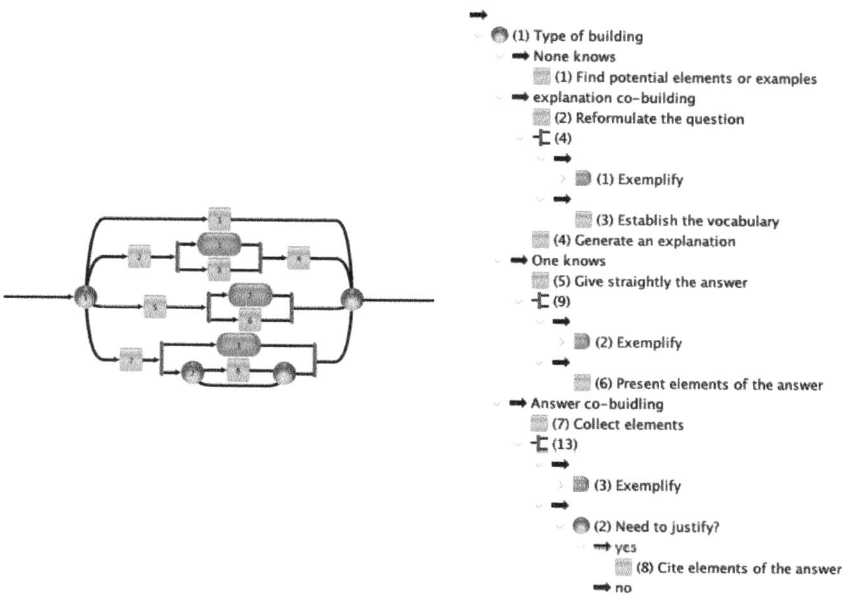

Figure 3.2. *Model of the collaborative answer building processes. For a color version of this figure, see www.iste.co.uk/brezillon/contextbasedmodeling.zip*

Figure 3.2 shows the four types of building an answer that depends on the familiarity of participants with the domain from where the question comes. Three main observations were made from the elicitation phase:

– Subjects had a problem finding the right granularity of their answer, but gathering contextual information helps to determine it. When subjects cannot identify the right level of granularity, they enter into a process of explanation to justify their proceduralized context.

– Subjects often begin by repeating the question to be sure they understand correctly and to look for some relationships between elements of the question and elements of the answer from their personal working contexts (personal experience).

– Subjects can know globally the answer without knowing the components. As a result, subjects express an external and superficial viewpoint. They provide explanations spontaneously to: (1) strengthen a known answer, (2) make progress in the co-construction of the answer and (3) be sure of the granularity of the answer. The explanation is generally less precise than the answer (generally at a too general level), but useful between them to reinforce their ties. Several groups of subjects were confused and provided an explanation instead of giving the answer (thus with additional details not necessary).

Once the activity is accomplished (selection and instantiation of contextual elements), mental model and proceduralized context enter the actors' mental representation. Later, the proceduralized context may be recalled to replay the mental model. Thus, the more actors experiment, the more they acquire structured operational knowledge, and the more actors work together, the more they reinforce their ties too.

Figure 3.3 shows proceduralized-context building from group working contexts (CE stands for contextual elements) and shared context. Actor_1 introduces the contextual element CE_1 from their working context into the shared context. Because CE_1 belongs to Actor_2's working context too, the contextual element is accepted. When Actor_1 proposes the introduction of CE_2, Actor_2, which has no reference to it in their working context, needs explanations for accepting CE_2, both agreeing on CE'_2 (compatible interpretation of CE_2 in shared context). For accepting CE'_2, the receiver builds an interpretation CE"_2 in their working context. Once Actor_2 agrees to the contextual element, contextual elements of shared context are combined into a proceduralized context for addressing the activity development.

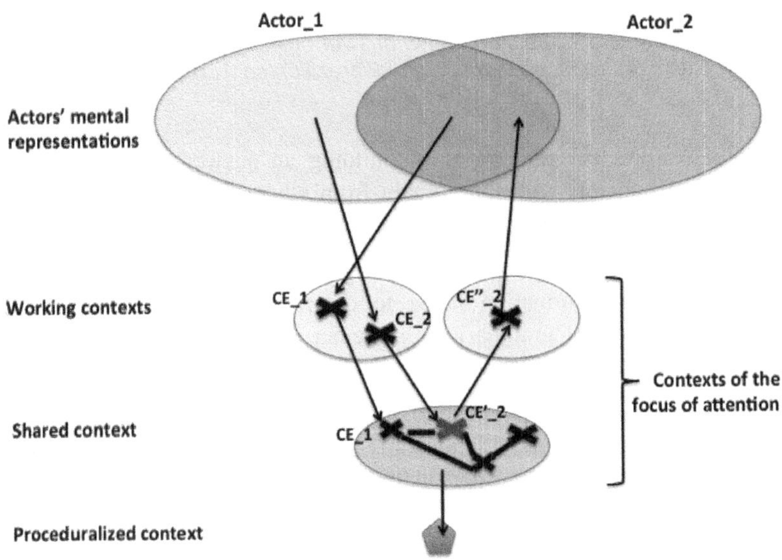

Figure 3.3. *Collaborative building of a proceduralized context. For a color version of this figure, see www.iste.co.uk/brezillon/contextbasedmodeling.zip*

The change of role (and turn) between group members during group-activity development supposes considering the contextual graph of the group activity jointly with shared context in order to introduce a notion of cycle in the representation during group-activity development by re-traversing the group contextual graph in an updated shared context.

This explicit modeling of shared-context building with the group contextual graph opens the door to more options, for instance to stop the simulation at the end of a turn, to introduce loops for managing a negotiation between two actors, the possibility to change the objective of an actor when an unexpected event occurs (e.g. the actor selects an object and discovers finally that the object is not adapted to their objective) and to introduce backtracking in actors' reasoning (or at the group level). This also makes it possible to open the door to the role allocated to different actors (reviewers in the submission example) and a new insight into the problem of cooperation versus collaboration discussed in the introduction.

3.2.4. *The turn*

Group-activity development corresponds to the course of a turn during which different actors intervene (including the possibility of parallel turns such as in the review process of the "Submission management" example). Turns, that is, intervention of a series of actors, are performed sequentially at different moments of the group-activity development. A turn is the local contribution of an actor to the group activity during the traversing of the contextual graph representing group activity. In an internal view, a turn is the local contribution of an actor to a reasoning step in the global reasoning of the group activity.

A turn corresponds to (1) selection of the actor, the manager of the next turn, (2) selection of the corresponding subtask in the activity, (3) development of a subtask and computation of the corresponding proceduralized context and (4) management of shared context for the next turn. Turn management also implies a management of roles and subtasks. In some sense, turn mechanism plays a role of synchronizer (coordinator) of the shared context (a kind of "hub") for all actors' activities because beyond contextual elements used for turn management, there is information exchange between independent subtasks.

Figure 3.4 represents a conceptual model of a turn, based on the part of the shared context (in yellow on the figure) that is associated with the subtask. This part of the shared context is composed of reserved contextual elements (see section 3.4.3), which are the activation conditions of the turn, and post-conditions concerns what to do once the turn is completed. This turn model, building block of a group activity, is domain independent because domain knowledge is at a finer granularity of the internal description of the independent subtask.

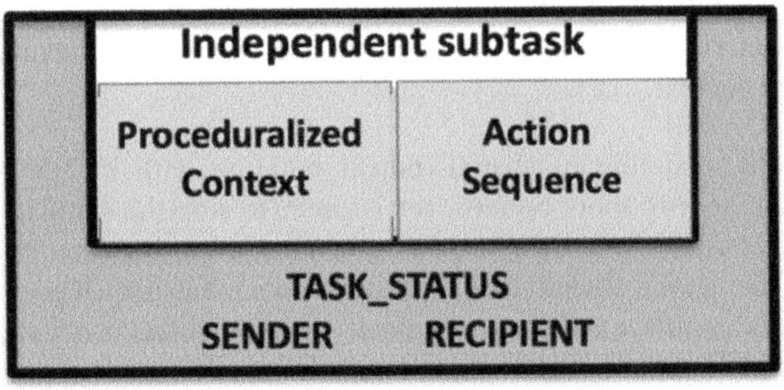

Figure 3.4. *Conceptual model of a turn. For a color version of this figure, see www.iste.co.uk/brezillon/contextbasedmodeling.zip*

Once the turn model is obtained, the next step is to represent movement across turns during group-activity development. Concretely, this supposes traversing in a cyclic way the directed contextual graph for realizing the next turn corresponding to the next role in the updated shared context. The links between turns into different activities are a way to model group-member interaction in real-time because it is not possible (and interesting) to store all the mental models.

3.2.5. *CxG-based simulation*

Usually, a simulation allows us to describe the evolution of a (formal) model from a set of initial conditions. The model expresses a statement about a real system that is based on formalized concepts and hypothesis about the functioning of the real system (see section 1.2). A model-based simulation is a top-down (deductive) model, while a CxG-based simulation corresponds to a bottom-up (inductive) model. In a CxG-based simulation, working (or shared) context evolves during mental-model development, not as a function of an independent variable like time, but along a variable representing the progression of the activity during its accomplishment. If a formal model is given initially, the mental model is developed progressively from a mental representation and evolves according to the reasoning associated with it. In that sense, a CxG-based simulation is a particular type of simulation, for which we consider reasoning as the variable representing the activity from its launching to its finalization.

The behavior of a CxG-based simulator is comparable with the usual model-based simulator's behavior, supposing that (1) contextual elements in the contextual graph can be compared to the parameters in the formal model (a change of parameter values impacts the model behavior as a change of instantiation modifies the mental model developed) and (2) variables in a model-based simulation are related to the result of the progressive formal-model development as a function of time. Conversely, the equivalent of a model for a group activity is a contextual graph at the implementation level and the progressive evolution of the mental model (the path in the contextual graph) can be followed along the reasoning development. The mental model also has another representation as a series of turns and is built dynamically, jointly with the mental-model development. In both situations, CxG-based simulation relies on the group-activity model and reasoning for describing group-activity development.

Table 3.1 gives a comparison of model-based simulation and CxG-based simulation according to seven characteristics.

	Model-based	**CxG-based**
Goal	Representation of a real system	Mental-model development as an activity
Real system	The model as internal viewpoint	Mental model as an external viewpoint
Tactical level	A formal model	A mental representation (contextual graph)
Operational level	Simulation from an initial state	Simulation by development of a mental model from an initial shared context
Working context	Initial set of values of variables and parameters	Contextual elements and real-time instantiations
Simulation	Temporal evolution of the model	Reasoning evolution in the mental-model
Type of support	Real-system centered	Use-centered

Table 3.1. *Comparison of the model- and CxG-based simulations (Brézillon 2018)*

In CxG formalism, a contextual graph implements a mental representation of a group activity that is structured by subtasks. A CxG-based simulation describes the progressive developing the mental model in the context at hand. Such a contextual model corresponds, on the one hand, to the whole mental representation as a contextual graph (the static part at the tactical level) and, on the other hand, to building and development of a specific mental model (the dynamic part at the operational level) corresponding to the given context, while a formal model is only static in a simulation.

For going further in the specification of CxG-based simulation, we consider that CxG-based simulation belongs to the class of discrete-event simulation (DES), although not completely. DES is one of the methods used to virtually model and analyze systems or processes (such as the frenzy of activity at an airport) where changes happen at specific, distinct points in time (Law and Kelton 2000; Babulak and Wang 2008). DES is intended to simulate systems where events occur at specific, separable instances in time. DES contrasts with a continuous simulation where events are tracked continuously. The core idea behind DES is to represent a system as a collection of entities with attributes and simulate how distinct events affect these attribute changes over time. There are three prevalent forms of expressing discrete event simulation programs: event scheduling, activity scanning and process interaction. The CxG-based simulation reproduces the development of an activity realized by an actor.

However, DES still faces some significant challenges: these include integrating human behavior; using simulation for exploration, not replication; determining return on investment and communication issues across a splitting community (Collins et al. 2023). The CxG-based simulation addresses such challenges: human behavior is an explicit source of context, replication and exploration of alternatives of mental-model behavior of an actor is the objective of our tool, and communication across a splitting community is ensured by the contextual graph containing all the known developments of an activity in different contexts. Globally, CxG-based simulation seems perfectly ascribed in the general line of DES tools with a correspondence between elements of DES tools (event, attribute, etc.) and the CxG-based simulation exists, but there is a divergence on their uses.

An attribute is a property or characteristic of an entity or the system as a whole, and the state of the system is represented by the combination of all attributes at any moment. The state of the system changes as events occur, reflecting updates in conditions or statuses (SoftwareSimm 2022). CxG-based simulation realizes an activity through the course of a path in a contextual graph (a mental-model development) as the entity or system, contextual elements play a similar role to that of attributes, the event would be the arrival at a contextual element for which we need to know its instantiation, and thus, the occurrence of the event is to know its instantiation. The event space is composed of external input events and external output events and internal events (Mansharamani 1997). External input events are events that are triggered from outside the system. In a CxG-based simulation, the instantiation is given from context sources, that is, like an internal input event, and the request for an instantiation is an internal event that is a change in state variables that do not affect the system environment.

In the example of the traveler traffic in an airport (Mansharamani 1997), we follow the movement of a unique traveler going to reach their boarding gate, while in the literature, all the travelers going to all their boarding gates (i.e. all travelers are in different contexts) are followed, and the instantiation will not change the system state but allow the course of the development. In our approach, we do not look for validating proposed changes (instantiations) but to find them for making a choice to continue activity development.

3.3. Operational level

3.3.1. *Introduction*

Actors use knowledge and experience to contextualize a procedure for developing an activity. From an external viewpoint, activity covers the actor, task realization, contextual information considered by actors and various choices made by them to reach the goal. We now extend the initial framework presented in Chapter 2 to a model group activity, the two concepts introduced at the conceptual level (shared context and turn), and the concept of interaction in the group activity, and we illustrate the extensions of the formalism on different examples. A turn mechanism is proposed to adapt CxG formalism to group activity. The types of interaction among group members are studied based on the distinction between contextual elements related to the task and those related to interaction management. The real understanding of group activity does not only help decision-makers but also provides designers with real requirements for building successful applications.

3.3.2. *The notions of group activity and interaction*

Group activity is not limited to the official objective. It may also concern, upstream, the setup of the group activity and, downstream, the use of the results of the group activity. There is no real modeling of the mechanism ensuring interaction between members during group activity because the type of interaction management depends essentially on the type of group activity. Finally, we address the lack of consideration in the literature of shared context that is associated with the group work and group-member interaction.

The notion of activity is particularly adapted to a collective viewpoint on an activity. In collaborative work, several actors work together as group actors. This requires an external viewpoint for "sharing out" an activity between group actors. Group activity is related to the way in which the group as a whole realizes the activity. Benítez-Guerrero et al. (2012) present the development of an activity (called effective activity) as an instance of an activity model that describes group actors that can participate in the activity, how the activity can be carried out, the family of objects that can be manipulated or produced, and which roles group actors and objects will play in the activity (what we call the context of the activity).

The introduction of the notion of group activity in the CxG formalism supposes a transition from one actor to a group of actors. Each group actor interventions are independent of the others. Each group actor generally intervenes at different moments during group-activity development. This transition from one actor to N actors necessitates an evolution of the conceptual approach, replacing an actor's mental representation (i.e. the set of mental models developed by the actor for a given activity) by a group-mental representation that also concerns mental models, which plays more of a role of archive of the group activity than for actor activity. We hypothesize that a group activity is a sequence of contributions coming from successive actors, an actor intervening several times in the group activity.

Interaction between actors during group-activity development can be understood as the execution of a sequence of independent subtasks during a cyclic use of the contextual graph, independent subtasks being taken in activities of group actors. Interaction between group actors corresponds to a shift of the focus from an independent subtask in one actor's activity to an independent subtask in another actor's activity. The type of interaction evolves along the group-activity development by the play of actors that intervene, their contribution to the group activity, the importance of what is expected, etc. It required a simple extension of CxG formalism for transposition of an activity into a sequence of independent subtask realization. Such an evolution of the conceptual approach is not a bifurcation point because – as a return on investment – task realization of each actor has benefit of a deep change in its modeling with the change of viewpoint, from an internal viewpoint (the task model) to an external viewpoint (set of independent subtasks) integrated in a group activity. Thus, a group-activity modeling, as a mental model, is assimilated to a sequence of interventions made by different actors.

The processing of a group activity (global level) consists of entering successively into an actor's activity (a local level) to realize the retained subtask at the actor's granularity. Thus, group-activity development is led in a kind of glocal approach, a step corresponds to the request of a sender and is taken charge of by a recipient. In an enterprise, each actor plays a role with attached subtasks. Group activity requires the collaboration of actors with specialized roles for different parts.

The main difference between group activity and actor activity is the incremental building of the group mental model as a sequence of actors' interventions in addition to the instantiation processing.

3.3.3. *The CxG_2.0 formalism*

The modeling of group activity is discussed in the "Paper submission" example (section 3.6.1) for illustrating the CxG-based simulator developed (Garcia and Brézillon 2015). The paper submission process requires interaction among actors with different roles: author, editor, reviewers and publisher. In the initial example, the representation is "document-oriented" and the editor does not appear explicitly in the process, when editor's role is important in the submission management. A translation of the "document-oriented" representation to an "actor-oriented" representation in CxG formalism opens the road for a richer representation including paper rejection and management by the editor of a conflict between reviewers, which are easily represented. However, it is a representation according to the editor's viewpoint only, and contribution of other actors to the submission-management example is limited to a role of "subcontractors" of the editor, not as actors in a group activity. Interaction between group actors corresponds to a movement of the focus from one actor's activity to another actor's activity and, more specifically, between precise subtasks inside actors' activities.

Figure 3.5 shows the idea of the conceptual modeling of turn management on the "paper-submission" example. A new cycle starts if shared context has been modified during the last turn. Shared context thus plays the role of an inference engine in the CxG-based simulation of the activity.

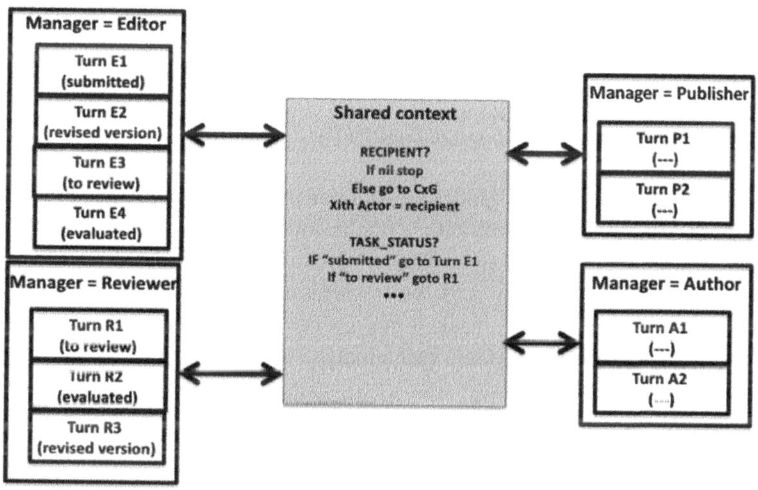

Figure 3.5. *An operational representation in terms of turns of the paper-submission example. For a color version of this figure, see www.iste.co.uk/brezillon/contextbasedmodeling.zip*

This supposes a particular organization of actors' activities based on the independent subtask considered at each traversing of the graph. An independent subtask is represented by a contextual subgraph (like in CxG_1.0 version). It may lead to different decisions according to shared context, and therefore, interaction in the group activity may move differently towards one or another independent subtask depending on the context.

3.4. Implementation level

3.4.1. *Introduction*

Mental-model building is a path in the contextual graph that corresponds to a sequence of independent subtasks performed during the activity development. At the operational level, the arrow from mental model to mental representation in Figure 3.1 points out the fact that, once built, the group mental model may enrich the group mental representation, that is, the collective experience of the group. The result of a subtask realization allows the specification of the following actor that will be the next manager (the recipient) and of the independent subtask to realize. Thus, the contextual graph is structured for supporting turns with (1) the selection of the manager (instantiated by an actor) for realizing an intervention, (2) the selection of an independent subtask in the manager's activity to be performed when crossing the contextual graph and (3) the designation of the next manager with its independent subtask to execute at the next turn. As such, a turn sequence is similar to a CxG-based simulation.

3.4.2. *From actor activity to group activity*

The proposed solution is a modeling of actor interventions in the group activity in terms of *independent subtasks*. Each independent subtask encapsulates operational knowledge, reasoning and actions that the manager has to perform at one intervention in a group activity and the transmission of the relevant results to the next actors. An independent subtask is represented by a specific contextual graph (like in CxG_1.0 version of the CxG formalism).

KP19	Independent subtasks are realized successively in a cyclic use of the contextual graph.

The global intervention of an actor (actor activity) in a group activity corresponds to a set of independent subtasks. An independent task may lead to different decisions and therefore requires reasoning to be built step-by-step in the group activity. As a result, the group-activity development corresponds to the assembling of a sequence of independent subtasks taken in different actor activities. It is a dynamic building of the group mental model, while the mental representation is composed of the independent subtasks of the group actors (in the contextual graph). The interaction between actors during the accomplishment of the group mental model corresponds to subtask realization and management of the reserved contextual elements for the next turn and implies a shared-context management. Group activity is more than the simple sum of actor activities because individual activities are interdependent.

KP20	A group activity is built by the assembling of a sequence of independent subtasks taken successively in actors' activities.

At the end of a turn during the building of the group mental model, the independent subtask just realized (with the instantiations and the proceduralized context) is added at the end of the assembling of the previous realized subtasks and thus added to the group mental model. This double operation of jointly building and developing the group mental model is made possible by management of reserved contextual elements that ensure the cyclic use of the directed acyclic contextual graph by determining which actor will take charge of the next cycle and for which independent subtask. Finally, we obtain the mental model (the assembling of the realized subtask), a proceduralized context (composed of the proceduralized contexts of the subtasks in the assembling) and the sequence of actors that have intervened. However, the global result being generally complex, we prefer to replay the CxG-based simulation.

3.4.3. *Reserved contextual elements*

The introduction of reserved contextual elements makes it possible to represent group activity as a sequence of group actors that communicate through their shared context. Based on the notions of roles and tasks, Garcia and Brézillon (2015) propose managing turns during mental model development with four *reserved contextual elements*, corresponding to roles and task, for controlling CxG-based simulation.

KP21	Reserved contextual elements, which are associated with roles and tasks of actors, allow the management of turns and the cyclic use of the directed contextual graph.

We distinguish them in upper case letters and yellow color in the contextual graphs. Thus, MANAGER is the actor who is responsible for the current turn (defined in the contextual graph of group activity). SENDER is the actor who is named (instantiated) MANAGER for executing the next turn. RECIPIENT is the actor that will be in charge of the turn after MANAGER. TASK_STATUS specifies the independent subtask in the manager's activity to consider. Instantiations of RECIPIENT and TASK_STATUS are modified consequently at subtask realization. In the "Submission management" example, the editor (MANAGER) receives a submission (TASK_STATUS = "Submitted") from an author (SENDER). At the end of the turn, the editor's decision is made (e.g. accept the submission), and the submission is sent to a reviewer (RECIPIENT) with TASK_STATUS instantiated to "to be reviewed" and editor becomes the new instantiation of SENDER for the next turn.

The processing of a turn corresponds to (1) select the actor that will be the manager of the turn (instantiation of SENDER and RECIPIENT), (2) select the independent subtask in the contextual graph of MANAGER' activity (instantiation of "TASK_STATUS"), (3) update of proceduralized context and independent-subtask realization and (4) manage the shared context for the next turn (instantiation of RECIPIENT and TASK_STATUS). At the level of the CxG representation, this supposes accessing the actor activity, to enter into the contextual graph for reaching and executing an independent subtask, to exit the contextual graph, to update the shared context and to re-enter the contextual graph in the updated shared context. It is the basic principle of the CxG-based simulation that is discussed later. Here, we discuss the modeling of a turn and of a turn mechanism in the continuity of the previous modeling (conceptual and operational) levels.

There is a hierarchical organization of actors and independent subtasks in group activity starting by identifying the instantiation of MANAGER and TASK_STATUS. The reserved contextual element, called TASK_STATUS, guides mental-model development towards a specific independent subtask inside MANAGER activity. After their instantiations just before entering the contextual graph, MANAGER and TASK_STATUS are instantiated just before exiting the turn at hand (i.e. according to the result of the independent subtask). These reserved contextual elements do not intervene in the independent subtask, except by their instantiations that are managed by particular actions (e.g. action "MANAGER = RECIPIENT" that push the instantiation of RECIPIENT in MANAGER), once the independent subtask is realized (with possibly different outputs). They play a role of synchronizer of actor interaction during group activity. The two categories of contextual elements and those specific to the group-activity management constitute the shared context.

These actions guide group-activity development and are a way to represent a mechanism for turn management (Brézillon 2015). Reserved contextual elements are used in combination (e.g. TASK_STATUS and RECIPIENT), but the change of instantiation of a reserved contextual element often is not systematic at the end of an independent subtask. For example, the reviewer may decline the editor's request and TASK_STATUS then keeps the instantiation "to be reviewed", and the editor, as a manager, will receive a document with the status "to be reviewed", which will lead to the independent subtask "look for another reviewer" before restarting the turn mechanism. It is a way to introduce loops in a directed and acyclic graph, due to the shared-context representation being made explicit for managing turns during group-practice development. Reserved contextual elements are task-independent, but their values have a semantic depending on the domain. For example, MANAGER may be the "editor" or "reviewer" in the submission process, and the "operator" and "simulator" in the TACTIC project.

The representation of all actors' activities must be made explicit in a uniform way. Figure 3.6 shows the generic structure of the contextual graph, which is defined by an initial frame based on (1) the role (manager) and (2) independent subtasks (TASK_STATUS) in actors' activities at the same level, and thus facilitating their coordination based on the notion of the role of manager held by the editor, the reviewer, the author or the publisher.

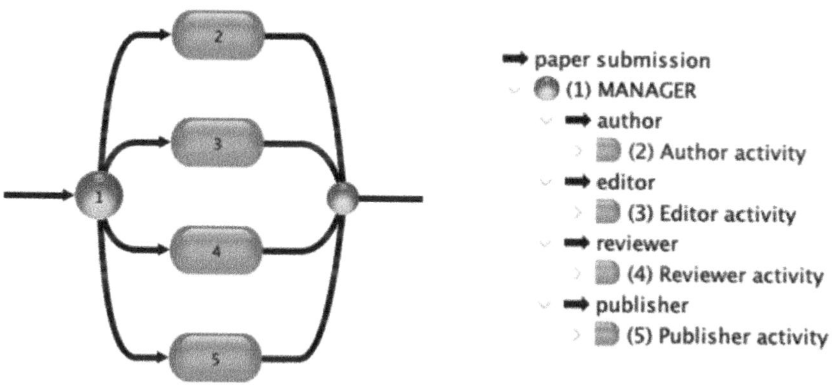

Figure 3.6. *"Submission management" example as a contextual graph. For a color version of this figure, see www.iste.co.uk/brezillon/contextbasedmodeling.zip*

Figure 3.6 shows the group-activity model of the "Submission management" example (section 3.5.1) in which each branch corresponds to a role's activity (i.e. the task associated with the role). Each activity in the figure has an identical structure that begins with a reserved contextual element TASK-STATUS with branches having each an independent subtask of the manager's activity. The current active manager role in the group activity corresponds to the instantiation of the contextual element MANAGER among the values "author", "editor", "reviewer" and "publisher".

3.4.4. *Mechanisms of the CxG-based simulation*

At a given step of group-activity development, an actor is the temporary manager of a specific part of the group activity. This specific part, corresponding to an independent subtask in the actor's activity, supposes entering into each actor's activity to follow at lower granularity group-activity development as a sequence of subtask realizations. Thus, there is local realization of subtasks for the global development of group activity (glocal approach). This allows the identification of the points of interaction among actors inside their activities. The turn mechanism is the keystone of the dynamic organization of actors' activities and group activity and the basis of the notion of CxG-based simulation. The turn mechanism in group-activity development can be automated easily and lead to a new type of simulation, the CxG-based simulation of group-activity development that opens new perspectives on previous types of simulation because the sequence of interactions between actors is built dynamically during the simulation and does not need a complex representation of all the combinations of turns in a group activity because possible combinations can be rebuilt at any time. The turn mechanism can be easily represented at the operational level (Figure 3.5). For example, when a turn ends, the system may detect what to do next. The rule presented in the figure will shift the focus onto the next actor or stop the simulation if RECIPIENT = <nil>.

The rule implements the first contextual element "MANAGER?" of the contextual graph. This leads to considering a CxG-based simulation as a cycle with (1) an initial shared context (i.e. a set of instantiations), (2) a turn-based development of group activity, (3) a comparison of initial and final shared contexts and (4) the triggering of a new cycle of the simulation if initial and final shared contexts are different (or "exit" if the next recipient is set to "nil" as in Figure 3.5).

The extension of CxG formalism in its CxG_2.0 version includes the management of several actors and the use of a directed acyclic series-parallel graph for describing group-activity development as the assembling of a sequence of subactivities realized by different actors. Shared context thus becomes a crucial place for interaction management as well as independent-subtask management in each actor's activity. When a subtask is realized, shared context is updated for determining which actor (recipient) must intervene next and which independent subtask that actor must realize.

KP22	A turn corresponds to a traversal of the contextual graph for realizing an independent subtask and shared-context management for the next turn.

Shared context plays a more important role than the working context in actor activity because shared context is updated collectively for building and developing group activity. In the CxG_2.0 version, shared context is attached to the group, not individual working contexts.

An important point here is the shared-context updating for preparing the next turn. This turn mechanism requires us to:

– Identify turns, i.e. decompose each actor's activity into *independent subtasks* structured by particular contextual elements that encapsulate operational knowledge, reasoning and actions that the manager has to perform and the transmission of relevant results to the next actors.

– Organize the turn sequence during group-activity development with a mechanism for ensuring the flexibility of the series building. Thus, a group contextual graph represents the knowledge needed for realizing independent subtasks in activities and the way in which this knowledge must be used all along the progress of the group activity.

A CxG-based simulation corresponds to successive traversals of the contextual graph for a sequential realization of subtasks as long as shared context is modified during the turn. Turn-sequence management is obtained by changes made in shared context during the previous turn, by execution of the actions in the subtask, and by instantiation of reserved contextual elements (Brézillon 2017).

KP23	A **CxG-based simulation** represents a sequence of turns by a cyclic use of the directed contextual graph as long as shared context is modified during the turn.

The group management (actors and independent subtasks) is performed in the contextual graph. The cyclic use of the contextual graph associated with shared context opens the possibility of backtracking into group reasoning as well as the possibility of cycles for negotiation between two (or more) group members.

KP24	The shared-context management associated with the cyclic use of the contextual graph opens a modeling of group activity larger than task realization.

Figure 3.7 shows the organization of the contextual graph in two windows (obtained from the CxG software). The window on the right is the graphical representation of the contextual graph with four contextual elements (blue circles, contextual nodes with a number and combination nodes without number) and six activities (pink elongated ovals containing each a contextual subgraph where each branch corresponds to an independent subtask). The window on the left presents the legends of all the items on the graphical part. By clicking on the arrow to the left of the items (left window), it is possible to aggregate or expand the item on the graphical window too. For example, the contextual elements (blue circles) are expanded, and activities (pink elongated ovals) are not.

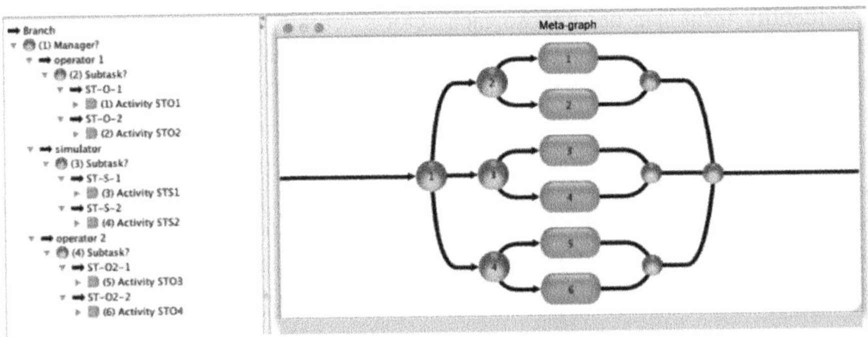

Figure 3.7. *Example of a conceptual graph. For a color version of this figure, see www.iste.co.uk/brezillon/contextbasedmodeling.zip*

In the CxG_1.0 version, mental-model development corresponds to a unique traversal of the contextual graph for representing the whole mental-model development that is obtained by following a path from the input to the output of the contextual graph. In the CxG_2.0 version, CxG-based simulation of group activity corresponds to a cyclic traversal of the contextual graph for progressively building on the mental model development.

KP25	Group-activity dynamics corresponds to the progressive assembling of independent subtasks in a sequence jointly with the mental-model development.

The advantage is to dynamically represent simply complex structures of group activities like mental representation for one actor. The inconvenience is the difficulty of giving a simple explanation, other than by CxG-based simulation, of the modeled group activity to the end-user because the mental-model structure (subtask assembling) depends on context. Note that proceduralized-context building is created in real-time at each subtask realization during group-activity development.

The shared context opens the door to CxG-based simulation for several options:

– CxG-based simulation can be stopped at the end of any turn (with an action "RECIPIENT = <nil>").

– The use of CxG-based simulation parameters introduces naturally the notion of cycles for managing conflict, negotiation, alternative checking among actors and realizing a given subtask (or sequence of subtasks) in different contexts, thanks to the association of the contextual graph and shared context.

– The same activity can be assigned to several actors (e.g. several reviewers in a paper submission).

– An independent subtask may have several possible outputs (identified by reserved contextual elements on different branches of the contextual subgraph). Outputs concerns the next subtask to realize and also may concern the study of variants by the manager, next actor or a subset of actors.

– Independent subtasks can be reused in a number of different combinations and several times with a unique representation at the implementation level.

– An actor may change the instantiation of a contextual element used in the subtask of another actor (or several other actors).

The dynamic modeling of group activity gives a new insight for addressing the focus of a unique actor with a "nonlinear" representation (i.e. with independent subtasks) of actor activity, for example, checking first different alternatives by simulation (cyclic use of the contextual graph for one actor) before making a decision.

Concretely, Figure 3.8 corresponds to the start of the CxG simulation for the turn O4 (see Figure 3.9 on TACTIC project). The shared context (the window with a red frame in Figure 3.8) initially contains all the contextual elements of the contextual graph because any subtask can be realized. The contextual elements in the shared-context window are ordered chronologically, and the operator selects the instantiation of the first contextual element (MANAGER) from the popup window just after the name of the contextual element where the known values are presented.

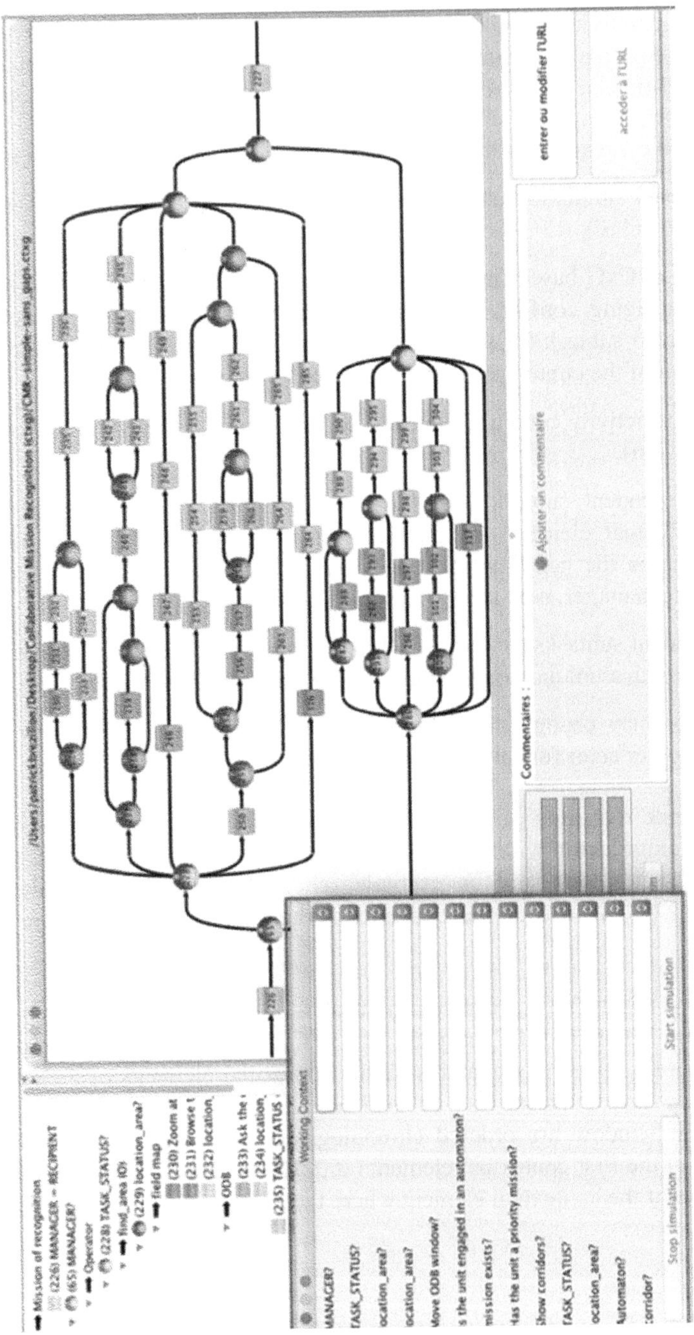

Figure 3.8. *Start of the CxG-based simulation of "Manage a unit" with the shared context in the red frame. For a color version of this figure, see www.iste.co.uk/brezillon/contextbasedmodeling.zip*

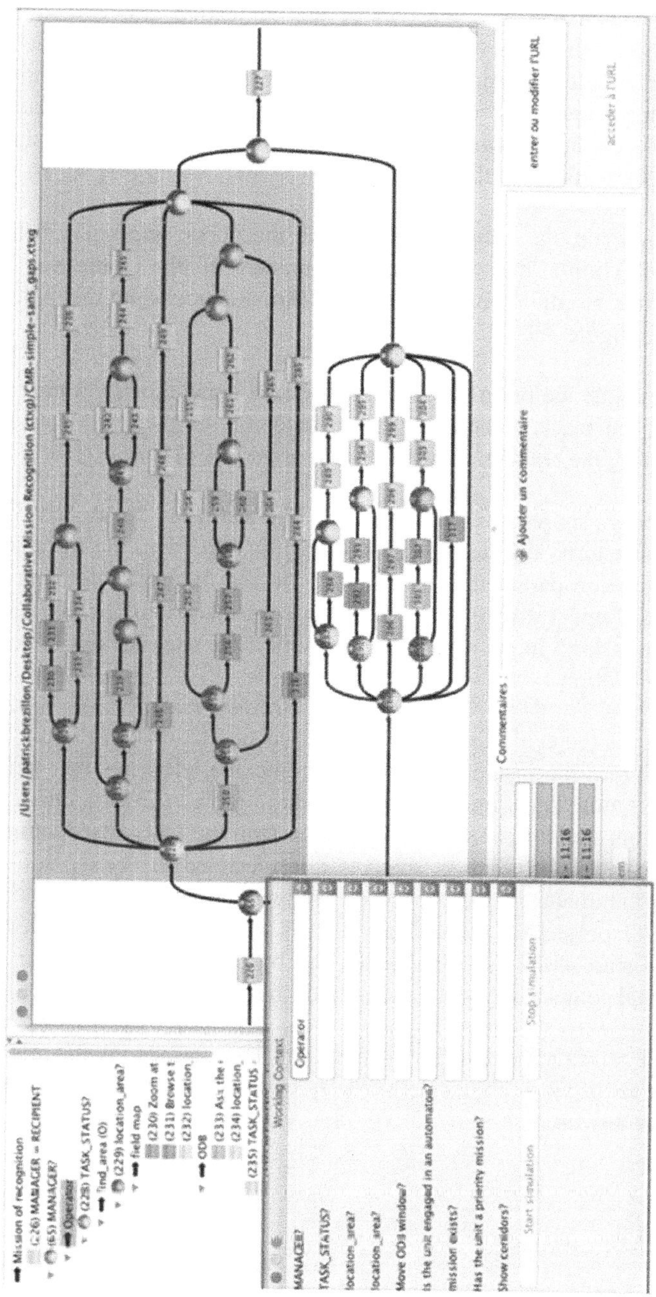

Figure 3.9. *Instantiations leading to the realization of the independent task O4. For a color version of this figure, see www.iste.co.uk/brezillon/contextbasedmodeling.zip*

At each instantiation, the left window of the shared context is updated with the relevant contextual elements, and the part of the contextual graph of interest is represented as a gray shade on the graphical window. The next instantiation of TASK_STATUS to “select mission-2” leads to the branch where the independent task O4 is (the gray shade is also reduced consequently to this branch). Once all the contextual elements on the path are instantiated, the simulation engine then starts the second phase of an effective simulation.

The instantiation (i.e. the choice of a value in the popup window) of the first contextual element limits the focus on the branch of the contextual graph corresponding to this instantiation and to the contextual elements on this part of the graph, as shown in Figure 3.9.

Figure 3.10 presents the progress of the CxG-based simulation by a progressive transformation of the black color into the red color of the path followed by the reasoning held during the realization of the independent task O4.

Figure 3.10 also shows the end of the simulation as expressed by the window “Show next turn” on the right part of Figure 3.10 with the instantiations made for the simulation parameters with MANAGER and RECIPIENT = “simulator”, SENDER = “operator” and TASK_STATUS = “define_course-corridor”, which will lead to the independent task S5 in the simulator’s activity if the user decides to continue the CxG-based simulation.

The actor controls the evolution of the CxG-based simulation by providing at the beginning of each turn the instantiations of the contextual elements that would be crossed at the next turn. Thus, the actor can decide to replay the turn, check a turn that is different from the normal successor or even stop the CxG-based simulation. Thus, the actor may try different alternatives to understand the best practice in a given context (or the impact of the context on the practice selection). That situation occurs in the SART project for the subway in Paris when an operator arrives in the control room and studies the practices developed by the previous operator during incident solving and compares them to alternatives they would have chosen.

The pre-filled information can be changed at any time, providing a flexible experience to the actor, who can decide to replay or skip the simulation of a turn or change the actor at any time.

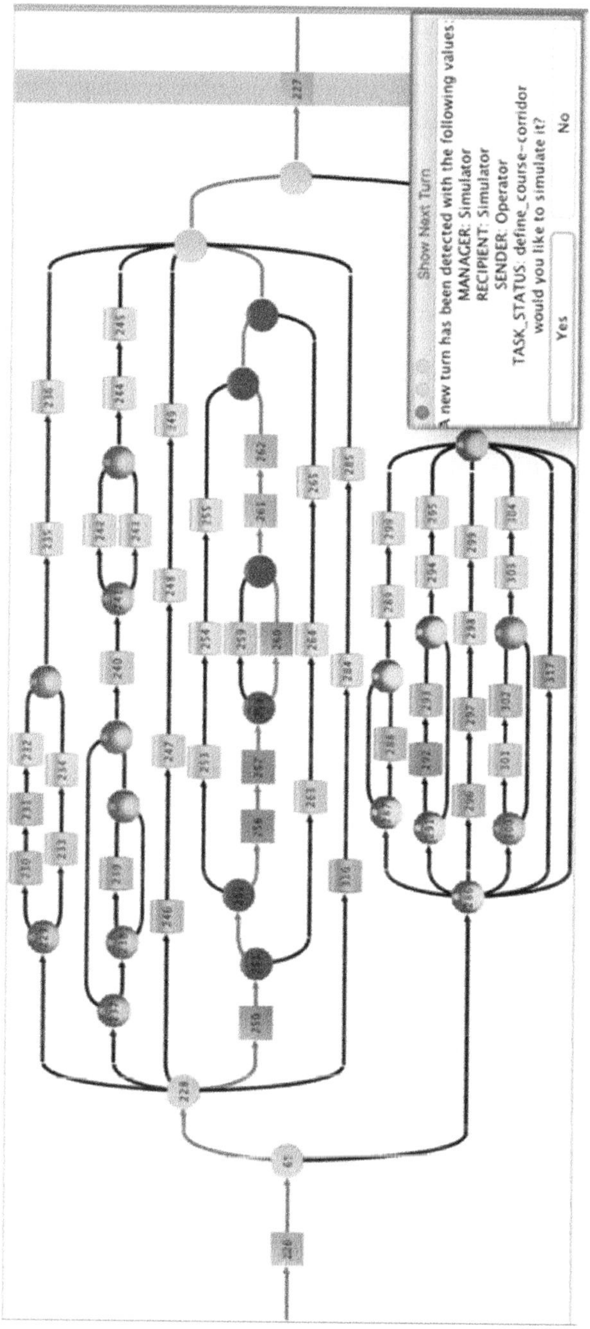

Figure 3.10. *CxG-based simulation of the turn S5 that follows turn O4. For a color version of this figure, see www.iste.co.uk/brezillon/contextbasedmodeling.zip*

The explicit association of the shared context with the contextual graph solves the main limitation of the contextual graph, namely the acyclic nature of contextual graphs that are considered without the working context. In the TACTIC-project (see Figure 3.21) example: (1) the turn O4 allows the operator to change their reasoning when an unexpected event is encountered (e.g. the chosen unit cannot accept the mission) and (2) the simulation parameter RECIPIENT = <nil> allows the turn mechanism to stop the simulation at the end of any turn, for example, when an action cannot be executed due to a lack of external resources. Moreover, the turn mechanism allows the introduction of loops for managing a negotiation between actors as well as for realizing an independent task several times (e.g. the review process allocated to several reviewers in the paper submission example).

Another effect in more complex models with several actors is to let the actor focus on the different types of interaction between actors and decide which interaction to promote in a given context. The strategy that is used for modeling group activity is to "divide and conquer" by decomposing the group task into "elementary" independent tasks that communicate only through the shared context. Thus, each independent task in the group activity corresponds to a step in the reasoning of an actor, and the interest of this modeling process is to consider interaction in group activity based on the turn mechanism. The methodology developed for a group activity would apply to an actor's activity too.

3.5. Environment level

In the actor activity, we concluded that the sources of context and the instantiation process were the two main points in the environment. The actor activity is linked to environment level only for having the answer to a question (i.e. instantiation of the contextual element) or for letting the actor solve unexpected problems encountered during activity development. There are more points to discuss about the environment of a group activity. The group activity has more links with the sources of context than with the instantiation process, links that include the management of actors and of the independent subtasks managed by reserved contextual elements. Reserved contextual elements (e.g. MANAGER, SENDER, RECIPIENT and TASK_STATUS) have their instantiations managed directly in the contextual graph at the implementation level, that is, prior to being used or directly implemented in the contextual graph, but it is possible to change their instantiation in another application of the approach. Reserved contextual elements have a special process different from the representation as a question like for those of the domain. Any intervention of an actor on them must be made directly at the level of the contextual graph.

The instantiation process in group activity concerns changes introduced by an actor about the selection of the actor, an independent subtask or the use of other options such as a "what-if" search, anticipation, negotiation and interaction with other actors. However, there is also the management of turns for the cyclic use of the contextual graph, the reserved contextual elements for actors (arriving or leaving the group) and subtask assembling of subtasks (selection, reordering, change of RECIPIENT for the next turn); changes by an actor may concern the instantiation of MANAGER and TASK_STATUS and the type of interaction (e.g. synchronous or asynchronous).

3.6. Two examples

3.6.1. *"Submission management" example*

The "Submission management" example is coming from Torres da Silva et al. (2005) who proposed a UML representation of the activity "submission management" example (Figure 3.11). It is a well-known model largely used in different formalisms of representation (but not modeling) such as production rules, UML, Bayesian networks, Petri nets and fluence graphs. The model describes (schematically) the activities of an author that submits a paper to the Editor of a Journal, the latter asking the advice of Reviewers before sending the accepted paper to the Publisher of the Journal. Submission management is considered from the Editor's viewpoint, while the Editor's activity does not intervene explicitly in the model. Indeed, the model is "document-centered" with three states (submitted, reviewed, published). We chose this example because it illustrates that a model (submission management) may be expressed in different representations (UML, Petri nets, etc.), and therefore, model and representation are two distinct concepts. We enrich the example with its modeling by additions of functions unfolded by an explicit representation of the activities of the editor, the author, the reviewers, and the publisher. Putting the editor's activity center stage is not sufficient for expressing contributions of other actors, which stay as "subcontractors" in the editor's activity, not as full actors like in group activity that is modeled after all the actors' contributions to the activity as a group.

There are several formalisms of representation such as Contextual Graphs: production rules, UML, Bayesian networks, Petri nets and fluence graphs. We can illustrate concretely the differences between model and representation on the "paper submission" example. This initial model is represented in Figure 3.11.

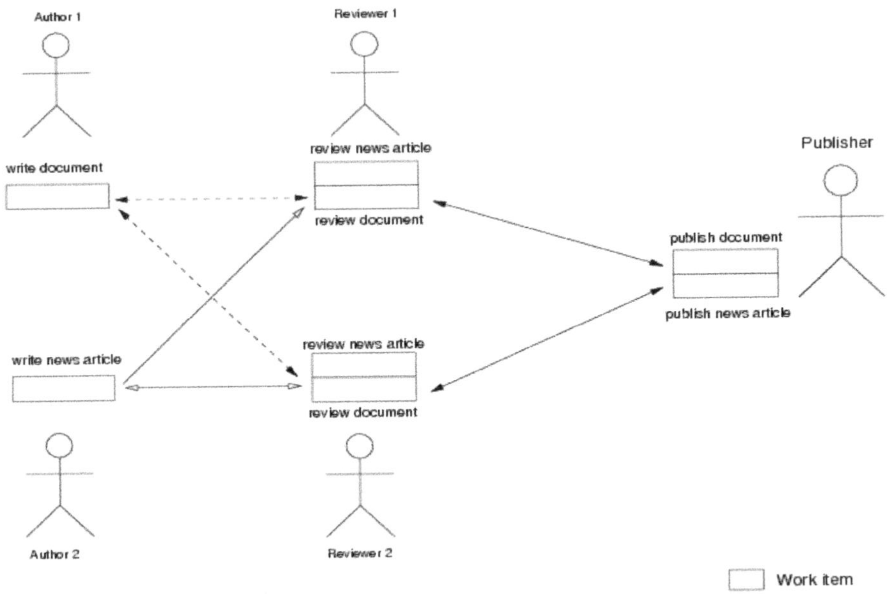

Figure 3.11. *Paper-submission example (Torres da Silva et al. 2005). For a color version of this figure, see www.iste.co.uk/brezillon/contextbasedmodeling.zip*

Figures 3.12 and 3.13 give the representation of this model in Petri net and in UML respectively.

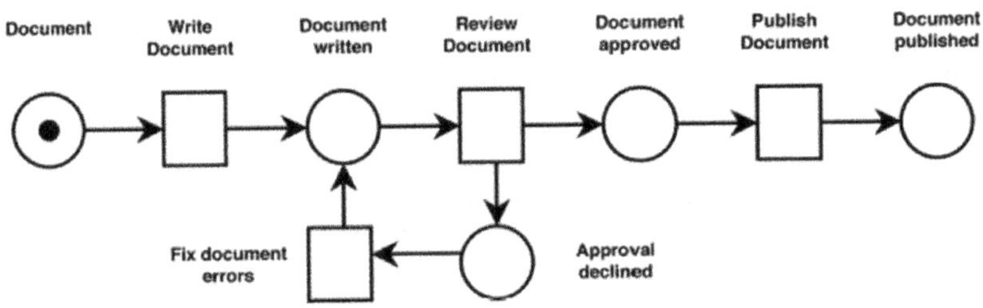

Figure 3.12. *Petri-net representation of the submission-process example. For a color version of this figure, see www.iste.co.uk/brezillon/contextbasedmodeling.zip*

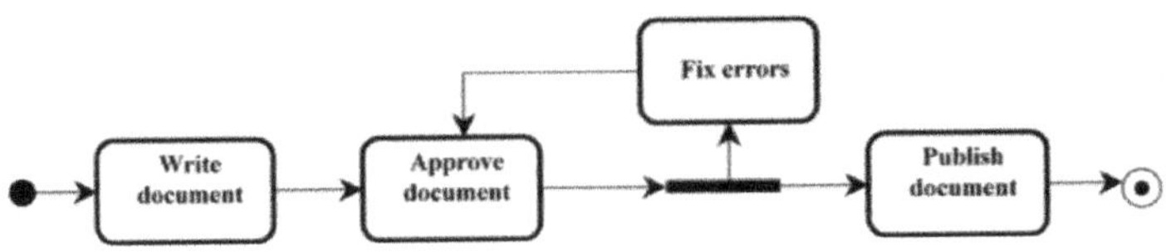

Figure 3.13. *UML representation of the submission-process example*

The representation in the CxG formalism of the initial model is shown in Figure 3.14 (green square boxes represent actions, blue circles contextual elements, and the two red vertical bars an ESIA). This initial model of editor's activity does not consider the possibility for the editor rejecting the submission, but we already added the possibility to ask for changes (contextual element 6) before publication but not the control of the revised version (Brézillon 2015). These limits come from the fact that the model is directed from start to end. We introduce later new options such as changing a reviewer and solving reviewer conflict in a group-activity model.

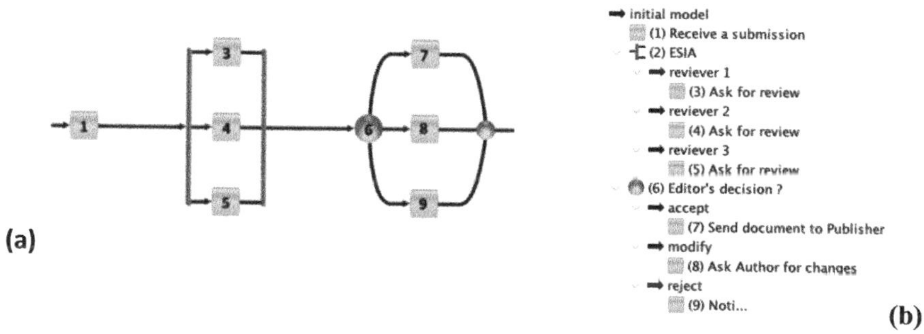

Figure 3.14. *CxG representation of the "submission management" example from editor's viewpoint. For a color version of this figure, see www.iste.co.uk/brezillon/contextbasedmodeling.zip*

In Figure 3.14, the example of the paper-submission process (Brézillon 2015), the editor's task "Submission management" makes reference to the reviewers as a simple action like "Ask reviewer" as long as we are not interested in the reviewer's behavior. However, the editor may need to collect different information from reviewers such as personal advice, comments on the submission and possibility to revise their judgment. It is supposed to detail the review process led by reviewers, as an independent activity described in another contextual graph and information exchanges realized through shared context as part of working contexts of editor and reviewers (discussed hereafter and in Figure 3.16). The questions then are (1) how to coordinate the different tasks and (2) how (contextual) information must be exchanged between tasks (and thus between actors).

Figure 3.15 shows an extended version of the editor's viewpoint by defining an initial working context (a set of instantiations). The graph being acyclic and directed, the mental representation does not consider that a revised version requires a new review process or that the publisher asks for changes due to editorial constraints.

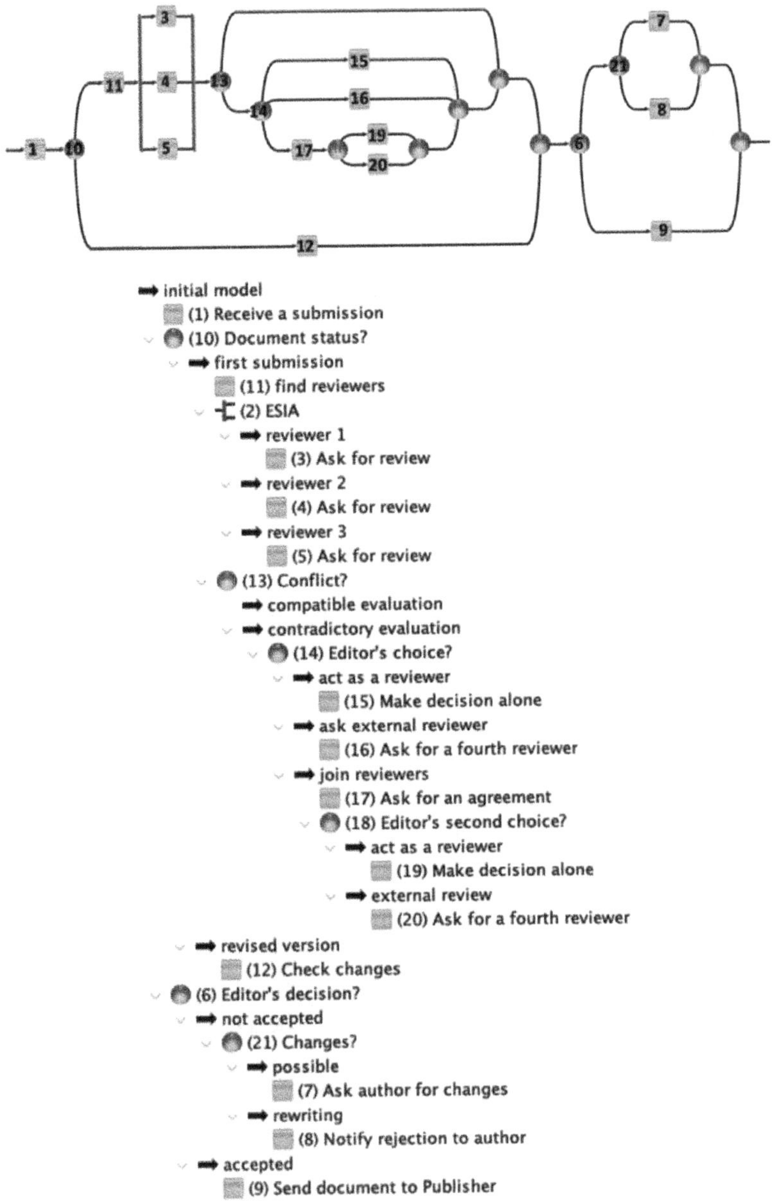

Figure 3.15. *An extended model of the editor's activity in the "submission management" example. For a color version of this figure, see www.iste.co.uk/brezillon/contextbasedmodeling.zip*

Simply, editor's activity consists of sequential parts: management of the submission, management of reviewers (selection, retrieving reviews, conflict), decision-making (send or not the final version to the publisher), information to the author (acceptance, rejection, changes required). Such a directed development of the editor's activity does not consider an editor rejection of the submission at reception of the document or a reviewer's refusal. Reviewer management is not always a simple step: a reviewer may reject the demand due to lack of time, because the reviewer knows the author of the submission, or due to lack of competence on the topic of the paper, conflict of interest with the work or conflict with other reviewers. The global evolution of the modeling of the "submission management" example is represented by the transition from Figure 3.14 to Figure 3.15 and later for group activity.

In Figure 3.15, for instance, one supposes that the Author sends back to the Editor the revised version of their submission (Document status = "revised version"), the Editor either accepted the new version (Editor's decision = "accept") or not but then checks nevertheless if minor changes would allow the version to be accepted (Changes = "possible"). The corresponding proceduralized context then is Document_status(revised_version)-Editor's decision(accept).

Figure 3.16 gives a representation of the editor's (top of the figure) and the reviewer's (bottom of the figure) activities. The arrows represent the location of three contextual elements existing in the two contextual models, namely "Document_status" (1), "Reviewer_decision" (2) and "Changes" (3) (the legends of the two contextual graphs are not presented in this figure). Document_status is instantiated by the author of the submission with one of the values "1st submission" or "revised version". The contextual elements "Reviewer_decision" and "Changes" are instantiated in the reviewer's task and used in the editor's task. The three contextual elements compose the shared context between editor and reviewer (in this model). Shared-context management proceeds in the following way: editor triggers activity "Ask for review" and editor's task realization will resume once the two reviews will be made by reviewers and received by the editor (contextual elements "Changes" and "Reviewer_decision" are then instantiated).

In a collaborative work, shared contextual elements are instantiated by an actor and user by the other. The values of a shared contextual element may be different from one task to another because it has different weights in the two task realizations. We also can observe that ordering shared contextual elements 2 and 3 is different in the two contextual graphs because, for arrow 2 (Figure 3.16), the reviewer relies on the importance of changes before making their decision, while the editor first has to compare all the reviewers' decisions to choose between reject (changes do not matter in this first step) and accept with minor changes or ask for a new submission if changes are important.

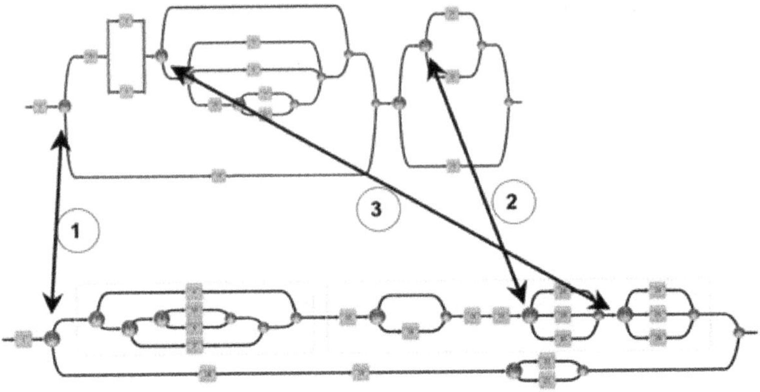

Figure 3.16. *Shared context between an editor (top) and a reviewer (bottom) tasks. For a color version of this figure, see www.iste.co.uk/brezillon/contextbasedmodeling.zip*

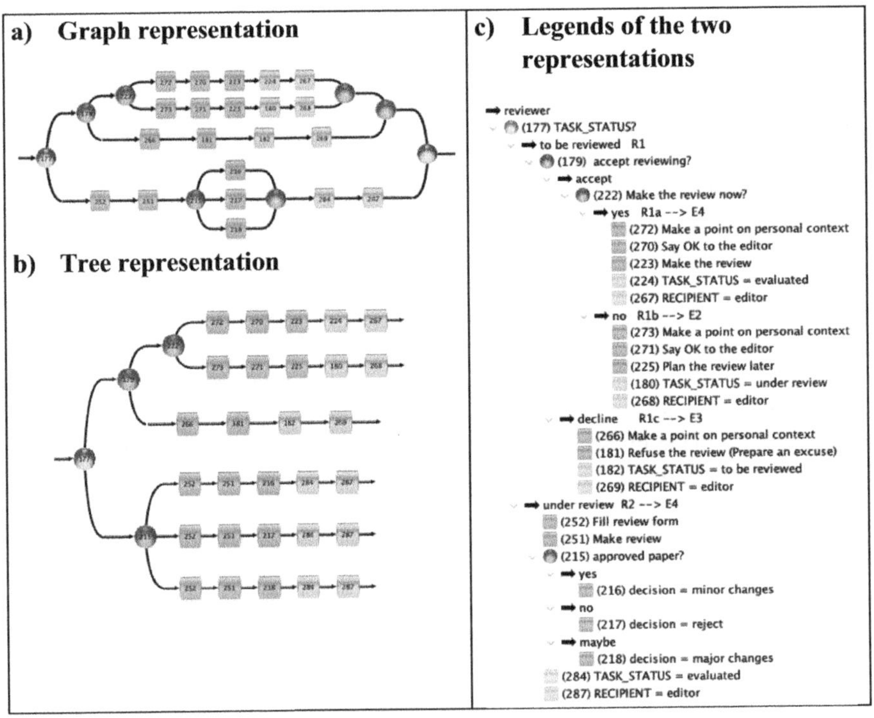

Figure 3.17. *Contextual graph (a), tree representations (b) and legends (c) of the reviewers' activity. For a color version of this figure, see www.iste.co.uk/brezillon/contextbasedmodeling.zip*

Figure 3.17 presents contextual graph and tree representations of the reviewer's activity. The structure being mainly parallel, the differences between the graph and tree representations are easily identifiable. Such a structure is explainable by the fact that reviewers generally have gained experience with this activity.

The tree representation of the reviewer's activity in Figure 3.17-b is very simple (only six mental models of the reviewer's activity). Comparatively, the simplified editor's activity presented in Figure 3.15 with two contextual elements in series leads to a tree with 19 mental models.

The shared context contains the previous results and normal and reserved contextual elements that the manager can reach during each turn. A new turn starts if the shared context has been modified during the previous turn. The contextual node, which is the input of the contextual element, is presented as a question, for example "MANAGER?", "TASK_STATUS?" and the instantiation corresponds to one answer to the question and is associated with an independent subtask on a branch between contextual and recombination nodes. This instantiation is specified by an action like MANAGER – "reviewer" at the end of the previous turn. If no instantiation is indicated, the value "nil" is taken by default, and the activity development will be stopped. During cyclic use of a contextual graph, shared context plays the role of an inference engine for the CxG-based simulation of the group-activity development. The shared context is the medium of communication among actors on the current state of the group activity when its development moves from one actor to another one. Shared context emerges out of interactions and experiences among group actors. The turn-by-turn building of a mental model offers the possibility to redo a turn for analyzing the intervention of an actor in different contexts in a "what if" search in a group activity.

Figure 3.18 shows a group-activity viewpoint of the "submission management" example, the actors being the author, the editor, the reviewers and the publisher. (It is a second extension of the model presented in Figure 3.15 for the editor as a unique actor of the activity).

Except for the first independent subtasks "submitted E1" in the editor's activity and the subtask "to be reviewed R1" in reviewers' activity that are totally unfolded (see Figure 3.18-a), all other independent subtasks are represented only by their names for concentrating our discussion on the role of the reserved contextual elements for assembling independent subtasks in the mental model. The first bold arrow (Paper management) at the top right of Figure 3.18 indicates the group activity. Then, arrows at the first indentation correspond to "MANAGER?" (editor, reviewer, author, publisher) and the second one to "TASK_STATUS?" (the independent subtasks of MANAGER) like submitted, to be reviewed, under review, evaluated and revised version for the editor. The independent subtasks are numbered

(E1, etc.) and often the next independent subtask is indicated (e.g. E1a → R1) towards the first independent subtask ("to be reviewed") of the reviewer to show how the assembling of the independent subtasks is made (and represented in a drawing by hand at bottom-left of Figure 3.18). Note that the first subtask of editor (E1) has two different outputs (E1a and E1b) towards independent subtasks of different actors (reviewer and author). The transition between two successive independent subtasks is implemented by the reserved contextual elements RECIPIENT and TASK_STATUS in the actions colored yellow at the end of subtasks.

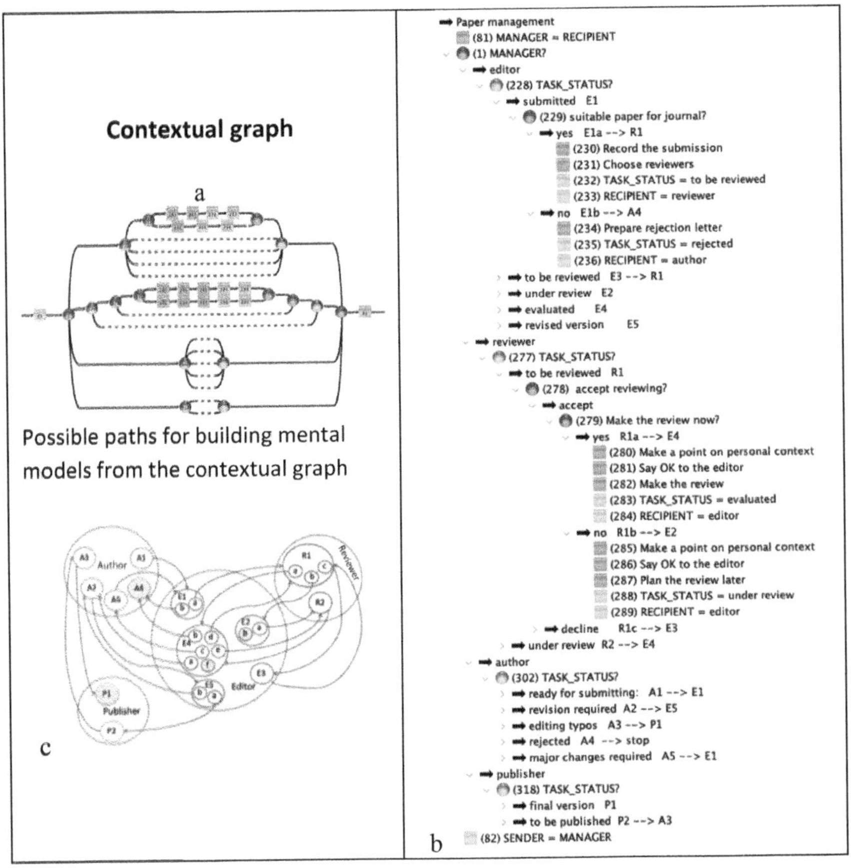

Figure 3.18. *Modeling of the submission-management example as a group activity. For a color version of this figure, see www.iste.co.uk/brezillon/contextbasedmodeling.zip*

There are two types of actions (Figure 3.18b): the actions in green, like "Choose reviewers" (action 231) in the activity model, and in yellow for reserved contextual elements, like "RECIPIENT = reviewer" (action 233) for simulation management. The latest actions have an expression for automatically changing the instantiation of a reserved contextual element in a CxG-based simulation. The reserved contextual elements are managed at the end of all actors' independent subtasks. Shared contextual elements, which transmit information between independent subtasks, are (1) instantiated by an actor and used by another one, like "Reviewer_decision" and "Changes" that are instantiated in the reviewer's subtask and used in the editor's subtask and (2) used differently according to their relative weight in the subtask, like the importance of "Changes" for reviewers for choosing either reject or accept, while the editor looks first for the global decision of the three reviewers before considering "Changes" for "accept with minor changes" or "accept a new submission for important changes".

Each actor is responsible in the contextual graph in Figure 3.18-b of different subtasks:

– Editor's subtasks are:

"to be reviewed" to find another reviewer to replace a failing reviewer,

"under review" for the *kind warning* to reviewers of approaching deadline,

"evaluated" for managing a very late reviewer or its replacement, match or mismatch of reviews and

"revised version" for checking the new version alone or under reviewers' control.

– Reviewer's subtasks are:

"to be reviewed" for accepting with or not an extended deadline and

"under review" to sum up changes requested and make a decision.

– Author's subtasks are:

"ready for submitting" once supposing to having addressed all requirements of the journal,

"revision required" for evaluating the degree of difficulty of the work to do,

"editing typos" for addressing publisher's request,

"rejected" for analyzing critics either to submit in another journal or not and

"major changes required" for creating a new version or abandoning.

This list is non-exhaustive. For example, the editor may decide to play the role of reviewer after a very late withdrawal of one reviewer. More generally, a system that develops a mental model also may check different types of development by qualitative simulation like stopping simulation at the end of a turn, changing actor's objective when an unexpected event occurs, introducing loops for managing negotiation between two actors, backtracking in actor's reasoning (or group reasoning), proceeding to a what-if analysis, allocating a role to different actors.

The graphical representation by hand at the left-bottom of Figure 3.18-c shows the complexity of all the possible paths that the contextual graph would exhibit if all the paths were unfolded. However, from a modeling viewpoint, it is important to find a compromise between the level of details and the ease of use of the model, but, from a practical viewpoint, a tree view (Figure 3.17) facilitates the identification of the right mental model as a whole. Moreover, the activity of a unique actor can also be represented as a group activity (with "group" of one actor). It provides two complementary representations of the same model of actor activity for choosing between two different interpretations on how the actor processes the activity.

3.6.2. *The TACTIC project*

Command & Control systems (C2 systems) provide operators with a view on the operational situation, which typically shows a map with symbols representing units. The operator interacts with a simulator for realizing different tasks like "Giving an order of recognition" that was modeled as a contextual graph (see section 1.3.4 for details and Figure 3.19). This task has three actions and three activities including "Manage a unit" (occurrences 62 and 67 of the activity count for one). The system gathers information from various sources and allows operators to interact and give orders directly. C2 systems are also used or being adopted in non-military areas, for example, in civil safety or by large private operators.

Such C2 systems have three complementary sources of information commonly used together: spatial coordinates of objects (field map), temporal coordinates (chronology) and socio-technical coordinates (ORBAT). The three sources of information constitute a cognitive tridimensional referential in which events take place in an evolving context. A unit is associated with a knowledge network about local information, such as life bar, and other global information such as belonging to an automaton. Such a knowledge network should allow different views adapted to the desired granularity of the context.

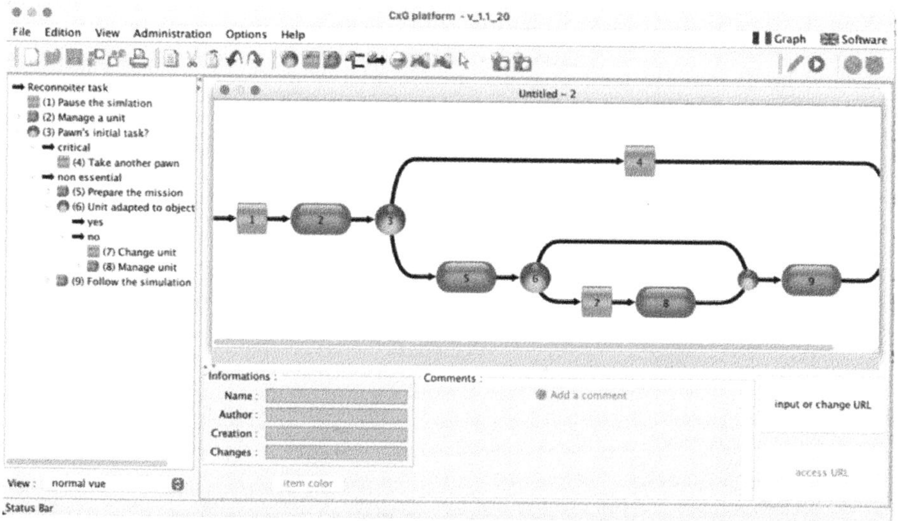

Figure 3.19. *Task realization "Giving an order of recognition" in CxG formalism. For a color version of this figure, see www.iste.co.uk/brezillon/contextbasedmodeling.zip*

Figure 3.20 represents the model of the activity "Manage a unit" from the operator's viewpoint as a contextual graph and its legend (in the CxG_1.0 version). The activity is rather sequential, beginning with (1) choice of where to select a unit (first contextual element), (2) choice of a unit (second contextual element), (3) checking if the selected unit may realize the required recognition mission and (4) positioning the unit in the center of the window of the field map (the different colors of actions in figures are explained in the following).

Operator–Simulator interaction goes through an interface (the place of cognitive interaction with the operator) and the screen (the place of physical interaction for simulation visualization). As a result, operators must deal with an interpretation of the domain (the simulation resulting from the operator–simulator interaction) intertwined with an interpretation of the interface functioning for translating actions on the simulation into commands to the interface. For example, by clicking on the pause button, the operator thinks to stop the simulation, while this action triggers on the interface a command to the simulator that suspends simulation. As a result, the operator associates simulation control with actions on the interface, the latter playing the role of the simulator.

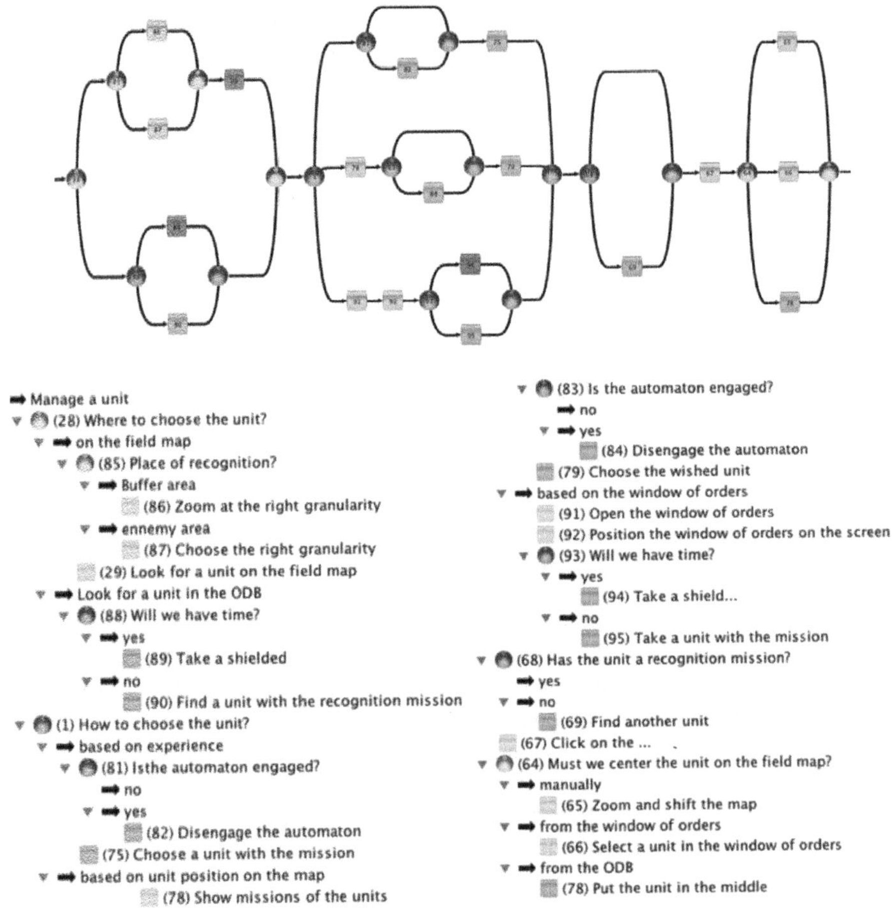

Figure 3.20. *Contextual graph of activity "Manage a unit". For a color version of this figure, see www.iste.co.uk/brezillon/contextbasedmodeling.zip*

The TACTIC project allows us to identify two main changes to simplify operator's task realization with a simulator. The first change aims to discriminate the interface and operator–simulator interaction. At the implementation level, this means separating domain actions (control of the simulation) and interface actions. The second change is to study relationships between the operator's mental model and the three sources of information of the simulator considered the "simulator's mental representation" (see Figure 3.22). Thus, making the two maps compatible is a way to tailor information presentation to the operator in an activity-oriented way.

Figure 3.21 shows the distinction between domain actions and interface actions based on the model of the turn mechanism discussed previously. The rectangles represent the parts of the turn corresponding to independent subtasks, and the arrows correspond to the implementation of conceptual representation in Figure 3.19.

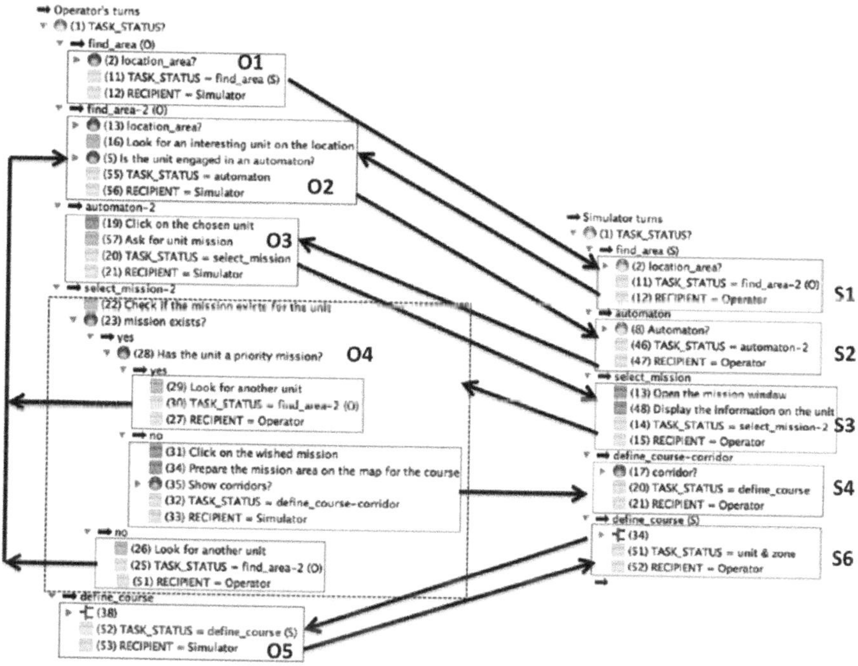

Figure 3.21. *Movement between turns in the model. For a color version of this figure, see www.iste.co.uk/brezillon/contextbasedmodeling.zip*

Figure 3.21 represents the first part of the mission "Manage a unit" as modeled in Figure 3.20 with the operator's activity on the left part and the simulator's activity on the right part. (Here, the contextual graph of the group activity contains two branches only, one for the operator and the other for the simulator.) Most of the independent subtasks are not detailed in Figure 3.21 to facilitate a focus on the turn mechanism symbolized by thick arrows.

The main features of the representation are:

– Colors. Items for independent subtasks keep their initial colors (i.e. dark green square boxes for domain actions and blue circles for contextual elements). Items for shared-context management are in light green. Actions in violet (both in operator and simulator activities) are interface actions (e.g. action 19 "Click on the chosen unit" in rectangle O3 on the left-up part of the figure).

– The use of reserved contextual elements for managing turn sequence through shared context introduces, in a natural way, the notion of cycle that does not exist in the CxG_1.0 version, thanks to the joint use of shared context with the contextual graph.

– A turn starts with the contextual element that checks the instantiation of TASK_STATUS and directs the focus on an independent subtask represented by a rectangle. For instance, the first turn in the operator's activity corresponds to Value (TASK_STATUS) = "find_area (O)" and rectangle O1 that contains the independent subtask with the closed contextual element "location_area?" and the actions in yellow that modify the instantiations of TASK_STATUS and RECIPIENT for the next turn.

– The turn with the rectangle O4 is particular in the sense that there are three outputs, two towards an operator's turn (arrows on the left) and one towards the turn S4 towards simulator's activity. The two arrows on the left correspond to a loop in actor's activity for changing of unit.

The turn-mechanism model presents three main characteristics in this application. First, in addition to reserved contextual elements discussed previously for managing the turn mechanism, there are other contextual elements in light green that are also instantiated in one actor's activity and used in another one and thus are shared by the different actors. For example, the contextual elements "local area" (in S1) and "automaton" (in S2) in Figure 3.21 are instantiated by the operator and guide to independent subtasks in simulator's activity (contextual elements 2 and 8). Second, the interface actions (in violet) show the need to consider the interface as a real partner (but not modeled in this study) at the same level as the operator and simulator. This will suppose a specific management of turns for the interface with reserved contextual elements RECIPIENT and TASK_STATUS. Third, the non-explicit consideration of the interface as actor is responsible for unnecessary turns. For example, for choosing a mission, the operator first has to ask the simulator to open the mission window (an interface action) and to fill the mission window (a domain action of the simulator) which is considered as a unique action.

The dissociation of turn definition and dynamic assembling of turns (turn sequence) brings an elegant solution to severe limitations of the initial version of CxG formalism that does not associate working context with the actors and activities in the contextual graph. The explicit association of shared context with the contextual graph thus solves the main weaknesses of the contextual graph used alone, namely: (1) the turn O4 allows the operator to change their reasoning when encountering an unexpected event (e.g. the reviewer decline the request) and thus compensates for the acyclic nature of contextual graphs and (2) the reserved contextual element “RECIPIENT = <nil>” allows us to “stop” the turn mechanism and to exit the group-activity development in any turn, say, when an action cannot be executed by lack of external resources.

The CxG_1.0 formalism can be a tool for editing contextual graphs if we are not concerned by the activity development. It also can be a manual simulation tool by considering jointly the contextual graph and the working context for modeling and simulating human reasoning in its complexity and nonlinear nature. However, the extension presented here in the CxG_2.0 formalism offers a way to model and simulate group activity from a general viewpoint (turns, shared context) to local viewpoints with independent subtasks, reserved contextual element and actor interaction. The tool for exploiting this new version of CxG formalism is the CxG-based Simulator.

Going back to the conceptual level, the actor performs a domain action through an interface action. There is no direct link between these two types of action, but the link is not natural for the actor because several interface actions may correspond to the same domain action. A main reason is that the actor uses their choice on contextual information such as their preferences, task, situation and environment. For example, the simulator has three sources of information: map, ORBAT and chronology. Thus, for selecting a unit, actor each time must look at what is the best information source in the current context because each of them has advantages and disadvantages (browsing a long list of items in the ORBAT, too many items on the map) that imply additional actions such as zoom on the map and use of a search engine for the ORBAT (Kabil et al. 2015). Thus, actor “compiles” each domain action with a contextualization of the interface actions in order to select the best one in a given context. Domain actions will be more easily associated with an interface action if shared context is made explicit, resulting in greater interface flexibility, not only with respect to the actor, but also with respect to the task realizations.

Figure 3.22 shows a conceptual view of the previous discussion in order to simplify the operator’s task realization with a simulator. The first one concerns a clear distinction of the interface with operator–simulator interaction. The consequence is the separation of “domain_ actions” and “interface_actions” and the possibility of establishing a simple mechanism of translation between domain_actions and interface_actions by shifting the main problem of translation at interface exchange level, not on domain actions. The second change is to compare the expert map of the operator with the “expert map” of the simulator (mainly the three sources of information) for making the two maps compatible, even across a translation in terms of “interface_actions”, for transmitting commands to the simulator and, conversely, for presenting results to the operator.

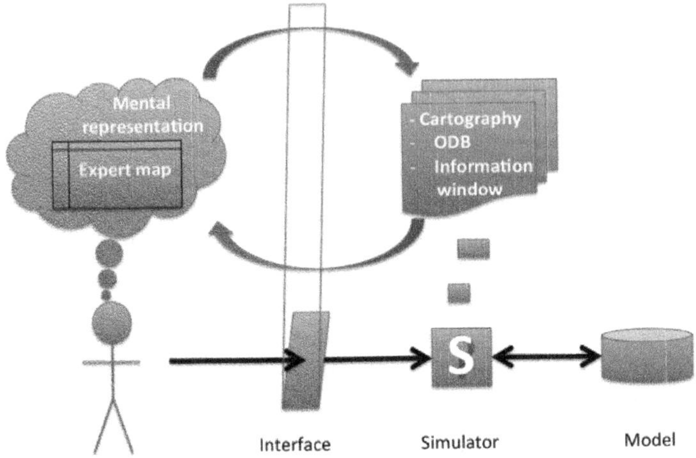

Figure 3.22. *Model of operator–simulator interaction. For a color version of this figure, see www.iste.co.uk/brezillon/contextbasedmodeling.zip*

The conventions for interacting are imposed by hardware that is used, and a change of hardware imposes a change in actors' habits. Some changes, like migration from computers to laptops, were well accepted. Acceptance depends on the relationships of actors with new technologies (as a counter-example, some actors always have difficulty with a trackpad 25 years after its creation). Device migration does not mean a simple translation of conventions but the introduction of new concepts and thus new conventions. For example, touch interaction allows an application to translate and use physical movements to emulate direct handling of interface elements.

3.7. Review of the chapter

Shared context plays a central role in group activity. It takes place between individual working contexts of group actors and collective proceduralized context. The collaborative development of shared context allows group actors to keep their individual mental representations compatible and adjusted to the joint activity and collective mental representation. Shared-context building is the first step of a collaborative process of decision-making and shared-context management consists of collecting and managing contextual elements, processing the proceduralized context and building group mental model.

The notion of "activity" extends the notion of "task realization" by exploiting the specific context at hand (i.e. mental-model development). An activity covers the actor, activity, contextual information considered by actors and various choices made by them to reach the goal. Group activity is more than the simple sum of actor activities because individual activities are interdependent. Interaction between group actors corresponds to the movement of the focus from one actor's activity to another actor's activity. An activity is the physical and mental behavior that the actor exhibits for realizing the task. Activity of each group actor is independent (but complementary). Each group actor generally intervenes at different moments during group-activity development. Each intervention is represented as an independent subtask, the actor's activity becoming a set of independent subtasks (like a set of elementary activities). Thus, the processing of a group activity consists of entering in an actor's activity to follow the realization of the actor's independent subtasks that are responsible for the progress of group-activity development (in a kind of glocal approach). The intervention occurs from a sender (another actor) and will be taken charge of by a recipient (a third actor). In an enterprise, each actor plays a role, and activities are associated with it. Building and developing group activity requires actor collaboration with different roles specialized for different parts of the group activity.

In a group activity, each actor's independent subtasks are incrementally developed like in CxG_1.0 version, while group activity is the object of complex nonlinear reasonings, including backtracking, negotiation, look-ahead, etc. It is possible to represent in a contextual graph very different contextual reasonings in a group activity. However, if design and development of a contextual graph are easy (one divides the problem to treat subproblems), nonlinear reasonings are difficult to follow mainly because they do not correspond to a simple path in the contextual graph like practice development in the CxG_1.0 version of CxG formalism. The example of the TACTIC project is relevant for this point.

Although this is not the object of this book, it appears from this study that the lack of consensus on the terms of collaboration and cooperation may come from the fact that (1) these terms evolve dynamically during interaction; (2) an activity takes a meaning with, upstream, group-activity setup and downstream the use of its results. It shows that an activity, conversely to a task, has several phases with different types of actions, these phases being initiation, preparation, development, finalizing and debriefing; (3) the type of turn management depends essentially on the type of group activity and (4) shared context plays a central role in a group activity. To be fully operational, an actor must know the request and context, in which the request is made. The more shared context is developed, the more efficient group decision-making becomes. Interaction between group actors corresponds to a movement of the focus from one actor's activity to another actor's activity and, more specifically, between precise subtasks inside the actors' activities that will be assembled. The type of interaction evolves along the development of the group mental model by the play of actors that intervene, their current activity in the group activity, the importance of what is expected, etc.

The transition from 1 to N actors in the four-modeling level framework implies the addition of modeling of group-actor management and what each actor does in the group activity from a global viewpoint. There are two options. The first option consists of group-activity management as a whole, with the actors' interventions being implicitly considered. A second option is to consider the contextual graph as a composite of the actors' contextual graphs. The two options lead to a highly complex representation of the collective task realization that would be difficult to model at operational and implementation levels. The third smart option chosen as a better solution was to change the representation of individual contextual graphs, considering that each actor intervenes on specific steps of the group activity.

A group activity is considered as a sequence of turns accomplished by different actors, first, for addressing the request of an actor (the sender), and, second, for preparing elements for another one (the recipient). Each actor's contribution is the realization of a subtask solicited by a sender in a particular shared context, and the result will trigger a new turn with a recipient for performing a particular subtask using the obtained results in a new shared context. As a result, the actors participate in the group activity with as many independent subtasks as possible interventions during collaboration.

The inputs and outputs of a turn, first, are context-dependent and cannot be planned in advance, and, second, are transmitted between turns through the shared context. As a result, there is a dynamic building of the sequence of turns (mental model) by the assembling of independent subtasks in the mental representation of the group activity that contains independent subtasks. Thus, a contextual graph has a partially fixed structure given by (1) choice of an actor (the manager of the turn), (2) choice of an independent subtask in the manager mental representation, (3) turn management and (4) identification of the turn series as a mental model built from a mental representation, while a mental model developed by an actor in the CxG_1.0 version exists in the mental representation. An independent subtask may have several possible outputs (defined by different instantiations of contextual elements on different branches of the contextual subgraph). Such outputs may concern the study of variants by the manager, the next actor or a subset of actors, or the next subtask to realize. Thus, interaction management is essential for a group activity that is simultaneously built and performed.

The main difference between the CxG_1.0 and CxG_2.0 versions is the explicit management of group actors because, if tasks are defined by roles in the CxG_1.0 version, a group-activity development depends on different roles in the CxG_2.0 version. Shared context, which is associated with the contextual graph, has a crucial place for interaction representation (i.e. the cyclic use of a directed graph). It ensures the exchanges of contextual information between turns and plays the role of an inference engine that analyzes contextual elements that have a modified instantiation to deduce what to do after the turn (e.g. If "task_status = <nil>", Then stop simulation). This opens the road for nonlinear reasoning with several options (stop, enter a negotiation phase, etc.). A tree representation, which is associated with a graph representation, is composed of branches with proceduralized context followed by the corresponding sequence of actions for an experimented actor, both representations corresponding to the same mental model, that allows us to focus on the process to apply to decision-making.

The first step was to leave the actor's viewpoint to an external viewpoint for making the group viewpoint explicit.

The second step was task realization not the task itself (i.e. on mental model). The main reason is to introduce the notion of activity as an extension of the notion of task realization by taking into consideration the notion of working context attached to it and, for a group activity, the notion of shared context for an operational modeling of group activity. Such a modeling is possible only in a formalism that allows a uniform representation of the elements of knowledge, reasoning and contexts.

The third step consists of considering independent subtasks in the contextual graph instead of group actors' task realization. This choice is based on group-activity assimilation at a sequence of punctual actor interventions; each intervention addresses the request of a sender (another actor) and sends the result of the subtask realization to a recipient (another actor).

The fourth step concerns the key elements of our approach, namely the notion of turn and the mechanism for going from one turn to the next turn for modeling interaction during group-activity deployment. The set of changes in our conceptual framework ensures a logical shift of the paradigm of contextual graphs in the representation of an actor activity to the paradigm of a contextual graph for group activity. Indeed, actor interaction is expressed as the cyclic traversing of the contextual graph by reapplying the model of the group activity (i.e. the contextual graph) in different contexts, which are attached to turns.

The fifth step is about the lessons learned from the contextual modeling of group activity. The type of interaction between group actors evolves along the progress of activity realization, and what is collaboration at one moment may become cooperation at another one. Thus, it is possible to qualify the type of interaction among group actors in a definitive way.

A turn mechanism is proposed to extend the CxG formalism to group activity. An activity is modeled as a sequence of turns, a turn being a local contribution of an actor to the group activity. The steps of a turn are: (1) selection of the actor that will be the "Manager" of the turn; (2) selection in the manager's activity of the subtask to realize according to the instantiation of "Task_status"; (3) realization of the independent subtask and of the proceduralized context and (4) change instantiations of reserved contextual elements for preparing the next turn. Thus, the turn-mechanism model covers the contextual elements instantiated in the manager's subtask and used in the subtask of another actor; a change of reasoning if an unexpected event occurs; possibility of negotiation, etc. The type of turn management depends essentially on the type of group activity.

Turns are executed sequentially because the output of the subtask includes actor and subtask of the next turn. This "turn mechanism" plays the role of a synchronizer of the dynamic combination of turns that offers the possibility of a nonlinear reasoning (e.g. backtracking, preliminary study of alternatives) and avoids a complex modeling of the group activity in any context. The cyclic use of a directed contextual graph corresponds to a CxG-based simulation, thanks to reserved contextual elements. There also are several abilities of the CxG_2.0 version not present in the CxG_1.0 version like exiting a simulation at the end of a turn (with recipient = "nil"), anticipation, checking alternatives, explanation generation, negotiation between a part of the group actors and even a resumption of the whole simulation if instantiation of a contextual element changes during the simulation due to an external event.

In the CxG_2.0 version, CxG-based simulation expresses the simultaneous building and development of a mental model and its proceduralized context. Mental-model building during its use is rather close to a numerical simulation of nonlinear systems (like nonlinear differential equations) without a theoretical solution. This approach also allows the CxG-based simulation tool for expressing an activity "one-shot" but with intermediate variants like the checking of alternatives with *what-if* mental simulations.

4

The Two Versions of the CxG Formalism

4.1. Introduction

This chapter starts with a summary of the key points identified in the previous chapters. The global picture of our approach begins with the contribution of the threefold approach (conceptual, operational and implementation) in the unification of the results as well as the interest to replace the results in the four modeling levels after having shown that decision-making was the foundation for the different activities discussed previously. The unifying framework also has benefited the CxG formalism with the introduction of the concepts of mental model and mental representation. The notion of experience base highlights the potential merging of contextual graphs developed around different activities in a given domain. In this chapter, we discuss the key points identified in Chapters 2 and 3, the links between these key points and the main concepts needed for modeling an activity, and the organization of the concepts pointed out in a lattice represented in the space of the four modeling dimensions. We thus propose a coherent picture of the whole for a definition of context associated with an activity and its development for modeling contextual reasoning with the required integration of the concepts discussed in other domains.

This chapter continues with a discussion of the theoretical results on an "Internship-offer analysis" application modeled in the two versions CxG_1.0 and CxG_2.0 of the CxG formalism on an experiment with master's students. If all the students are concerned with the same objective, to realize the "Internship-offer analysis" activity, each student has the private goal of finding the "right" internship for themselves. Section 4.3 gives our interpretation of the results based on different organizations of the contextual elements that lead to a collective task modeling in the CxG_1.0 formalism and as activity modeling for each actor of the group in the CxG_2.0 formalism (after the initial experiment). We then compare the results obtained in the modeling of the "Internship-offer analysis" activity with those obtained for the modeling of the "DVD-reader diagnosis" activity (also modeled by students).

4.2. The key points of the research

This section meets the key points identified in previous chapters in Table 4.1 mainly as a global reminder. The table allows us to summarize the keypoints for: proposing a discussion of the concepts put center stage, explaining their definition with respect to other concepts depending on the modeling level and their evolution throughout the approach, pointing out why some concepts like "context" are difficult to define in a static way due to their different facets according to the levels of the modeling we are doing.

4.2.1. *Discussion on key concepts of the approach*

The key points introduced in Chapters 2 and 3 are met in Table 4.1 in their original ordering. They are presented in the table followed by the four modeling levels, namely conceptual, operational, implementation and environment with a particular attention to their relationships in order to have an integrated view at the framework level.

Key point	Definition
1	The focus of attention of the actor divides context into contextual knowledge and external knowledge.
2	Contextual knowledge is assimilated to contextual elements that come from four sources, namely, the actor, the activity, the situation and the environment.
3	The proceduralized context is the expression of the operational knowledge in contextual knowledge that is used in the focus of attention for the current step.
4	We cannot speak of context in an abstract way: context and focus of attention are interdependent.

5	The means and methods to accomplish an activity are as important as the focus itself.
6	A mental model is the contextualization of a mental representation in a specific context.
7	The contextual graph is a unified implementation of the mental representation representing all mental models realized.
8	The focus of attention supposes a partial ordering of the contextual elements.
9	There are four sources of contextual elements: the actor, the focus, the situation and the environment.
10	The contextual element and its instantiations must be processed separately.
11	Mental models are at the operational level, while their development in specific contexts corresponds to a path in the contextual graph at the implementation level.
12	The mental representation is like a local experience base containing all the known mental models for a given activity in different contexts.
13	A contextual graph is a directed, acyclic, series-parallel graph with exactly one root and one exit.
14	A contextual element is implemented as a pair {contextual node, recombination node} with as many exclusive branches as known instantiations of the contextual element.
15	The proceduralized context is the ordered sequence of contextual elements that are instantiated during the crossing of the contextual graph along a path.
16	The building of the proceduralized context is part of the development of the mental model.
17	Contextual elements structure mental representation at the operational level, and their instantiations are processed dynamically at the environment level.
18	Shared-context building is the first step of the development of group activity.
19	Independent subtasks are realized successively in a cyclic use of the contextual graph.

20	A group activity is built by the assembling of a sequence of independent subtasks coming from actors' activities.
21	Reserved contextual elements, which are associated with roles and tasks of actors, allow the management of turns and the cyclic use of the directed contextual graph.
22	A turn corresponds to the traversal of the contextual graph for realizing an independent subtask and shared-context management for the next turn.
23	A CxG-based simulation represents a sequence of turns by a cyclic use of the directed contextual graph as long as shared context is modified during the turn.
24	The association of shared-context management with cyclic use of the directed contextual graph opens a modeling of group activity larger than task realization.
25	Group-activity dynamics corresponds to the progressive assembling of independent subtasks in a sequence jointly with the mental-model development.

Table 4.1. *List of the key points for modeling and use context*

Then, we have collected the key concepts and established an empiric graph of dependency between them and represented it in the four-level framework given in Figure 4.1 where blue circles indicate the key concepts directly related to the actor, and green circles only make clear that the same key concept "contextual element" appears twice at two different levels. We discuss only the key concepts that are directly related to the framework. The chosen ordering in the presentation is based on the appearance of the concepts on the table, that is, as introduced in the approach from the conceptual level to the environment level. However, some concepts at a low level may have reverse effects at upper levels, such as the representation of a contextual element as a pair of two nodes at the implementation level because the reasoning step, associated with the contextual element, may have as many expressions as branches between the two nodes making reasoning nonlinear. Other key concepts appear either at a unique level (e.g. contextual graph at the implementation level) or at several levels (e.g. contextual element at context-based formalism and CxG software are implicitly used at the operational, implementation and environment levels).

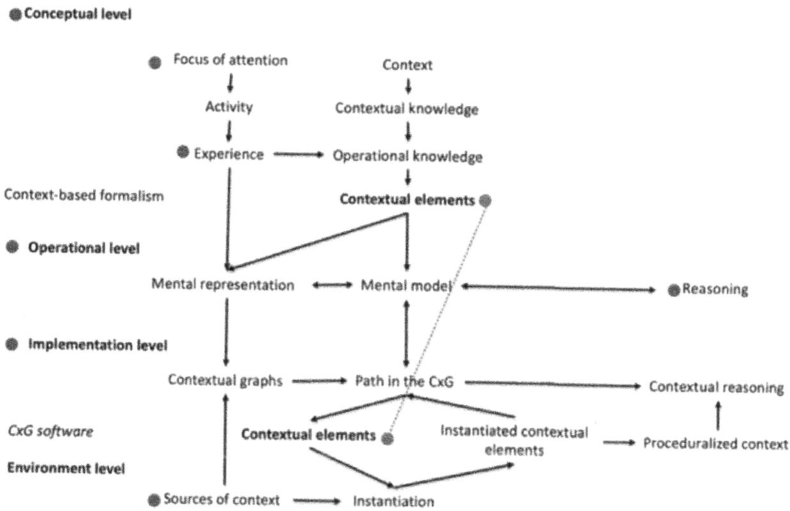

Figure 4.1. *Key concepts and their evolution in the four-level framework. For a color version of this figure, see www.iste.co.uk/brezillon/contextbasedmodeling.zip*

Globally, the two vertical lines correspond to the modeling of an activity (on the left in Figure 4.1) and its context (at middle in Figure 4.1) with strong connections between the key concepts of the two lines. Context cannot be discussed out of the activity that is accomplished by an actor in a given situation with available means in the environment considered as "the four sources of context" that we briefly summarize now. The 25 key concepts are discussed after, especially respectively to their relationships.

The modeling of an *activity* is the object of the four-level approach described in Chapters 2 and 3. Activity modeling is a more global approach than modeling a task because an activity has four phases distinguished by particular verbs of action like: to accomplish or to plan (before to start), to initiate or to launch (at the triggering of the activity), to perform or to carry out (during the execution of the activity) and to realize or to close (upon completion of the activity). Context intervenes differently at each phase of the activity. Under the umbrella of "activity", we consider different tasks such as decision-making, diagnosis and problem-solving, such tasks being context-dependent. Based on the concepts selected at the conceptual level, activity is modeled at the operational level through a mental representation and mental models and at the implementation level as a contextual graph corresponding to the mental representation and paths in the graph for mental models. Finally, the environment level concretizes the limits of an activity, that is, what is not in the activity but intervenes in it as sources of context that punctually intervene in the development of a mental model. In Figure 4.1, activity is associated with the concepts "focus of attention", "experience", "operational knowledge", "mental representation", "mental model", "contextual graph", "paths in the contextual graph" and "sources of context".

In the scientific approach in Biology (Brézillon 1983), the human is an observer, the *actor* is responsible for the activity during all its phases: planning the work and collecting contextual information, setting up the elements necessary to start the activity, following or real-time control of the execution of the activity, completing the activity and concluding it with a final report. In Figure 4.1, the actor is the master of the work at the conceptual and operational levels and the pilot of the execution of the activity at the implementation level, and one of the sources of context is associated with the activity. In this title, modeling an activity is also modeling the actor's reasoning. In some sense, activity corresponds to the objects upon which the actor's reasoning acts as a process.

A *situation* is the set of physical and human circumstances in which an actor accomplishes an activity. Such circumstances feed the sources of context. The situation is established in the first phase of the activity, for example, to identify in contextual knowledge what will be operational knowledge and the actor's goal and objectives. A situation evolves according to the context at hand (e.g. rush hours or not) in which the activity is accomplished. In Figure 4.1, the situation may be associated with operational knowledge and sources of context and evolves depending on the interaction of implementation and environment levels.

We now discuss the 25 key concepts in Figure 4.1 along the two "bloodlines" (static on the left for the activity, dynamic on the right for context) across the modeling levels of the framework because a key concept makes sense only in the global view of the four-level framework. Downward arrows correspond to concept refinement across levels, refinement and not only change of representation. The representation of contextual elements as pairs of nodes at the implementation level leads to considering a contextual element at the operational level as a nonlinear step of the reasoning. Horizontal arrows represent the impact of activity on context (e.g. the mental models coming from the mental representation) and, conversely, of context on activity (e.g. contextual element and mental model on mental representation at the operational level). Now, the key concepts in Figure 4.1 can be discussed.

Actor's *focus of attention* (KP-1, 3, 5, 8) concerns an activity on which the actor leads a *reasoning* on its progression. The focus may concern the *activity* either as a whole or a specific reasoning step depending on the effort required by the actor.

Contextual knowledge (KP-1, 2, 3) is the part of context more or less related to the focus of attention of actors considering an activity through their experience. *Operational knowledge* is the part of the contextual knowledge that intervenes in the focus of attention, that is, activity accomplishment. If contextual knowledge is related to *mental representation* (the global view on the activity), operational knowledge is related to the *mental model* that is in the focus of attention in the specific context at hand. Actor's *experience* (KP-12) is what the actor knows after frequent accomplishment of the activity in different contexts, what the activity is (as an object), as well as how to realize it (as a process). Experience is *operational knowledge* that is used in activity realization, transformed into a *mental representation* by the actor and punctually developed as a *mental model* in the specific context at hand. The mental representation is implemented as a *contextual graph* at the level below. Finally, heterogeneity of the *sources of context* (actor, activity, situation, environment) requires refining the notion of operational knowledge in the concept of the *contextual element*.

Actor's *reasoning* explains activity realization in a kind of *simulation* of decision-making, action organization and desired outcomes during the *development of a mental model* in a given context and a *path* in the *contextual graph* by instantiating *contextual elements* according to the sources of context. In that sense, the *instantiation process* (KP-10) is part of the reasoning leading to the generation of the proceduralized context that appears as a context-based model of reasoning. The *proceduralized context* (KP-3, 15, 16) is, conceptually, the part of the *operational knowledge* that is put center stage by the *focus of attention* during activity accomplishment and is pragmatically, an ordered sequence of instantiated contextual elements obtained along a *path in the contextual graph*. It allows us to replay the mental-model development by *CxG-based simulation* and offers a powerful tool for context-based intelligent assistant systems (CIASs). It also offers alternative checking for selecting the right instantiation of a contextual element. Indeed, the proceduralized context is a kind of contextual signature (fingerprint) of the activity in the specific context.

Figure 4.1 shows the difficulty of establishing a simple definition of context that appears under different aspects according to activity phases and the four modeling levels. Top-down, context is assimilated to (1) contextual knowledge, (2) operational knowledge, (3) contextual elements, (4) instantiated contextual elements and (5) proceduralized context. Contextual knowledge concerns the mental representation and comes from four sources (actor, activity, situation and environment). Operational knowledge is the part of contextual knowledge used in the development of a mental model and exploited by the instantiation process for producing the instantiated contextual elements in the proceduralized context associated with the mental model. *Contextual element* (KP-2, 8, 9, 10, 14, 17) is the key concept for a working definition of context because it structures the contextual graph and any activity model, including reasoning. The assimilation of a contextual element to a *pair of contextual and recombination nodes* at the implementation level gives a directed, acyclic and series–parallel structure to the contextual graph. In addition, contextual elements act as *units of reasoning* that acquire an expression according to the instantiations of the contextual elements.

The mental representation (KP-6, 7, 11, 16) is an operational representation of actor's experience resulting from the accumulation of mental-models obtained in different contexts. A mental representation is personal to an actor and difficult to transmit directly. However, the contextual graph, its implemented representation, is externalized and thus sharable. It is important to note that the mental representation and contextual graph are two complementary context-based representations of an activity realization by an actor as well as a group. An actor accomplishes an activity by developing a mental model (KP-6, 7, 12, 17) in a given context. This mental model is extracted from the actor's mental representation and implemented as a path in the contextual graph. The challenge here is to find the right instantiation of the contextual elements on the path that corresponds to the context at hand as provided by the sources of context. In terms of reasoning, there is a double aspect, the path to follow and the instantiation of the contextual element encountered, a consequence being to have a context-based model of the reasoning as an ordered sequence (i.e. the path in the contextual graph) of instantiated contextual elements (use of the instantiation process). The contextual graph (KP-7, 13, 19, 21, 22, 23, 24) is in the line of the mental representation after experience. The implementation keeps the properties identified previously like the uniform representation of activity accomplishment in the different contexts. It adds a directed acyclic series–parallel structure that provides a context-based modeling of reasoning held in the activity. A path in the contextual graph corresponds to the contextual reasoning held during mental-model development representing activity accomplishment. A contextual element that appears on the path is like a question, and the instantiation is the answer to the question in the context at hand coming from the sources of context.

The situation in which one actor is responsible for an activity can be extended to situations in which a group of actors intervenes in the realization of the activity. There are two classes of changes. The first class concerns the evolution of initial functions, such as a new definition of actors' activity with the consequence of a different structuring of the contextual graph at the implementation level and the replacement of the working context for an actor with a shared context for a group. The second class of changes concerns mainly the introduction of new concepts at the implementation level like assembling actors' interventions from the cyclic use of the contextual graph, turn and actor management by reserved contextual elements (RCEs) and CxG-based simulation. Three main differences exist between the modeling of actor activity and group activity. First, the notion of a group experience is difficult to comprehend and the difficulty persists for group mental representation, because different actors contribute to the accomplishment of the activity, and actors have a partial view of the activity. Second, each actor intervenes on a part of the group activity, an intervention can be unique or multiple during the accomplishment of the activity with the consequence of building the mental model jointly with its development for following the (real-time) accomplishment of group activity. Third, new concepts are introduced for the management of actors in a group. On the one hand, the working context of each actor must be enriched by the *shared context* associated with the group activity. On the other hand, actors' interventions must be assembled at the group level. Thus, the activity of each actor in a group is expressed as a set of *independent subtasks* in the group activity. This implies a *cyclic use of the directed contextual graph* with a structure for identifying the actor that will be the manager of the turn and the independent subtask that must be realized, and a management of the turns between successive crossings of the contextual graph where shared context ensures information transfers between the successive turns. Thus, before being developed in a specific context, a group mental-model must be built, that is, by assembling a sequence of independent subtasks taken in the activities of different actors.

For actor activity, there is a direct link from experience to the mental representation and contextual graph after, with a parallel between the mental model extracted from the mental representation and the path followed in the contextual graph. For a group activity, the mental representation (operational level) and the contextual graph (implementation level) contain actors' activities considered as sets of independent subtasks from which the mental model is built. As a result, a mental model cannot be extracted from the mental representation directly, and the cyclic use of the directed contextual graph is required for developing one-by-one independent subtasks that will be assembled at each turn with the instantiation process (at the environment level) to build the group mental model at the operational level. Concepts such as reasoning, contextual graph, RCEs, proceduralized context undergo exaptation to build the mental model but always keep the same meaning.

Shared context (KP-18, 23, 24) makes explicit the mental-model building and development for a group of actors. It concerns communication between actors (compatibility of actor mental representations), interaction between their independent subtasks, step-by-step building of the mental model from a base of independent subtasks with a contextual graph structured by RCEs for cyclic use of the contextual graph and building of the proceduralized context of the group mental model. On a more general level, shared context plays the role of inference engine for a CxG-based simulation and a key element in a "passport" for CIAS. Independent subtasks (KP-19, 20, 22, 25) are the representation of actors' individual activities that are in the mental representation and in the contextual graph corresponding to the group activity. An important technical point is the possibility of a cyclic use of a directed contextual graph and the possibility of proceeding to CxG-based simulation on the basis of a one-off intervention of actors, which leads to the possibility of checking alternative steps on the path from a given step (e.g. negotiation among actors). At an operational level, the group mental model is built by the progressive assembling of the developed independent subtasks, but the mental model emerges from the path followed in the contextual graph, not from the mental representation like in the actor activity. *RCEs* allow management of the actors' interventions and selection of independent subtasks during activity accomplishment and behave as activation conditions of a turn by instantiating MANAGER and TASK_STATUS and as post-conditions for the next turn by managing SENDER, RECIPIENT and TASK_STATUS. RCEs also ensure the control of the CxG-based simulation (cyclic use of the directed contextual graph, stop of the simulation at any turn, etc.). A *turn* (KP-21, 22, 23) corresponds to an actor's intervention in a group-activity accomplishment, that is, the realization of an independent subtask during the traversal of the contextual graph. Knowing the initial shared context, is it possible to replay a turn with different variants before making decisions. At the end of the turn, the independent subtask realized is added to the subtasks already assembled. Subtask realization and assembling other subtasks provides a turn-by-turn building of the mental model controlled by RCEs. The turn-by-turn building of the group mental model opens the possibility to proceed to a what-if approach before integrating a turn in the existing assembling. *CxG-based simulation* (KP-23) offers a pragmatic understanding of the evolution of a group activity instead of a cognitive simulation of an activity accomplished by a unique actor. It allows a visualization of the dynamic of the reasoning held during the development of a group mental model, because a multi-actor reasoning is more complex than for a unique actor because the group reasoning includes the building of the mental model by the RCEs in addition to its development. It is also a support for shared-context building and exploitation by different actors during group mental model development. It also is an important tool for CIASs.

4.2.2. *Definition of the context of an activity*

We identify the context of an activity to the proceduralized context that is built during the realization of that activity, or the mental-model development at the operational level or the path followed in the corresponding contextual graph at the implementation level. In Table 4.1, two definitions of the proceduralized context, namely a conceptual definition that defines it as the contextual knowledge usable in the focus of attention at a current step (KP-3), and an implemented definition that defines it as the ordered sequence of contextual elements that are instantiated during a contextual-graph run (KP-15). The identification of the context of an activity to its proceduralized context is a pragmatic extension of our initial definition of context in 1999 ("context is what constrains a task realization without appearing in it"). Task realization has no visible links with context, while it is possible with activity accomplishment that dynamically embeds the instantiation of its contextual elements from the sources of context in a way more efficient than in Logic, where the attachment of the premises P1, P2, ... as TRUE to the conclusion C1 gives a contextual meaning to C1 (see hereafter).

The originality of the definition relies on:

– the joint building of the proceduralized context with the realization activity;

– a real-time definition is always synchronous with the step at hand in the activity realization;

– the possibility that activity and context may modify the evolution of each other;

– the reuse of the proceduralized context for CxG-based simulation of activity realization;

– the strong explanatory power of the proceduralized context on the manner by which an activity is realized.

4.2.3. *Contextual reasoning*

Moreover, activity accomplishment relying on the actor's reasoning that makes a decision at each contextual element by choosing the instantiation according to the sources of context. As a result, the proceduralized context, which is based on instantiated contextual elements, is a kind of contextual reasoning. Locally, the reasoning held during the accomplishment of an activity in a specific context is contextual because of the intervention of the actor in the choice of the instantiation of contextual elements. Globally, instantiation corresponds to the selection of an expression for the reasoning step among several branches that leads to as many different types of reasoning as branches in different contexts. This instantiation process makes reasoning nonlinear in activity accomplishment. For a better understanding of the impact of context on reasoning at the implementation level, consider that the contextual node in a contextual element is a question (e.g. what is the weather?) and instantiations of the branches between the contextual and recombination nodes correspond to different known answers (e.g. it is sunny, it is raining) and each branch contains a particular expression for the reasoning step (e.g. if it is sunny, take a T-shirt, if it is raining, take a raincoat). The recombination node allows us to delimit the effect of the instantiation on the reasoning to a unique step.

The model of a group activity (CxG_2.0 version) differs from that of an actor activity (CxG_2.0 version) mainly at the implementation level due to the change of representation of actor's activity as a set of independent subtasks. This is a strong argument for the positioning of our modeling approach since the common conceptual level implies a coherence of all the possible extensions of the activity modeling. For instance, it is possible to change actor-activity representation from one model to a set of independent subtasks with the same result but moving from an external viewpoint on the activity model to an internal viewpoint as previously captured in a contextual graph. It is an interesting aspect, especially for group activity that is the object of the next two sections on the analysis of an internship offer and the diagnosis of a DVD reader.

A reasoning generally cannot be separated from the context in which it takes place. The contextual nature of reasoning appears when the conclusion, for example in a rule-based system, is intertwined with conditions as developed hereafter. Such reasoning concerns activities such as decision-making, interpretation, diagnosis, pattern recognition, which are context-dependent. Moreover, reasoning in one context may influence reasoning in other contexts when reasoning is formalized as a set of deductions, each deduction carried out inside a context, connected by appropriate "bridge rules" (Giunchiglia 1997) and lifting rules (McCarthy 1993). Reasoning involves a time-based decision-making process, where decisions made imply actions that change the context at hand and therefore affect the agent's subsequent decisions. Thus, operational knowledge explains how to behave (what to do and not do) while knowledge and reasoning allow the identification of the context in which the activity is accomplished, as well as when it changes. As a result, transition knowledge needs to be built in real-time because context may change after action execution (Gonzalez 2014).

An actor holds contextual reasoning, which is based on personal experience, is expressed as the joint play of activity development and instantiation process of contextual elements. Contextual reasoning includes the gathering of contextual information, structuring of contextual elements, decision-making and triggering of actions. There are two main parts: first, the proceduralized context and, second, the sequence of actions to perform in this specific context, as represented in the Mental-Model Tree view (see section 2.4.4). As such, we see that any reasoning can be considered as contextual reasoning. The contextual graph is the implementation of the mental representation of contextual reasoning in the actor's experience. There are numerous examples of contextual reasoning like, for example, the clinical reasoning of a physician (Konopasky et al. 2020) that may arrive at two different diagnoses for two patients with the same symptoms, findings and diagnosis but different contextual factors (factors that are not directly linked to the activity potentially influencing reasoning).

Contextual reasoning can be nonlinear reasoning that can be revisited on the fly because instantiation of contextual elements can be modified at any moment. This leads to decision-making to use different strategies such as depth- and breadth-first strategies, glocal search (where global solutions are adapted to local needs), the contextualization-decontextualization-recontextualization approach (when no task model exists). At the implementation level too, CxG formalism gives a parallel and series structure to a contextual graph and uses logic of use of actors rather than logic of functioning of designers. We also show that other context-based formalisms such as CxBR and CMB propose interesting approaches close to the CxG formalism.

A mental model belongs to a mental representation that is the actor's experience. Mental models and mental representation are in long-term memory. Actors exploit their experience from the mental representation for building numerous mental models corresponding to the reasoning in different contexts. As the first consequence, mental models are integrated in the uniform mental representation and structured by contextual elements used in different mental models. The first contribution of mental models to CxG formalism is to point out the central role of contextualized objects and the contextual reasoning using these objects. Initially, the focus was on task realization as an extension of the task model. In the new modeling framework, we consider mental-model development in a specific context as expressing the reasoning leading to this development. This notion of contextual reasoning is not new. In section 2.2.2, we show that a practical unit of reasoning in a rule system like "IF P1, P2, … THEN C1" supposes the attachment of the premises P1, P2, … as TRUE to the conclusion C1 that gives a contextual meaning to C1 and makes contextual the reasoning that cannot be separated from the context in which it takes place. In the CxG formalism, contextual reasoning follows the structure of a contextual graph (the mental representation) and exploits the particular structures of the contextual elements (the branches between contextual and recombination nodes, and selected instantiations), activities (as independent contextual subgraphs) and ESIA (the set of independent local units of reasoning). The course followed by the contextual reasoning in the contextual graph is mainly guided by the play of instantiations at the instant at which the value of a contextual element is required. Saying it differently, the actor facing an activity: (1) uses their experience for identifying the right mental model, (2) identifies the relevant contextual element in the mental model, (3) looks for its instantiation at the current step of the reasoning, (4) performs the reasoning step (action, activity, etc.) and (5) goes to the next contextual element up for a clear view of the way to address the activity. Thus, contextual reasoning covers mental-model development and proceduralized-context building at each step.

Arriving at a contextual element, its instantiation is mandatory to choose the right expression for the reasoning step. The different known instantiations of the contextual element go down to the operational level to select the instantiation. The instantiation process is performed in working memory to determine which value can be the candidate according to context awareness. An instantiation could be a known value (i.e. in an existing mental model) or not. If the value is unknown to the CxG software, the actor has to provide it as a variant of an existing one by defining the new mental model (using the editor of the CxG formalism) by adding a new branch between contextual and recombination nodes of the contextual element, defining the value associated with the new branch and creating the reasoning step to perform for this new instantiation of the contextual element, thus in this new context. From the CxG-system viewpoint, it is learning by assimilation. There is also the possibility of learning by accommodation for a more consequent change (e.g. addition of a new contextual element, for example), but the spirit stays the same.

If the acquisition of a new mental model in the mental representation is easy (often, an addition of a new value and the corresponding step of the reasoning to perform), conversely, the visualization of a specific mental model in the mental representation is difficult because the contextual graph is not centered on the mental model but on contextual elements. In section 2.4, we propose a "mental-model tree view" associated with the contextual graph where contextual reasoning in a mental model is associated with a proceduralized context followed by the sequence of operations to execute in order to realize the right mental model. The important point is that contextual reasoning must be considered at two decisional levels: the operational level where the mental representation (long-term memory) resides and at the implementation level where contextual elements in the mental model are instantiated from the environment level (working memory) thanks to "context awareness". Gonzalez (1974) does a similar observation with the context-based reasoning (CxBR) formalism (section 2.6.4). Contextual reasoning involves a time-based decision-making process, where made decisions imply (at operational level) actions that change the context at hand, which, in turn, affect the agent's subsequent decisions. Actors hold contextual reasoning on the basis of their experience.

In CxG formalism, contextual reasoning is following mental-model development (i.e. a path in a contextual graph) with: (1) a uniform (mental) representation of mental models structured by contextual elements, (2) a series of reasoning steps corresponding to the crossed instantiated contextual elements and their various expressions, (3) an association with the building of the proceduralized context and (4) an explanation of each reasoning step in terms of contextual elements, their instantiations and ordering.

Explaining a contextual reasoning at the level of an activity accomplishment is possible from the proceduralized context that can be broken-down in terms of the contextual elements encountered (and instantiated) during the mental-model development and the alternatives (i.e. mental models corresponding to abandoned values of contextual elements, etc.). In CxG formalism, it is also possible to access contextual information such as authors of the mental model and date of creation. Moreover, making explicit proceduralized context allows the automatic identification of the sequence of actions to perform for this specific proceduralized context, as represented in the Mental Model Tree view of the CxG formalism. A mental model is extracted from the mental representation when contextual elements are instantiated in working memory. Mental representation gives the background on how to address an activity in different contexts, while a mental model makes explicit how to address the activity in a specific context. A mental model is developed at the same time as it is used. The sequence of the joint instantiation process and mental-model development corresponds to a CxG-based simulation. A CxG-based simulation is clearly developed in working memory, while mental representation (contextual graph) and mental models (paths in the contextual graph) are in long-term memory. The introduction of the concept of mental model in the CxG formalism extends naturally the CxG formalism to any object in reasoning (task realization, decision-making, problem solving, etc.) and simplifies the use of the CxG formalism at the current step of contextual reasoning held during mental-model development, where all reasoning steps in a contextual element are exclusive.

Reasoning involves the process of drawing logical conclusions and making judgments based on available information and evidence in the context. Context provides elements of the framework within which reasoning takes place. Reasoning is inherently contextual because it is influenced by the specific circumstances, background knowledge, values and objectives that constrain the interpretation and use of information, that is, the four sources of context discussed previously. Different contexts lead reasoning to different conclusions when engaging in rational thought processes. By explicitly acknowledging the contextual nature of reasoning, we can appreciate that actors may arrive at different conclusions based on their personal contexts. Contextual factors can significantly impact how information is interpreted and understood, and failing to consider the context may lead to misinterpretations or misunderstandings of someone's reasoning or argument. By taking context into account, we can better understand the reasoning process of others and reduce the likelihood of miscommunication. As said for decision-making, we must gather (contextual) information, then determine available options for planning and, finally, perform the retained plan. Contextual reasoning leads actors to consider the various contextual factors that may influence their own reasoning process and encourages them to evaluate the strengths and weaknesses of different arguments within specific contexts in a "what if" approach. Thus, the comprehension of context allows us to identify relevant information, weigh different factors and make more informed decisions.

In group activity, CxG-based simulation must be discussed with respect to long-term memory and working memory. The visualization of mental-model development results from a cycle of uses of a directed contextual graph (the mental representation). This cyclic use of the contextual graph is required because, if independent subtasks are known in advance, the sequence of subtasks depends on the instantiations of the contextual elements made during each cycle by context awareness. Figure 4.2 shows that (1) mental representation and mental models inside are in long-term memory, (2) instantiation of crossed contextual elements is retrieved from working memory and then (3) once back to long-term memory, the reasoning step in the mental model is performed, and the cycle is repeated. Thus, in the CxG-based simulation of a mental-model development in Figure 4.2, the instantiation value(C1) of the contextual element C1 in long-term memory is obtained in working memory, and the reasoning step A1 is then executed in the mental-model development at long-term memory level. The cycle continues up to the next contextual element (if any) to instantiate. The mental-model development is associated with an ordered sequence of instantiated contextual elements, that is, the proceduralized context. All elements of known mental models already exist in mental representation. A new mental model is built for integrating changes in a new context of task realization as illustrated in the example of the "coffee preparation" introduced in section 2.4.

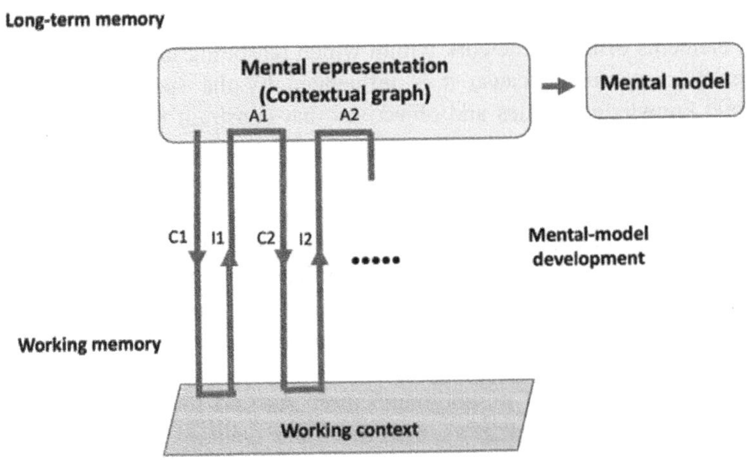

Figure 4.2. *Conceptual model of a CxG-based simulation of a mental-model development. For a color version of this figure, see www.iste.co.uk/ brezillon/contextbasedmodeling.zip*

The distinction of the two processes, contextual-element instantiation and mental-model development, explains the observation in the SART project that actors, once an incident is declared, first look to identify the context (i.e. relevant contextual elements for the development of the mental model and their instantiations) in which the incident occurs (a qualitative building of the proceduralized context) and, second, make a decision by developing a plan of actions relevant for the identified context. This observation is at the origin of the mental model tree visualization associated with the contextual-graph representation discussed previously.

It is possible to express a given model of a living system in different representation formalisms, especially tree and graph representations. We do it in the SART project, starting with a rule-production formalism, then a decision-tree formalism and finally a graph formalism. A formalism of representation leads to a type of visualization that selects the features judged important for an actor and excludes other features. For example, the software Freemind used in the TACTIC project is based on a tree representation of the contextual elements expressing mainly knowledge structure, and (contextual) reasoning which is marked by additional arrows between contextual elements on different branches (see TACTIC project). An alternative visualization in the CxG formalism is a path in a contextual graph, and knowledge structures appear as support to the actions executed by the actor. The choice of a formalism must be made after the definition of the conceptual framework and the way in which relevant concepts must be formalized. Conversely, developing a conceptual framework supposes a confrontation to a real-world system that requires its implementation. The two versions CxG_1.0 and CxG_2.0 of the CxG formalism offer two representations that differ essentially by the possibility of having either a mental model obtained as a path in the contextual graph because all the known mental models belong to the contextual graph (version CxG_1.0) or a dynamic building of a mental model from assembling independent subtasks used for representing actors' mental models in the contextual graph (version CxG_2.0).

In the different projects on which we worked (SART, TACTIC, etc.), the contextual graph is a powerful tool for representing and managing the representation of actors' experience during task realization, but it was necessary to associate the contextual graph with a mental model tree representation (see section 1.2.2) with the two parts, the proceduralized context and the required sequence of reasoning steps as a "macro-action" corresponding to the proceduralized context. This ascertainment is also found in the literature. For Logan (1988), cognitive processing of experts has a high level of automaticity through a single-step retrieval of actions from memory. Klein and Calderwood (1991) show that decision-making may proceed directly from recognized situations to predefined actions. Both accounts point to a situation where skilled knowledge is accessed and used in ways that don't necessarily lend themselves to easy verbalization. Our initial modeling in the SART project was in a decision-tree representation (the procedures being expressed as production rules, another representation formalism). We move towards a graph representation for various reasons (Pasquier 2002). CxG formalism was very relevant for mental-model development. However, actors preferred a more direct visualization with, first, identification of the proceduralized context (i.e. an ordered sequence of instantiated contextual elements) and, second, the scenario (i.e. the sequence of reasoning steps as a macro-action) to apply. The interest is to let the actor reason with a mental model, first, by looking for the more realistic proceduralized context and, second, on the macro-action that is associated with it. Thus, mental models are easily developed in a CxG formalism and used in a (mental model) tree representation.

Concepts such as reasoning, a contextual graph, RCEs and proceduralized context are exaptated for building the mental model. Modeling an activity accomplishment also is modeling actor's reasoning as a kind of simulation of the decision process. The proceduralized context, which is associated with the activity accomplishment, appears as a context-based model of reasoning. This context-based model is expressed as an ordered sequence (i.e. a path in the contextual graph implementing the mental-model development) of instantiated contextual elements (use of the instantiation process). The instantiation process is part of the reasoning leading to the generation of the proceduralized context. Contextual elements act as units of reasoning that acquire an expression according to the instantiations of the contextual elements. An instantiation corresponds to the selection of an expression for the reasoning step among several branches that leads to as many different steps of reasoning as branches in different contexts.

The explicit integration of context in the representation (through contextual elements and their instantiations) allows us to respect the human approach of actors' work (collect information, make a decision, act) as shown in the SART project. The CxG approach was used by persons not necessarily experts (e.g. such as students in Cognitive Psychology) in more than 20 very different applications. The extension of the CxG software for including CxG-based simulation led to model collaborative work, the main changes concerning the cyclic use of the contextual graph, of the working context and the decomposition of the task of each group member into independent subtasks for representing exchanges among group members (see Brézillon (2017), for research on group work).

In the SART Project (section 1.3), the first reaction of the operator (responsible for a subway line) being informed of an incident is to look for contextual information on the whole subway line and on lines having a connection with the line before seeking a reason for the incident. Thus, the operator has a global view of the situation and then can act locally for incident solving. The global part corresponds to different sources of contextual information such as the operational control board (see Figure 4.3), information from colleagues in the control room, some phone calls at the station where the incident occurred and from the train driver. The local part is the incident solving with decision-making based on the contextual information and direct action on the operational control board and indirect action of the train driver. This result is similar to the use of "zones of interest" in the FlexMim project.

Figure 4.3. *The glocal approach of the subway-line responsible. For a color version of this figure, see www.iste.co.uk/brezillon/contextbasedmodeling.zip*

4.2.4. *Global and local contexts*

4.2.4.1. *Procedure, practices and "best practices"*

A contextual element, with its different potential instantiations is a unit of contextual reasoning that intervenes as a step in the global reasoning of the activity. As a result, a mental model results from a contextual reasoning, while procedure does not result from such a reasoning because context is excluded from the procedure. For example, Ohm's law is stated as "the voltage U across a resistor is proportion to intensity I of the current flowing through it" (U = R x I is similar to the procedure). However, this law does not take account of the context that says when the temperature increases, the electrical resistance also increases, and the voltage will be different.

In the literature, a best practice is considered a method or technique that has been proven to be effective in achieving a particular goal or objective. A best practice is identified in a given context as producing the most efficient and effective results based on research, experience or benchmarking against industry standards. A best practice is a method or technique that has been generally accepted as superior to other known alternatives because it often produces results that are superior to those achieved by other means or because it has become a standard way of doing things, for example, a standard way of complying with legal or ethical requirements. A best practice specifies what we ought to do without regard to whether we do it, while a standard practice is what we have agreed we will in fact do, to some specified level of detail. Best practices are applied in various fields, such as business, healthcare, education, technology and many others. They are intended to improve the quality of work, enhance productivity, reduce costs and ensure consistency in performance. Best practices are related to how to carry out a task or configure something. Adopting best practices requires a willingness to learn, a commitment to improvement and a willingness to implement change. It involves identifying the most effective processes and procedures for achieving specific goals and then implementing them consistently and continuously. It also involves monitoring and evaluating performance to ensure that best practices continue to be effective over time. Overall, they are a way to optimize performance and achieve the best possible outcomes in any given situation or field. A key strategic talent, which is required when applying best practice to organizations, is the ability to balance the unique qualities of an organization with the practices that it has in common with others, that is, a transversal contextualization of the practice.

Determining best practices to address a particular policy problem is a commonly used but little understood tool of analysis because the concept is vague and should therefore be examined with caution. Vagueness stems from the term "best" which is subjective. While some research and evidence must go into determining a practice the "best" it is more helpful to simply determine whether a practice has worked exceptionally well and why. The best practice is found by the progressive assembling of the components that are relevant in the working context (especially when the practice is built and used at the same time). Scott (2011) offers an alternative view to "best practice": "contextual practice", in which the notion of what is "best" is specified in a particular context. In the CxG formalism, a contextual graph contains all the best practices in their proceduralized contexts (context-based practices). This solution accounts for the whole context of the application of the practice, while the "best practice" that is built with only a few contextual elements found in a large number of practices. Context in which a best practice is being applied plays an important role in determining its effectiveness. Best practices are not universal solutions that can be applied to all situations in the same way. The effectiveness of a best practice can depend on the specific circumstances and environment in which it is being applied. For example, a best practice that works well in one organization may not be effective in another organization with a different culture, structure or mission. Similarly, a best practice that works well in one country may not be effective in another country with different laws, regulations or social norms. Moreover, the context of best practice can also influence the level of customization required to adapt the best practice to local conditions. Some best practices may need to be adapted to the local culture, language or values to be effective in a specific context. Therefore, it is important to consider context when selecting, implementing and evaluating best practices. This includes understanding the specific goals and objectives, the organizational structure, the cultural and social norms, and the legal and regulatory environment in which the best practice will be applied (i.e. the global part of the context, what is called the local environment in the four sources of contextual elements). By first considering context, organizations can select and adapt the best practices that are most appropriate for their unique situation and improve their chances of success.

Computer programming and development are areas where establishing and following best practices is common and beneficial. This is because there are an infinite number of ways to write computer code that works, but setting standards make the code easier to read by others, simple to maintain and more fault-tolerant. The most common coding best practice is to add comments to the source code for explaining why the practice is the best in the context. While comments do not affect functionality, they make the code easier to use in a group. It is a kind of implicit introduction of the context of the best practice but is not directly usable. Thus, a best practice involves identifying the most effective processes and procedures for achieving specific goals and then implementing them consistently and continuously. A key strategic talent required when applying best practice to organizations is the ability to balance the unique qualities of an organization with the practices that it has in common with others, that is, the contextualization of the practice. However, the concept is vague and should therefore be examined with caution. In the CxG formalism, a "best practice" is the mental model that works in its specific context not a generic one.

4.2.4.2. *Contextualization-Decontextualization-Recontextualization*

The direct reuse of known mental models in a domain where knowledge is weakly (or not) formalized allows experts to rely on highly compiled experience and try to directly reuse their experience in numerous specific contexts if possible, but from the mental representation, not from mental models that are unknown. The past experience is reused in three steps for obtaining an idea of the mental-model realization: Contextualization, Decontextualization and Recontextualization (CDR), the objective being to determine how to change instantiations of contextual elements. In the CxG formalism, we start from the contextual graph, look for an interesting path and apply the reasoning with other instantiations of the contextual elements on the path. The initial "contextualization" of instantiated contextual elements in a known past experience close to the experience at hand. In other terms, it comes down to finding contextual elements that have been instantiated in the previous mental model. The decontextualization of the past mental model leads to the general activity model with its contextual elements that now may be instantiated again but differently. It comes down to find the location of the mental model in the mental representation and the contextual elements to instantiate. The recontextualization of the activity mental model, supposed to be the good one for the new context, consists of re-instantiating its contextual elements in the context at hand. This CDR approach is particularly useful when the activity is on something too complex to comprehend, like the "black box view" on wine fermentation. In the "Contextualizing scientific workflows" project (section 1.7), Fan et al. (2011) point out the CDR process in the search of a scientific workflow (SWF) in virtual screening (see Figure 4.4): A researcher extracts from a repository an SWF close to their working context (phase of contextualization), extracts the SWF model (phase of decontextualization) and, finally, instantiates the SWF model in their working context (phase of recontextualization). Then, a workflow engine ensures the execution phase in which input data is consumed according to the formal model and output data are produced as results. If it is a success, the new SWF is put in the repository available to other scientists. Otherwise, a new iteration is needed by reconsidering either the phase of decontextualization for finding a new model or by trying a different recontextualization of a new SWF. Figure 4.4 presents the SWF lifecycle form where the way to make the context explicit in the process was studied (the details are given in Fan et al. (2011)).

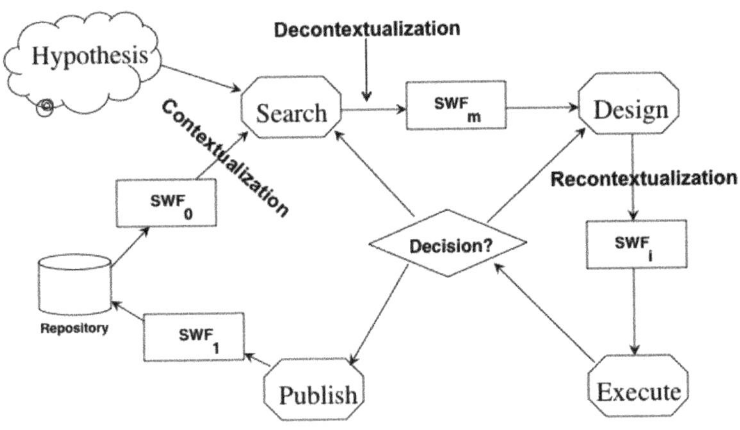

Figure 4.4. *Flexibility inside workflow lifecycle (Fan et al. 2011)*

Figure 4.4 presents the approach for SWF lifecycle with the five steps (search, design, execute, make a decision, publish), in which we identify three context-based processes: (1) the contextualization process that identifies the published SWF in a context close to the context at hand from the repository; (2) the decontextualization process that extracts the part of the published SWF – the SWF abstract model – to be reused for the problem at hand and (3) the recontextualization process that designs the SWF concrete model before executing the SWF to find the best one that is adapted to the current context. At the decision-making step, scientists either go back to the repository to search for a completely new SWF concrete model for a new contextualization, after potentially re-designing the current SWF concrete model and its fragments. The research cycle is resumed as long as the scientist is not satisfied, and finally, the instantiated model (SWF_i) is published in the repository for a sharing purpose with other scientists. Generally, the phase of decontextualization (leading to the abstract model (SWF_m) and the assembling of components leading to the instantiated model are not recorded because they are considered too specific to the SWF at hand. The contextualization–decontextualization–recontextualization process is found in different domains (e.g. ecology and petrol) where a solution is built from known solutions in different similar domains (Brézillon 2010). As a result, an SWF repository contained instantiated SWF concrete models (similar to the practices considered in the CxG formalism) not the abstract SWF models (i.e. the procedures). Most scientists need to re-do the docking multiple times to evaluate the parameters until they are satisfied. Scientists use implicitly contextual knowledge. For example, the answers to the question "what are sources of hidden contexts for choosing software?" show that the main sources of hidden contexts are: (1) familiarity with the software, (2) availability of resources and (3) the situation at hand. This allowed the identification of the relevant contextual elements and their values, and the actions executed for each instantiation. This leads to the automatic generation of the relevant SWF concrete models among which the scientist chooses one.

4.2.4.3. *Glocalization*

Glocalization[1] represents the fusion of "globalization" and "localization", emphasizing the need for global entities to tailor their offerings to suit the unique characteristics of local regions or communities. Glocal, an adjective, by definition means "reflecting or characterized by both local and global considerations". The term "glocal management" in a sense of "think globally, act locally" is used in the business strategies of companies, in particular by Japanese companies that are expanding overseas. Glocalization (a portmanteau of globalization and localization) generally is considered as a case in which a global product is transformed into another

1. Wikipedia (see: https://en.wikipedia.org/wiki/Glocalization).

shape in order to meet the needs of local consumers. However, local solution does not mean specialization of the global solution. In a reverse innovation view, the goal is not to simplify the global problem but to simplify the local uses of the solution. Top-down innovation overlooks the true inventiveness and specialized understanding possessed by local individuals for a model that has worked in an entirely different region and for a unique population. Radjou et al. (2013) explain that processes and methods (such as Six Sigma) are not capable of delivering agile solutions. Six Sigma is useful when mass producing in a predictable environment but acts like a straitjacket: once we get in, we stay in it. The authors propose the Jugaad approach as the art of spotting opportunities in the most adverse circumstances and finding ingenious, improvised solutions using simple means. It is doing more with less. In the context of the CxG formalism, the mental representation corresponds to global and a mental model corresponds to local for one actor (for in the case of group activity, the mental representation corresponds to the global activity accomplishment in various particular contexts, but the mental model must be built in a given "local").

The concept of "Globalization" (different from glocalization) expresses the important shift in economic and political organization of the world economy. The concept moved rapidly into the cultural domain too. Virtually every (local) government has taken measures to align its social and economic policy to the "exigencies" and "requirements" of this new competitive world (dis)order and the forces of a new "truly" free-market-based world economy. The strong stance was "local must be global or die". The discourse of neoliberal internationalism has become the *Pensée Unique* (Swyngedouw 2004), a hegemonic, incontestable and virtually naturalized and self-evident set of arguments and beliefs for an international elite of economists and policy analysts. The adoption of the term "globalization" implied a profound geographical reorganization of capitalism, making many of the presumptions about the "natural" geographical units within which capitalism's historical trajectory develops less and less meaningful. The "global" companies like GAFA are above "local" countries and escape the laws of local countries and do not pay taxes. The example of Silicon Valley, the geographical clusters of companies in "the Third Italy" or the concentration of financial services in Manhattan or the City of London illustrate the process of intense territorial concentration combined with a global reach and outlook. In other words, a scalar transformation of the networks of economic organization has taken place. Globalization concerns business or eventually economy, not local people, agriculture, companies and their (small) countries. The image of the global village may have become a standard cultural icon of the time, but many places have in fact suffered from a diminished interdependence.

Glocalization is different from Globalization because it relies on the coordination of global and local concerns. In the 2010s, we knew the limits of globalization, and we observed the importance of the local concerns, especially with the strong emphasis on ecology. The carbon fingerprint looks like an indicator of the mandatory needs to reduce globalization for the benefit of glocalization, that is, coordinating roles of global and local. "Glocal" attempts to capture the melding of international and local realities. The concept behind the idea is essentially that someone is aware at a global level of the process of globalization, the interchange of cultures and ideas, but it is also aware of the distinctiveness of their own culture at the local level. In economy, globalization is the systematic elimination of the "local". Globalization is not a spontaneous convergence of cultures, policies and economies, but rather the reshaping of various local structures in order to accommodate global capital and its cultural needs.

In the MICI project, digital slides are analyzed at two levels in a cyclic way with a phase of fast exploration for finding zones of interest (global search) followed by a phase of fine-grained analysis of the zones judged of interest (local search). At the global level, Anatomical Pathology Physicians (APPs) follow procedures that include a gross examination (visual examination of organs), dissection and sampling of surgical specimens according to standardized protocols (global search). They enter an exploratory phase that is guided by their knowledge (their mental representation of the problem). Global properties of an image allow distinguishing objects and zones of interest in complex scenes for working on them (selection, recognition and control of action). At the local level, APPs make a microscopic examination of stained tissue sections (local search) with a zoom further down to the zone of interest. The grain size at which APPs choose to zoom (magnification at either x20 or x40) affects not only what they can discern but also what becomes indistinguishable, thus permitting the mind to ignore confusing details. Moreover, APPs cannot use tools like pattern recognition because object identification is not binary. Instead, they select and combine features as criteria in favor of the presence, the absence or uncertainty on features (in a kind of "image wall"). APPs give a value of the feature for evaluating the criterion that depends on APPs' experience. The modeling of the glocal search is an important process of their decision-making.

The glocal approach is also illustrated on the second example given in Figure 4.5 that comes from the MICO project (section 1.8) for digital counting of mitotic score in breast cancer. Mitotic counting is mandatory for classification and prognosis of breast carcinomas.

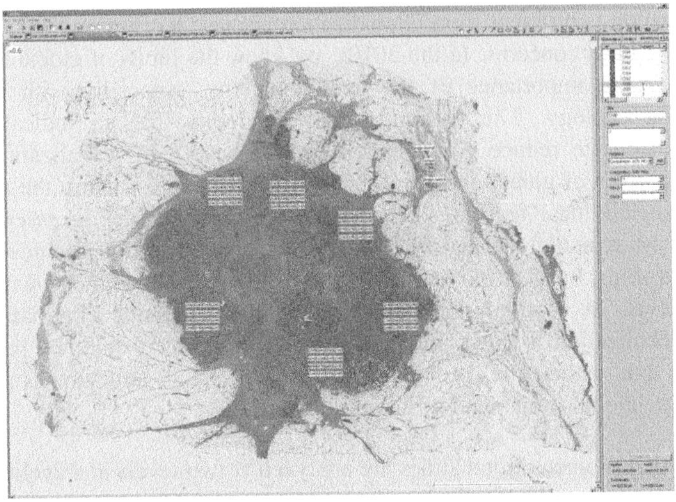

Figure 4.5. *Virtual slide of invasive ductal carcinoma with six positioned C10 frames on tumor periphery. For a color version of this figure, see www.iste.co.uk/brezillon/contextbasedmodeling.zip*

The count usually stands as a decisive point for treatment. Counting mitoses is done by screening routine glass slides. Slides are made of 3 microns in thickness, and scanned at 40 magnification using a scanner. In Figure 4.5, the global approach consists of finding zones of interest on a slide of the tumor. Four to six frames corresponding to a 10x magnification (C10) of a microscope were localized at the periphery of a tumor. Each of these frames was then divided into four subframes corresponding to a 20 magnification (C20), and each of the latter was divided into four others (C40) corresponding to a 40 magnification of a microscope. This procedure respects thus the recommendations of mitotic count in SBR (Scarff-Bloom-Richardson) grade, that is, 10 contiguous fields with 40x high magnification at the tumor periphery.

The local approach in the MICO project (Figure 4.6) concerns the count of mitosis in the 10 zones of interest at C40 on a C10 frame. Two pathologists examined all the virtual slides. On one chosen C10, mitosis count was made on 10 C40 contiguous fields. Each mitotic figure was located by annotation. C10 territories chosen on each virtual slide were located on the corresponding slide.

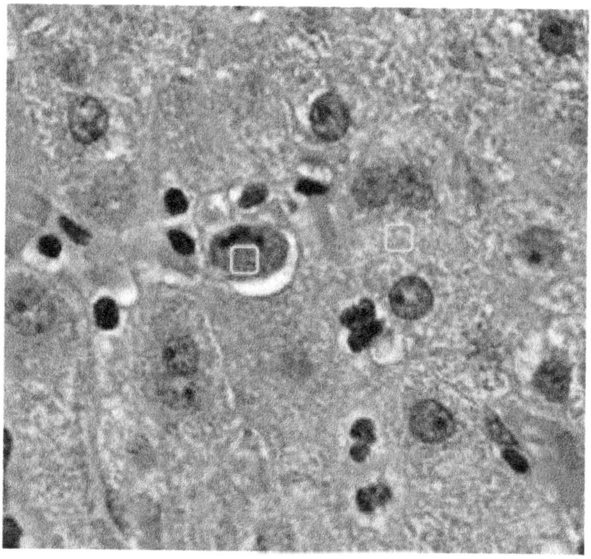

Figure 4.6. *Located mitosis on a C40 field of the virtual slide in Figure 4.5. For a color version of this figure, see www.iste.co.uk/brezillon/contextbasedmodeling.zip*

The two pathologists then evaluated mitotic count on these 16 located territories, on 10 contiguous fields with a microscope field diameter of 0.55 mm. While counting mitosis on virtual slides, pathologists annotated "mitosis" on one part and other figures which are morphologically similar to mitosis called "likely mitosis" or not at all mitosis called "no mitosis" on the other part. During mitotic count, pathologists annotate "mitosis" and also other figures which morphologically look like mitosis, called "likely mitosis" and others that are not mitosis called "no mitosis". A recent study used quite the same methodology to improve agreement between pathologists and a computerized detector. Moreover, difficult cases on slides benefit from double counting and agreement. The mitotic figures non-visualized by one pathologist are reviewed and discussed by the other and vice versa. Furthermore, the main advantage of scanned slides is to annotate the figures and thus have a traceability which is not only a medico-legal value and also allows the discussion between pathologists of the diagnosis through telepathology.

In the TACTIC project (section 1.5), there are two types of glocalization. The first one is at the operator-C2 system interaction level, as shown in Figure 4.7. The C2 system has three sources of information: A map, which can be considered as a Global Information System (GIS); An ORder of BATtle (ORBAT), which contains the unit's hierarchy; and Action windows, which allows users to visualize and give orders. The three sources of information are complementary. As they are generally used together, it would seem wise to consider them as a 3D cognitive repository in which events take place: an object has spatial (cartography), temporal (chronology) and sociotechnical (ORBAT) coordinates. This means that by clicking on a unit, all the information related to this unit should be able to be automatically extracted to be presented to the operator. Each unit would then be associated with a knowledge network, with close information, such as the life bar, and other more distant information such as belonging to an automaton. Such knowledge organization should allow presentations at the different desired levels of aggregation. The first two sources of information correspond to the global part of the operator-C2 system containing the "mental representation" of the simulator, while the third source of information (the action window) concerns the specifications of the "mental model" of the simulator that are managed by the operator, with clicks on an item for having local information on it.

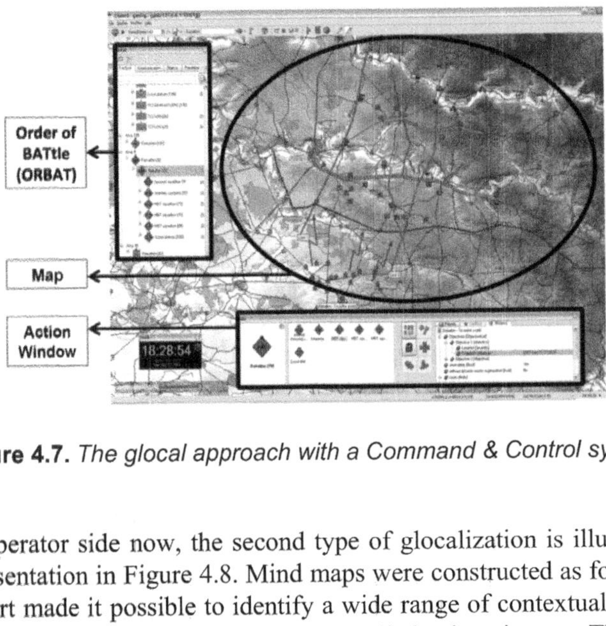

Figure 4.7. *The glocal approach with a Command & Control system*

On the operator side now, the second type of glocalization is illustrated by the mental representation in Figure 4.8. Mind maps were constructed as follows. First, a state of the art made it possible to identify a wide range of contextual elements that an operator was likely to mobilize, which was called a domain map. This map of the domain served as a starting point for operators. Second, we asked the operators to adapt this map of the domain to their personal needs according to the tasks they have to perform. The adaptation could lead to a reorganization of the map as well as a complete overhaul of the map. The map thus drawn up by each operator is the image of the mental representation of the operator's experience. Third, at the end of the task, the operator was asked to realize the task "Analysis of a tactical situation" and indicated in mental representation contextual elements used during task realization. The result of the task realization is the mental model.

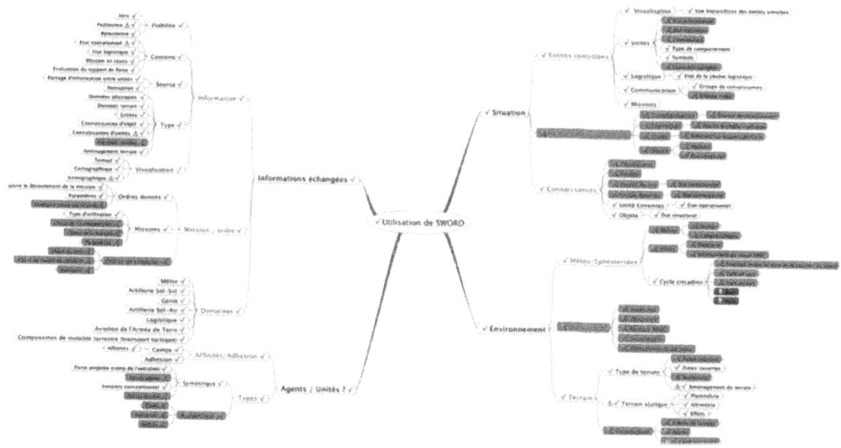

Figure 4.8. *The global and local approaches in operator's mental representation. For a color version of this figure, see www.iste.co.uk/brezillon/contextbasedmodeling.zip*[2]

Each mental map (mental representation and mental model) is specific to each actor and the task at hand. Mental representation corresponds to all the items on the figure (green, blue and darkened) that are associated with operator's experience with the task chosen during a session. Mental model corresponds to the items used during a session with the C2 system (thus not darkened in the figure). Here, the mental model is strictly included in the mental representation. This example leads to associating a global approach with a mental representation and a local approach with a mental model. Thus, glocalization could be associated with the modeling of the experience of an operator, and, in this sense, a global view of the operator's experience is a contextual graph and the local view concerns the development of a practice (mental model).

To sum up, the glocalization approach allows reasoning to use a global and local association. The options are (1) a global solution imposes a simplification of local uses (top-down way) with the extreme case of elimination of the local by the global (globalization); (2) homogenization of local solutions at the globalization level and (3) global (e.g. search of zones of interest) guides local (e.g. zoom in zone of interest). The third option concerns especially pathologists, where the global search guides the search of criteria and the zoom allows the identification of features for

2. The data contained in this figure is irrelevant. Its purpose is to provide a visualization of knowledge organization.

using these criteria by decision-making on magnified images like in mitosis diagnosis. We come back to the notion of glocalization in the section on the application of our theoretical framework to chronic inflammatory bowel diagnosis.

4.3. The "Internship-offer analysis" example

4.3.1. *The actors*

Students registered for the Innovation-Management Master of Sorbonne University for acquiring a second competence in management after the first acquisition of a disciplinary competence (Biology, Chemistry, Engineering, Mathematics, etc.). Thus, they were familiar with elements that intervene during realization of the "Analysis of an internship offer" activity and had an experience to share during the collaborative exercise in Innovation-Management Master. Here, the mission given to students was to work collaboratively to gather all contextual elements they had already considered as important during their past experience with this activity. The mission was to model the activity as a contextual graph in CxG_1.0 formalism. Thus, the task modeling is rapidly becoming an activity modeling in which subjective contextual elements were introduced by students.

A major concern of all Master-2 students was to find a position in an enterprise (internship first and employment second), but each student realizes the "Analysis of an internship offer" activity in a personal context that is different from other students' contexts. It was due to their disciplinary origin, and their personal preferences, motivations, goals for their professional life, social environment, their capacity, etc. The first step of the modeling was to gather the contextual elements considered as important, to organize them into a few classes and to structure them. It was an important challenge because students agreed on the selection of contextual elements to consider for analyzing an internship offer but opinions diverged on the way to use them, beginning by ordering, combining and using them in the specific analysis of their internship offers. Peer groups' cohesion is determined and maintained by factors such as group communication, group consensus and group conformity concerning attitude and behavior. Discussions help them to think through a problem or discover alternative approaches to solving the problem. The difficulty is not the theory but how to apply the theory. Peer discussion provided opportunities to express ideas about the problem in more detail, to explore alternative viewpoints, different approaches and to ask for and hear different explanations. It is easier to understand an explanation given by another student (same language) who had just grasped the solution, than an instructor's explanation (at a "much higher level"). No need to know the rationale for using something (we do it with a number of pieces of equipment in our home such as TVs and fridges). The "internship-offer analysis" activity is particularly interesting because students experiment the same contextual elements, but in different contexts, and thus classify them differently from other students. Moreover, experience acquired on the "Internship-offer analysis" activity is directly reusable on the task "find a good hiring" that each student will face just after.

The role of the instructor was voluntarily limited to the role of facilitator, providing explanations on terms used during the session and the context of terms. The instructor also may intervene for suggesting ways to analyze an internship proposal. The instructor uses a depth-first language (the deep meaning behind everything), while students' exchanges are in a breadth-first language to learn a piece of knowledge in their mental representation. Students being directly concerned by the result (i.e. the list of relevant contextual elements), quickly appropriated the concept of collective task realization, by first defining their personal criteria as the best combination of contextual elements; and, second, a global view on how other students led the same search with their criteria, which were not necessarily the same. The collaborative work was organized through a class-wide discussion experiment for analyzing an internship proposal with the collective digital means available (overhead projector, access to the Web, public and private communication tools, etc.).

4.3.2. *Conditions of the experiment*

The session concerned a group of 25 students of Master-2 level coming from different disciplines. They were willing to be trained in Innovation Management because their disciplinary masters are strongly "research-oriented" while they wanted to work in enterprise. The group of students is composed of 8 males and 17 females, coming from Biology (9), Chemistry (5), Computer Sciences (2), Engineering (6) and Environment (3). Only the first steps were based on the students' experience for analyzing the internship offer because it was not possible to have a unique internship offer interesting to all students. Our hypothesis was that analysis of different offers in different domains relies on the same foundation of contextual elements.

The experiment was led in their usual computer room. An overhead screen acted as the shared context of the students. Students had thought of the problem beforehand, a preliminary step in small (disciplinary) groups, results posted for all the class on Google Drive. Technology provides the opportunity for a collaborative-work space, but the quality of the negotiation will rely on coaching and face to face discussion. Students worked on the shared document in Google Drive and used the chat window for extra work interaction. Conflicts or questions were fixed orally. Any student could modify the shared document but a specific student plays the role of the leader. Indeed, students rapidly decide to elect a leader for managing changes in the shared document, one or two other students playing the role of secretary for arranging the shared document (spelling, ordering of items, coloring categories, etc.). The session was developed in six steps: (1) Gathering elements in order to establish a relevant shared context, (2) Identification of the relevant elements, (3) Classification of the elements, (4) Categorization of the elements, (5) Search of the instantiations of the elements and (6) Modeling of the activity.

The list of contextual elements was established from different sources: student (objective, plans for the future, etc.), enterprise and context of the task realization (e.g. an internship as a pre-employment). Thus, collaborative work goes to a consensus (same goal) for the set of contextual elements that have to be considered, then to task modeling as a contextual graph and, finally, specific instantiation of the model for each student.

4.3.3. *Development of the experiment*

Students understood that it was not an academic example but a real preparation for the search of an internship as a "springboard" for their forthcoming search of a job. Table 4.2 presents the list of contextual elements resulting from the collaborative work classified by category (Table 4.10 presents a classification by "Meaning" of the contextual elements). Students interacted orally with the leader when allowed by the leader and used a chat window for kidding on the side, jokes on students intervening and the student "nominated as volunteer to be the leader of the group". Indeed, collaborative work allows an informal effort, while cooperation is a formal effort.

Table 4.2 presents 30 contextual elements that all students consider as important for an efficient analysis of an internship offer. An interesting lesson learned at this step is that objective and subjective contextual elements come from different sources (from the offer, from the enterprise and from students' preferences, the "candidate") and are mixed in the table (see ranking), showing that some subjective contextual elements were judged more important than objective ones. The goal was to determine the importance of each contextual element guiding the modeling of the "internship-offer analysis" activity as a contextual graph. A vote was organized on the importance of each contextual element for all the students, from 1 (not important) to 5 (very important), and the average vote was automatically computed (and rounded) on the 25 votes (see column 4 in Table 4.2). Global ranking (column 5) shows that the student tries to build a global picture of the internship offer from all the categories in column 3 (the offer, the enterprise and their preferences).

Ranking	Contextual elements	Category	Votes (1 - 5)					Average value	Meaning
			1	2	3	4	5		
2	Public transport	Entreprise	0	0	5	6	14	4.36	mandatory
3	Working atmosphere	Entreprise	0	0	3	11	11	4.32	mandatory
9	Business Type (Type & Size)	Entreprise	0	3	8	10	5	3.65	mandatory
10	Work timetable	Entreprise	3	0	7	8	6	3.58	personal
12	Is the company hiring?	Entreprise	1	2	10	9	4	3.50	indifferent
14	Company turnover	Entreprise	1	0	16	5	3	3.36	indifferent
20	Location	Entreprise	5	2	4	7	7	3.12	personal
24	Competitors	Entreprise	6	3	10	2	4	2.80	indifferent
27	Confidentiality	Entreprise	15	0	0	0	10	2.60	binary
26	University partnerships?	Entreprise	8	4	6	1	6	2.72	personal
29	Listed company	Entreprise	14	4	3	2	2	1.96	personal
5	Teamwork	Offer	0	0	8	10	7	3.96	mandatory
7	Travels during internship?	Offer	0	4	2	13	6	3.84	mandatory
15	Perspective of employment	Offer	4	3	6	4	8	3.36	personal
18	Specification of the offer (e.g. From Bts to Bac+5)	Offer	4	0	10	9	2	3.20	indifferent
19	Internship period	Offer	4	1	10	7	3	3.16	indifferent
21	Is it my expertise field?	Offer	2	6	8	9	1	3.04	personal
22	Remuneration	Offer	1	6	13	3	2	2.96	personal
28	Advantages (Restaurant coupon, etc...)	Offer	7	7	6	2	3	2.48	personal
1	Interest of the proposed missions	Candidate	0	0	0	16	9	4.36	mandatory
4	Responsabilities	Candidate	0	0	3	17	5	4.08	mandatory
6	Initiatives	Candidate	0	2	3	15	5	3.92	mandatory
8	Autonomy	Candidate	0	0	8	16	1	3.72	indifferent
11	Compatibility with the professional project	Candidate	2	2	7	8	6	3.56	mandatory
13	Company reputation	Entreprise	3	2	7	6	7	3.48	personal
17	Previous professional experience	Candidate	1	5	9	6	4	3.28	personal
16	Profile compatibility with the offer	Candidate	4	1	8	8	4	3.28	personal
25	Language	Candidate	8	3	5	8	2	2.73	binary
23	Driving license required	Candidate	13	0	0	0	12	2.92	binary
30	Importance of required competences	Candidate	12	6	6	0	1	1.88	personal

Table 4.2. *List the contextual elements retained for modeling of "Internship-offer analysis"*

If it was easy to reach a consensus on the list of contextual elements to retain, conflicts appear on their ordering because interests and motivations of students in the choice of an internship were very different and generally non-negotiable (e.g. internship may be a preliminary condition for employment or not).

Three examples will illustrate the large dispersion on how contextual elements are considered. First, as expected, "interest of the mission" (rank 1 in Table 4.2) is the key element for all the students (internship must allow validation of acquired competences in management at least). Second, conversely, the "competences required" in the offer (rank 30) were considered necessary because they had a double competence disciplinary-management but not sufficient because students already considered this contextual element for selecting the offers. Three, the contextual element "location" (rank 20), although found relevant by students, corresponds to a weak consensus of students because "location" is strongly related to other contextual elements like the importance of the enterprise for the student (requiring motivation if the enterprise is far), the possibility of using a personal car (if they have a "driving license") or "public transport", the student's ambition to be accepted in the enterprise, etc. This observation points out the interest to study the correlations between contextual elements (this constrains the modeling as a contextual graph). Four, the contextual element "Driving license required" (rank 23), as the contextual element "confidentiality" (rank 27), shows two binary positions without intermediary votes. Students without a driving license and personal car (and also students opposed to this idea) will reject offers that required that candidates have a driving license, while student with a driving license will see the possibility to be mobile during their internship (e.g. go and visit customers).

The important lesson learned here is the difficulty of having a unique general model for analyzing an internship offer: each student has their own preferences for analyzing an internship offer and may weight a contextual element differently from other students. Students often weight a contextual element depending on the presence or absence of some other contextual elements. For example, driving license is important if the offer suggests the possibility to go and visit customers or the lack of public transportation for going to the enterprise (another extreme alternative being to rent a room close to the enterprise). Moreover, students associated contextual elements of different natures without considering first their rank in the classification. For example, students put in the same category "transport" (to go to the enterprise) and "work ambiance", although these two contextual elements belong to two different ontologies. Indeed, students created three categories in a goal-oriented way, not in a task-oriented way, namely the candidate (student's preferences), the enterprise and the offer content (column 6 in Table 4.2). The classification of contextual elements in a category was based on votes for allowing the expression of personal and context-based strategies of the students, which may include some side effects that are interesting for them but not others (e.g. when they like to travel). For analyzing an internship offer, students addressed first the internship mission but rapidly the contextual elements related to their preferences (e.g. "responsibilities", rank 4) and the enterprise, not the content of the internship offer directly (the first contextual element in this category is "teamwork" with rank 5).

The category "candidate" is not a classical user model or user profile but the result of a consensus among students. For example, students were especially sensible to the relationship of the internship with their professional project. They also were aware that "work experience" is a discriminating factor for a recruiter that supposes they find something to say to the recruiter (previous internships or summer jobs must be presented differently, for instance). The category "enterprise" describes the students' mental representation of an enterprise. Generally, parameters used by an enterprise for its presentation are not the first priority for students (e.g. they prefer listed enterprise, competitors, etc. to have something to say during their motivational interviewing). If keywords in the offer are well identified by students, students are also interested by "hidden keywords" like the possibility of hiring after the internship and do not hesitate to go onto the website of the enterprise to interpret the terms of the offer (eventually to find the person with whom they would work).

Instantiation of contextual elements can be obtained by application of production rules. Consider the contextual element "confidentiality" (rank 27) for which there are only two groups of students that find it "important" or not. This could be a blocking factor for different reasons, like a foreign student that will not be accepted for an internship in the French army. Another reason can be that the enterprise works on a topic that is interesting for a student, but the student may not want to stay in the enterprise after the internship and knows that they will not be authorized to work with a competitor during the next four years. It could be a severe pre-requisite for some students. However, "Confidentiality" has a low rank (27) and then a global model would consider this contextual element after other contextual elements. Conversely, foreigner students will check this condition early in their analysis because if they do not fill this mandatory clause, it is not necessary for them to continue the analysis of the internship offer. This point shows that a unique model for all students is not possible. Some different variants are presented in the contextual graph of Figure 4.9. (Note that at the time of the experiment, only the CxG_1.0 formalism existed.)

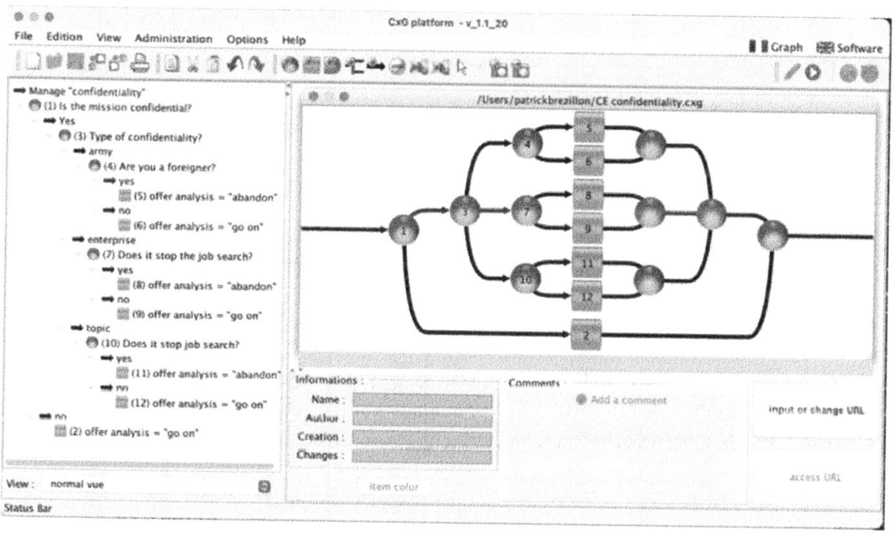

Figure 4.9. *Different consequences of the contextual element "confidentiality". For a color version of this figure, see www.iste.co.uk/brezillon/contextbasedmodeling.zip*

Figure 4.9 presents a model of the use of the contextual element that considers the reasons for confidentiality (the employer would be the army or a special enterprise, or the topic is highly delicate politically or commercially). From the student's viewpoint, for each of these reasons, we just check (for this example) if this could stop internship-offer analysis or not. Other paths may exist, such as the student is ready to lobby to be accepted.

4.3.4. *Interpretation of the results*

In Table 4.3, the list of contextual elements is reorganized with respect to the meanings according to students of the nature of the contextual elements. Four categories were retained concerning "mandatory", "indifferent", "personal" and "binary".

Ranking	Contextual elements	Category	Votes (1 - 5)					Average value
			1	2	3	4	5	
	Mandatory							
2	Public transport	Entreprise	0	0	5	6	14	4.36
3	Working atmosphere	Entreprise	0	0	3	11	11	4.32
9	Business Type (Type & Size)	Entreprise	0	3	8	10	5	3.65
5	Teamwork	Offer	0	0	8	10	7	3.96
7	Travels during internship?	Offer	0	4	2	13	6	3.84
1	Interest of the proposed missions	Candidate	0	0	0	16	9	4.36
4	Responsabilities	Candidate	0	0	3	17	5	4.08
6	Initiatives	Candidate	0	2	3	15	5	3.92
11	Compatibility with the professional project	Candidate	2	2	7	8	6	3.56
	Indifferent							
12	Is the company hiring?	Entreprise	1	2	10	9	4	3.50
14	Company turnover	Entreprise	1	0	16	5	3	3.36
24	Competitors	Entreprise	6	3	10	2	4	2.80
18	Specification of the offer (e.g. From Bts to Bac	Offer	4	0	10	9	2	3.20
19	Internship period	Offer	4	1	10	7	3	3.16
8	Autonomy	Candidate	0	0	8	16	1	3.72
	Personal							
26	University partnerships?	Entreprise	8	4	6	1	6	2.72
13	Company reputation	Entreprise	3	2	7	6	7	3.48
17	Previous professional experience	Candidate	1	5	9	6	4	3.28
16	Profile compatibility with the offer	Candidate	4	1	8	8	4	3.28
15	Perspective of employment	Offer	4	3	6	4	8	3.36
10	Work timetable	Entreprise	3	0	7	8	6	3.58
20	Location	Entreprise	5	2	4	7	7	3.12
21	Is it my expertise field?	Offer	2	6	8	9	1	3.04
29	Listed company	Entreprise	14	4	3	2	2	1.96
30	Importance of required competences	Candidate	12	6	6	0	1	1.88
22	Remuneration	Offer	1	6	13	3	2	2.96
28	Advantages (Restaurant coupon, etc...)	Offer	7	7	6	2	3	2.48
	Binary							
27	Confidentiality	Entreprise	15	0	0	0	10	2.60
25	Language	Candidate	8	3	5	8	2	2.73
23	Driving license required	Candidate	13	0	0	0	12	2.92

Table 4.3. *Student-centered categorization of contextual elements*

Student votes (mandatory, indifferent, personal, binary) must be contrasted with the global ranking of contextual elements. Students consider as mandatory 50% of contextual elements concerning the candidate against 25% for the enterprise and 25% for the offer. Students want to develop their personal values (responsibilities, initiative and autonomy), preferentially to what concerns the enterprise (and teamwork could be considered as related to the candidate). In the category "Indifferent", the values of the enterprise are not a priority (50% of contextual elements) and, again, 80% of contextual elements matter to students. Personal choices: 75% of contextual elements concern the enterprise and the offer, and 25% concerning the candidate are thus supposed to be normal implicitly in an offer. In the 75%, some contextual elements are external to the offer (e.g. timetable, location, reputation, university partnerships) but important for the student. For example, "location"[3] may be a problem for the student if the enterprise is in the far suburbs of the city, with no public transport, no restaurant, maybe a choice of moving close to the enterprise with the cost of an apartment, etc. Indeed, such contextual elements must be evaluated jointly with other contextual elements (e.g. location, transport, stores, etc.). Binary choices: one can say 100% concern the candidate (confidentiality is decided by the enterprise but concerns directly the candidate, like a foreigner). Contextual elements "confidentiality", "language" and "driving license" do not concern directly the interest of the offer but constrain strongly the student's decision-making. Half mandatory contextual elements belong to the class "candidate" (interest of the mission, responsibilities, initiatives, compatibility with the personal project).

Collaborative work was a success for students to identify contextual elements that are important for analyzing an internship offer, even though the importance of some contextual elements is a personal matter, especially when several contextual elements must be combined. During the collaborative work, each student benefits from hearing other students explain problems in their own words and thus learn more easily than from the teacher. Orally, students argue in their usual language and terms while what is written in the shared document is immediately corrected. The shared document has never been a battlefield for negotiation. Negotiation was led orally in an open way by students because it was faster in this way to reach an agreement on ideas, concepts, etc. than on sentences and development. The first steps of the collaborative modeling in the CxG_1.0 formalism, based on accepted contextual elements, saw the difficulty of assembling all contextual elements in a coherent global picture. The main reason was the difficulty of summarizing the importance of contextual elements for each student. Coupling a few contextual elements was possible (e.g. "location", "public transport", "advantages" like restaurant) but often concluded with diverging positions (e.g. need of a personal car

3. Cars do not have the same importance in France as they do in the USA, distances and the accessibility of public transportation is quite different too.

due to the lack of public transport in an industrial area where the enterprise is in the far suburbs). As a result, no global modeling of the task "internship-offer analysis" was possible. The solution would be to make a checklist of contextual elements up to each student to make a decision. Thus, the collaborative work led finally to identifying the building blocks of the offer-analysis model, while the real global modeling of the offer stays essentially personal.

Students retained the lesson that their decision-making depends crucially on contextual elements that had nothing to do directly with the internship offer. The experiment was reconducted the following two years with new promotions of students, but with different results according to different initial choices. For example, the following year students voted only for contextual elements they were interested in. The initial goal was not considered as a rigid procedure by any student, but a "skeleton of model" that students can flesh out to their personal needs and preferences.

The lack of a consensual model in the CXG_1.0 formalism leads us to modeling the task "Internship-offer analysis" in the CxG_2.0 formalism (five years after the experiment), that was developed for collaborative work but could be used for task realization by a unique actor and allowing intermediate variants during activity development. The main difference (with respect to the initial experiment) between the CXG_1.0 and CxG_2.0 versions of the CxG formalism concerns the mental representation that has a fixed structure in version 1.0 and a dynamic building of mental models (from contextual elements) in version 2.0. The modeling of the "Internship-offer analysis" activity in the formalism CxG_2.0 supposes a consideration of the contextual elements in Table 4.3 as independent subtasks. However, we decide to gather the 29 contextual elements (excluding the "interest of the mission, rank 1, accepted before the analysis) according to five groups in the following order: (1) the offer, (2) the enterprise, (3) personal context (sensible contextual elements for the students at the origin of the work), (4) social aspects and (5) practical aspects. The distribution of contextual elements is given in Table 4.4.

The offer		**Personal context**		**Practical aspects**	
21	Is it my expertise field?	**4**	Responsibilities	**20**	Location
18	Accuracy (e.g. M2 or master)	**8**	Autonomy	**2**	Public transport
11	Compatibility Profile-offer	**6**	Initiative	**23**	Driving license

27	Confidentiality	**11**	Compatibility with prof. project	**28**	Benefits (restaurant coupon, premium, etc.)
7	Travel during internship	**17**	Previous profession experience		
The enterprise		**Social aspects**			
13	Company reputation	**3**	Working atmosphere		
9	Business type	**5**	Teamwork		
12	Is the company hiring?	**10**	Work timetable		
15	Perspective of employment	**19**	Internship period		
14	Company turnover	**25**	Language		
24	Competitors	**30**	Required competences		
26	Univ. partnership				
29	Listed company				

Table 4.4. *Grouping of the contextual elements*

We thus obtain a contextual graph with five branches for representing the groups. RCEs RECIPIENT and TASK_STATUS were used respectively for designing a group of contextual elements and representing a particular contextual element (or a subgroup of them). The results (complete graph and tree representations) being too large for the book, we proceeded with the CxG-based simulations to illustrate how a student can proceed to their analysis of an offer and show only a small part for the explanation. Figure 4.10 gives the part of the contextual graph that represents the group "The offer".

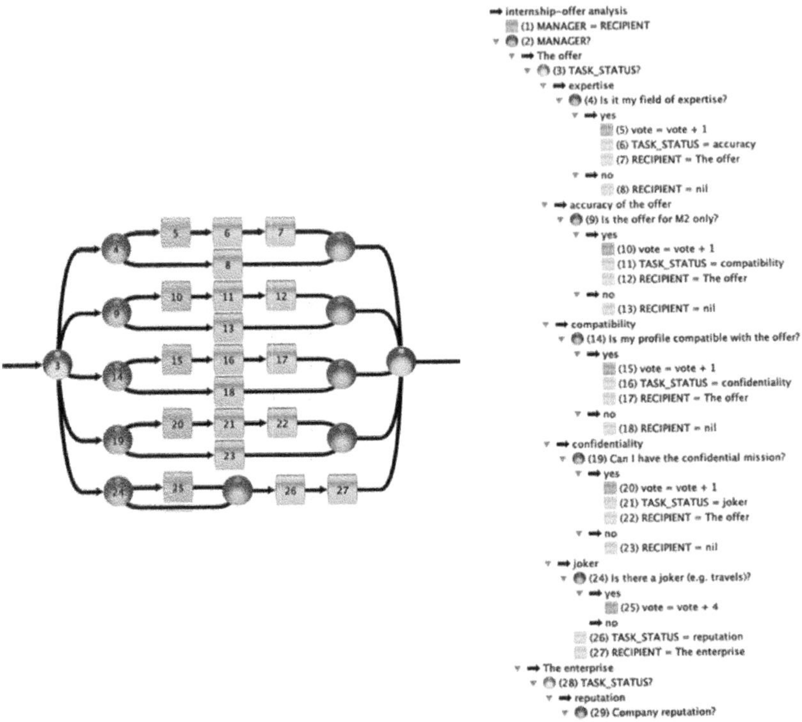

Figure 4.10. *Part "the offer" of the contextual graph representing "internship-offer analysis". For a color version of this figure, see www.iste.co.uk/brezillon/contextbasedmodeling.zip*

RCEs RECIPIENT and TASK_STATUS represent what will be done at the next step of the simulation, the group (RECIPIENT) and the contextual element checked (TASK_STATUS). The last RCEs (numbers 26 and 27) in the group "The offer" gives the link for going to the next group "The enterprise". RECIPIENT = "nil" indicates stopping the simulation at the end of the step if the student finds a reason to reject the offer (e.g. the student has no driving license as required). The action (green square box) shows a counter (vote) that indicates the number of contextual elements positively considered by the student (not used in this task modeling, but the total gives the student's subjective evaluation of the offer).

Figure 4.11 shows that the CxG-based simulation begins with the presentation of the initial working context (see part on the left) with all the contextual elements for the selection of their instantiations (popup menu at the right of each contextual element) with possible instantiations shown for the first contextual element (MANAGER).

Contextual elements are ordered according to their ranking in each class. Each time a contextual element is instantiated, the list of possible contextual elements to be instantiated decreases. For example, once MANAGER = "The offer", it is not necessary to consider contextual elements in the other groups. The process ends when all instantiations on the path are known and the simulation can run. The right part of Figure 4.11 shows the simulation trace corresponding to the simulation in Figure 4.12. This trace is accessible to students and contains additional information like the evolution of the voting system. It is also possible to have a sequence of images corresponding to changes for an animated gif.

****

Simulation Trace

****

internship-offer analysis

MANAGER = RECIPIENT

MANAGER?

The offer

TASK_STATUS?

expertise

Is it my field of expertise?

yes

vote = vote + 1

TASK_STATUS = accuracy

RECIPIENT = The offer

SENDER = MANAGER

internship-offer analysis

MANAGER = RECIPIENT

MANAGER?

The offer

TASK_STATUS?

compatibility

Is my profile compatible with the offer?

yes

vote = vote + 1

TASK_STATUS = confidentiality

RECIPIENT = The offer

SENDER = MANAGER

Figure 4.11. *Working context at the start of the simulation (left part) and simulation trace (right part). For a color version of this figure, see www.iste.co.uk/brezillon/contextbasedmodeling.zip*

Figure 4.12 shows the instantiations of MANAGER (first contextual element to instantiate), of TASK_STATUS (the contextual element "Is my profile compatible with the offer?") and the result of the simulation where the path follows is in red in the graph window. At the end of the simulation (in our experiment, at the instantiation of the last contextual element, vote is incremented by 1 and the instantiation of TASK_STATUS is changed for "confidentiality", the next contextual element to reach), the small window at the bottom of the graph allows us to confirm the pursuit of the CxG-based simulation or not.

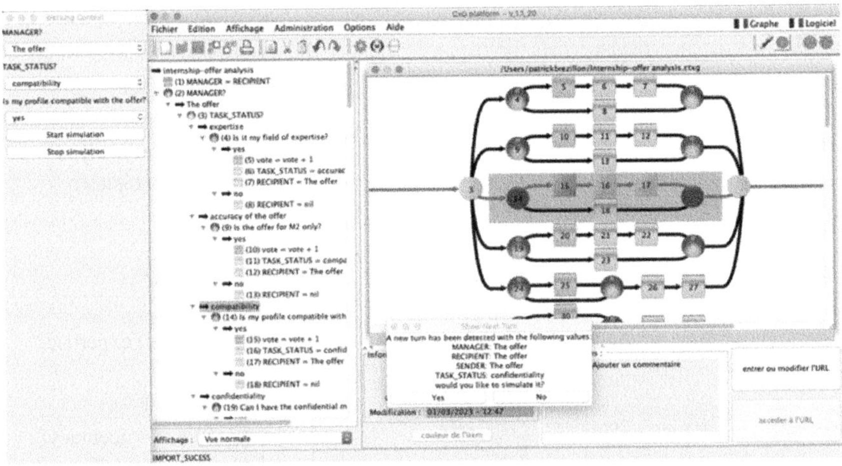

Figure 4.12. *Intermediary results of the CxG-based simulation. For a color version of this figure, see www.iste.co.uk/brezillon/contextbasedmodeling.zip*

In our experiment, an independent subtask is just a contextual element. Then, the interest of the model in the CxG_2.0 formalism (normally for collaborative tasks) is that each student can select among the consensual list the contextual elements that they consider significant for them. In the CxG_2.0 formalism, students have the possibility of an *a la carte* exploration of the contextual graph (i.e. the list of contextual elements) according to their choices of instantiation of the contextual elements (e.g. choosing first MANAGER = "Social aspects" or going back on "The offer" for a different set of instantiations for simulation of alternatives).

The purpose of this experiment is different from what we thought initially. The previous promotions acted as a community of interest by sharing the same goal (internship-offer) analysis but only for their personal benefit. Students had not looked for a collective solution to the problem but only a support for each solution building for their personal quest from the list of contextual elements considered as a skeleton for their practice building. It is why students were ready to accept unpleasant solutions of others because they knew they could change them for their personal use, while a collaborative solving of the same problem (e.g. how to go together somewhere) is a radically different situation. This version lets students compare alternatives before choosing and finding arguments for the motivational letter and interview, understanding the choice of a fellow, etc. The voting system also adds factual (subjective anyway) information on decision-making to comfort students.

4.3.5. *Comparison with the "DVD-reader diagnosis" task*

In the example of the DVD reader, collaborative work concerned a task realization for which all students had the same personal goal, "see a movie", but each student had a particular movie in mind and a particular device. Thus, when a fault occurs on the DVD reader, the collaboration was only on the modeling of the task realization "DVD reader diagnosis". The personal knowledge and personal experience shared among students concerns movies and the general use of a DVD reader, that is, more its functioning than its technology. Thus, their decision-making is mainly at the operational level (while decision-making in the internship-offer is more at the tactical level). The diagnosis of a hardware system aims to determine the origin of the fault from information recorded by observations, check and test them. Indeed, it is similar to diagnosis in general medicine, that is, disease identification from its symptoms. In these two domains, only external perception of the item's (device or body) behavior is concerned (Brézillon 2007).

First, the procedure relies mainly on the natural structure of domain knowledge. In the user manual concerning DVD-reader diagnosis, the designer organizes domain knowledge (e.g. electrical part, mechanical part, video part, etc.) in a parallel structure, which corresponds to the usual paradigm "divide and conquer". Conversely, users developmental models based on a use-oriented organization of the domain in a serial structure of knowledge needs for their task realization: (1) switch on the TV and the DVD reader (and thus potential power supply problems can be identified and solved), (2) introduce a DVD in the device (and thus, potential mechanical problems are discovered and considered), etc. The engineer (as expert) develops a prescribed task in a logic of functioning (a parallel structure), and users (as novices) apply an effective task in a logic of use, that is, a serial structure (Richard 1983).

When a DVD reader presents a troubleshooting problem, users may (eventually) refer to the user manual provided with the device. Generally, there is a one-page aid for troubleshooting in a 40-page manual. However, the effective task (solving the troubleshooting problem) of users may be either to follow instructions in the user manual or to identify the problem by themselves. We first translated the troubleshooting page of the user manual (the prescribed task) into a contextual graph by defining each problem as a specific activity with all the details given in the user manual. The contextual graph resulting from the troubleshooting page is presented in the simplified view (Figure 4.13) (C stands for contextual element and A for activity).

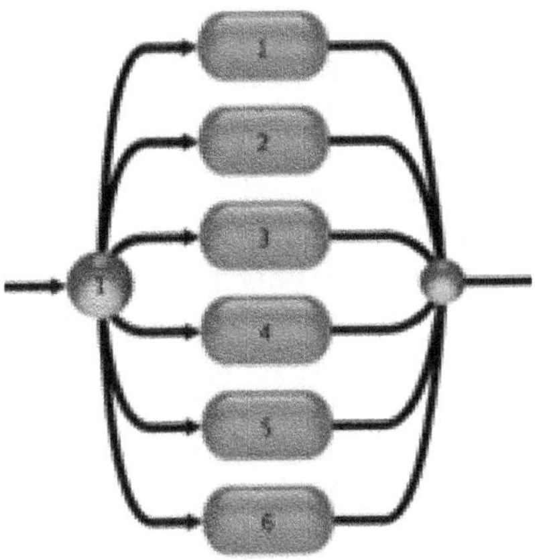

C1: Type of problem?
- A1: Power problem-solving
- A2: Video problem-solving
- A3: Audio problem-solving
- A4: Password problem-solving
- A5: Mechanical problem-solving
- A6: Other problem-solving

Figure 4.13. *Representation of the diagnosis page in the user manual of the DVD reader. For a color version of this figure, see www.iste.co.uk/brezillon/contextbasedmodeling.zip*

According to the engineering viewpoint (prescribed task), the knowledge structure is top-down because the task model relies heavily on domain knowledge and its structure in terms of mechanics, power, audio, video, etc. This "logic of functioning" is represented as exclusive alternatives in the contextual graph (no combination of faults is considered) because each step in the engineer's reasoning is based on a hypothetical-deductive approach. The user model in this troubleshooting presentation impacts the level of detail to be provided (but all the users, novices as well as experts are represented at the same level in the troubleshooting page). As a result, for a novice with a supposedly very low level of understanding, the explanation is "If you do not see a red light at the front of your device, then check if the device is connected to the power source", and, on the same fault page, there are other explanations like "Change AV" for experts with specialized knowledge without explaining what AV means (AV means audio-video). Figure 4.14 gives the detailed part of the "Video problem solving" activity from the engineers' viewpoint.

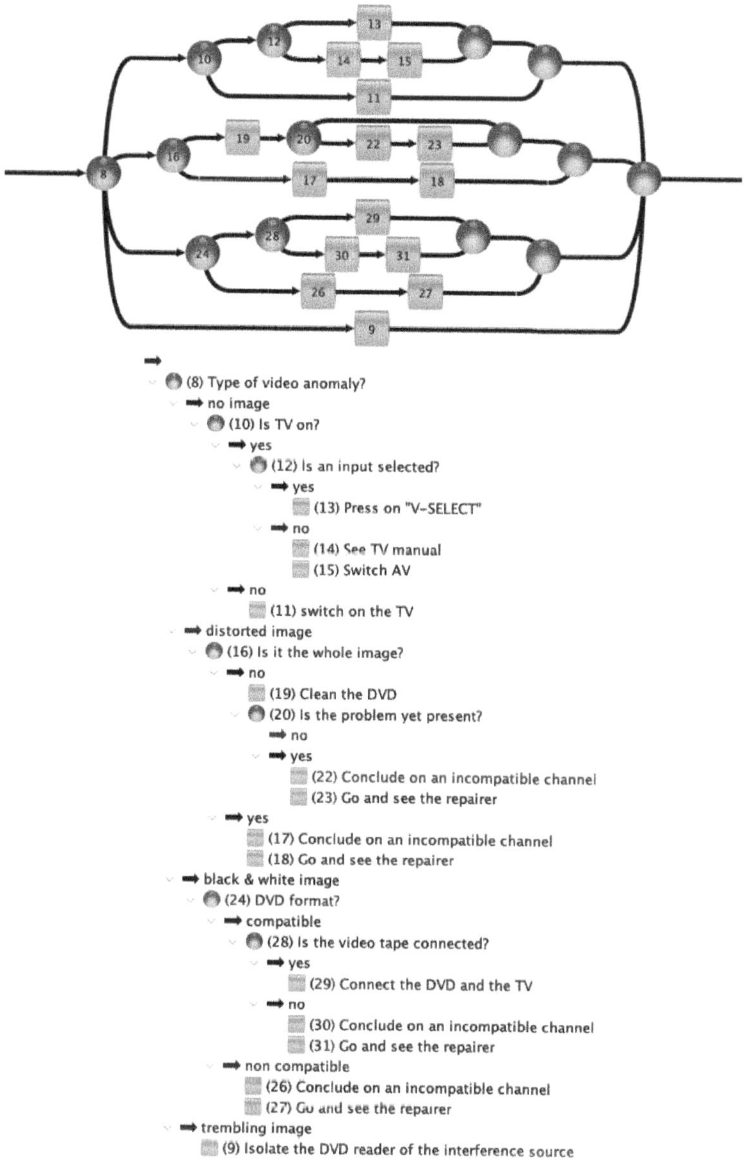

Figure 4.14. *The video problem-solving activity (Activity A2 in Figure 4.13). For a color version of this figure, see www.iste.co.uk/brezillon/contextbasedmodeling.zip*

The mental model for the DVD reader diagnosis was the result of the collective work of a group of 17 students in the second year of the Innovation-Management Master at Université Pierre et Marie Curie (Paris, France, previous name of Sorbonne University). After numerous critics of the fault page in the user manual, students decide to attack the problem from their user viewpoint. The goal of the experiment was to express in the CxG formalism their collective understanding of instructions, not to compare their individual understanding. All students were aware of how to use a DVD reader, although with different perceptions and experience but with the same goal: "See a movie on DVD", which is a usual task for a user. This (normal) task is accomplished regularly by users, and each time with success. Rapidly, students were confused with the logic of functioning in the user manual ("Why put password problem on the same level as video problems?"). It appeared rapidly that users move from their normal task to the troubleshooting task only when a problem occurs at one step of the routine (sequential) task. Thus, the step of the normal task where troubleshooting occurs is immediately known, knowing that previous steps of the normal task are accomplished correctly. Figure 4.15 presents the contextual graph easily obtained consensually.

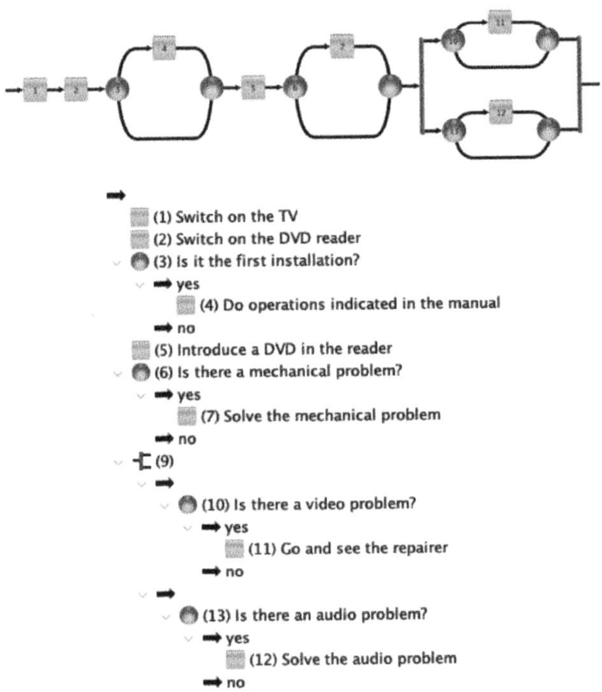

Figure 4.15. *Collaborative modeling of DVD-Reader diagnosis. For a color version of this figure, see www.iste.co.uk/brezillon/contextbasedmodeling.zip*

The result of this collaborative work is heavily experience-based. For example, it is natural for them to switch on the TV first (not explained in the user manual) because instructions on the DVD appear on the TV screen before playing a DVD because "I know that the contents of the DVD (i.e. the menu and the movie choice) are shown on the TV screen", and I know that the DVD reader is "on" because the TV and DVD reader are on the same plug (a contextual element that is not considered in the user manual). As a result, first, they contextualize the modeling within their environment and, second, they begin modeling a troubleshooting mental model at the step of their "See a movie on DVD" task where a discrepancy appears with what they expect. They follow a logic of use, but it is not a bottom-up approach, which would contrast with the top-down approach in task model (it would be a perpendicular approach). Indeed, a mental model of a normal functioning is sequential, and potential problems will appear sequentially (first power problems, second mechanical ones, etc.) and are ramified when different experiences and/or contexts intervene at each step. While the task model considered by the engineer has a parallel architecture (Figure 4.13), the mental model has a series architecture (Figure 4.15). There is also a strong difference at a finer level of description. Users have bought their DVD reader, and this operation is not made frequently (it was relatively expensive in 2005). Moreover, engineering parameters that are too subtle for the user (e.g. "Is the image completely or only partially distorted?") may lead the user to carry out the wrong action, which consequently could lead to the destruction of the device (that is expensive too). Users then prefer to sum up the technical instructions in one action "Send to the repairer".

Unlike the engineer's concern, users pay attention to whether the device is under warranty or not, whereas this is not considered in the user manual. Users are also perfectly aware that they have special actions to do the first time they install the DVD player. This knowledge relies on their experience and the similarity between the new device and devices already installed at home. A DVD reader needs power supply, an image appears on the TV screen, which therefore must be switched on first and connected to the DVD reader, the remote control needs a battery and user–device interaction will take place through the TV screen. There is also new information to learn, generally when a step of the mental model is new, like the first time the user watches a movie on several DVDs (e.g. The Lord of the Rings) or on a double-sided DVD. All other problems will cause users to go and take the device to the repairer.

For the "Internship-offer analysis" activity, the "specificities" of the analysis of the internship offer matter a lot in each student's experience. Students share contextual elements on the enterprise and the offer, but their interpretation may differ largely, and thus, specificities of the offer intervene. The knowledge involved in the analysis of an internship offer is domain and personal knowledge. To analyze corresponds to determining the constituent elements of the internship offer. Thus, the goal is to look for the information in the offer, both visible and also hidden, and attached information on the enterprise, for example, start-ups recruit flexible profiles of students, while international enterprises prefer candidates coming from other international groups. The offer specifies the researched profile of the student (training, experience, know-how). Indeed, the "internship-offer analysis" activity is only a subtask of the global activity: "Have an internship before the beginning of the internship period", with other subtasks like "Write your cover letter" and "Succeed in your motivational interview". These subtasks are strongly "student-driven", that is, based on personal contextual elements of the student. "Internship-offer analysis" must be considered with a large spectrum of contextual elements that each student needs to instantiate in a specific way according to their individual context. All the students share the same contextual elements, but their instantiations are specific to each student (salary, transport, etc.). Thus, it is a large spectrum of instantiations rather than of contextual elements that explain the dispersion of votes on some contextual elements in Table 4.4.

4.4. CxG formalism for CIAS Design

Four generations of AI systems testify to an evolution in the design of AI systems, namely expert systems, knowledge-based systems (KBSs), joint cognitive systems (JCSs) and intelligent systems. Our testimony relies on different real-world applications in different domains, especially for the French national power company, the subway company in Paris, in medicine, a platform for e-maintenance, road safety and open sources (Brézillon 2023). Each generation tried to address the failures previously encountered for modeling human expert knowledge because operational knowledge allows the contextualization of theoretical knowledge used in formal representations.

Expert systems separated the representation and the use of declarative knowledge instead of procedural knowledge. However, part of the knowledge, which comes from technical domains, has an organization and a structure that were not considered explicitly and thus not used directly by expert systems. As a result, implicit knowledge (e.g. screening clauses) was used to control the inference engine. For example, the SART expert system for real-time diagnosis in extra-high voltage substations (400,000 volts) was developed from the technical knowledge on equipment in substations (section 1.3.3). The expert system was validated in an EHV substation near Paris (flat ground) with success, but a second validation failed in an EHV substation in the Alps (the station was in a narrow valley in mountains). The technical knowledge did not deal with the difference of contexts of the two substations (e.g. line spacing). The retained solution was to develop a knowledge configurator of the expert system (we would call it now a "contextualizer") for each substation instead to tackle the modeling of context.

KBSs worked on knowledge acquired prior to its use (i.e. decontextualized), while experts always provide knowledge in a specific context that knowledge engineers did not consider because they modeled couples (problem, solution), not triples (problem, context, solution). For example, a KBS for incident solving in the subway of Paris was developed based on procedures established by the company from the practices recorded during incident solving on subway lines. The formalization of a practice set as a procedure corresponded to a decontextualization of the practices (specific details were pushed to the side). As a result, operators were obliged to contextualize the procedure to address the specificity of the incident at hand. For instance, the time of occurrence of an incident may be rush hour or night hour. The operator will use a fast procedure at rush hour to avoid a degenerated incidental situation, whereas they will use a safe procedure at night hour. Thus, two aspects of context appear (but were not distinguished at that time): the contextual element (here, "time of occurrence of the incident") and its instantiation (here, rush hour or night hour).

Nevertheless, four failures of the use of early AI systems are pointed out (Brézillon and Pomerol 1996):

– The user is excluded from the problem-solving process, while the user knows the context in which the problem occurs.

– The system does not use knowledge correctly because its contextual dimension is not acquired with it.

– The system cannot initially possess all the required knowledge, which must be acquired incrementally when needed, jointly with its context of use.

– The system cannot generate relevant explanations because the system and user do not share enough knowledge for constructing explanations.

Then, AI systems moved from the view of KBSs towards two close approaches, namely *Situated Cognition* and JCSs. The *Situated Cognition* approach insists on the necessity of considering the environment of problem-solving, but it was more conceptual claims than implementation. The JCS approach concerns the complementarity of the human (the user) and the system with respect to problem-solving, especially on their cognitive asymmetry (Woods 1985). This complementarity supposes that AI systems are able to realize several tasks for interacting with users, such as knowledge acquisition, learning, simulation and explanation. This means that the AI system must be able to acquire new knowledge incrementally when needed, that is, with the context of the missing knowledge. This requires making the context explicit (i.e. modeled) in AI systems and associating knowledge, reasoning and context. However, few context-based approaches exist. Moreover, the context model must not be a layer between data and applications or a middleware or ontology like those found in the literature because context is intimately linked to knowledge and reasoning. Thus, it appears that context plays a central role in the modeling of knowledge and reasoning in an activity for reinforcing the "intelligence" side of AI systems.

Two approaches to context-based systems generally are evoked in AI: formal and pragmatic approaches (Turner and Brézillon 2022). Formal approaches concern formal properties and relationships between a set of discrete contexts and only try to solve real problems, while pragmatic approaches focus first on solving real-world problems and then on abstracting general principles from what has been done. Later, Artificial Intelligence (AI) systems aim to understand actor(s) through their decisions, actions and behaviors, not from some abstract actor model or profile from a library but with the support of algorithms. Despite the great success of AI systems over everything that existed before, it is still impossible to know in advance all the contextual variants of a solution. Context-based explanations are an intrinsic part of the construction (Brézillon and Abu-Hakima 1995).

We distinguish Intelligent Assistant Systems (IASs) and "Intelligent systems" (or AI systems) because the latter is a term used in formal approaches like algorithms where experts' knowledge is in the machine, but humans do not participate in the activity (task realization, decision-making or problem-solving) like with an IAS. On the one hand, expert systems were rejected by users that considered them a black box addressing 80% of the problems users understood but missing 20% of the problems for which users want support, On the other hand, users abandoned KBSs due to their too limited knowledge. This shows that intelligent systems are efficient when the experts' knowledge can be put in the form of an algorithm for problem-solving, that is, without the help of a user. However, it is not enough. Intelligent systems' knowledge about context is often sparse. It may rely on location (GPS), internet-based services (weather, etc.) and expected properties of the task, as well as an actor profile based on statistical considerations and augmented, or selected, with the help of available sensors (e.g. biometric sensors for identification or determining physiological state).

In situations where the intervention of the users in an activity is mandatory, especially in non-formal or non-technological domains where the unexpected events are the norm, the task must be co-realized jointly by the user and the system, the main reason being that users and systems have complementary competences. However, the decision power must stay in the hand of the users in domains, such as the control room of a nuclear plant. An IAS exploiting experience bases will be able to propose more effective support to users than previous KBSs. The experience bases developed for an activity also can be used by humans for training future experts on how to behave in the different ways to make a decision according to the variants of the working context (Tahir and Brézillon 2013). In that sense, IASs interact at the tactical decisional level with users (the choice of a solution), while previous systems (especially those aiming to replace users) are at the lower operation decisional level. However, most IASs lack any attention to the full panoply of facts, knowledge and details that is the total context in which IASs and actors cooperate.

We thus prefer to recall these IASs that use context as a central component of their behavior, CIASs. The actor stays the decision-maker and the CIAS mainly proposes satisfying alternatives and may justify them, including recalling relevant points from previous interactions, and even from previous realizations of an activity in different contexts. Actors' expertise is highly compiled contextual knowledge built mainly by experience and is generally used in decision-making process leading to critical and definitive decision. A CIAS is a decision-support system for actors that have such a high level of expertise in a domain that is not well-known or too complex. First, the CIAS must be able to follow what experts are doing and how they are doing it and anticipate their needs. This means that the system must have some model of the experts' reasoning (e.g. like a mental representation of users' experience), but it needs to be a competent secretary, solving all the simple problems the experts encounter by itself and preparing dossiers on complex situations to enable the experts to make their own decisions. A CIAS must work like a human and must be understandable to a human.

The CIAS's line of reasoning relies on human experts' line of contextual and nonlinear reasoning as available in their mental representation. A CIAS developed in the CxG formalism offers the possibility of exploiting reasoning in a contextual graph (a mental representation) and developing a mental model (a line of reasoning in a specific context) using a CxG-based simulation that presents other abilities such as explanation, browsing, knowledge acquisition, learning, training and communication. As such, CxG-based simulations allow a CIAS the exploitation of a contextual graph as an experience base (Brézillon 2023). As a simulator, the CIAS builds progressively a mental model with the possibility of going back in the reasoning developed. The CIAS can easily monitor a contextual graph, thanks to the description of contextual elements as questions (e.g. temperature?) with its known values (e.g. "warm" and "cold"). The CIAS, arriving at such a contextual element, looks for the instantiation in the shared context that is attached to the contextual graph. A "manual" version of the CIAS is presented in the CxG simulation presented in section 3.4.4.

Note that the CIAS finds an instantiation of the contextual element by using the sources of context, if this is not possible, the CIAS can ask the actor for the value and the new reasoning step, but it also can access the internet to find a proposal to submit to the actor. A CIAS is a decision-support system for actors that have a high level of expertise in a domain, which is not well-known or too complex. There are several consequences. The CIAS must be able to follow what experts are doing and how they are doing it and anticipate their needs. This means that the system must have some model of experts' reasoning (e.g. experience bases). To be a competent secretary, the system can solve simple problems and prepare documents on complex situations to enable experts to make their own decisions. CIAS's line of reasoning relies on human experts' reasoning as represented in a mental representation.

A CIAS also requires several abilities.

Simulation. A CxG-based simulation develops the dynamic of a given reasoning on domain knowledge for various reasons (validation purposes, checking alternatives, playing or replaying a reasoning sequence in different contexts, explanation purposes, etc.). The simulator is a tool that allows the system to provide rich explanations of different types and levels of details on group-activity development and to be a decision-support system by analyzing all the features of a mental model at any moment of an activity and thus proposing an anticipation capability. It is often the unique means for nonlinear reasoning.

Explanation. Explanation facilitates the development of the shared context between the CIAS and the actor. The generation of an explanation can be viewed as a contextualization process where the system accepts explanations from the actor and then change its knowledge organization accordingly. In order to align the actor's and system's reasonings, the actor and the system must cooperate to co-construct the explanation in the current context of the activity at hand. Explanations thus are considered as an intrinsic part of the activity, and, therefore, the reasoning line of the system may be modified by explanation. This leads to cooperative activity development where the proceduralized context, which is associated with the mental-model development, can be unfolded to explain the rationale behind the development of the mental model in a given context.

There are different types of context-based explanations that are possible thanks to the real-time development of a mental model, such as visual explanations, dynamic explanations, actor-based explanations, micro- and macro-explanations and real-time explanations; these different explanations can be combined in different ways such as visual and dynamic explanations for presenting future alternatives and abandoned options (Brézillon 2008). The main categories of explanations identified in the CxG formalism are as follows:

– Visual explanations are linked to the graphical presentation of a set of complex information: contextual-graph growth, the mental-mode development, changes introduced by an actor, etc.

– Dynamic explanations are associated with the progress of the mental-model development, anticipation and presentation of alternatives, explanations with different granularity and chronology for introduction of the practices (items can be introduced anywhere in the contextual graph).

– Actor-based explanations concern the information known by the system regarding practices that have been developed by actors (detailed explanation on unknown parts by the actor and sum up parts developed by the actor).

– Context-based explanations for presenting why an activity is "good" in one context and "bad" in another one, thanks to proceduralized contexts as ordered sequences of instantiated contextual elements.

– Micro- and macro-explanations use activity representation either as an entity (for macro-explanation) or a subgraph (for micro-explanation), thus at different granularity levels. A macro-explanation is given from an external viewpoint on the location of the activity in the contextual graph. A micro-explanation presents how the activity is realized step-by-step.

– Real-time explanations are composed of (a) learning-support explanation asked by the system during a problem-solving when it fails to match the actor's activity in its experience base; (b) reading-support to the actor to follow a mental-model development realized by another colleague and (c) activity-support by the IAS to the actor for preparing in parallel their work.

Browsing is quite different from simulation with respect to time in the decision-making process. A CxG Browser works at a tactical level where time is not considered explicitly (e.g. duration of an action and loop on routine action do not matter) because browsing concerns more practices in a comparative way rather than the effective development of a practice in a specific context (e.g. comparison of a given recipe in different cookbooks like at an operational level). Reasoning is more on the realizability of the task than its effective realization (i.e. the first step in the decision-making process). Browsing a contextual graph is a kind of qualitative simulation of experiences for two reasons. Firstly, observing only the reasoning contained in the contextual graph (e.g. to know that a particular action must be executed, but without concern about the effective execution of the action). This concerns only a description of the experience base, the presentation of all the practices known by the system. It is important for learning and explanation capabilities. Secondly, looking at how the relevant contextual elements are intervening, their instantiations in different working contexts and the actions to assemble for developing the different practices. For developing an activity, the CxG Simulator considers (1) time and (2) the qualitative effect of an action execution (e.g. its duration that may constrain the start of another action).

Incremental knowledge (and context of use) acquisition is the answer to the fact that a system cannot have all the needed knowledge at the design time. Incremental knowledge acquisition plays an important role in two situations. Firstly, when the knowledge is missing in the current context, the actor adds new knowledge through explanations, and the system acquires new knowledge in its context of use. Explanations enable the proceduralization of contextual knowledge with the new knowledge pieces. Secondly, a chunk of knowledge may be known by the system but incorrectly used, that is, a link to the current context is missing. Here, incremental knowledge acquisition will be on the refinement of the proceduralized context, and explanation will support that refinement. The approach relies on the fact that experts' knowledge is essentially a justification (i.e. explanation) of their judgment in that context. In the CxG formalism, the incremental acquisition of new practices allows the retrieval of the history of the uses of a given practice, its application in different contexts and/or the use of alternative practices in a given context. An actor can thus replay the solving of a given incident and apply different practices to check the consequences and how the changes of context can affect the quality of the practices and, finally, retain for the next time the strategy that is the most relevant in the particular context.

Learning allows CIASs to "learn by interacting with actors" and become increasingly familiar with actors and their way of accomplishing their activity. This type of learning does not rely on training datasets (i.e. a kind of decontextualized learning) but from activities accomplished by actors (a kind of contextualized learning). Learning occurs incrementally and concerns new mental models developed by the actor not yet in its experience base. There are two types of learning, either the actor learns from the system or the system learns from the actor. In the former situation, with mechanisms such as explanation, generation and simulation, the system plays the role of a trainer for novices not familiar with mental-models developed by other actors. During this learning by the actor, the experience base is exploited in a kind of procedure-based learning. The second type of learning occurs when the actor stops the system for specifying a variant of a reasoning step that does not exist in the experience base. Thus, the system plays the role of a learner that will have to modify its experience base. In the CxG formalism such a variant occurs generally when a contextual element was not considered up to now (e.g. it kept the same instantiation during all the task realization), but in that specific context, the instantiation is different and the actor decides to execute a different action. During its learning, the system will enrich incrementally the experience base in a kind of learning by assimilation. There is a learning by accommodation when it is a new contextual element that is introduced instead of an instantiation change. Note that during the two types of learning, the system is in a phase of incremental knowledge acquisition (see the "coffee preparation" example in section 2.4.3).

Training. Conversely, the CIAS may be a trainer for actors not quite familiar with mental models for accomplishing an activity as described in the experience base of the CIAS. The training here consists of explaining elements used during mental-model development, especially contextual elements and their instantiations in the proceduralized context and the variants abandoned (for other instantiations of the contextual element).

Communication. Communication is a key ability of a system for actor–CIAS interaction during their joint activity. Communication component must be able to handle interruptions, reorient as needed and resume work at any point by using the other abilities for explaining, learning practices and acquiring knowledge. Communication also concerns interaction among the tools of the CIAS, which are interdependent, and, on the contrary, between tools and actors. Thus, the actor has a unique interlocutor that avoid the cognitive overload of actors with as many languages to know as tools by managing complex questions in which several modules may intervene partially. A part of the interaction manager in charge of interruption, reorientation, resuming facilities at any point and the possibility to obtain information on the status of the search (Where are we? What can be done from this state?, etc.).

The CxG Platform (Brézillon 2014) contains an editor with the usual functions for managing a contextual graph, reading practices, browsing alternative of the practice that is developed, exploring a contextual graph at different granularities (an activity can be expanded as a contextual subgraph), analyzing (contextual) information attached to each item (date of creation, author, comments, etc.) and managing data. The CxG software, available under GNU license, is written in Java, and contextual graphs are stored as XML files to be available to other software (an activity and a contextual graph are stored as independent XML files). Design and development of the software are user-centered for easy use by non-specialists in computer science and mathematics (students, physicians, psychologists, etc.) and 15 min training is sufficient for starting a modeling in a contextual graph. It also is possible to link an item in the contextual graph to an external document (Word, PDF, etc.), to run an external piece of software, etc. The CxG platform offers the possibility of implementing into the CIASs all the cited abilities (explanation, browsing, incremental knowledge acquisition, learning and communication) that operate on the same experience base (a contextual graph) as a shared medium for them.

The CxG-based simulator is the main tool of a CIAS that allows real-time decision-making and anticipation of outcomes even when there is a lack of comprehensive a priori planning. Thus, the CIAS may determine how to behave according to predictions, anticipating future states that may affect its present states. It also allows the exploration of different types of nonlinear reasoning: validation, checking alternatives, replaying reasoning in different contexts, negotiation between group actors, explanation, etc. CxG-based simulations may provide the generation of explanations for predictions and make the CIAS an effective decision-support system. In that sense, a CxG-based simulation is a particular type of simulation, but with specific properties quite different from the more usual model-based simulation.

Figure 4.16 proposes a general architecture of a CIAS. In addition to the tools already discussed, there is a base of external facts that allows the transfer of data or information between the different external applications and services triggered by an action in the contextual graph. The CIAS manages this fact base because some information at the operational level may be relevant for it (e.g. the change of instantiation of a contextual element). Domain expertise is contained uniquely in the CxG experience base, and data and information of the domain are contained in the base of external facts. Thus, this architecture may be applied in different domains just by changing these databases, and, in a given domain, the expertise of one or several actors can be combined over these databases.

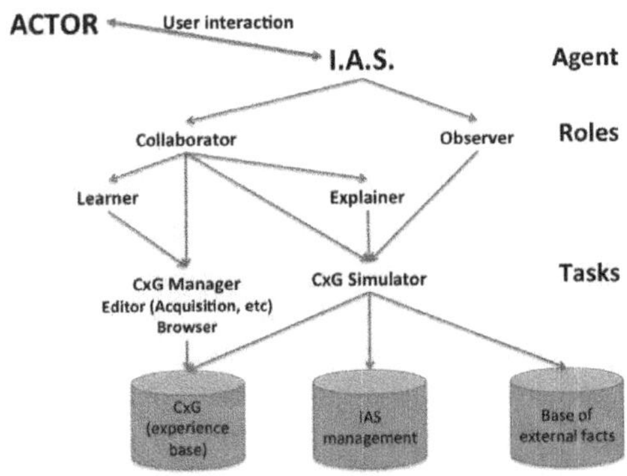

Figure 4.16. *Proposal of an architecture of CIASs. For a color version of this figure, see www.iste.co.uk/brezillon/contextbasedmodeling.zip*

The CIAS can take different roles with the actor, such as collaborator and observer, and its architecture is organized at three levels: agent, role and task. Each role corresponds to different tasks at two (sub-) levels and is controlled by the CxG_Manager and the CxG_Simulator. The CIAS exploits three bases. Firstly, experience base corresponds to contextual graphs representing domain expertise as the actors' mental representation. Thus, this architecture can be applied in different domains with limited changes. Secondly, the base of external facts allows the transfer of some data or information between different external applications and services triggered by an action in the contextual graph. The CIAS manages this fact base because some information at the operational level may be relevant for managing mental model development at the tactical level as a source of context. For example, an action may cause a change of instantiation of a contextual element that leads the CIAS to modify its mental-model building.

The CxG_Manager helps the actor in contextual-graph management incrementally acquire new knowledge and learn new mental models enriching the experience base. CxG Simulator automates, under the control of the actor, mental-model development according to the context associated with the contextual graph, integrating the consequences of action execution. The modules shared-context management and action management are part of the "personal experience base" and belong to the CIAS management module. The personal-experience base also contains knowledge (described in a contextual graph too) about coordination of its different modules (action, shared context) and a module for interaction management with the actor. Working on a human experience base, a CIAS would behave similarly to a human, and thus, it is possible to have a description of tool management made by the CIAS in contextual graphs too.

The next step is to study the possibility of mapping between the actor's mental model and the simulator "mental model" for modeling their actor–system interaction. The situation seems relatively simple in battlefield simulation (see TACTIC project) because it was possible, on the one hand, to help the operator express their mental models as expert maps, and, on the other hand, identify data sources of their simulator as three databases. However, it may not be as direct as in other applications (i.e. between human actors). As an assistant, a CIAS is a decision support system for actors that has a high level of expertise in a domain not well known or too complex. Actors' expertise is highly compiled like chunks of contextual knowledge built mainly by experience. Such an expertise is generally used in a decision-making process leading to a critical and definitive decision. The consequences are as follows:

1. The CIAS follows what the expert is doing, how they are doing it, anticipating a potential mental model as the target, thanks to the representation of the experts' reasoning. The system must be an excellent secretary, solving alone all the simple problems of human experts and preparing a complete file on complex situations letting experts make their decision.

2. The CIAS work from mental models developed by experts with the contextual elements used by the expert during their development. The line of system reasoning is drawn from lines of experts' reasoning described in the experience base. This gives an actor-centered representation of the domain (Brézillon 2003).

3. The CIAS must be able to develop a decision-making process in real-time to analyze the association diagnosis and action built by experts during their reasoning (Brézillon and Pomerol 1999). Indeed, the system simultaneously develops the decision-making process and its context-specific model (i.e. the mental model).

4. The decision-making process being highly contextual, the CIAS must benefit from its interaction with the expert to learn new practices by acquiring the missing knowledge incrementally, and thus enriching its experience base.

5. Making context explicit in the experience base leads to the possibility of generating relevant explanations for: presenting the rationale behind a mental model with the abandoned alternatives; training (future) experts from the different mental models developed; facilitating experience sharing among experts in a kind of dynamic corporate memory and allowing the first step towards the certification of their protocol.

6. The main tool of a CIAS is the CxG-based simulator. Its originality is to build and develop at the same time the mental model. Indeed, the CxG-based simulator is the key element of a CIAS for real-time decision-making because it is possible to account for unpredicted events, thanks to an explicit modeling of context as contextual elements covering, the user, the task realization, the working situation and the local environment with its available resources. All the items are interdependent and also time-dependent. Thus, CIASs cover a more general problematic than context-aware applications. This seems the key point for mobile decision-making because the instantiations of contextual elements are taken on-the-fly at the moment it is necessary.

Finally, the CxG formalism is a passport for intelligent systems based on human experience. The "hard kernel" of our approach is the explicit modeling of context in activity, which leads to a homogeneous view of how a class of AI systems can become context-based intelligent systems, especially context-based IASs (Brézillon 2023), which aim at reuse and extend human experience based on how this experience grows. CIASs developed in the CxG formalism offer the possibility to model contextual reasoning with context-based simulation, a powerful modeling tool for CIASs. The goal is not a direct discovery like for machine and deep learning, but a reuse and an extension of the human experience in the spirit of generative AI. For deep learning, the goal would not be to accumulate contextual knowledge (infinite dimension of context) but to identify in the situation and environment contextual elements that can be relevant for a robot to accomplishing its task and develop its mental representation in a kind of a "modeling by acting". The CxG formalism provides powerful experience bases that can serve as a basis for deep learning in order to complete the known practices.

4.5. Review of the chapter

This chapter starts with the summary of the key points from the two previous chapters. The key concepts are discussed in the framework of the four modeling levels, with their characteristics and evolution from the conceptual level to the environment level. Then, we comment on the interdependency of these concepts for a holistic view on the four-modeling level proposed. The 25 key points, found during the years of research on context modeling and use, lead to a robust CxG formalism (based on only four items, action, activity, contextual element and ESIA) implemented in a piece of software easy to use for modeling a large number of very different problems in a large spectrum of applications (subway, power systems, management, medicine, psychology, etc.), thanks to making contextual element and instantiation explicit with knowledge and reasoning. A contextual element can be considered as containing a step of the contextual reasoning developed from the mental representation in a mental model, the former appearing as a uniform description of all the mental models.

The term of "activity" covers different tasks such as decision-making, diagnosis and problem-solving, such tasks being context-dependent. The four phases of an activity are identified by verbs of action: to accomplish or to plan (before to start), to initiate or to launch (at activity triggering), to perform or to carry out (during activity execution), to realize or to close (upon completion of the activity) and context intervenes differently for these phases. In the four-level framework, there are different views on an activity. At the conceptual level, an activity is the focus of attention of an actor accomplishing the activity and therefore acquiring experience about it. At the operational level, an actor comprehends experience as a mental representation that corresponds to the accumulation of the mental models developed by the actor during interaction with the activity at different moments and then contexts. A mental representation is personal to an actor and difficult to transmit directly, but its implemented representation, the contextual graph, is externalized and thus sharable. Both the mental representation and contextual graph are two complementary context-based representations of an activity accomplishment by an actor as well as a group. The processing of an activity in a specific context requires an implementation for dealing with the realization of the activity and its consideration in the context at hand (environment level). In the CxG formalism, the mental representation is implemented as a contextual graph, and mental models are paths in this contextual graph for describing the actor's reasoning held in specific contexts during activity accomplishment, these specific contexts being identified at the environment level.

The actor's focus of attention is on an activity or one of its steps that the author accomplishes, launches, realizes or finishes. The focus of attention divides the context of an activity into contextual knowledge and external knowledge. Contextual knowledge is the part of the context that is more or less related to the focus of attention. The part of the contextual knowledge that effectively intervenes in the focus of attention is operational knowledge. At the operational level, contextual knowledge is related to mental representation, and operational knowledge is related to a mental model. Context comes from four sources, namely the actor, the activity, the situation and local environment. Knowledge heterogeneity in the notion of operational knowledge is clarified in the concept of a contextual element. Contextual elements structure the contextual graph and any activity model, including the reasoning associated with it. When a contextual element appears on the path followed for mental-model development, it is as a question, and its instantiation is an answer to the question in the context at hand as contained in the sources of context. Thus, the interaction of context and activity intervenes in a contextual element that is modeled at the implementation level as a pair of contextual and recombination nodes with, between them, as many branches as known instantiations. The assimilation of a contextual element to a pair of contextual and recombination nodes at the implementation level gives a directed, acyclic and series–parallel structure to the contextual graph. On each exclusive branch between the contextual and recombination nodes, there is an independent subtask that leads to considering a contextual element as a step in the reasoning held in activity realization at the operational level. Thus, the choice of an instantiation makes reasoning nonlinear. Instantiation of a contextual element comes down to finding its value in the context at hand in one of the sources of context in the environment.

Activity realization results from the actor's reasoning in a kind of simulation of decision-making. The instantiation process is the part of reasoning generating proceduralized context that appears as a context-based model of reasoning. The proceduralized context is an ordered sequence of instantiated contextual elements obtained all along the activity development. It is the signature (fingerprint) of the activity accomplishment in a particular context that allows CxG-based simulation of mental-model development and offers a powerful tool for CIASs because it also allows for checking alternatives during activity development.

The main differences between an actor activity and a group activity are at the implementation level because concepts such as experience, mental representation and mental models are difficult to comprehend in a group activity. Moreover, each actor has punctual intervention on activity realization, the mental model being built from independent subtasks during a cyclic use of the directed contextual graph. New concepts like turn and shared context are introduced for the management of actors in a group. Thus, before being developed in a specific context, the group mental-model first must be built by assembling a sequence of independent subtasks taken in the activities of different actors and second be developed like an actor activity at each turn. RCEs behave as activation conditions of a turn and as post-conditions for the next turn. Shared context concerns actor communication, information transfer between independent subtasks, the step-by-step building of the mental model and plays the role of an inference engine for the CxG-based simulation. RCEs provide a structure on a contextual graph for the cyclic development of one-off interventions of actors. The cyclic use offers the possibility of checking variants on the path from any step (e.g. negotiation among actors). The main result is the building of the group mental model at the operational level by assembling the developed independent subtasks at the implementation level. The CxG-based simulation offers a pragmatic understanding of the evolution of group activity realization instead of a cognitive simulation like for activity accomplishment by a unique actor. It is a visualization of the dynamic of the reasoning held during mental-model development. CxG-based simulation is also an important tool for CIASs. The model of a group activity differs from that of an actor activity mainly at the implementation level due to the change of representation of the actor's activity as a set of independent subtasks. This is a strong argument for the positioning of our modeling approach since the common conceptual level implies a coherence of all the possible extensions of the actor-activity modeling. For instance, it is possible to change the representation of a model of an actor activity from one unit to a set of independent subtasks with the same result but moving from an external viewpoint on the activity model to an internal viewpoint as previously captured in a contextual graph. It is an interesting aspect, especially for a group activity in the analysis of an internship offer and the diagnosis of a DVD reader.

A short definition of context is "the context of an activity is the proceduralized context associated with its accomplishment". The proceduralized context appears in two key points. First, at the conceptual level, where the proceduralized context was seen as the contextual knowledge usable in the focus of attention at a current step. Second, at the implementation level, the proceduralized context is specified as the ordered sequence of contextual elements that are instantiated during a contextual-graph run. However, a more important unfolding is necessary because its originality relies on:

– a real-time definition that is synchronous with the step-by-step progression of activity realization;

– a joint proceduralized-context building and activity realization with the influence of each on the evolution of the other;

– a reuse of the proceduralized context for the CxG-based simulation of activity realization;

– The strong explanatory power of the proceduralized context on the manner by which an activity is realized.

Activity realization is the result of an actor's reasoning, and the instantiation process corresponds to the selection of an expression of the reasoning step in a contextual element that makes reasoning nonlinear. The proceduralized context then can be assimilated to a context-based model of the reasoning that makes reasoning contextual and contextual elements steps of the actor's decision-making. As a result, decision-making is a contextual nonlinear reasoning.

After, we discuss the global approach that has been realized collaboratively during a course in the Innovation Management Master and show that mental models of a task realization (associated with each student) may differ deeply from the group model (resulting from a consensus): each student agreed on the global model (i.e. the list of contextual elements) but said that they will never use it directly for themselves (personalization of instantiations of contextual elements). Each group member brings a unique perspective that frames the peer group experience. Knowing that the member might be called upon to explain the thought behind a response encouraged them to formulate explanations in advance. A major function of the CxG_2.0 formalism is the CxG-based simulation for building and visualizing task realization according to actors' real-time choices like in the task "internship-offer analysis". This "replay" mode is important for actors that do not know exactly what to do. CxG-based simulation is interpretable at the operational level (where the task realization is), and the progress of the mental-model building is ensured at the implementation level. Thus, the CxG-based simulation is a modeling tool for CIASs, but a modeling tool quite different from numerical simulation.

An observation concerns the different types of ordering of contextual elements: temporal ordering for the "wine making" project (section 1.9), functional ordering in the TACTIC project (section 1.5) and the "paper-submission" example (section 4.2.2), and no complete ordering in the "internship-offer analysis" due to subjective contextual elements. However, a temporal ordering of contextual elements is not a real modeling of time like a function of time, F(t), mainly because context-based mental models are more conceptual than formal due to the activity.

In the "Internship-offer analysis", each subtask corresponds to a unique goal for everybody, but activity realization is deeply "actor-driven" (each student has a personal view on the objective). The main reason is the intensive consideration of personal contextual elements in students' working context at the same level as the contextual elements linked to the shared context. For instance, the interest of a student for tourism traveling (a totally external contextual element for analyzing the internship offer) was important for them, although there was nothing to do with activity realization. As a result, there are as many different decisions as students. The point to retain here is that, even with a clear mental representation, external contextual elements allow the actor to generate mental models at the operational level that are different from the procedure established by the company at the tactical level but respect company goals at policy and strategy decisional levels to protect travelers. Thus, it is important to consider all decisional levels for evaluating results of decision-making at the operational level. The "Internship-offer analysis" task has a very superficial "model" that we can sum up by: (1) checking if the proposed mission is acceptable; (2) seeing if the mission can be ascribed to the professional project and (3) controlling if the practical information is satisfactory. Such a model is highly decontextualized to concern all students regardless of their scientific discipline, and, as such, it does not leave room for the contextual knowledge of students like "autonomy" and certainly not for contextual information about tourist trips. As shown in the study, external contextual elements are as important for students as the role of the mission in the personal project. Classically, reasoning modeling in a context-based formalism of representation corresponds to a contextual reasoning (a sequence of steps), and contextual elements are allowed to introduce "light" variants of the way to lead a contextual reasoning. However, examples (e.g. the SART project and the "Internship-offer analysis") show that external contextual elements cannot be neglected in the contextual and nonlinear reasoning of the decision-maker at the operational level.

The CxG_1.0 formalism is used for modeling activity where mental models developed differ between them by small variations and are represented in a unique experience base (the contextual graph). Conversely, the CxG_2.0 formalism allows us to model the activity using mental models with heterogeneous expressions (e.g. with negotiation, waiting for an answer, looking ahead for potential ways). The contextual graph is an expression of the mental representation in the CxG 1.0 formalism, but this mental representation is built on the fly in the CxG_2.0 formalism because a mental model is built by assembling the independent subtasks in the mental representation depending on their results. To sum up, the CxG_1.0 version, initially designed for an activity accomplished by an actor, does not work for a group activity (no model exists), but the CxG_2.0 version allows the individual use by each actor in a group-activity model when all actors have the same objective (find an internship), but each student has their own criteria and preferences.

5

Use of the CxG Formalism in Different Modeling

5.1. Introduction

Chapter 5 presents four applications in different domains, and a fifth application is an attempt at illustrating the possibilities of our approach in Semiotics. We revise these works in a context-based way. The first example concerns a high-level summary about all that was known in the 1990s about breast cancer diagnosis. Logan-Young and Hoffman (1994) were experts in critical decision-making (anatomo-cyto-pathologist diagnosing women for breast cancer) and rely on a highly compiled experience, act under temporal pressure and are very concerned by the consequences of their decision. They sum up their experience on breast cancer diagnosis in three books, the first one concerning the procedures (or best practices) when no formal knowledge was available. The authors were considering practices (in the sense of "best practices") instead of procedures to cover a large class of patients (but supposing that all physicians behave in the same way). The modeling of their expertise is represented in a complex set of 13 figures (but in an "optimized" representation), representing extensive flow charts for solving every possible type of problem.

The second example concerns hierarchical task analysis (HTA) (Shepherd 2001). The interest of HTA is in system goals, sub-goals and plans, with feedback loops. Originally developed for training process control tasks in the steel and petrochemical industries, HTA has been used for a range of applications in both individual and team tasks. It is a strategy for examining tasks and especially understanding task contexts. HTA-knowledge elicitation relies on a tree representation, mainly for reuse in training, but not in task-realization simulation.

Thus, the objective of HTA is for conducting task analysis, not for modeling behavior. The choice of a relevant method for task analysis is error-prone with, on the one hand, different people that adopt different methods for carrying out the same task, and, on the other hand, individuals that may use different strategies for dealing with similar situations in different contexts.

The third example is the ACA application (Brézillon 2010). The ACA method (for Adequate Category Learning in French) is a training process (for a human) based on a typology of known behaviors, a situation for the analysis, in which the behavior of the learner is analyzed in different contexts, and specific scenarios that carry out the learning. The domain is road safety. The driver has a mental representation of a car-driving activity to understand a particular situation, driving being an on-the-fly construction of a contextualized knowledge structure. The goal is to anticipate behaviors of other drivers and make a decision consequently for managing (potential) critical situations based on contextualized information, two drivers reacting differently in the same situation. The approach allows the mental representation to capture "good" and "bad" behaviors.

The fourth example presents a contextualization of the anatomical and cytology pathology (ACP) workflow for analyzing nonconformity during reception and registration steps in the ACP Department. The workflow monitors work quality in the ACP Department, the actions, detection and correction of nonconformities as well as a base for intelligent software creation that links different modules in medical care. Its organization relies on rooms and floors that samples cross from the room at reception to the room where the physician signs, through different rooms on two different floors for preparing and analyzing samples. A nonconformity situation may occur during the process. Such situations are difficult to identify to correct the problem and to learn how to avoid it again because generally the result appears as more important (critical) than the process leading to it.

The fifth example (Brannen 2004) is chosen in a semiotic approach of the transfer of the Walt Disney Company made during internationalization in Tokyo Disneyland (1983) and Disneyland Paris (1992) with the same international strategy, but there are two opposite results: a success in Japan and a failure in France. In Disneyland Paris, European visitors come from different sociocultural environments and take advantage of Disneyland Paris during their vacations in France. Generally, firms transfer their whole organizations, including business models, steeped in image-based, ideological, people-dependent management that are even more closely related to context and sociocultural environment in which they are enacted. However, if the source is significantly foreign from the target, the transferred assets may not fit the target context in the host country. The notion of semantic fit was considered as a necessary complement to strategic fit and leads to a formalization of a conceptual model of recontextualization – the process by which firm assets take on new meanings in distinct cultural environments. We revisit this study in terms of context-based approaches of the sociocultural environments of the source (USA) and the targets (Japan and France), and finally replace this study in the CDR paradigm.

5.2. Breast cancer diagnosis

The books of Logan-Young and Hoffman (1994) represent the sum of all the known procedures, such as clinical breast examination and breast self-examination, the technical aspects of mammography and ultrasound, fine-needle aspiration cytology, core biopsy and preoperative needle localization. They also present methods used by Loga-Young for obtaining patient histories and examine various clinical problems and diagnostic results (Freig 1996). Problem-solving flow charts sum up Logan-Young's experience with a user's viewpoint on the appearance of the breast in mammography, sonography and ductography. Anatomic sites of various benign and malignant breast conditions are diagrammed. The focus was on the presence of any breast disease signs and symptoms and to evaluate their cause if present. At an upper level, an emphasis was put on the clinical breast examination (CBE) and the need to "see" the patient, not only the X-ray radiography. The problem was that malignancy may mimic benign disease and benign disease may mimic malignancy on both mammography and CBE; this compartmentalized approach allowed too many patients to fall through the cracks. The books include material from both clinical and mammographic examinations and prone breast self-examination. It also gives an outstanding review of the physics and technical aspects of equipment selection such as ultrasound. The authors underline that it is now mandatory that the same physician perform and interpret the examination made with the newer units used. More generally, the author shares her experience in the domain in a very detailed way. Their Chapter 13 is supplemented by 13 extensive flow charts for solving every possible type of problem. Although these charts may seem daunting to comprehend at first glance, they contain as close to "cookbook-like" details as can be provided for the art of patient management. We present a global context-based representation of these 13 flow charts.

Figure 5.1 shows one of the 13 figures. The colors identify different classes in the domain that does not concern us. We added to the figure (1) arrows for indicating links with other flow charts (and pages), and (2) a dotted rectangle that corresponds to an isolated activity, to point out how we can identify the different granularities of the knowledge.

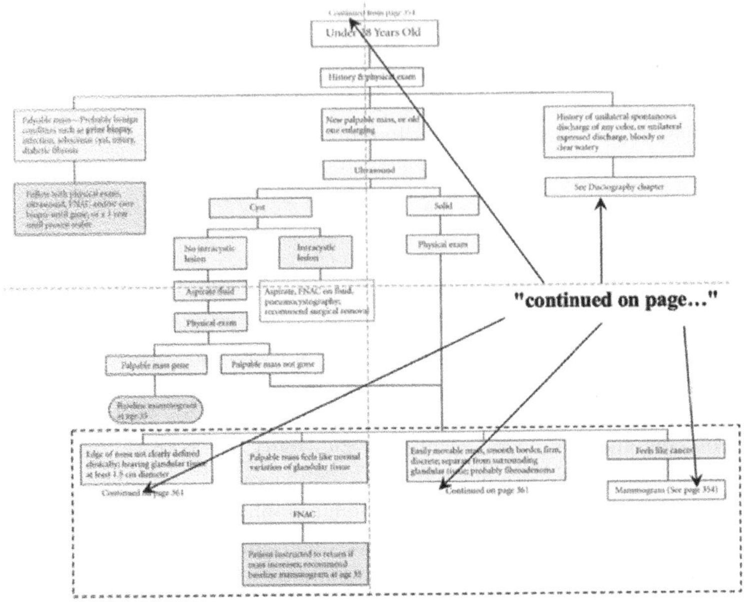

Figure 5.1. *One of the flow charts in Logan-Young and Hoffman (1994). For a color version of this figure, see www.iste.co.uk/brezillon/contextbasedmodeling.zip*

When actors are experts that make critical decision (e.g. anatomo-cyto-pathologist diagnosing a woman for breast cancer), they rely on a highly compiled experience, generally act under temporal pressure and are very concerned by the consequences of their decision. Our goal is to show that it is a problem of representation formalism (and also of new technology). The first point is to translate their representation in a context-based representation. The second point is to underline the new insight brought by this context-based formalism that allows dynamic views on the whole picture, on the one hand, by explicitly introducing the notion of activity (a kind of sub-graph clearly identified by physicians such as mammogram and ultrasound), and, on the other hand, by some mechanisms of aggregation and expansion that allow reasoning on a specific part of the whole graph without losing the global picture.

Our first point was to translate this representation in a context-based representation (Brézillon 2013). The second point concerned the new insight brought by this context-based formalism that allows dynamic views on the whole picture, on the one hand, by explicitly introducing the notion of activity (a kind of sub-graph already clearly identified by physicians such as mammogram and ultrasound), and, on the other hand, by some mechanisms of aggregation and expansion that allow a specific part of the whole graph without losing the global picture. The first step in the processing of the representation is a transformation of the initial graph in a (decision) tree by untangling some parts more on paths than on elements on the paths. Our goal is to simplify the representation that was initially optimized in size. However, this does not yet correspond to a simplification of the understanding of the figure. A simplification is illustrated by the transformation of the content of the dotted rectangle in Figure 5.1 that contains an activity that is called from two different branches above with the same activity added at each branch as shown in Figure 5.2 (and the other flowcharts of the book).

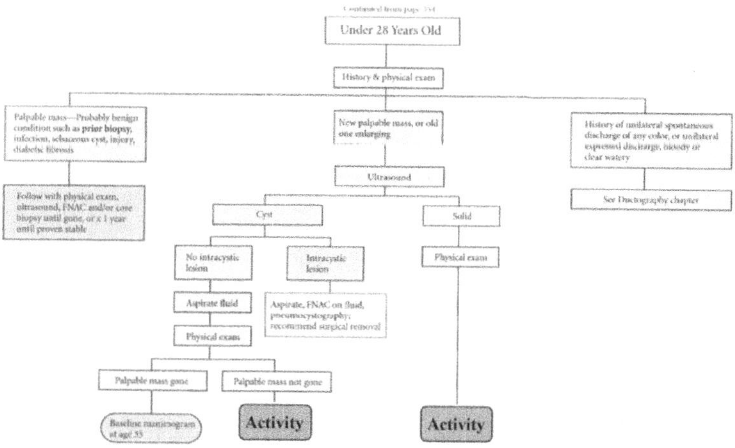

Figure 5.2. *Introduction of activities in Figure 5.1 with two lower parts as activity. For a color version of this figure, see www.iste.co.uk/brezillon/contextbasedmodeling.zip*

A second step concerned the replacement of questions about the state of the world (with their different instantiations) by the introduction of contextual elements. For example, "Physical exam?" (bottom left in Figure 5.2) has two possible instantiations "palpable mass gone" and "palpable mass not gone" (the first boxes just under the fork). This adaptation of the figure corresponds to a contextual element ("Physical exam?") and its possible instantiations ("palpable mass gone" and "palpable mass not gone"). This allows the introduction of a uniform representation of the elements of knowledge, reasoning and contexts and to emphasize the role of context in the decision-making process of the physician. For example, the activity introduced in Figure 5.2 is considered only in the context "palpable mass not gone" and in the context "ultrasound shows solid" palpable masses. Once the method corresponding to the instantiation of the contextual element is executed (the activity continues on another figure of Logan-Young's book), it is possible to merge the branches again. After propagating this processing through the 13 initial figures putting the whole into a unique figure (and correcting two small problems), we obtain a complex contextual graph as shown by a global view in Figure 5.3, which is shown only for the general scale of the initial problem.

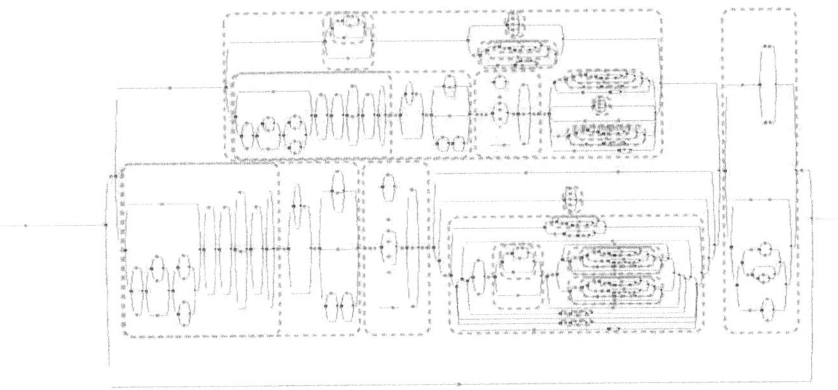

Figure 5.3. *The complete representation as a contextual graph (with unfolded activities). For a color version of this figure, see www.iste.co.uk/brezillon/contextbasedmodeling.zip*

Figure 5.3 gives an idea of the complete and complex representation of the expertise on breast cancer described in the 13 figures of Logan-Young and Hoffman (1994). Among the changes made, it was possible to transform some groups of actions into complex activities (red dotted frames), for example, ductography, ultrasound, physical exam, FNAC (fine-needle aspiration cytology) with some medical background (the student doing this work was a physician). Some activities contain other (sub)activities with domain knowledge at a lower granularity. It shows the coherent representation of knowledge at different granularities in the initial figures of Logan-Young.

The association of a contextual element to a question makes it possible to handle different types of values: data (e.g. yes or no), information (border thickness vs. 8 mm) and knowledge (cyst or solid, stable or enlarged). Again, the separation of the contextual element and of its instantiations clarify the representation. Moreover, the diagnosis obtained at the exit of the contextual graph may have a different answer (e.g. return in one year or immediate surgical removal) according to the path followed in the graph (i.e. the history of the patient and the right practice to develop in the specific context of the patient). Finally, by recursively applying the notion of activity in the representation, the graph given in Figure 5.1 (and the 12 other flow charts not shown here) becomes the contextual graph given in Figure 5.4 (without the content of the activities). Note that in this "simple" representation, there are 400 initial items organized according to the granularity of the data, information and knowledge.

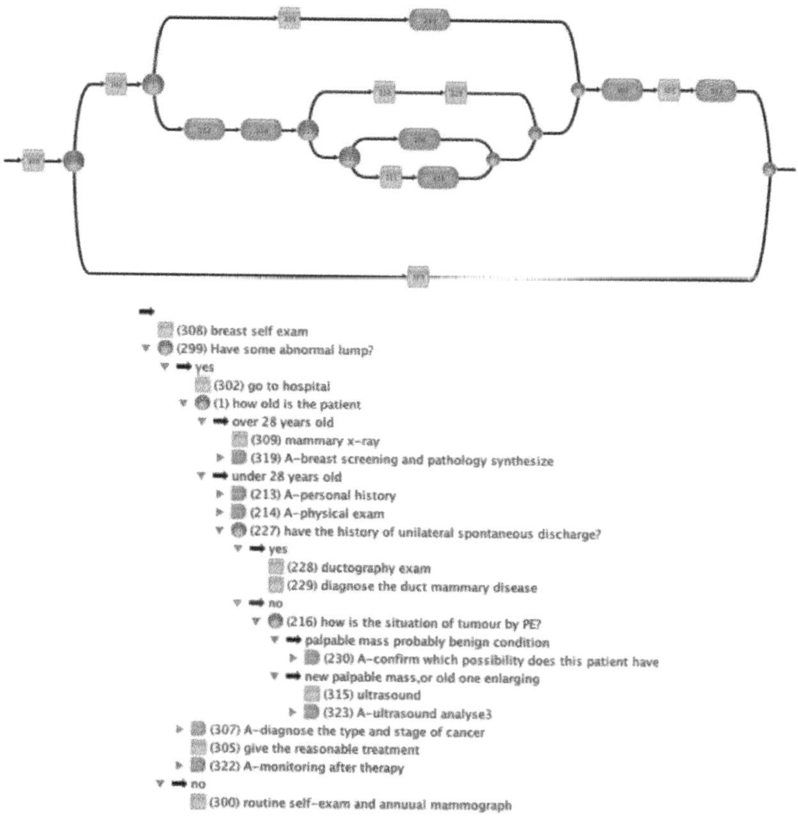

Figure 5.4. *The contextual graph in Figure 5.3 with activities. For a color version of this figure, see www.iste.co.uk/brezillon/contextbasedmodeling.zip*

To sum up, the different steps: (1) often domain structures are not sufficient to avoid complex representations of large amounts of data, information and knowledge; (2) the notion of activity tackles the representation at different granularities of reasoning and objects of this reasoning; and (3) the explicit representation of context as contextual elements and instantiations allows the organization of the expert's reasoning in relevant chunks of knowledge. An interesting difference between the initial representation of Logan-Young and Hoffman (see Figure 5.1) with the contextual-graph representation (see Figure 5.4) is the transformation of a flat representation into a representation structured by the expert's reasoning, not components of this reasoning. For example, "control visit" is realized after a period of either one year or two years according to the context in which the visit is realized. In the initial representation, this content was represented twice to differentiate the control-visit date (i.e. the instantiation of "control visit?"). In the contextual graph, we have the same activity on two branches with an action "Fix date of the control visit at X" with X = 1 year in one context and X = 2 years in the other context. Another interesting difference is to avoid implementation simplification of the problem modeling to stay in the limits of the representation formalism. For example, "border thickness versus 8 mm" appears several times while complexity is less for activities such as mammogram, ultrasound, etc., because they are not at the same level of granularity. In the initial representation, it was represented by arrows that were separated or jointed more for technical reasons (e.g. for economy of the representation) than for semantic reasons. Indeed, this problem was also found initially in the SART project.

We obtain the same results in the FlexMim project on another type of cancer (IBD) where most of the same knowledge is used. Physicians have to make a decision on the basis of a large quantity of data, information and knowledge. They tackle these sources by using the domain structure for their decision-making. For example, in the application "breast cancer diagnosis", some data, information and knowledge are specific to subtasks (mammography, fine-needle aspiration cytology, etc.), and can be organized according to independent domain structures. In the contextual-graphs representation, the notion of activity (as defined by users) allows the association of the notion of granularity with the representation of domain structures. This is particularly important when actors collaborate on different aspects of the same problem or with different viewpoints. Always in the FlexMim project, the task "Diagnosis of chronic inflammatory bowel disease (IBD)" was executed by experts separately with personal methodologies, but it was the modeling (and not the realization) of the task that was the object of the collaborative work of the anatomo-cyto-pathologists, and all had to conclude on IBD or not. Their diagnosis related to sources of information at different granularities (macroscopic and microscopic examination of patients' tissue samples and cells) that concern anatomy, histology and cytology for finding molecular abnormalities. The diagnosis is made on digital slides of a microscope scanned in 30-Go files. The modeling was led by a specialist that did not belong to the group. Thus, the knowledge involved in the IBD task was essentially domain knowledge for the initial information (digital slides) and the result (IBD or not), but the methodologies used by experts were essentially the personal contextual knowledge of each expert based on their experience, the weighting of criteria and the combinations of the contextual elements shared by all experts.

However, we can go one step further for tackling a large quantity of data, information and knowledge by exploiting contextual cues used by users for organizing their reasoning in an objective way. The main difference between domain structures and context structures is the dynamic building of the latter. This is like a conceptual schema used in databases, but built dynamically to address the specific query of the user, and not the preliminary view of the designer of the database. We encountered the same situation in other applications in the same domain (FlexMim project). In the SART project for subway monitoring where operators explained to us that, when they inform on an incident, they first look for contextual information about the state of the whole line, eventual problems with other lines, etc., and only afterwards on the incident. This obeys the general paradigm "gather contextual information, make a decision, and act" in decision-making.

5.3. Hierarchical task analysis (HTA)

Task-analysis approaches tended to observe aspects of performance, whereas hierarchical task analysis (HTA) sought to represent system goals, sub-goals and plans, with feedback loops in a nested hierarchy (Stanton 2004). HTA was first developed by Annett and Duncan (1967) to overcome the limitations of classical time-and-motion methods in analyzing complex non-repetitive cognitively loaded tasks and explaining human-skilled performance (Shepherd 2001). Originally developed for training process control tasks in the steel and petrochemical industries, it has been used for a range of applications in both individual and team tasks, including interface design and evaluation, allocation of function, error prediction, workload assessment, training, job description, work organization, manuals design, job aid design, error analysis, team task analysis and procedure design. HTA is a strategy for examining tasks, aimed at refining performance criteria on constituent skills, understanding task contexts and generating useful hypotheses for overcoming performance problems. Task examination leads to redescription into sub-operations and a plan that governs the conditions where each sub-operation should be carried out. It is a way to introduce nonlinearity into a linear representation. The main characteristic of HTA is knowledge elicitation in a tree representation, eventually a reuse in training, but not in task-realization simulation. While the basic approach can be trained in a few hours, it is generally acknowledged that the sensitive use of the method will take some months of practice under expert guidance.

HTA is a framework for conducting task analysis, not a tool for modeling behavior. The choice of a relevant method belongs to the analyst with the possibility of bias, error of judgment and unfocused work, unsuited to an applied setting. Moreover, different people adopt different methods for carrying out the same task, and individuals commonly vary their strategies for dealing with similar situations in different contexts. Shepherd (2001) proposes the example of a supermarket checkout task where the checkout operator waits for the next customer, then processes items from the customer's trolley, then establishes the charge to be made and obtains appropriate payment (see Figure 5.5). The context not being considered, there are five principal sub-operations, namely, #2 that is further broken-down into six more of which #4 is further broken-down into two more and #5 into four and #6 into five sub-operations, one of which (#3) is described in five sub-operations. The box for each operation contains no more than a brief title, which stands for both the goal and the principal action involved. The operation 2.5.3 (enter price) is identified as at the third level of decomposition and is itself finally re-described as five sub-operations that are listed at the bottom of the table. These can be identified in the diagram as operations 2.5.3.1–2.5.3.5. HTA relies on several concepts, namely the notion of plan, flexibility, stopping rule and methodologies such as the formalism of representation, the simulation and the implementation view.

Many parts of tasks correspond to procedures. However, decision-makers also need to have flexible approaches when they encounter situations outside of what is expected to perform with credit. They must deal with the unscheduled or unexpected, rather than routine predictable events, so they have to plan and make decisions. A plan specifies the order in which the task and subtasks are performed. It concretes the "rationale" that refers to the immediate reasons for the action and answers the question why an action was carried out.

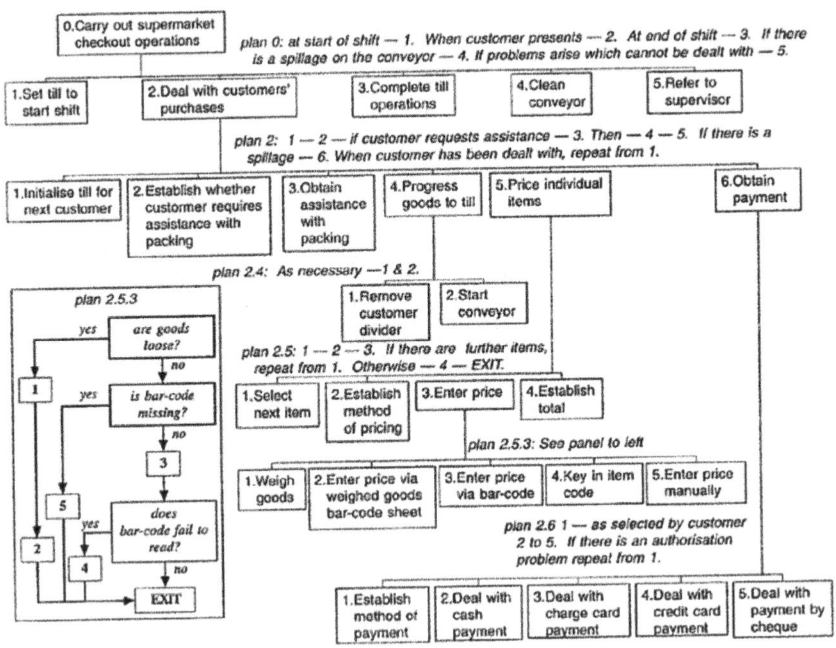

Figure 5.5. *Supermarket checkout task (Shepherd 2001)*

In Figure 5.5, the supermarket checkout task contains different choices within plans represented in different ways:

– In “deal with customers’ purchases” (operation 2), one responsibility is to ensure that customers obtain assistance with their packing if they wish. Thus, plan 2 contains a choice element where a decision is made concerning the customer’s requirements.

– In “obtain payment” (operation 2.6), the operator must establish how the customer wishes to pay – presumably by asking them. The alternatives are set out for the operator to follow according to the customer’s choice.

– In “enter price” (operation 2.5.3) without access to context, the operator must determine how each item will be dealt with. Plan 2.5.3 has been set out as a decision flow diagram. It could equally have been set out as the following set of rules:

If goods are loose - 1 - 2.

If goods are not loose, but the bar-code is *missing - 5.*

If goods are not loose and bar-code is available - 3.

If bar-code fails toregister - 4.

The *plan* is necessary because the taxonomy does not always flow in order of events and it is necessary to see the options available in the sequence of tasks. In HTA, a plan does state the events, not their frequency and predictability. The plan describes the contextual-information sources that the worker must attend to, in order to signal the need for various activities. Thus, the overall goal is broken-down into a next level of sub-goals. Such a control structure enables the analyst to capture the contextual conditions that trigger the sub-goals under any super-ordinate goal. A context might include time, environmental conditions, completion of other sub-goals, system state, receipt of information, etc. This provides more information about how to accomplish the task; however, it can still be broken-down into smaller units, which will describe the individual operations (performed via the visual, manual or cognitive modes) that need to be performed. Recursively, plans describe how to perform the operations in each sub-goal level of the hierarchy. Moreover, experts’ intuition implicitly relies on experience as a complex combination of contextual elements.

Plans are implicit in the decomposition structure of a HTA, but they are made more explicit by adding the appropriate algorithm to the HTA diagram. Figure 5.5 shows different representations of plans. (Plans are written next to the branches to describe the way in which the branched operations should be carried out.) The plan for #0 comprises a simple procedure, operations #1, #2 and #3 with two conditional operations, #4 and #6. The plan for operation 2.5.3 is described in the form of an algorithm that contains three tests (Are goods loose? Is the bar code missing? Does the bar code fail to read?). Decision-makers may need to adapt as they get tired, as the characteristics of the materials they are dealing with vary, and as tools they are using wear down or change their operating characteristics.

Flexibility is an important part of task analysis. People change with circumstances and differ from one another in view of their personal histories and factors such as their individual tendencies to take risks or the extent to which uncertainty causes them to become stressed. Making flexibility explicit in plans, the HTA approach is then used to describe many ends: from person specification, to training requirements, error prediction, team performance assessment, and system design (Stanton 2004). This encourages a systematic examination of the task to identify requirements for flexibility, the cognitive operations that operators carry out in order to work flexibly and the context in which these cognitive operations are carried out (Shepherd 2001).

Decision-makers use their experience to recognize the key aspects of the situation at hand as familiar that gives them a sense of what goals are feasible, what (contextual) cues are important, what to expect next and what actions are typical in that situation (Klein and Calderwood 1991). Generally, the decision-maker looks at a branching tree of responses and estimates the probability and utility of the different possible future states. Both multi-attribute utility analysis and decision analysis strategies are often disappointing in practice. They do not work under time pressure because they take too long and lack flexibility for handling rapidly changing field conditions (Klein and Calderwood 1991). Experienced decision-makers are not searching for the best option. They only want to find one (but without ordering all the options) that works, a strategy called "satisficing". The comparison of options is replaced by a "look ahead", "what-if" cognitive simulation to detect any pitfalls.

Experienced decision-makers cope with time pressure and dynamic conditions. Rather than trying to change the way they think, we should be finding ways to help them by developing techniques for broadening their experience base through training, so they can gain situation assessment more quickly and accurately. The level of description is highly dependent upon the purpose of the analysis. Progressive re-description of the sub-goal hierarchy could go on indefinitely, and knowing when to stop the analysis is one of the most difficult features of task analysis. The concept of stopping rule is the solution that is used in HTA. A stop rule specifies the level of detail beyond which no further redescription is of use. A stopping rule, which is simple enough in its conception, was proposed: if the probability of failure (P) times (x) the cost of failure (C) is acceptable, then stop the task analysis. If P x C is unacceptable, then the analysis should continue (Stanton 2004). Under most situations, probabilities and costs are not known and the analyst has to apply an approximation of this rule, although it may not be clear what they are basing this judgment on. The proposed P x C stopping rule is a rough heuristic, but analysts may have trouble quantifying the estimates of P and C.

There are different common representations for task modeling: graphical trees, universal modeling language and contextual modeling. A representation essentially is a mapping of concepts and relationships (and possibly attributes) to the visual domain. Some aspects may also concern the appropriateness of the mapping in relation to the purpose and audience. Paterno et al. (1997) propose a compact and graphical notation, immediate both to use and understand to describe task models, which can specify a wide range of temporal relationships among tasks. Its logical structure and the related automatic tool make it suitable for designing even large sized applications. However, the choice of a representation formalism depends essentially of the nature of the application. HTA description is based on two types of format, namely the diagrammatic and tabular formats. Diagrams are more easily assimilated but tables often are more thorough because detailed notes can be added. Both charts are based on binary choice decisions and intervening operations. Decision/action charts have only a single level of task description, and when complex tasks are analyzed, the diagrams become unwieldy and difficult to follow. The tabular format contains a task taxonomy that analyzes the context and constraints of the tasks and their associated sub-goals.

The taxonomy comprises 12 factors that need to be considered when investigating the adequacy of design decisions in support of task performance. These factors are: the difficulty of the task; the predictability, controllability and frequency of events; the severity of consequences of error and possibility for recovery; information representation and feedback; the presence of environmental, situational and task stresses; access to help and advice; physical and environmental constraints; and legal, industrial and cultural compliance. A hierarchical list and a hierarchical diagram present exactly the same information on the sub-goal hierarchy in two different forms (representation formalisms). The advantage of the diagram is that it represents the groups of sub-goals in a spatial manner, which is useful for gaining a quick overview of the HTA. The hierarchical lists show the same information in a more condensed format, which is useful for very large analyses (Stanton 2004).

Attempts have been made to develop software support for HTA to simplify the production of the hierarchical diagrams and the tabular format by allowing direct manipulation of the data objects and easy editing of the analysis. Other examples have been developed for specific applications, such as error prediction or workload analysis (Stanton 2004). As HTA involves reiteration and revision, the software tool should enable the sub-goal hierarchy and plans to be edited with ease (Stanton 2004). Any change made in one form of the representation is propagated through the other forms of the representation.

In HTA domain, simulation proposes a simplified version for the trainee, or when the system feedback provided in the real situation may be too delayed to help the trainee learn and so additional feedback must be provided by the instructor (Shepherd 2001). By practicing tasks on a simulator, the trainee would be able to apply the same skill in the real task. Often, the justification for simulation is to provide the trainee with experience of events that occur infrequently, to master critical skills that would, otherwise, never be experienced. This creates a major problem for the training designer. In practical tasks, people often gear their responses to expectation, so the trainee learns to anticipate events in the simulator but cannot transfer these expectations to the real world. Figure 5.6 presents the contextual graph (upper part) of the initial representation and just below the legends of the graph. We keep this unfolded version, which is strongly simplified by the introduction of activities (in pink dotted ovals in the figure) for a better isolation of the different subtasks, for a direct comparison with the initial representation in Figure 5.5. Roughly, the "plans" which appear as comments on the initial figure are made explicit in the activities and the nesting of some activities (activity 3 contains activities 10, 24, 21, and activity 21 contains activity 29).

The checkout task is normally relatively linear (accept the next customer, process goods to cash register, price individual items, obtain payment, close the transaction). This task is at the level of a procedure, that is decontextualized. Plans are introduced for managing alternatives depending on the context (e.g. the type of payment). They are specified outside of the procedure because this representation is not a context-based representation. We developed another model (in the CxG_2.0 formalism) of HTA considered as a collaborative task between the cashier, the customer and the supervisor of the store for detecting eventual new aspects of HTA. The model is given in Figure 5.7. The first contextual element (25) concerns the selection of the actor (the cashier, the customer and the supervisor). The task of each actor was broken-down in independent subtasks, which are described in the legend of the graph (second part of Figure 5.7).

Figure 5.7 shows the contextual graph (upper part) and just below the legends of the graph in two columns (the last arrow "non-payment" at the bottom of the first column corresponds to the first arrow "non-payment" of the second column). The non-integration of plans in the HTA representation supposes reasoning simultaneously in different representations, and not in a uniform representation, of the elements of knowledge (taxonomy), reasoning (plans) and contexts (flexibility) as in the CxG formalism instead of the redescription process described by the authors (activities allow us to differentiate knowledge pieces at different granularities). Indeed, the redescription process existing at the corresponding nodes of the initial tree representation is like contextual information for understanding the HTA (such as in the breast cancer diagnosis in the previous section).

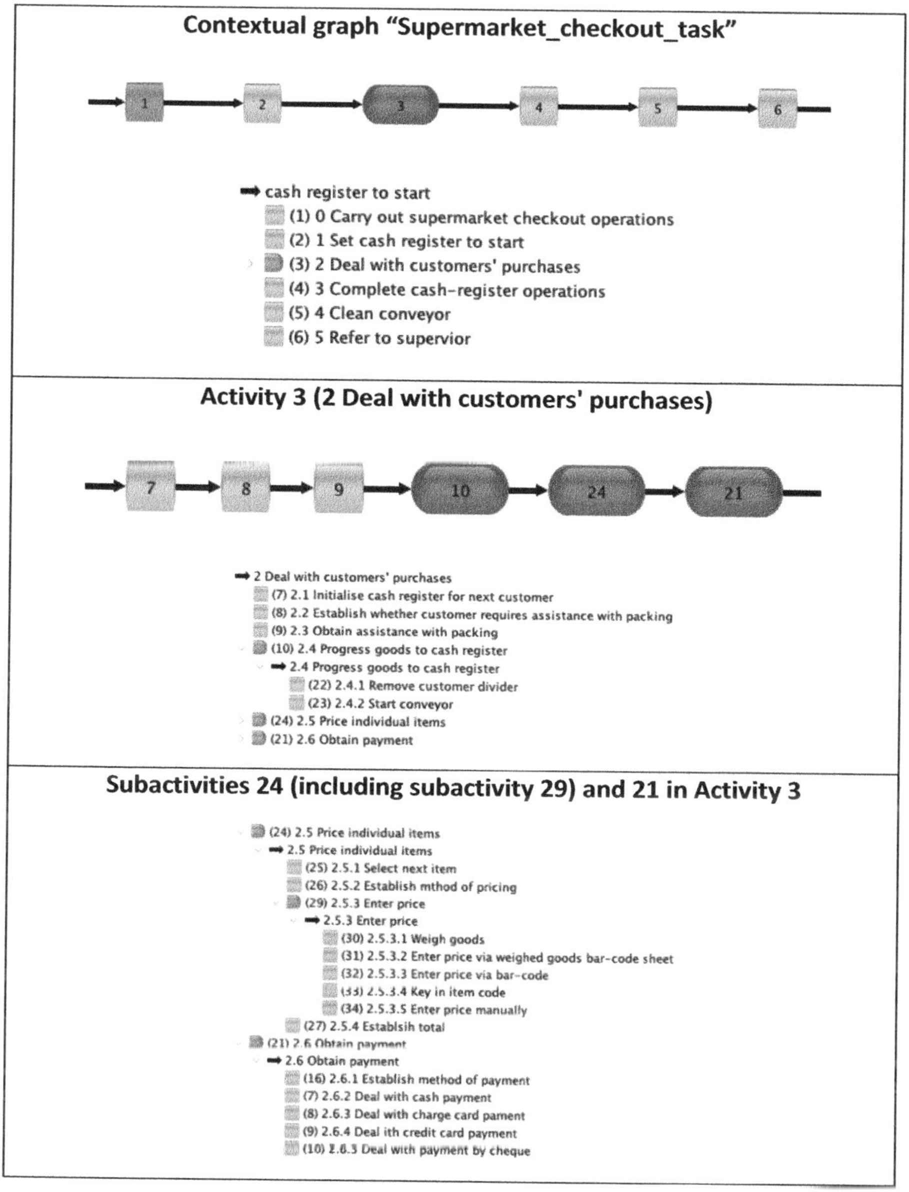

Figure 5.6. *CxG representation of the supermarket checkout task with details on activity 3 and subactivities 24 (including 29) and 21. For a color version of this figure, see www.iste.co.uk/brezillon/contextbasedmodeling.zip*

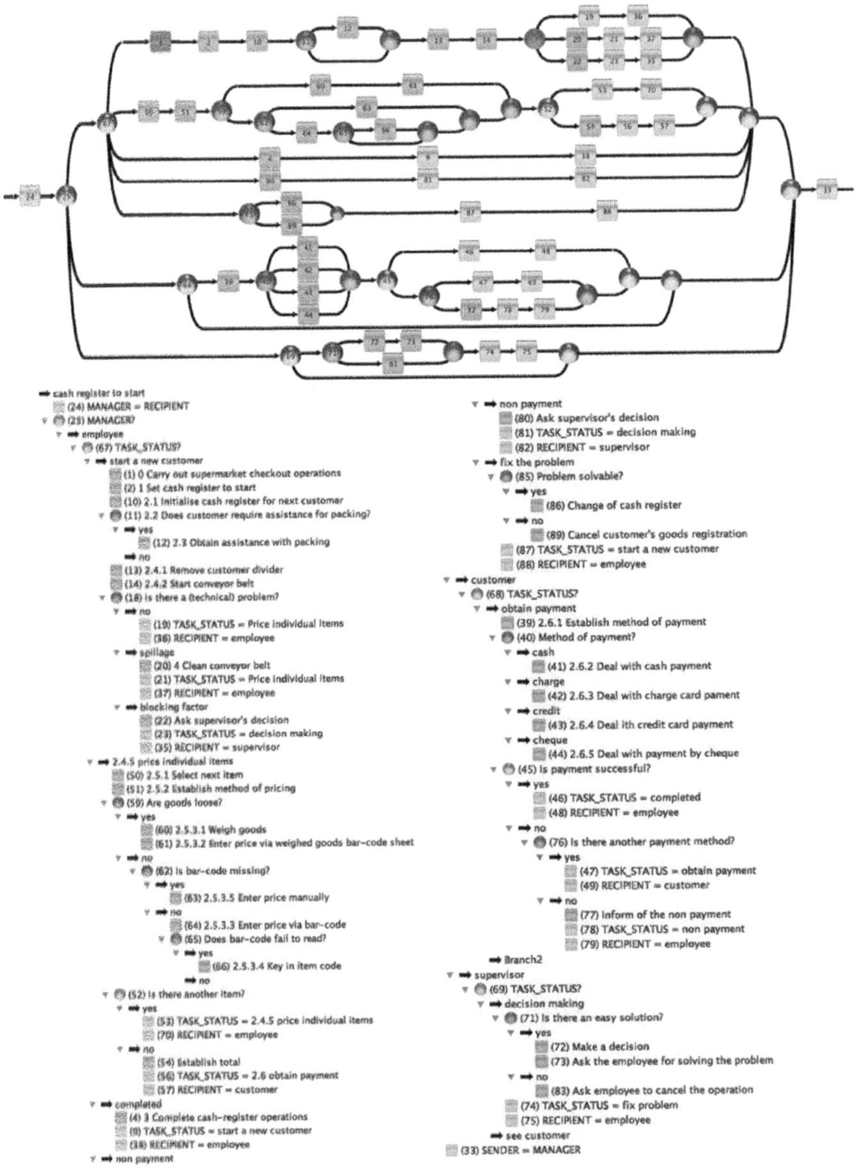

Figure 5.7. *CxG version of the supermarket checkout task in Figure 5.6. For a color version of this figure, see www.iste.co.uk/brezillon/contextbasedmodeling.zip*

Beyond the fact that the two representation formalisms are, globally, different and, locally, identical, we note more conceptual differences in the two representations in Figures F1 (5.6) and F2 (5.7):

– simplification by organization of the tasks by actors (cashier, customer, supervisor) in a collaborative view of the checkout task;

– simplification by introduction of activities for distinguishing the different main activities in F1 (4 Progress goods till, 5 Price individual items and 6 obtain payment);

– making explicit plans which were implicitly represented in F1 (e.g. plan 2.5.3 is isolated in Figure 5.6);

– version CxG_2.0 of the context-based formalism integrates loops such as plan 2.5 “If there are further items repeat from 1 Otherwise Exit” as a cyclic use of the contextual graph.

– easy introduction of new products and innovations (coupons, loyalty card, contactless payment, real-time management of products, etc.);

– contextual elements are not limited to binary choices, and even choices may be between items of different domains;

– there is no need for stopping rules; a contextual graph is directed and acyclic with one input and one output and the contextual reasoning stops when the shared context becomes unchanged.

CxG_1.0 and CxG_2 representations of the checkout task could be a way to guide the reorganization of the checkout task among actors and extend the representation to new options (e.g. contactless card or the “click & collect”).

5.4. The ACA project

5.4.1. *Introduction*

Based on the ACA project, we show the interest of capturing mental models for “good” as well as “bad” behaviors, and finally explain how the formalism of the contextual graphs comes from a decision-tree formalism (Brézillon 2010).

5.4.2. *The ACA method*

Table 5.1 presents the GDE matrix goals for driver education (see the ACA project in section 1.6). The matrix contains elements to take into consideration for modeling the driver’s behavior at the four decisional levels (plus the upper social-environment level). This vertical modeling of actors' behaviors allows powerful explanations. The degree of contextualization increases in the top-down approach of behavior studies, and the cause of an action at the operational level may be at the policy level.

Hierarchical levels of driver behaviour (Higher levels directly influence lower levels)	Essential elements of driver training: Knowledge and skills to master	Awareness of risk-increasing factors	Self-evaluation
Level 5 Social environment	*Knowledge of and control over:* • cultural and sub-cultural issues • work-related issues • group goals, values and motives • social environment and position	*Risks related to:* • cultural or work issues impacting on driving • context of journey such as work or pleasure • passengers	*Self-evaluation and awareness of:* • how culture or work issues impact on driving decisions and judgements • how placement within social group or work environment influences choices
Level 4 Personal goals for life and skills for living	*Knowledge of and control over:* • how life goals and personal tendencies affect driving behaviour • personal motives and competencies • lifestyle/life situation • age-related issues • personal values and ambitions	*Risks related to:* • acceptance of risk • self-enhancement through driving • high sensation seeking • susceptibility to social pressure • use of alcohol or drugs • personal values and attitudes to society	*Self-evaluation and awareness of:* • personal skills for impulse control • attitude towards risk • introspective competence • risky tendencies and habits • safety-negative motives
Level 3 Goals and context of driving	*Knowledge and skills concerning:* • purpose of the journey • route planning • evaluation of required driving time • evaluation of necessity of journey • safety and control of passengers	*Risks connected with:* • driver's physiological condition • purpose of the journey • driving environment such as rural/urban or day/night • social context and in-vehicle company	*Self-evaluation and awareness of:* • own physiological condition • journey planning skills • typical journey goals or expectations • typical risky driving motives • self-critical thinking skills
Level 2 Mastery of traffic situations	*Knowledge and skills concerning:* • traffic rules • observation • signals • anticipation • speed adjustment • safety margins	*Risks caused by:* • wrong expectations/assumptions • vulnerable road users • disobeying rules • unpredictable behaviour • information overload • difficult conditions such as darkness	*Self-evaluation and awareness of:* • ability to deal with a variety of traffic situations • observational skills • planning and anticipation • personal driving style • personal safety margins
Level 1 Vehicle control and manoeuvring	*Knowledge and skills concerning:* • control of direction and position • tyre grip and friction • technical aspects of vehicle • physical handling when cornering, accelerating and braking	*Risks associated with:* • insufficient skills • poor speed adjustment • difficult road conditions • improper use of seat belt, head restraint, etc. • under-inflated or worn tyres	*Self-evaluation and awareness of:* • understanding of essential knowledge and skills • strengths and weaknesses of basic vehicle control • ability to control the vehicle in challenging conditions

GDE Matrix - Based on the work of Hatakka et al. (2002) and Keskinen et al. (2010) — This version © Ged Wilmot & Claire Wilmot, 2018

Table 5.1. *The GDE matrix for modeling drivers' behaviors*

Contextual elements in this table are at different decisional levels. It is a flat inventory of all the contextual elements identified as related to the behavior of drivers, but difficult to exploit directly without a goal (a common thread). The goal in this project was to address a strategy-oriented training-driven as an alternative strategy to (financial) punishment-driven. In France, a driving license is associated with 12 points. For each offense (driving too fast, failure to respect traffic light, responsible for an accident), the driver loses from two to six points each time, and is not allowed to drive when they have lost the 12 points. A number of drivers face such a situation (loss of the 12 points, thanks to automatic radars, for example), but the French government has been obliged to find a way to allow those drivers to be able to reuse their car. Thus, there are training centers for drivers having lost their driving licenses (it is just necessary to attend the course for recovering the 12 points). It is a tactic corresponding to the strategy of money punishment.

The tactical goal relies on another strategy for helping bad drivers to understand their fault and to be trained to correct it. For that, we use the GDE matrix (Hatakka et al. 2002; Peräaho et al. 2003) to identify contextual elements that are the most relevant for our purpose. Sessions were followed in specialized centers for correcting bad behaviors (driving license with the 12 points lost) in order to, first, determine some profiles based on our selections of contextual elements of the GDE matrix, and, second, interrogate the bad drivers on their feeling on the official approach. The ACA method (for Adequate Category Learning in French) is a training process (for a human) which is based on two notions of similarity. The ACA method uses: (1) a typology of known behaviors, (2) a situation for the analysis, in which the behavior of the learner is analyzed in different contexts, and (3) specific scenarios that carry out the learning. Apprentices themselves determine their specific needs for knowledge in the form of an objective that the method will help to achieve. Different categories of "theoretical" drivers are assembled on the basis of contextual elements.

A category corresponds to a particular set of instantiations of variables (the contextual elements) that describe a theoretical behavior in the problem at hand; each behavior (or category) corresponds to a level of expertise of the category members. Examples of instantiation are "people knowing or not knowing the highway code and knowing or not knowing how to drive" and "people who know the highway code (and know how to drive or not)". A link between two categories is established from the comparison of behaviors through a comparison of the instantiations of contextual elements in each category. A link corresponds to the change of the instantiation of a single variable. The analysis situation is chosen so that apprentices react in their own way to the problem and their behavior can be identified from the categories of the typology.

A particular scenario is designed to progressively change instantiation of all contextual elements of categories in the typology. It checks whether the learner behaves similarly to the behavior represented by the appropriate category. Learning, which is concretely represented by these specific scenarios, is associated with a change of category over the links following from an inadequate category to a more adequate category. Thus, the ACA method makes it possible to adapt learning for each apprentice in three stages: (1) categorization of the apprentice in a starting category, (2) use of a list of intermediate categories between the starting and goal categories and (3) verification that the apprentice's behavior has approached that of the category goal. Three steps are based on two similarity measures. First, the similarity of membership intervenes to find which category can be related to apprentice behavior. This similarity is a distance between the learner behavior and known behaviors associated with categories. Second, the transformation similarity makes it possible to calculate the path, that is, the list of intermediate categories, between the starting and goal categories. The known behaviors associated with categories were established from a questionnaire established and posted on the

Internet to instantiate contextual elements that define categories. (For the statistical methods used in the formal part of the project, we have been obliged to only use binary values "yes" and "no" as possible instantiation of contextual elements.) The questionnaire included 162 questions for instantiation of 61 contextual elements. It was completed by 420 people who answered all the questions.

The questionnaire leads to a typology established on a set of behaviors to bring out the categories of behaviors. The techniques for establishing such a typology are generally derived from unsupervised automatic classification techniques (more specifically agglomeration methods in this work). A typology of 15 categories (see Figure 5.2) was obtained by agglomeration methods of the 420 responses to the online questionnaire. The data from the questionnaire being binary, a simple criterion of distance is sufficient to group data. Hierarchical classification methods seemed the most suitable for the application of the ACA method. The analysis situation aims to study the behavior of an apprentice faced with a given problem. The specific scenario is built to help the learner to change behavior depending on the correction of the instantiation of a variable (e.g. "aggressive?" from "true" to "false"). Goal-category validation is based on membership similarity. This validation step of the ACA method that guarantees the result of the learning.

5.4.3. *Application in road safety*

The application of the ACA learning method concerns road safety. The driver has a mental representation of the car-driving task that is constructed from inferences and the context in which the inferences are made. This coherent minimal mental representation allows us to understand a particular situation (the development of a mental model). Driving is the on-the-fly construction of a contextualized knowledge structure (Van Elslande 1992), and the mental-model building depends essentially on context awareness.

Categories describing behaviors of risky drivers have been identified from categories of general driving behaviors. Knowledge of driving errors makes it possible to determine those made by the learner driver and to select the scenarios that are suitable for correcting these driving errors. The relevant variables of each category have been identified. For example, if a category has the variable "aggressive" with the value "true" and all other classes have the variable "aggressive" with the value "false", then all aggressive drivers are grouped in the first class, and the "aggressive" variable is considered as a relevant contextual element for category 1. A subset of relevant contextual elements was then selected to identify categories that, each, characterize risky driving behavior. Only relevant contextual elements associated with driving errors were selected.

The procedure followed for the experiment is (Brézillon 2010):

– The apprentice first passes eight scenarios.

– At the end of each scenario, the apprentice answers a short questionnaire which allows them to instantiate their feeling at the time.

– At the end of the series of scenarios, the apprentice must answer a longer questionnaire that aims to make the apprentice aware of their behavior and their driving errors.

– Finally, the apprentice goes through the last three scenarios of validation.

One situation of analysis is a crossroads without priority in the form of T (see Figure 5.8(a)). The black car of the learner driver comes from the bottom road and goes straight. A white car is coming from the perpendicular road and wants to turn right (the lane of the black car), but the white car has a "give way" sign. An expert has identified the five scenarios of all the possible behaviors in the analysis situation (see Figure 5.8(b)); these behaviors have been modeled in a contextual graph associated with a space of situations; the latter details the complexity of the situation (normal, pre-critical and critical). (They will be shown in scenario 3 discussed just after this example.)

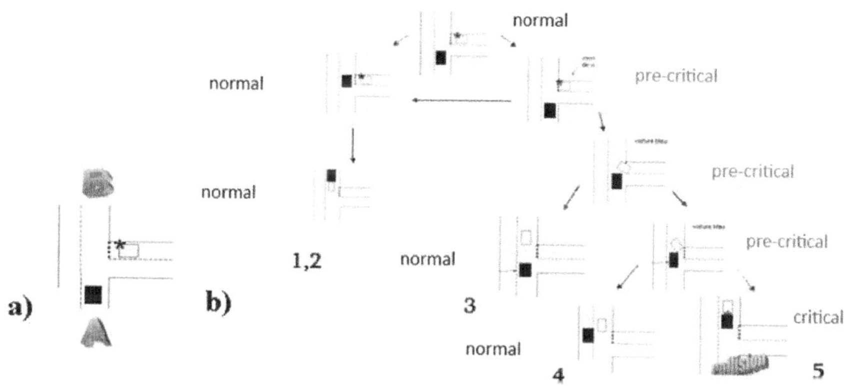

Figure 5.8. *Different possible situations defined by the expert. For a color version of this figure, see www.iste.co.uk/brezillon/contextbasedmodeling.zip*

Scenario 1 corresponds to the normal situation: the driver of the black car moves forward and the driver of the white car waits for them to pass, then turns right behind them. In scenario 2, the driver of the white car moves forward a little to reach the lane marking. Several reasons can explain this behavior. For example, the driver of car B wants to see if there is another car behind the black car, to decide if it can move on right after or not. The white car moves forward, but does not engage. The driver of the black car reduces speed, pays attention to the behavior of the driver of the white car and passes the intersection at reduced speed. The white car then enters the lane and turns right. Scenarios 1 and 2 come together since they end in the same way.

After two scenarios (3 and 4) leading to two pre-critical situations finishing on a normal situation, in scenario 5, the driver of the white car is still trying to pass the black car, but this time the driver of the black car is absolutely not attentive to the white car: the driver is convinced that they are within their rights, and that the white car must give way to them. The driver of the black car therefore does not consider the fact that the white car does not respect the signs. When the driver of the black car realizes that the white car is about to enter, they no longer have time to brake, nor to try to avoid them by passing in the left lane. They brake, but it is insufficient, and a collision occurs between the two cars. Thus, changes in a situation are context-dependent, with contextual elements concerning the user, the task realization, the situation and the local environment.

The description of scenario 3 (Table 5.2) is chosen among the 12 scenarios that were defined in collaboration with INRETS-BRON for carrying out the experiment. Each scenario is illustrated by:

– a screenshot of the critical situation present in the scenario as it is seen by the participant in the simulator (left part);

– comments on the reasons for choosing this situation, its degree of criticality and error variables that are instantiated thanks to this situation (right part);

– the space of behaviors shown as a contextual graph of the possible behaviors of a driver in this situation;

– the space of situations makes up the scenario is represented by a grid in which the columns represent the evolution of time and the lines of the situations;

– the correspondence between the contextual graph of the possible behaviors and the situations.

Each situation presents one of the three states of criticality: normal situation (white), critical situation (in which an accident occurs, in red), pre-critical situation (ultimate situation where the driver can still avoid the critical situation if it reacts quickly, in yellow).

<table>
<tr><th colspan="2">Scenario 3</th></tr>
<tr><th>Description</th><th>Comments</th></tr>
<tr><td>Critical situation
</td><td>Comments: T-junction requiring anticipation
Scenario:

The first oncoming vehicle turned sharply to the left at the crossroads just before the participant’s arrival. The Vehicle following this car (the black car in the picture) will also turn left when it should give way.</td></tr>
<tr><td>Behavior space

</td><td>Graph of the possible behaviors
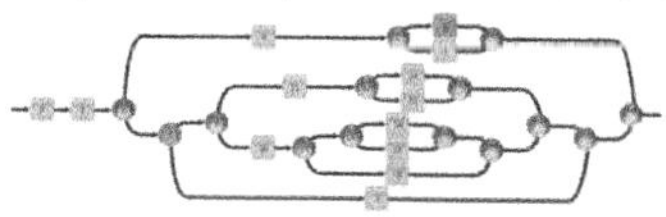
The graph models the way the driver analyzes the situation by first checking if there is a car on the right, then looking at the vehicles in front, before deciding whether or not to reduce his speed and manage a possible collision risk.</td></tr>
<tr><td>Situation space
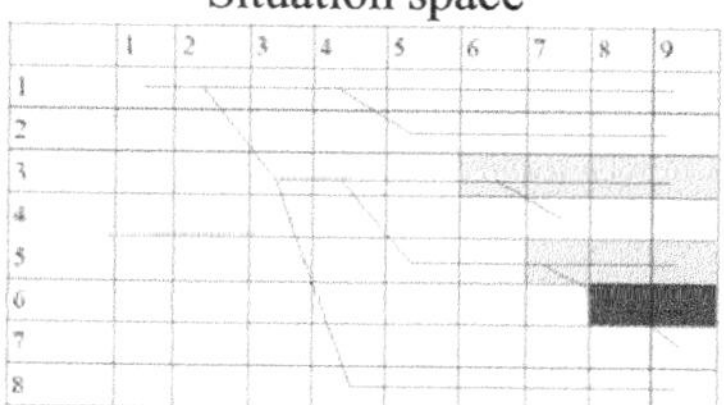</td><td>This scenario has a critical situation (in red in the figure) where the driver passes between two vehicles that are too close together and two pre-critical situations (in yellow in the figure) where the driver takes risks.</td></tr>
</table>

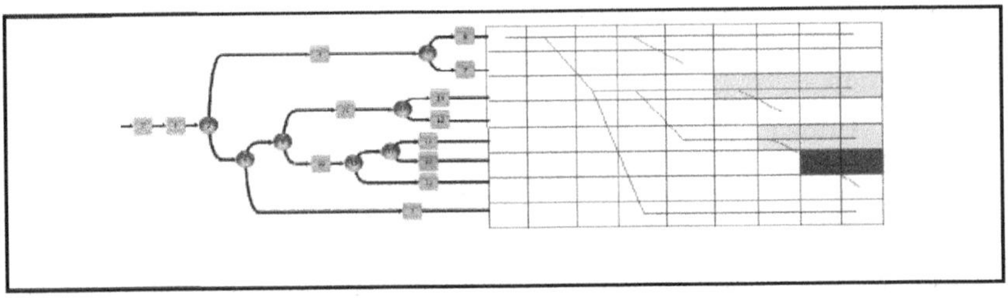

Table 5.2. *A critical situation, a behavior space and a situation space. For a color version of this table, see www.iste.co.uk/brezillon/contextbasedmodeling.zip*

Table 5.2 presents scenario 3 in Brézillon (2010) for analyzing a situation proposed to the apprentice that corresponds to a crossroads without priority with two vehicles. This situation analysis has been broken-down into several scenarios. A scenario corresponds to the instantiation of particular conditions (contextual elements) of the situation of analysis. In this scenario 3, several errors can be checked at the same time: basic competences, good prediction, good speed adjustment and compliance with safety margins. A scenario allows us to test several errors at the same time, each error being tested in several scenarios. In order to classify the apprentice in a starting category, the instantiation process of each contextual elements takes place according to the protocol with the following methods:

– A statistical method analyzes traces of apprentice's behavior for finding the first instantiation of the contextual elements.

– A cognitive method analyzes the behavior of the driver using the same traces and instantiations found by the statistical method, verifies and corrects this first instantiation. The purpose of the cognitive method is to explain certain errors too. The result is a new, more accurate instantiation of the variables of the apprentice's behavior.

– A decision method finally determines the theoretical category that is the closest to that found for the driver. The apprentice is then placed in the category that best describes their behavior.

The objective of the transformation is to determine the course among the categories that the driver must follow in the typology to arrive at the category-goal through progressive learning. For this purpose, we determine (1) all the links between the categories of the typology, but only the paths that lead to the category-goal of the driver are retained; (2) the errors that the driver must correct in the category to arrive at the category-goal are determined. Each scenario makes it possible to correct a driving error, which blocks the driver in a category other than their category-goal. The driver goes through the specific scenarios one by one (and therefore progresses from one intermediate category to another) and, at the end of each scenario, the validation of the arrival category confirms the appropriate change of category.

Figure 5.9 gives an example of validation where the highlighted lines show the path taken by a driver from the initial category through the categories to their appropriate category.

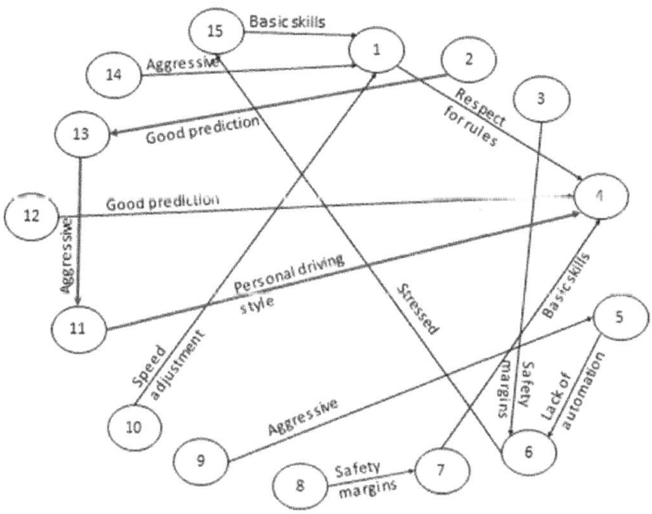

Figure 5.9. *Example of the path followed among intermediary categories by the learner (Brézillon 2010). For a color version of this figure, see www.iste.co.uk/brezillon/contextbasedmodeling.zip*

A second kind of results are indirect consequences of application of the ACA method. The data from the questionnaire provide other interesting contextual information. The main errors initially identified included:

– failure to assess the need for a journey before taking the car;

– failure to respect the rules of conduct;

– good predictive power of the driver;

– failure to respect the safety margins;

– the feeling of having your own driving style;

– concern for fuel economy;

– lack of automatism;

– driving for no specific reason;

– stress at the wheel;

– the lack of objectivity in their self-assessment of their driving abilities.

Figure 5.10 shows the evolution of five of these errors. The drivers have been grouped into four age groups: 18–25 years old, 26–36 years old, 36–55 years old and 56–65 years old representing an evolution of temporal context of the drivers.

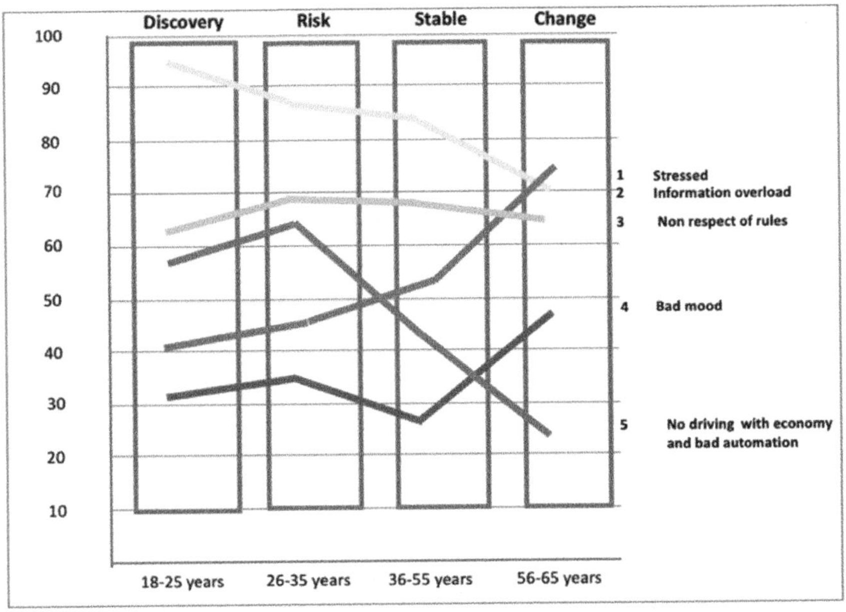

Figure 5.10. *Evolution of a some driving errors. For a color version of this figure, see www.iste.co.uk/brezillon/contextbasedmodeling.zip*

The aim was to check whether errors had the same importance for all the apprentices:

– The discovery period (18–25 years) with problems of safety margins, information overload and failure to assess the need for a journey. The main concern of this group is skill issues. They have acquired a driving license for their mastery of the highway code and a minimal experience of driving a car with a side monitor to correcting driving errors. However, the real experience relies on the skills acquired as a complete driver alone.

– The risk period (26–35 years) is marked by the development of their own driving style (acquisition of personal skills), and all that concerns its relationship to risk (safety margin, obedience to rules, information overload). It is the period when the driver gains self-confidence and explore the limits of their competences.

– The stability period (36–45 years) when the drivers "found themselves" and stabilized their relationship to risk. They have found their driving style in their previous period and established a stable "perimeter" of this driving style. In this period, generally the driver has a new social life, like a wife and children, or begin to have health problems. Thus, the search to put back its limits is over.

– The driving change period (56–65 years) with an evolution of the driver's skills with age, although that age does not modify the relationship of the driver with driving. The driver becomes obliged to keep new skills and driving compatible and to revise the initial driving style. It is a problem especially when new skills are less efficient than the previous ones.

In Figure 5.10, we only present five contextual elements selected to identify the theoretical categories established previously. The goal is to show that the few contextual elements selected initially (called variables) can be associated with other contextual elements to give a more complete image of the driving errors. (Driving supposes a context covering a large number of situations.)

Driving error 1 concerns the stress that appears increasingly with age. Older drivers are stressed on the road due to diminishing skills, and an increasing lack of self-confidence. Conversely, there are different reasons for explaining the limited stress of young drivers such as weak driving experience and thus a lack of pragmatic knowledge about problems with driving (e.g. let a correct distance with the car followed for avoiding a sudden brake, especially if it is raining). Stress also can be due to awareness of an information overload and the feeling to be unable to correctly analyze a situation, thus expressing the fact that contextual elements may be related to each other.

Driving error 2 concerns information overload. This contextual element shows that in the beginning, the young driver is very prone to information overload because driving is a new experience with no pragmatic knowledge (such as proceduralized contexts) and there is a lot of information to contend with. In the following two groups, experience grows with the acquisition of driving skills (concretized by accumulation of proceduralized contexts for identifying specific contexts requiring attention), and thus the need for information being less important. In the last group, senior drivers, on the one hand, have proceduralized contexts covering a large part of information and thus rely on their automatisms, and, on the other hand, they reject information on, say, new devices they do not use or old devices became unsuitable over the years. The main weakness here is the lack of updating their contextual knowledge.

Driving error 3 concerns the non-compliance with the rules. This contextual element has similar importance for the four groups with a significant weight (about 70%). However, the reasons may be quite different for each group. For the first group, rules, maybe, are not well assimilated (or forgotten), and young drivers are discovering that practice may be interpreted differently of the official rules. The rules (e.g. the orange traffic light says normally to stop while drivers prefer speed up to reach the other side of the crossroad before the red traffic light and being stopped in the middle of the crossroad). For the senior group, rules can be forgotten, compiled with other rules or deliberately ignored because never used (e.g. the signal "watch out, falling rocks" does not concern a driver staying in cities).

Driving error 4 concerns bad mood. Generally, young drivers love to drive whatever their mood. Thus, bad mood is not important and concerns 30% of the drivers in the two first groups, and even less than 30% in the third group in which drivers have a stable driving style with automatisms coming from robust proceduralized contexts. Conversely, almost 50% of senior drivers often have a "mood-dependent" behavior, thinking at a number of problems during driving that becomes backstage with respect to personal problems, up to thinking about problems disconnected from driving (e.g. prepare an intervention at the meeting where they are going).

Driving error 5 concerns the lack of consideration for economy and automatisms. It is an error common for young drivers that favor pleasure to drive over considerations of economy and automatisms. They often take the car for the pleasure of driving aimlessly and drive fast. This is particularly striking at a time like now when the price of gasoline is double of 5 years ago. Conversely, senior drivers take their car for a precise reason difficult to satisfy by public transport. However, now (10 years after the study), we think of problems such as the future, the pollution, the climate, the cost to fill the tank of the car, etc., and young drivers may be sensible to the ecological problems too.

The results show that the statistical method alone improves driver behavior in the majority of cases (57%), but this improvement is stronger afterward (73%) with the use of the cognitive method in which context plays an important role on car driving. Moreover, the mental models developed now (10 years after the study) depend essentially on contextual elements, such as ecology and climate, far from the mental-model building. As a consequence, we are obliged to change our habits and develop new mental models. The same observation makes in the different age groups can have radically different contextual reasons more or less related to the activity. For instance, the respect for speed limits in France is more related to the wish to avoid to pay an (expensive) ticket or/and lose the driver license than to respect the law. Conversely, some drivers slow down arriving at a green traffic light because the traffic light may become orange.

Simplifying assumption of statistical methods (binary values for each contextual element) was a limiting factor of the study to exploit the entire context of car driving. The context evolves during the mental-model building: content of the car tank decreases during car driving, and gasoline stations are not frequent on a highway; speed limits are different in a street and on a highway. Thus, to answer the question “Respect of speed limit?”, we must to know where we are driving (another contextual element). On a county road, the speed limit is 80 km/h but when the county road crosses a village, the speed limit becomes 50 km/h, and the transition county-village is not always indicated clearly because the size and topography of the village may be subject to interpretation by the car driver. Driving a car implies the building of a mental model based on a contextual reasoning for each task realization. Thus, we have a collection of mental models of other drivers' behaviors, and on the road we have frequently to identify which mental model applies to the driver before, after, on the left or right side our car. Is the other driver aggressive? Driving fast or dangerously? Our collection of information on other cars moving around us (e.g. fast-moving car indicates a fast-reacting driver may be aggressive) makes mental model as a micro-simulator on the potential behaviors of the other drivers. We update our mental models in real-time to maintain a “shared context” with the other drivers to avoid an accident.

An important aspect of the mental model is the possibility of anticipating the behaviors of other drivers and make a decision consequently. For example, a car coming from the right with a “give way” must let us cross the crossroad (our first mental model of the situation). But... the first difference of the other driver's behavior (e.g. the car continues to move despite the “give way”) from our mental model triggers an alert of a change of context and the activation of a new mental model for managing the (potential) critical situation. Information coming from the others are data that we interpret based on our experience. It means that, first, information is contextualized, and, second, two drivers in the same situation will react differently.

5.5. Workflow modeling in an ACP Department

5.5.1. *The initial work*

Attieh et al. (2013) present a contextualization of the anatomical and cytology pathology (ACP) workflow for analyzing nonconformity during reception and registration steps. The workflow monitors work quality in the ACP Department, the actions, detection and correction of nonconformities as well as a base for intelligent software creation that links different modules in medical care. Its organization relies on rooms and floors that samples cross from the room at reception to the room where the physician signs, through different rooms on two different floors for preparing and analyzing samples. Anatomical and cytology pathology is essential in oncology. ACP physicians macroscopically and microscopically examine patients' tissue samples and cells in order to establish diagnosis and factors of severity of the disease, thus contributing to medical care. ACP physicians follow procedures that include a gross examination (visual examination of organs), dissection and sampling of surgical specimens according to standardized protocols and then a microscopic examination of stained tissue sections. Several techniques such as immuno-histochemistry, cytogenetic and molecular allow us to identify abnormalities in cells or tissue.

The ACP process follows a workflow that starts with a request form associated with a sample and after each action, information collected is integrated in the laboratory information management system file related to the ACP examination. While conformity is the fulfillment of a requirement, nonconformity is defined as "the failure to fulfill the requirements of a standard, in whole or in part" which may be prejudicial to the patient. Beyond the large spectrum of data, information and knowledge about the task to realize, other contextual elements intervene such as the type of task to accomplish, the actor realizing the task (technician, pathologist…), the situation in which the task is realized and the available resources in the immediate environment. Such contextual elements may impact task realization, and, if they are not integrated in the reasoning, they could lead to nonconformity.

Task automation in the ACP Department is limited because it depends largely on human decision-making, especially at reception and registration where actors rely implicitly or explicitly on many contextual elements to decide which actions must be done. The decision-making process includes assembling, organizing, structuring a large number of heterogeneous contextual elements, to arrive at an action sequence. A quality process guarantees each patient an assortment of diagnostic and therapeutic acts, which ensures the best result in terms of health. This supposes that all actors adhere to rules and standards to find out who did what, how and why. Therefore, it is required to elaborate recommendations, written procedures and protocols, to guide the workflow and the quality control. Nonconformity situations, which may occur during the process leading to the result (or the conclusion), are difficult to identify to correct the problem and to learn how to avoid it again because generally the result appears as more important than the process leading to it. Attieh et al.'s (2013) paper details contextual elements intervening at the two first steps of the process, namely the reception and registration activities (see Table 5.3).

Room	Tasks and subtasks	Actors	LIS and connections	Constraints
Reception Registration	• To receive (sample and request form): - Stamp date and time - Assign an examination number - Check the conformity - Contact the pathologist or technician concerned - Check the conditioning and the fixing fluid volume • To register immediately or later: - Identity verification on GILDA, origin of the examination - Protocols - Assign to the proper benches: cytology, Frozen section/fresh tissue, gross examination, cassette processing	Reception's technician	SGL Gilda Printers labels	Nonconformity Emergency situations' management Decision making and choices

Table 5.3. *Workflow table at reception and registration areas of ACP Dpt*

Table 5.3 presents a part of the workflow in terms of location, task to realize, actors that are concerned, laboratory identification system (LIS) and connection systems with the hospital information system and constraints. It is an important tool that highlights and identifies different key elements in the reception/registration step, for instance, to identify the task and who is doing it.

Samples and request forms reach the ACP Department by two possible paths: (1) the pneumatic system, from the clinical wards, operating rooms, the sorting center; and (2) a messenger for large surgical specimens and samples from other services not connected to the pneumatic. A request form is attached to each sample, which is a paper document and therefore not yet computerized. An ACP technician takes charge of the sample and the request form; stamps the date and time of reception on the request form; and checks the conformity of both the sample form (e.g. evidence noted on pot) and the request form (e.g. identification label of the patient, sample nature, clinical diagnosis). If the sample and request form are compliant, the ACP technician registers the information on the sample, prepares a folder for eventually renumbering bottles and the request form, registers actions and results concerning the sample, and alerts the duty doctor (the decision-maker for the sample). The nonconformity that does not block the completion of the examination must be declared to the sender department, and identified anomalies are recorded through a keyword entered in the computer file. Nonconformity blocking examination completion requires a form to be filled out explaining the reasons. In the latter nonconformity situation, the ACP technician records the incident and waits for the final decision to be made by the Head of the AP Service. Once the reception part is completed, the same technician that initially has taken charge of the sample will proceed with the registration task that includes a number of actions, a large part of them depending on human decision-making, which relies on training, competence and experience.

5.5.2. *Contextual modeling of the workflow*

The functioning of an ACP Department is associated with a set of contextual elements mainly about nonconformity and related domain knowledge, nonconformity generally leading to a whole series of inadequate actions. Thus, it is an important challenge to limit, as much as possible, risky situations by detecting them at the source (information meetings, observation and controls…). If measures are necessary conditions, they are not sufficient because they do not make explicit at which particular level the error did happen and which contextual(s) element(s) could be controlled to avoid it next time. The modeling of the task realization in the contextual graph (CxG) formalism is based on the four sources of contextual elements coming from the actor, the task, the situation and the local environment.

The actor

ACP technicians (actors) at reception and registration desks constitute a highly qualified staff trained to accomplish their tasks under control of the medical staff. Non-habilitated actor (with different skills) will generate a risk of nonconformity. Even with technicians working routinely, there are risks of nonconformity because technicians may rely too much on their experience and be less attentive to task realization (e.g. emergency situation, noncompliance with instructions, trying to help another actor, etc.). Moreover, several samples may arrive simultaneously, the technician normally handles them one by one. Nevertheless, an error may occur during task execution, especially if samples have the same nature. Another risk is the mixing or confusion in examinations if the technician tries to deal with multiple samples simultaneously. The actor responsible for any action is clearly identified (signed initials, IT code); otherwise, responsibility of the mistake cannot be allocated to a specific actor, which could affect the follow-up and nonconformity management. In addition, signing the request form provides written evidence and thus a trail to explore if any error occurs. Cultural and organizational diversity of actors also is an important element that could be considered as well as the age and experience of the technicians.

The task

The task is modeled in the workflow as a multi-step (sub)process. Checking request-form conformity is made in eight items. The ACP technician controls them in one order or another depending on preferences for control and other contextual elements. A similar procedure is applied for checking sample conformity. Conformity of the move from one step to the next is also checked. The move may concern a unique technician or a transfer of tasks between technicians. As a consequence, context switching plays an important role (contextual dimension of the task). The nature of the task is another contextual element, for instance, deciding if everything is compliant with norms or not, if the conformity blocks the sample processing, choosing medical and technical sectors, and evaluating situation emergency. Moreover, decision-making depends on multiple factors. For example, the implicit rule in the ACP Department "What I touch, I treat" imply a mandatory transfer of work responsibility from one person to another because its non-respect is a risk of error. Responsibility transfer supposes information transfer, situation assessment to manage with all the necessary details, especially with a new technician.

The situation

The ACP technician selects a method among different ones based on training and contextual information such as "the patient is known", "the surgeon is waiting the answer". Such contextual information (and others such as "it is vacation time and the team is reduced" or "the device X is busy") is characteristic of a situation. The simultaneous deposit of several samples may lead to errors by mixing examinations. The emergency of the examination and work overload generate stress, implicitly or explicitly, on actors' actions. This stress is handled differently from one actor to another. Nonconformity situation requires specific actions on the usual process. Thus, the working context must be replaced by a specific and independent nonconformity context for problem solving before returning to the working context.

Local environment

Environment includes all the entities (objects, space rooms, people and events) that are external to the current task but with a potential impact on task realization. The environment is all that may modify the normal status (1) of the task realization (e.g. software crash following overvoltage, intranet problem, broken pot containing the sample, empty or missing glove box), (2) of the actor (physician on duty having problems and thus unable to concentrate), (3) of the situation (e.g. power supply failure, poor conditioning of a sample, any ventilation or cooling system problem, as well as personal discussions during working hours). A major risk is a failure in the pneumatic system generating either delay to the reception or possible sample loss. Fortunately, degraded procedures are implemented for emergency situations to avoid interrupting or interfering with the work.

Figures 5.11–5.15 represent integration of the workflow and contextual elements identified above. The contextual graph contains a series of activities representing workflow components. Each activity is a contextual graph itself.

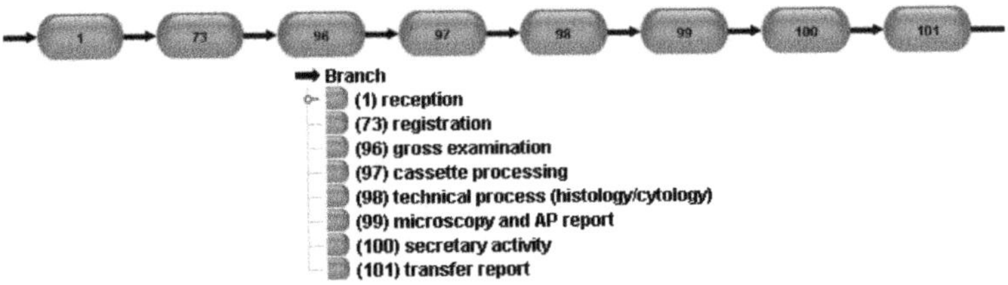

Figure 5.11. *Examination processing in the ACP Department. For a color version of this figure, see www.iste.co.uk/brezillon/contextbasedmodeling.zip*

The activity in the reception room (first activity in Figure 5.11) is described by the contextual graph shown in Figure 5.12.

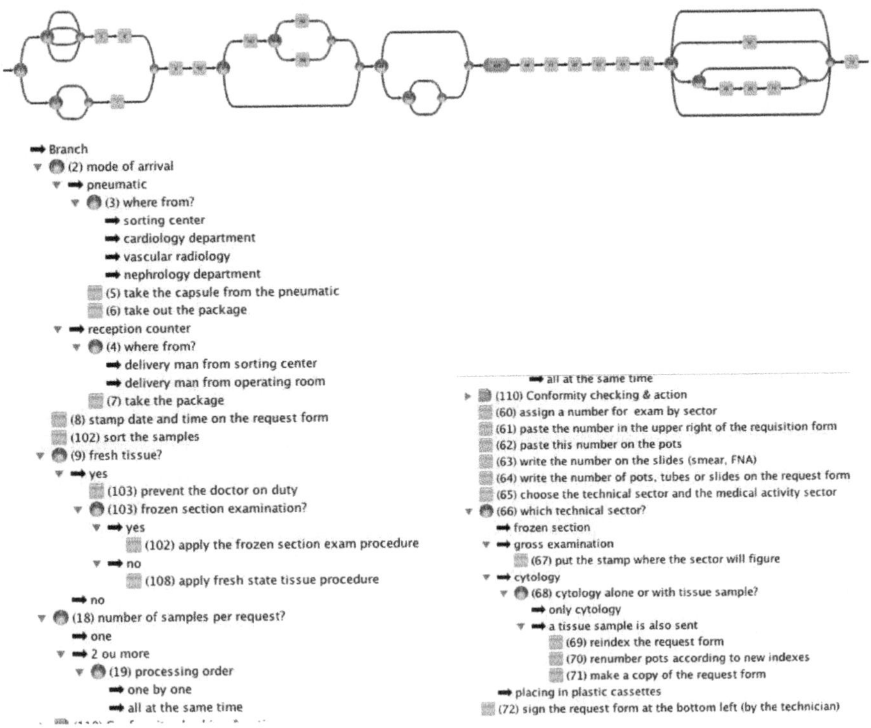

Figure 5.12. *Modeling of the reception workflow. For a color version of this figure, see www.iste.co.uk/brezillon/contextbasedmodeling.zip*

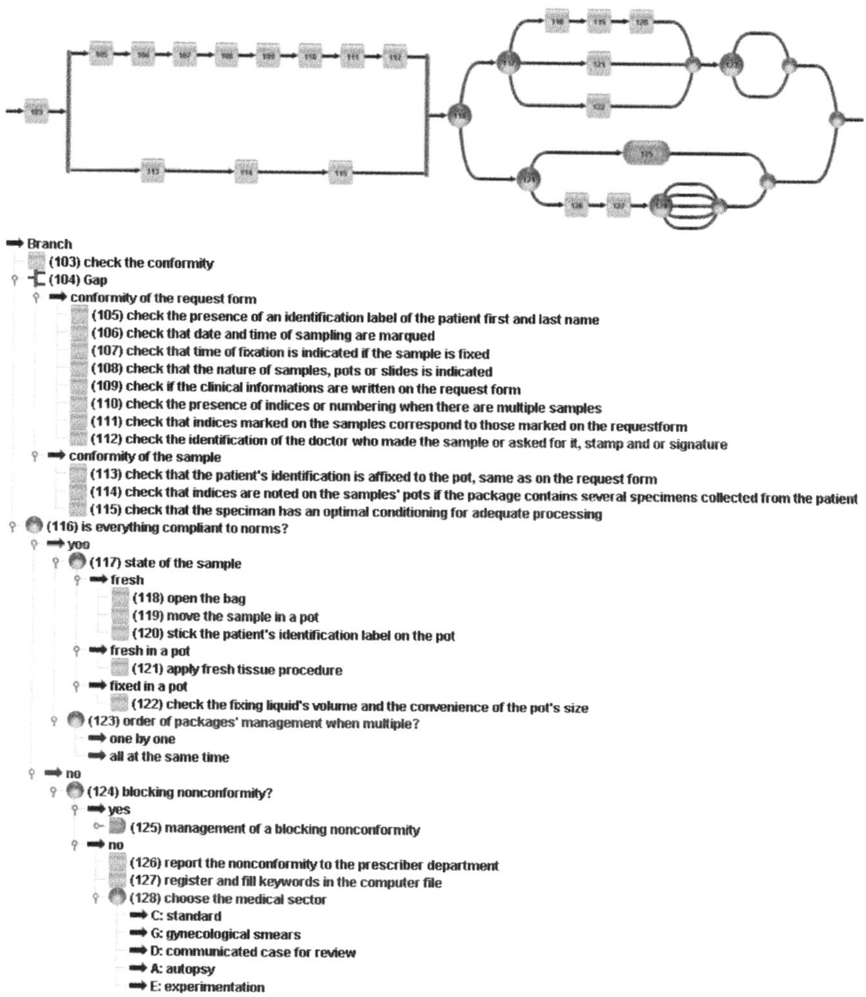

Figure 5.13. *Conformity checking and actions (activity 110 in Figure 5.11). For a color version of this figure, see www.iste.co.uk/brezillon/contextbasedmodeling.zip*

The management of a blocking nonconformity (activity 125 in Figure 5.13) is obtained by a sequence of actions (see Figure 5.14).

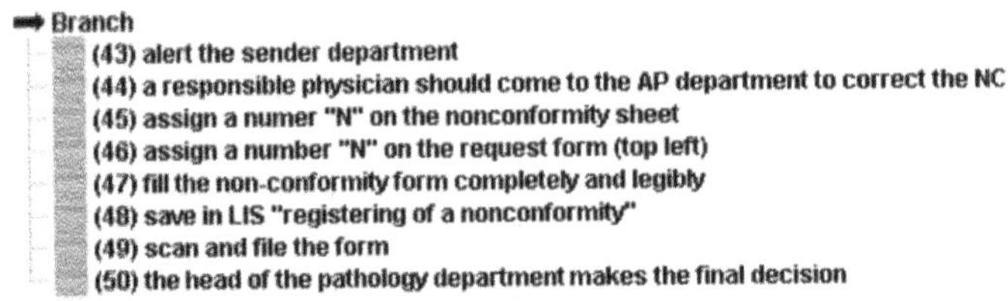

Figure 5.14. *Management of a blocking nonconformity (activity 125 in Figure 5.13). For a color version of this figure, see www.iste.co.uk/brezillon/contextbasedmodeling.zip*

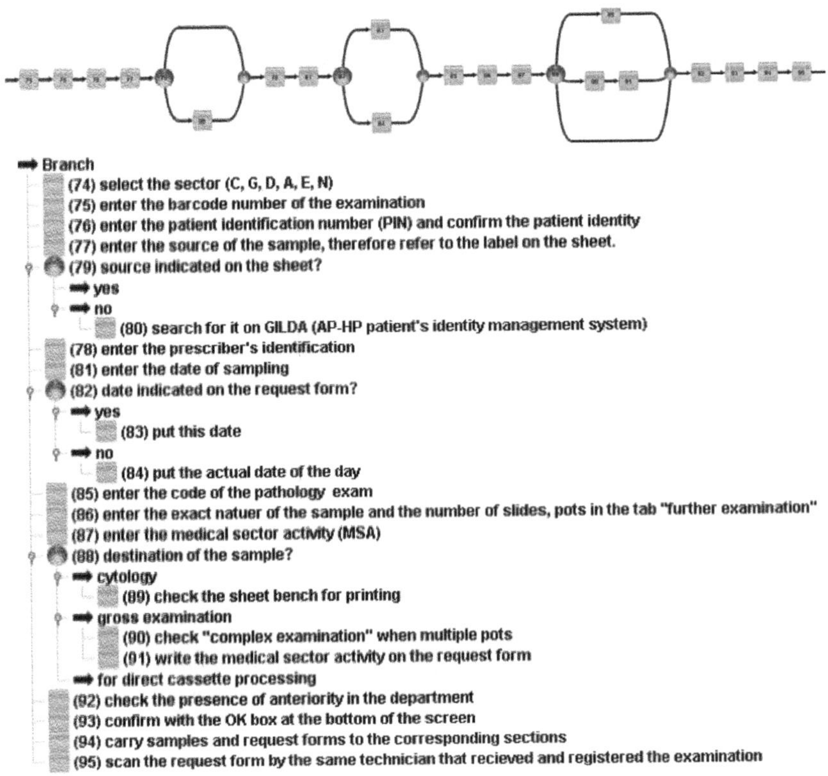

Figure 5.15. *Modeling of the registration workflow. For a color version of this figure, see www.iste.co.uk/brezillon/contextbasedmodeling.zip*

5.5.3. *Discussion on context-based modeling of workflow*

A contextual graph gives a unified view on the relationships between actors, tasks, documents or links to a specific action, the working context, new situations acquired from learning by assimilation or accommodation and finally on allowing analysis. Analysis of the contextual graph reveals the deficiency of the standard procedure documents, and accordingly the necessity of improving procedures and quality control. In other words, a contextual graph is a way to objectify events influencing the AP examination process and development of practices. Therefore, the contextual graph can be considered as a monitoring tool on work quality. Practices in the contextual graph (all paths from the input to the output of the graph) can by analyzed at different moments. Identifying in the contextual graph step-by-step the real practice developed by an actor allows the detection of a discrepancy that could lead to noncompliance of the real practice with respect to the path followed in the contextual graph. It is then possible to explain the reason for the occurrence of nonconformity. Generally, it is bad identification of the instantiation of a contextual element that leads to an incorrect decision.

The CxG formalism also may point out when a new problem occurs when not yet encountered. It is due to the absence of a contextual element in the contextual graph that always had the same instantiation till now. Then, a new practice must be developed and introduced in the contextual graph for this new instantiation. Arriving at a contextual element CE1, its instantiation is either known, the activity on the branch is performed and the system continues, or the actor must provide the new instantiation and specify the new practice. However, CE1 may also not be expected because, prior to CE1, another contextual element CE2 is missing. For example, when we prepare coffee, there is the action "Take water", that implicitly is supposed to be running water, but one actor may use mineral water for preparing coffee. For acquiring this new practice, it is necessary to introduce the new contextual element CE2 "Which type of water?" with the possible instantiations "running water" as previously and "mineral water" for the new action "Use mineral water". Adding a new instantiation to CE1 (and the specific action) is learning by assimilation, while adding CE2 and distinguishing between the two practices according to the type of water is learning by accommodation. Such an evolution of the contextual graph comes down to develop an experience base with all the practices developed and enriched incrementally. Moreover, it is possible to provide in a few clicks different statistics such as the nonconformity source, cause, examination number and description, correlation with the day, the sample sender, the technician at reception, etc., the goal being to allow an incremental revision of the contextual graph. It is also a way to keep technicians aware of their work and let them react immediately to correct a degrading situation. Complete information could then be provided in a "patient record" in preset files, where the prescriber has to fill in the boxes and whose access is limited to persons involved and protected by passwords. Explanation can be reinforced by introducing "bad practices" in experience bases for the purpose of training new technicians by allowing an AI system to know that what the technician is doing wrong.

The context-based representation of practices (i.e. mental models) developed by actors is richer than procedures and recommendations generally proposed because the latter covers a large class of problems but does not apply to any particular problem because a procedure never fits the specific contexts at hand. In the CxG formalism, contextual elements structure operational knowledge (practices). The interest of representing technicians' practices instead of procedures at the ACP Department is: (1) to identify risky practices, (2) to understand how a mistake has been made, (3) to train new ACP technicians and (4) to know how to manage nonconformity. It is the situation also found in car driving where the highway code does not replace the practice of driving. The main point here is that nonconformity appears when a contextual element was left implicit or forgotten. For example, between two examinations, a woman gets married and comes the second time with a new name, and the physician does not find the results of the previous examination. Another reason is the change of instantiation of a contextual element. For example, sample status is modified by inattention of the AP technician distracted by a phone call. A risk may become a prejudice because context is not considered, underestimated or lost among too many other contextual elements. Thus, context-based modeling of a technician task is essential to anticipate, control and avoid possible risks. It is particularly important when the workflow of the ACP Department activities contains a sequence of interrelated actions where an error at a particular step of the process leads to a cascade of wrong events or may be identified only at the final step of the sample processing. Modeling the context of a workflow in an ACP Department and representing the different steps in a contextual graph leads to structure-relevant practices (the effective task) instead of official procedures (the prescribed task) that are not applied directly but instead guide the use of the contextual graph.

5.6. Context modeling and semiotics

The notion of recontextualization discussed by Brannen (2004) in semiotics seems close to the process of contextualization–decontextualization–recontextualization (CDR) discussed previously. In the CDR process, contextualization is the process identifying an instantiation associated with a contextual element, decontextualization is the extraction of the contextual element of an instantiated contextual element and recontextualization is the allocation of a new instantiation to the contextual element instead of the previous one (the origin). However, the meaning of recontextualization in AI and semiotics are different.

Brannen (2004) analyzes the two first attempts of the Walt Disney Company made at internationalization: Tokyo Disneyland (1983) and Disneyland Paris (1992), with the same international strategy: 49% owned (profits) by Disney, 51% owned by a separate company, and commission rate (10% of admission fees and 5% of food and merchandise revenues). The goal was to implant a strict copy of the initial park (Anaheim, US) in Japan and in France, and the internationalization challenge was assessing the fit of what they wish to transfer abroad with the new host environment. Generally, firms transfer their whole organizations, including business models, steeped in image-based, ideological, people-dependent management that are even more closely related to context and sociocultural environment in which they are enacted. However, if the source is significantly foreign from target, the transferred assets may not fit the target context in the host country. Foreignness means dissimilarity (i.e. of lack of fit) in operating contexts of a multinational enterprise (MNE)'s home and host environments. Exemplar MNEs are Coca-Cola, Levi Jeans and McDonald's whose products have been successfully marketed with a global marketing strategy capitalizing, in part, on their foreignness. Disney success in Tokyo was the catalyst for Disneyland Paris internationalization. However, Disney drew the wrong conclusions from the apparently problem-free "copy-exactly" strategy it used in Japan. Even with an opening of a cold and rainy Spring day, Tokyo Disneyland was an immediate success with, after a while, 90% of repeat visitors and a replacement of traditional end-of-year school graduation outing sites such as temples. The opening Disneyland Paris was far under expectations in attendance, with a loss of $1.5 billion two years later. Firm assets are vulnerable to misalignment, because they are closely embedded in the sociocultural environment of the recipient culture and, therefore, resulting in misconstrued meanings associated with the transferred firm assets. In Disneyland Paris, European visitors come from different sociocultural environments and take advantage of their vacations in France for going to Disneyland Paris. This point was misunderstood at the source country because in US (and Japan) going to Disneyland is part of vacations, which are short in time and money-intensive, while in Europe, vacations are time-intensive (four weeks with a controlled budget). This misunderstanding was surprising because, on other aspects, the US is closer to France than to Japan (e.g. in US, Statue of Liberty, and Sleeping Beauty's castle in the theme park centerpiece originated in France). This point should have been essential before to automatically apply a problem-free "copy-exactly" strategy.

Using semiotics and the Walt Disney Company's experiences in internationalization, Brannen developed the notion of semantic fit as a necessary complement to strategic fit and formalize a conceptual model of recontextualization – the process by which firm assets take on new meanings in distinct cultural environments. We revisit Brannen's study in terms of context-based approaches of the sociocultural environments of the source (USA) and the targets (Japan and France). The core competence of Walt Disney (USA) relies on excellent human resource management practices, and the creation of the "happiest place on Earth". However, this "hyper normal" US theme emphasized commonality (inside US) and differences with others (non-US). One method for reaching happiness (in US) is employee training in its Disney University. This human resource competence has produced disparate results abroad. At Tokyo Disneyland, the US core competence fits into Japanese cultural norms of harmony, cleanliness and order where service is customer-oriented and hygienic. Conversely, freedom of dress and personal expression in France are opposed to Disney's human resource policies. This gap led to Disney violating French labor law (and raising the strong opposition of syndicates) by imposing the US dress code onto French workers in January 1995. The lack of consideration for the sociocultural context of the host has been responsible for a serious loss of money for the Walt Disney Company.

Brannen defined recontextualization as a change of meaning in a new cultural context. Recontextualization is a process, which follows a phase of decontextualization for extracting meanings from the initial context, into another context leading to a change of meaning and of the communicative purpose. Managers did not anticipate how the export meaning can be contextualized in a foreign environment. They expected that translation and training at the target place (i.e. recontextualization) were enough to transfer organizational resources intact (i.e. with the US contextualization). However, it was an attempt of recontextualization of the target host, not transfer of the US core competence at the target host. This myopia was due primarily to export process or cultural transmission (source viewpoint) rather than that importation or cultural acquisition (target viewpoint). By assimilating recontextualization to the whole context processing, the slip of meaning is explainable. First, the target culture is not passive but imparts its own meaning onto the transferred assets. For example, in Japan, Mickey Mouse was used to sell money market accounts, while in France, Mickey was a detective in the *Journal de Mickey*. Second, target environments have preexisting interconnections with the source culture: meanings attached to the assets of a firm already known implied the attachment of target meanings to the assets. Thus, firm assets receive pre-existing meanings given by sense-making filters as they enter the target environment. Moreover, foreign employees and consumers may see new uses for the assets, make different associations for product complements or substitutes, or even extract new meanings leading to innovations. This type of recontextualization concerns intangible skills and assets such as reputation or organizational culture as well as various aspects of the theme parks that are constrained by pre-existing contexts. For example, in US, a cowboy is the pride of his work; in Japan, cowboys are in groups around the campfire, working together like in a team, and in France, Lucky Luke is the lonely cowboy with his carefree, anti-establishment attitude, often outwitted by his horse. A second type of recontextualization corresponds to the possible emergence of a new meaning for source assets over time when integrated within the new cultural environment. Examples of such a second internal recontextualization are, in the US, the evolution of Mickey from the flamboyant rat-like figure (1920) to cherub-faced mouse now. In Japan, Tokyo Disneyland status evolves from a foreign vacation to the place to go to celebrate the New Year, and, in France, Disneyland Paris (several years after the opening) evolves towards a popular place with restaurants and live-entertainment mall right before the entrance of the park as a safe and fun place for youngsters to hang out, meet people and generally have a goodtime, even if it's far from the center of Paris and crossing sensible suburbs.

For Brannen, the process of recontextualization explains how transferred organizational assets take on new meanings in distinct cultural contexts. Recontextualization understanding depends on the process of transnational transmission and on the dynamics of host country reception (transmission and reception). In semiotics, recontextualization is considered as a key aspect of the cultural context in communication, "*language being a conduit for gaining deep contextual knowledge*". Brannen (2004) proposed a conceptual model of recontextualization, for representing the process by which new meanings are attached to transferred firm assets in host country contexts. In the semiotics approach, contextualization is the process by which the hearer/transferee makes sense of their world. Shared codes are context-dependent – the encoding and decoding of which are shaped by the particular sociocultural environments of the transferor and transferee. The starting point for understanding how signs convey meaning is the basic taxonomy of linguistic sign systems originally offered by Saussure (1916) who developed taxonomy to identify and made explicit the rules governing the process of signification. According to Saussure, words are signs that are composed of two components: (1) an image or "signifier" and (2) a concept or "signified". The relationship among signifier, signified and sign is shown in Figure 5.16. The main point is that significance of signs is based solely on a system of relationships between signifier and signified.

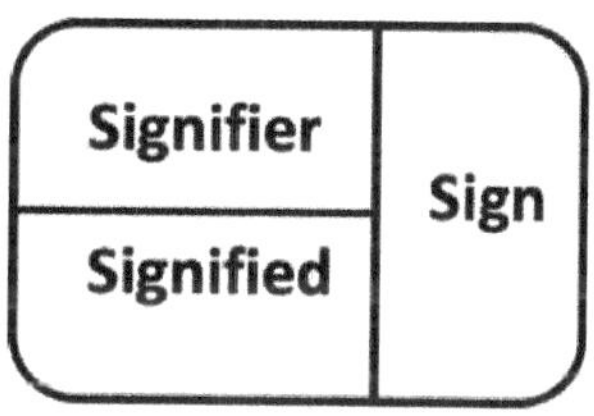

Figure 5.16. *Saussure's signification system*

In this taxonomy, the *signifier* and *signified* represent the two fundamental levels of language. The term signifier refers principally to the material world of sound and vision (i.e. the form, the expression) and the term *signified* relates to the concept or idea expressed by the sound or icon. A *signifier* cannot connote more than one *signified* at the same time. The relationship between the signifier and the signified is referred to as "signification". Note that, in the semiotics approach, the signifier plays a more important role than the signified. We make meanings through our interpretation of "signs", and a sign supposes an interpretation of someone (Pierce 1931). No sign makes sense on its own but only in relation to other signs. Its meaning depends on its context in relation to the other signs with which it is used. The main point we retain in relation with our context-based approach is that meaning of a sign depends simultaneously internally on the relations between the signifier and signified within the sign, and externally on relations between signs.

In the Japanese context of 1994, Brannen gave the example of a person who is wearing a black-and-white formal kimono with black-knotted obi-sash (the *signifier*) for a funeral (*signified*). The sign corresponds to the person that is in mourning (specific kimono for going to a funeral). However, the real signifier is more the color than the kimono (another garment can be considered for a funeral). Note that now the color for a funeral is white, and it would be better to consider the *signifier* "black-and-white formal kimono with black-knotted obi-sash" itself a *sign*, which would be associated with a *signifier* "black-and-white with black-knotted obi-sash" and the *signified* "kimono". The *signified* "kimono" can also be associated with another color as a *signifier* for another situation. Brannen pointed out that the sociocultural environment intervenes too. For example, if a western woman wears the same black-and-white kimono to a party in the United States (same *signifier*: a person wearing a black-and-white formal kimono with black-knotted obi-sash), but may have a different significance for other guests at the party such as a certain cosmopolitan chicness (or eccentricity) for Americans, and erroneous assumptions for a Japanese person.

Figure 5.17 (from Brannen (2004), but in a different presentation) provides a framework for analyzing recontextualization as semiotic patterns in cross-national shifts in systems of signification.

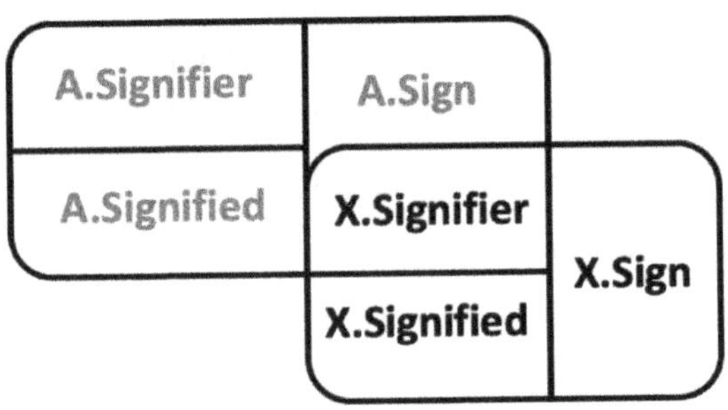

Figure 5.17. *Recontextualization model for transfer from country A to country X*

In Figure 5.17, A.sign in the country A becomes X.signifier in the country X with a new X.signified. Therefore, in the target firm, X.sign is built on a second recontextualization of X.signifier (i.e. A.sign) with the new X.signified. Managers expect us to understand how firm assets are recontextualized into new host environments (i.e. X.signifier replaces A.sign). They expect that, with some care in translation and training, they will be able to transfer organizational resources (X.signified) relatively intact. However, "translation and training" try to impose the source meaning as the target meaning without paying attention to the target context (i.e. the effect of the recontextualization). Such a recontextualization process is considered only on the exportation viewpoint, not the importation viewpoint.

In semiotics, there are important differences between Peirce's (1931) and Saussure's (1916) concept of the sign that contributes to theoretical ambiguities regarding the relations between the components that constitute *signs*. Researchers working on sound or word for analyzing signs, apparently, have different semiotician approaches. They, however, agree, first, to give more importance to the signifier rather than the signified, and, second, on the weak role of the actor in any semiotics model. Conversely in context-based approaches, an instantiation (the *signifier*) is a qualifier of the contextual element (*signified*). The selection of an instantiation is based on an external context (generally by the intermediary of a user). Thus, if semiotics approaches put the *signifier* center stage, context-based approaches put the contextual element center stage (the *signified*) and the instantiation backstage (the *signifier*). The AI viewpoint on the relationships between contextual element and instantiation allows us to assemble in a signification system built on a contextual element all its known instantiations, with the clear consequence being different instantiated contextual elements (different *signs*). Thus, the meaning of signs is attached and managed by an external context. Moreover, an instantiation can be a quantitative qualifier (a value) or a qualitative qualifier (another contextual element). This latter situation, which corresponds in semiotics to the recontextualization of the transfer from a source to a target, opens the door for an organization of knowledge and reasoning based on a contextual-element structure similar to the CxG formalism. The "translation" of the Saussure's signification system presented in Figure 5.16 is given in Figure 5.18.

Figure 5.18 presents a model of a contextual element inspired from Saussure's model that has three (exclusive) instantiations, value-1 and value-2 (e.g. the kimono is black-and-white or white) and contextual element-1 (e.g. the contextual element "garment" may have for instantiation "kimono", trouser, dress, etc.). This allows us to represent the structure that may exist on contextual elements. In the kimono example used by Brannen (2004), the "kimono" would be a contextual element with the instantiation (the attribute "color" of the contextual element "kimono") "black-and-white with black-knotted obi-sash". The choice of an instantiation depends on the external context (it is for a mourning at funeral). As said previously, there are other possible instantiations for the color of the kimono such as "white" (shiro-muku) in another external context (it is for a bride at a wedding). Figure 5.19 shows an interpretation of the recontextualization model for transfer from country A to country X in the CxG formalism.

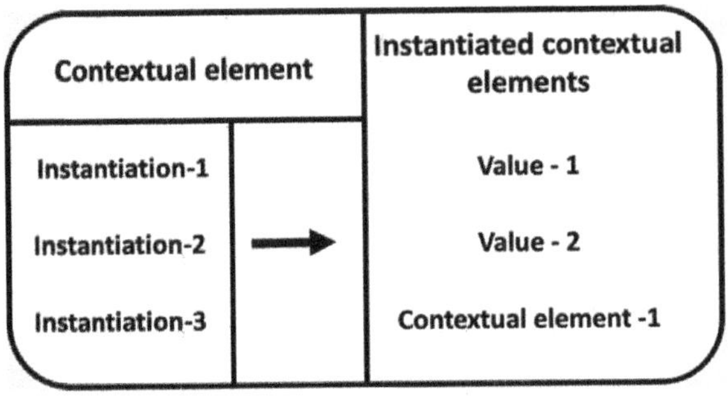

Figure 5.18. *The revisited Saussure's signification system in Figure 5.16*

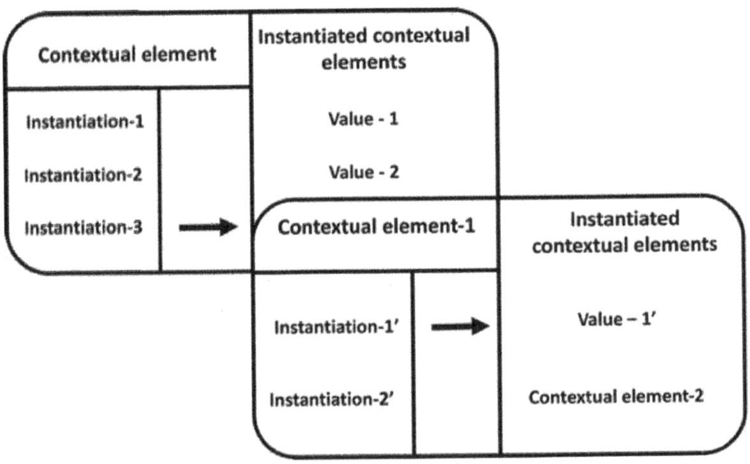

Figure 5.19. *Double role of contextual elements as signified and sign in AI*

In the CxG formalism, the conceptual model represented in Figure 5.19 corresponds to its implementation as a contextual graph shown in Figure 5.20.

Figure 5.20 is a translation of Figure 5.18 in the CxG formalism. In our knowledge, the effect of the limited life of an instantiation, that is, of a signifier life is not considered in the semiotics approach. The meaning of an instantiated contextual element is relevant in the external context at hand. Context coming from the user, the activity, the situation and the environment, the context-based approach brings an elegant solution to the problem evoked by Brannen about the difficulty with people management for the transfer of a firm core competence from a source to a target, because people management is part of the external context of the transfer and would act in the selection of instantiations.

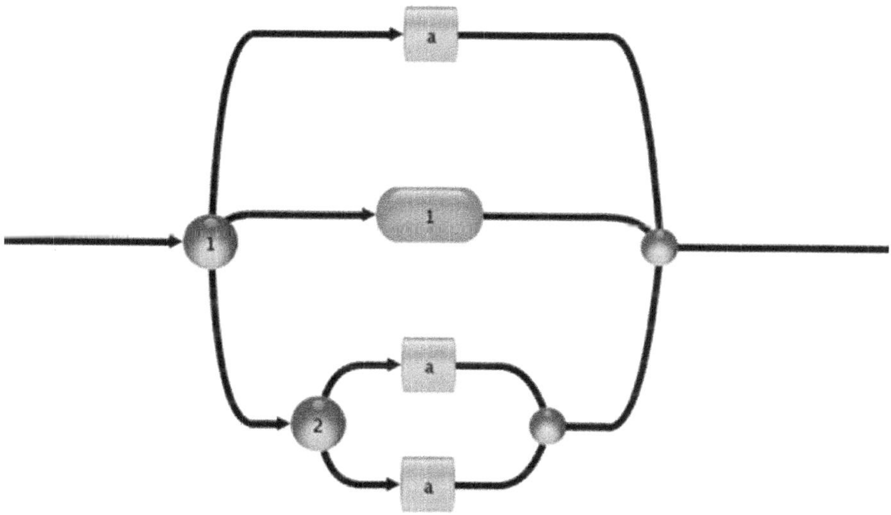

Figure 5.20. *Contextual graph of the model given in Figure 5.19. For a color version of this figure, see www.iste.co.uk/brezillon/contextbasedmodeling.zip*

Decoupling the contextual element from its instantiations avoids the semiotician problem of "one *signifier*–one *signified*" in the study of Disney because, first, a contextual element will have three instantiations, namely Disney-Anaheim, Tokyo Disneyland, Disneyland Paris, and, second, Disneyland Paris is for European people, the strategy then can be one *signified*-multiple *signifiers*. In AI, "re-contextualization" concerns only the last step of a whole process which includes three steps (see Figure 5.21): (1) identification of the contextualization associated with the instantiated contextual elements (CEs) from their current instantiations in the source context, (2) dissociation of the contextual element from its instantiation (decontextualization) and (3) allocation of the new instantiation valid in the target context to the contextual element (recontextualization). This process of contextualization, decontextualization and recontextualization (CDR) leads only to replace the instantiation of the contextual element given at the source with the instantiation coming from the target context. The change of instantiation (and of meaning) depends on the external context at the moment of entering the target context. The contextual element is supposed to be "initialized" with the first instantiation in the source context, which correspond to the other side of contextualization. Figure 5.21 shows how the CDR process (and related processes) is perceived in context-based approaches.

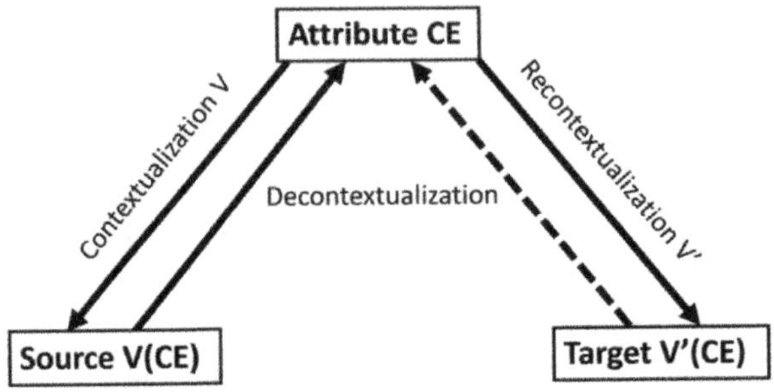

Figure 5.21. *A representation of the CDR process and its variants*

The recontextualization occurring during the firm-asset transfer is not a translation of the initial meaning. Brannen (2004) shows it on the "contextual element" Mickey Mouse, which has the US instantiation "all American boys" as a contextualization, while the Japanese instantiation is "safe and reliable" (first recontextualization) and the French instantiation "a resourceful detective" (second recontextualization).

5.7. Review of the chapter

Some attempts of modeling a problem in a bottom-up way without a domain model from data propose a view of their problem without considering context modeling. In this chapter, we present four different situations, the breast cancer diagnosis, the hierarchical task analysis, the ACA project, the workflow modeling in an ACP Department and a parallel with semiotics.

Breast cancer diagnosis is a task that has been the object of a very exhaustive accumulation of knowledge and experience (reasoning) on its realization (the objective-goal). In 1995 some authors proposed a global view on all the methods and techniques used for realizing this task. It was not an explicit modeling of context, but of the best practices to develop (i.e. in a given context for us). However, it was easy to identify contextual elements as questions guiding the reasoning of the practitioner for different answers to the question (potential values). For example, "Physical exam?" has two exclusive instantiations "palpable mass gone" and "palpable mass not gone". Making these contextual elements explicit leads to making explicit the organization of the expert's contextual reasoning with relevant chunks of knowledge. The second point is the isolation as activities of specific methods used such as ductography, ultrasound, physical exam, etc. As a consequence, the representation is lightened. A third point is the management of the representation of domain structures at different granularities.

Hierarchical task analysis was proposed in 1967 for conducting a task analysis, but not for modeling behavior. The strategy was examining tasks in terms of subtasks and especially understanding task contexts to represent system goals, sub-goals and plans, with feedback loops in a nested hierarchy. However, plans were not in the tree representation of the objects, but only associated with it. Plans were introduced because decision-makers also need to have flexible approaches to be able to perform with credit when they encounter situations outside of what is expected. They must deal with the unscheduled or unexpected, rather than routine predictable events, so they have to plan and make decisions. The idea is to break-down the overall goal into a next level of sub-goals in order to capture the contextual conditions that trigger the sub-goals under any super-ordinate goal. Thus, experts' intuition implicitly relies on experience as a complex combination of contextual elements that were considered in the initial approach as flexibility in plans as a way to make context explicit, but controlled by a branching tree of responses and estimates the probability and utility of the different possible future states. Moreover, the non-integration of plans in the HTA representation supposes simultaneously reasoning in different workspaces of the elements of knowledge (taxonomy), reasoning (plans) and contexts (flexibility). The redescription process (activities allow us to differentiate knowledge pieces at different granularities) is like contextual information for the understanding of the HTA. In the CxG approach, the notion of activity simplifies the representation, and the "plans", which appear as comments on the initial figure, are made explicitly operational in the activities and the nesting of some activities. The two versions 1.0 and 2.0 of the CxG representation formalism show that contextual elements are not limited to binary choices, and even choices may be between items of different domains.

The ACA project shows the interest of mental models for capturing "good" and "bad" behaviors in a bottom-up approach. Different categories of "theoretical" drivers are assembled on the basis of contextual elements. A category corresponds to a particular set of instantiations of variables (the contextual elements) that describe a theoretical behavior in the problem at hand; each behavior (or category) corresponds to a level of expertise of the category members. Changing driver's behavior consists of the computation of the path across intermediate categories between starting and goal categories. Path computation corresponds to the building of a scenario, allowing us to check several error variables at the same time. Driving a car implies the real-time building of a mental model based on a contextual reasoning, including anticipating events forthcoming and behaviors of other drivers. Driver's behavior is analyzed in two spaces, a behavior space (a contextual graph of possible behaviors) and a situation space (with three types of situation, normal, critical and pre-critical). The analysis is led in the two spaces to determine if a behavior is normal or not. The interview of the driver at the end of the scenario allows them to understand the reason for their bad behavior in a situation (e.g. non-identification of pre-critical situation where it was yet to correct his driving.

The contextual approach presented or modeling workflow tackles nonconformity situations and prevents medical error and eventual prejudice. It supposes tracing the origin and the cause of nonconformity to correct the problem and avoid it moving forward. For achieving such progress, it would be wise to do regular reports on the nonconformity found, and to improve communication between the different actors internal and external to the ACP Department. A contextual graph contains practices effectively developed by doctors and technicians, and not procedures as a decontextualized average over practices. Therefore, it is possible to compare step-by-step the real practice that is developed by an actor with existing practices in the contextual graph. Indeed, a contextual graph is a kind of "base of experiences" and the comparison of a practice under development can be automated easily by a context-based intelligent assistant system that manages in real-time the experience base. In addition, improving communication between actors would be possible with 2.0-collaborative tools, secure and easy to use in a similar way to a multi-objective microscope for collective diagnosis on slides.

In semiotics, the conceptual model of recontextualization proposed by Brannen is the process by which firm assets take on new meanings in distinct cultural environments. In Brannen's taxonomy, the *signifier* and *signified* represent two fundamental levels of language. The term *signifier* refers principally to the material world (i.e. the form, expression), and the term *signified* relates to the concept or idea expressed by the sound or icon. This implies that the signifier plays a more important role than the signified in semiotics. Conversely to the approaches proposed in semiotics, in context-based approaches, the instantiation (the *signifier*) is a qualifier of the contextual element (*signified*) that is more important than the signifier (a signified can correspond to several signifiers in AI, for example, a contextual element can have several possible instantiations). The selection of an instantiation is based on the external context (generally by user intermediary). AI viewpoint on relationships between the contextual element and instantiation in a model *a la* Saussure allows us to assemble in a signification system, a contextual element with different instantiated contextual elements (different *signs*) with the double role of the contextual element as the signified and sign. We have considered in the CxG approach the recontextualization problem in semiotics as the last step of a three-step process, the contextualization (identification of the initial instantiation in the source), decontextualization (extraction of the contextual element) and recontextualization (use of the new instantiation corresponding to the target). This process allows us to replace one instantiation with another because a contextual element has a unique instantiation at each time. CDR approach, thanks to the distinction of the contextual element from its instantiation (or its possible values). This is important because we do not consider binary instantiation, but with a variable number of values, of numerical or conceptual values, with the possibility of having a graph representation where nodes are contextual elements.

Conclusion

The approach presented in this book is ascribed in the realm of AI on the basis of separation of representation and use of knowledge in a given implementation with an emphasis on the modeling of context for real-world use. We consider a stricter separation of representation and use than in previous works: on the one hand, knowledge is not "tailored" for entering the representation formalism, and, on the other hand, the formalism does not depend on some (more or less hidden) simplifying objectives for using knowledge. For example, the production-rule formalism only accepts declarative knowledge under the expression "If <conditions> then <conclusion>" and introduction of procedural knowledge generates a syntax/semantics confusion such as screening clauses and rule packets for controlling this procedural knowledge.

The CxG formalism of representation has been used with success in 20 very different real-world applications because actors' expertise is modeled at the conceptual level, and its cognitive use through mental models is at the operational level. The CxG formalism has no hidden objectives such as control of rule firing by the inference engine in expert systems where the designer, for example, uses rule ordering for firing one rule before another one. The "human dimension of knowledge" plays a central role in acquisition, representation and use of expert knowledge that is highly contextualized. The CxG representation formalism only has four "generic" entities (action, contextual element, activity, ESIA). The real separation between representation and use comes from a modeling at operational and implementation levels, both being complementary. At the implementation level (with the software piece), complex behaviors may result from various combinations of a small number of contextual reasoning units (i.e. the independent subtasks).

The general lessons learned explain that the difficulty was to define context in an abstract way because context is related to activity, a larger notion than task. There is a chain of concepts: activity supposes an actor and a task that the actor realizes in a situation with the resources of a local environment. As a consequence, context finds its origins in four sources, namely the actor, the activity, the situation and the local environment. Two common denominators in the four sources of contextual elements are knowledge and reasoning that are used to describe what happens. The research on context was initiated in the technological domain where formal models of equipment to monitor exist, but context is interdisciplinary. Globally, domain knowledge is accessible like reports or rules, but it is important to consider some external knowledge concerning how to use domain knowledge because external knowledge may constrain the normal accomplishment of the activity.

Modeling context supposes a reasoning of the actor on the realization of the task, not on the task model. This supposes embedding task realization and its context in an activity, a pre-requisite for developing an intelligent system. Actors interpret task model (e.g. procedures of the company that are considered as mandatory) according to the contextual information collected to determine how to address the activity in a specific context. As a consequence, context is strongly related to operational knowledge and reasoning, both in mental models and in the heads of actors. Indeed, reasoning has an intrinsic contextual nature that supposes approaching an activity modeling with a uniform representation formalism.

During the 10 projects and applications presented in this book, we made progress on the modeling and use of context. Each project concerns some specific aspects of context, as well as specific contextual elements of other projects. Other applications mainly concerned the validation of results of our research without new findings about context modeling. The sequence of projects was an implicit guideline for our research on the modeling and use of context for the realization of an activity by an actor and for an actor group. The research is presented in four interdependent levels, namely, the conceptual level, the operational level, the implementation level and the environment level. The first version (CxG_1.0) of the CxG formalism is the result of research led jointly on these four levels of an actor's activity modeling.

Context is composed of contextual knowledge and external knowledge. Contextual knowledge is the set of elements more or less related to the activity in a flat way, and external knowledge concerns contextual elements that are not important at the moment the actor considers it. It is the focus of attention that distinguishes between contextual knowledge and external knowledge. Its evolution during the actor's reasoning provides dynamics to knowledge elements between the two types of knowledge, and thus, the frontier between contextual and external knowledge is porous. The selection of contextual elements in the four sources of context is a kind of first instantiation of contextual knowledge (or background context) but specifications of contextual elements (as a second instantiation) are required to be effectively used in actor's reasoning at the current step. Specifications result in a proceduralization process that transforms contextual knowledge into operational knowledge, the latter corresponding to the contextual elements that will be effectively instantiated and used to finally produce the proceduralized context.

A working definition of context was proposed in Brézillon and Pomerol (1999): "context is what constrains the focus without intervening in it explicitly". Context and focus of attention are interdependent; context makes focus explicit, and focus defines contextual elements in contextual knowledge that are relevant at each step (operational knowledge). In the four-modeling level framework, it is shown that the best definition of context is the dynamic view of the proceduralized context, that is, the ordered sequence of instantiated contextual elements of the mental-model development. A proceduralized context is the temporal signature (fingerprint) of an activity accomplishment, the key for its simulation by leading the development step-by-step of the reasoning included in the activity.

The actor uses operational knowledge and experience to develop practices (task realization in a particular context) that (re)contextualize the official procedure in the specific context. Practices differ from each other by a few elements, and, thus, summing up all the practices can be expressed in a unique global representation, in other terms, a mental representation that covers all mental models (task realization or practices) made by an actor in different contexts. The CxG representation formalism is able to express the mental representation in a unique contextual graph. There are other approaches for dealing with context, knowledge and reasoning. The general notion of "best practice" has a precise definition in our approach. A key strategic talent in an organization is the ability to balance its unique qualities with the practices that it has in common with other organizations. A "best practice" produced in a given context is the most efficient and effective results based on research, experience or benchmarking against industry standards. Best practices involve identifying the most effective processes and procedures for achieving specific goals, and then implementing them consistently and continuously. In CxG formalism, the mental model of an activity is the best practice in the context at hand, and there are as many "best practices" as contexts.

There is also the use of the two different notions of globalization and glocalization. "Globalization" means "local must be global or die". Glocalization is the transformation of a global product into another shape in order to meet the needs of local consumers. This specialization of the global solution does not correspond to a contextualization that is sought in glocalization that is a coordination of global and local. The glocalization approach was used in our research, and discussed in the projects SART, MICO and TACTIC.

Contextual knowledge is assimilated to a set of contextual elements coming from the four sources of context that provide instantiation of the contextual elements at any given moment. However, contextual reasoning progresses and the context provided by the four sources may evolve. What is changing is not contextual elements but instantiations. For example, the actor can see that the temperature (a contextual element) evolves from normal to critical (two instantiations). Thus, it is important to differently process contextual elements and their instantiations. Contextual elements determine the conceptual frame of the task realization (i.e. the stable part) and their instantiations provide the operational context at hand (the dynamic part). As a consequence, first, knowledge, reasoning and context must be managed jointly and need to be modeled in a uniform representation formalism such as the CxG formalism. CxG formalism uses a representation of contextual elements (the operational framework) as pairs {contextual node, recombination node} at the implementation level. The different possible instantiations of the contextual element correspond to branches between the two nodes, each branch containing a particular model of the reasoning step held during the corresponding instantiation. Contextual elements are organized in a contextual graph in the spirit of "Russian dolls" (matriochka) and are always defined (embedded) with respect to another contextual element: any contextual element is itself in a context. The separation of contextual elements and instantiations presents several interests: contextual elements are nested, one within another, without partial overlapping; Working context contains contextual elements, all known values of each contextual element and the chosen instantiation; there is a partial ordering of contextual elements; implementation as contextual and recombination nodes gives a directed, acyclic and series-parallel structure to a contextual graph; the instantiation process defines (1) the selection of a branch in the contextual element (i.e. the model of the reasoning step), (2) the path in the contextual graph that describes the reasoning held during the task realization, and (3) the ordered series of instantiated contextual elements that corresponds to the proceduralized context that is associated with mental-model development. A contextual element behaves as a unit of contextual nonlinear reasoning. The main steps of contextual reasoning are: gathering contextual information, structuring them, making decisions and acting. In a more pragmatic way, contextual reasoning is composed of two parts, the proceduralized context and the sequence of actions to perform in that specific context. For example, the operator in the subway control center, alerted of an incident, first looks at the situation and functioning conditions (proceduralized-context building), and, second, makes a better decision in this proceduralized context and finally applies the decision. An interesting aspect of contextual reasoning is the possibility of being nonlinear, this aspect does not appear in other reasoning models. Reasoning generally is between a "depth-first" strategy and a "breadth-first" strategy. The "depth-first" strategy goes to the finest possible granularity on a line of reasoning in order to anticipate, as much as possible, the course of events from a maximum of instantiated contextual elements. This strategy relies mainly on operational knowledge. The "breadth-first" strategy is applied when it is necessary to consider first all the possible options (potential lines of reasoning) before choosing a line for decision-making.

Actors are guided by personal mental representation (actor's experience) for extracting a mental model for addressing an activity. Mental representation corresponds to *operational knowledge* that the expert mobilizes in different contexts for accomplishing a given activity, while they develop a mental model for a specific context at hand. The joint play of mental-model development and instantiation process (mental-model building) makes their reasoning contextual. Contextual graph (CxG) formalism provides a uniform representation of elements of knowledge, reasoning and contexts that intervene in task realization. The CxG formalism calls on four elements (action, contextual element, activity, ESIA) that are sufficient for modeling complex real systems, thanks to the new functionalities that can be unfolded and contextual-element implementation as pairs of contextual and recombination nodes. When a reasoning arrives at a contextual node, it needs to be instantiated (known initially or asked of the actor) to select the corresponding branch and progress in the development of the mental model at the reasoning step. At the recombination node, instantiation does not matter anymore since the corresponding action (and not those on the other branches of the contextual element) has been completed. This modeling of contextual elements offers a context management in the CxG formalism, and the trace of mental-model development is kept as the proceduralized context.

The CxG software is an excellent tool for modeling a problem, but not adapted for simply visualizing its solution. Thus, the CxG formalism has been associated with a mental-model tree view for end-users. The contextual graph is at the implementation level and represents a mental representation at the operational level of an activity. Conceptual and operational aspects of context modeling have required a design and implementation level for the contextual graph (CxG) software, which, reciprocally, leads to reinforcing the conceptual modeling of context. Context-based intelligent assistant systems can easily exploit a contextual graph as an experience base. The consideration of several activities in a domain may lead to a set of experience bases that can be assembled in a unique repository (e.g. incident solving on a subway line concerns the exploitation of a subway line).

A contextual graph is a kind of support of contextual reasoning. However, modeling can reach a high degree of refinement due to concern for an intensive specialization. Granularity of the model depends on the goal of the modeling. The more we refine mental models, the more details are introduced, and, thus, the more we enter into details, the more mental model becomes complex, heavy to instantiate and time consuming for the actor. Thus, it is important to find the right level of granularity for modeling. For example, each natural mineral water has a particular mineral composition (calcium, magnesium, sodium, sulfate, etc.) that gives it health-promoting properties. However, the quantity of minerals leads to different effects on people. Thus, modeling a type of water to select may lead to a complex contextual graph to know the deep reasons of users. For example, magnesium acts on cardiovascular health, fatigue, muscle cramps, irritability, etc., and has a laxative effect. The user has after to choose the trademark of the mineral water because they have different tastes (and prices of the bottles intervene too).

The CxG_2.0 version was drawn from the CxG_1.0 version and enriched with additional new concepts. The shared context plays a central role in group activity. Its management consists of collecting and managing contextual elements, processing the proceduralized context with the building of the group mental model. The shared context takes place between individual working contexts of group actors and collective proceduralized context. The collaborative development of the shared context allows group actors to keep their individual mental representations compatible and adjusted to the joint focus on the collective mental representation. The shared-context building is the first step of a collaborative process of decision-making. The shared context evolves continuously jointly with group activity and additions of contextual elements by group members.

The notion of "activity" extends the notion of "task realization" by explicitly including context in which mental models are developed. The task is what an actor must do, and the activity is the (physical and mental) behavior that the actor exhibits for realizing the task. An activity covers the actor, the contextual information considered by actors, and the various choices made by them to reach the goal. A group activity is more than the simple sum of actor activities because actors' activities are interdependent. Interaction between group actors corresponds to movement of the group reasoning from one actor's activity to another actor's activity. Each group actor generally intervenes at different moments during group-activity development. Each intervention is represented as an *independent subtask*. Thus, group-activity processing consists of entering in an actor's activity to realize an actor's independent subtask. The intervention request comes from another actor (the sender) and will be taken charge of by a third (the recipient). In an enterprise, each actor plays a role, and tasks are associated with each role in the enterprise. In group activity, task realization requires actor collaboration with different roles specialized for different parts of the group activity. In actor activity (CxG_1.0 version), each actor's contextual graph is incrementally developed with small differences between practices (often in a unique contextual element), while group activity is the object of complex nonlinear reasoning, including backtracking, negotiation, look-ahead, etc. It is possible to represent very different contextual reasoning in a contextual graph representing a group activity. However, if the design and development of the contextual graph is easy (we divide the problem to treat sub-problems), nonlinear reasoning is difficult to follow, mainly because such reasoning corresponds to a complex path in the contextual graph instead of mental-model development in the CxG_1.0 version of the CxG formalism.

Although that it is not the object of this book, it appears that the lack of consensus on the terms of collaboration and cooperation comes from the fact that (1) these terms evolve dynamically during interaction; (2) a group activity must take into consideration, upstream, the setup of the group activity and, downstream, the use of its results; (3) the type of turn management depends essentially on the type of group activity; and (4) the shared context plays a central role in a group activity. Interaction between group actors corresponds to a transition of the reasoning from one actor's activity to another actor's activity, and, more specifically, between particular independent subtasks inside actors' activities. The type of interaction evolves along group-activity development by the play of actors that intervene, their current task realization in the group activity, the importance of what is expected, etc. The transition of 1 to N actors implies the addition of an (implicit) modeling of the management of a group of actors and what each actor does in the group activity, but from a global viewpoint. There are two options. The first option consists of group-activity management as an entity, actors' interventions being implicitly considered in the group contextual graph. A second option is to consider the group activity as composed of actors' contextual graphs. The two options lead to highly complex representations of the group activity difficult to model at operational and implementation levels. The third smart option chosen is to change the representation of individual activities for taking into account that each actor intervenes on specific steps of the group activity by a set of independent subtasks instead of a mental model. Group activity is considered as a sequence of turns accomplished by different actors for, first, adressing actor's request (the sender), and, second, preparing elements for another one (the recipient). Each actor's contribution is the realization of an independent substask sollicited by a sender in a particular shared context, and the result will trigger a new turn with a recipient for performing a particular subtask using the obtained results. As a consequence, actors participate in the group activity by as many independent subtasks as possible interventions during the collaboration.

The inputs and outputs of a turn are context-dependent and cannot be planned in advance. They are transmitted between turns throught the shared context. As a consequence, there is a dynamic building of the sequence of turns (the mental-model building) based on the contextual graph of the group activity that contains independent subtasks and parameters of the turns. Thus, a contextual graph has a partially fixed structure given by the choice of the manager during a turn, the choice of an independent subtask of the manager, turn management and identification of the turn sequence at the group level as a (group) mental model emerging of (group) mental representation. It is quite different to the CxG_1.0 version, in which the mental model developed by an actor exists in mental a representation. Moreover, an independent subtask may have several possible outputs (defined by reserved contextual elements on several different branches of the contextual subgraph). Such outputs may concern the study of variants by the manager, the next actor or a subset of actors, or the next subtask to realize. Thus, interaction management is essential for group activity that is simultaneously built and performed.

The main difference between the CxG_1.0 and CxG_2.0 versions is the explicit management of group actors because, if tasks are defined by roles (of actors) in the CxG_1.0 version, activity realization in a group depends on different roles in the CxG_2.0 version. Shared context, which is associated with the contextual graph, plays the role of a turntable for interaction representation (i.e. with the cyclic use of a directed graph). It insures the exchanges of contextual information between turns. Shared context also plays the role of an inference engine that analyzes contextual elements with a modified instantiation to decide what to do after the turn (e.g. If "TASK_STATUS" = nil, Then stop simulation). This opens the road for a nonlinear reasoning (e.g. stop, enter a negotiation phase, etc.) that can be observed by a mental model tree view of the contextual graph, which is composed of a proceduralized context followed by the corresponding sequence of actions for an experimented actor. It is an alternative representation of the contextual graph, both representations corresponding to the same mental model, that allows the process to apply the decision-making. Shared context emerges out of interactions and experiences among peer group members and affects each individual in the peer group. The voting system (as a type of reasoning) is a concept particularly useful for group activity, especially when group members are all expert in a domain where science is more an art than a science, that is, where experience is the main tool of the expert.

A turn mechanism is proposed to adapt the CxG formalism to group activity. A group activity is modeled as a sequence of turns, a turn being a local contribution of an actor to group activity. The turn mechanism is based on: (1) selection of the actor that will be the "manager" of the turn; (2) selection in the manager's activity of the subtask to realize according to the instantiation of "TASK_STATUS"; (3) computation of proceduralized context to find the part of group activity to realize; and (4) change of the instantiations of the reserved contextual elements for preparing the next turn. The main features of turn-mechanism model are: contextual elements instantiated in the subtask of one actor and used in the subtask of another actor; a change of reasoning if an unexpected event occurs; the possibility of negotiation, etc. Turns are executed sequentially because shared context contains the actor and the subtask selected for the next turn. This "turn mechanism" plays the role of a synchronizer of the dynamic combination of turns that offers the possibility of nonlinear reasoning (e.g. backtracking, preliminary study of alternatives) and avoids a complex modeling of the group activity in any context. Cyclic use of a directed contextual graph corresponds to a CxG-based simulation, thanks to reserved contextual elements for managing it. There are also several abilities of the CxG_2.0 version not present in the CxG_1.0 version such as exiting a simulation at the end of a turn (with recipient = "nil"), anticipation, check of alternatives, explanation generation, negotiation between a part of the group members and even a resumption of the whole simulation if the instantiation of a contextual element changes during the simulation due to an external event.

Thanks to the use of shared context and independent subtasks in the contextual graph of the CxG_2.0 version, the CxG-based simulation exhibits the simultaneous building of a temporary mental model with the associated proceduralized context. Mental-model building during its development is rather close to a numerical simulation for nonlinear systems (such as differential equations without the theoretical solution). This approach also allows the CxG-based simulation tool for expressing task realization "one-shot" but with intermediate variants such as the checking of alternatives by a kind of *what-if* mental simulations. A conversion of the contextual graph in a tree representation is proposed for allowing a fast understandability of the focus by actors with explicit proceduralized context and sequence of actions to do. The tree representation, in the CxG formalism, expresses the high level of automaticity through a single-step retrieval of actions from memory. It is not a simple decision tree.

Reasoning generally cannot be separated from the context in which it takes place. The contextual nature of reasoning appears when conclusion in a rule-based system is intertwined with conditions. Such reasoning is found in decision-making, interpretation, diagnosis, pattern recognition. Moreover, reasoning in one context may influence reasoning in other contexts when reasoning with contexts is formalized as a set of deductions, each deduction carried out inside a context, connected by appropriate "bridge rules" (Giunchiglia 1997).

Although the CxG formalism has been applied successfully in several fields (e.g. medicine, transportation, business management and military operations), there are some limitations. Actors have difficulty following the development of a specific practice in the contextual graph and to make the decision that is associated with it. Often, experts need to quickly identify the right practice that matches the specific context at hand and the resulting sequences of actions to execute (especially in emergency situations). Thus, experts evaluate first proceduralized context (context fingerprint of mental model) and the situation at hand to make an immediate decision (e.g. handle an incident in the subway), and, second, infer the type of object of the reasoning corresponding to the content of a given mental model. An object involved with reasoning can be either a physical object (e.g. a digital image in medicine) or a cognitive object (e.g. a diagnosis). A collaborative work led during a course in the innovation-management master shows that mental models (associated with students) of task realization may differ deeply from the global mental model of the group (resulting of a consensus): each student may agree on the global model (i.e. list of contextual elements) but say that they will never use it directly for themselves (personalization of instantiations of the contextual elements). Each group actor brings a unique perspective that frames the peer group experience.

Knowing that a student might be called upon to explain the thought behind a response encouraged them to formulate explanations in advance and, effectively, increased attention levels during the class.

There is an important evolution from CxG_1.0 to CxG_2.0 versions: the activity being led by either one actor or a group of actors. The CxG_1.0 formalism is used to incrementally bring together mental models, which differ among them by small variants, in the mental representation of the actor activity as a unique experience base. Conversely, the CxG_2.0 formalism relies on the punctual interventions of actors as independent subtasks stored in the group mental representation that leads to more complex activities and mental models with the possibility of negotiation, waiting for an answer, looking-ahead simulations. Moreover, a mental model, extracted from the mental representation in the CxG_1.0 formalism, must be built on the fly in the CxG_2.0 formalism. Interestingly, the CxG_2.0 version of the CxG formalism developed for group activity stays applicable to a unique actor with the interests: modeling nonlinear reasoning, nonlinear exploitation of an activity, integration of the environment state, change due to an unexpected event during mental-model development, replay of a particular independent subtask for checking different hypothesis before making decisions, backtracking in the reasoning held. This possibility offers two different viewpoints on the actor's activity, first, how the activity is accomplished, and, second, what is accomplished by the actor. Moreover, these two representations may compare the reasoning of different actors accomplishing the same activity. In the FlexMim project, experts reach the same diagnosis on slides with different strategies due to: different criteria, different weights given to criteria, different interpretations of criteria, consideration of different combinations of criteria, that is, on the method to apply for diagnosing. A similar situation exists in the project "internship-offer analysis" where all the students had the same objective (find an internship) but each student has their own criteria and preferences because students make an intensive use of personal contextual elements at the same level as contextual elements linked to their common focus. The important difference with the FlexMim project is that students make as many different decisions as actors because each actor has a personal focus of attention on the common objective.

A key element of the CxG_2.0 formalism is to use a CxG-based simulation for building and developing a mental model according to the actors' real-time choices with a "replay" mode for actors that do not know exactly what to do. CxG-based simulation is at the operational level (where mental representation and mental-model development are at hand) and is a modeling tool for context-based intelligent assistant systems. An observation concerns the type of ordering of the contextual elements: temporal ordering for the "wine-making" project, functional ordering in the TACTIC project and the "paper-submission" example, but there is no complete ordering in the "internship-offer analysis" application due to the class "candidates" with contextual elements such as "autonomy". Classically, reasoning modeling in a context-based formalism of representation may integrate contextual elements to introduce "light" variants of the way to lead a model-based reasoning. The two examples from the SART project and the "Internship-offer analysis" show that external contextual elements cannot be neglected in the contextual reasoning of a decision-maker. The contextualization of the reasoning developed by the actors is so important in some cases, that actors' private goals cover a spectrum of results larger than the objective of the task realization in the activity.

There are links between context and decisional levels too, especially when decision-making plays a central role. Decision-making presents four interdependent decisional levels, namely policy, strategy, tactic and operation. In our research on modeling and using context, we made several choices at the policy and strategy levels, such as the four sources of context, the choice of an operational definition of context, the emphasis on the relationships between context, operational knowledge and reasoning, and the choice of a context-based representation formalism, in which contextual elements are represented as pairs {contextual node, recombination node}. Throughout the presentation, we showed that the formalization of several concepts during our research operates simultaneously at the tactical and operational decisional levels. In the same spirit, four sources of context (the actor, the activity, the situation and the local environment) have specificity at decisional levels (e.g. the actor at the strategical level, the situation at the tactical level and the local environment at the operational level). Thus, context-based applications should be modeled and used by considering them simultaneously. Moreover, the CxG formalism does not impose a type of reasoning (such as production rules), and it is possible indeed to model in the same formalism different types of contextual reasoning found in real-world applications such as a voting system, CDR approach, glocalization for facing nonlinear problems. With respect to the four-modeling level framework, policy and strategy are covered by the conceptual level, the tactic decisional level corresponds to the operational level and the operation decisional level corresponds to the implementation and environment levels. The duality that is observed with most of the concepts, such as procedure versus practice, mental representation versus mental model, contextual element and pair of contextual and recombination nodes is addressed by the same problem at two different levels. It is also true in their use: "tactical" expert versus "operational" expert in the TACTIC project, the operator of a subway line is a tactical actor and the train driver is the operational actor in the SART project with the consequence that "Make your train empty of travelers" said by the operator implies a complex activity to follow for the train driver, the operational actor (make an announcement in the train, stop at the next station, etc.).

Fortunately, the research has a stronger positive side than a negative one. A model has predictive power that a representation does not because it's limited to observation smoothing. A model can be expressed in different representation formalisms, with more or less expressiveness, although each formalism has strengths, weaknesses and limits. As a consequence, the role of a model and of a representation are different. However, the choice of representation formalism is crucial for a good modeling because it has the role of reveler of concepts. Thus, it is not possible to assimilate a mental representation to mental model. Mental representation is an expression of the actor's experience about an activity, that is, an accumulation of mental models developed by the actor in different contexts. A reason is a difference of levels, mental representation and mental-model development are at the operational level for any context, while mental-model building, which required instantiation of contextual elements in a specific context at the environment level, is at the implementation level. In cognitive science, the notion of "chunk" plays a role similar to a mental model. A chunk is a collection of basic units that are strongly associated with one another (i.e. contextualized), and have been grouped together and stored in a person's memory. Mental models play the role of chunks of knowledge, but their building is made explicit in a proceduralized context.

This book gives a summary view of 25 years of research on how to model and use context in 20 real-world applications on a spectrum from technology-centered (SEPT, SART) to human-centered (e.g. FlexMIm) applications, that is, from well-defined domains to more fuzzy ones. Real-world applications impose strong requirements and imply the rejection of simplifying assumptions: the operator in a crisis unit and the surgeon in an emergency room have to rapidly make a critical decision that will be definitive. Thus, an answer to a question such as "Well, in 80% of the cases, the solution is…" is not acceptable, because the decision is made in a precise context that constrains that urgent decision-making.

The 25 key points, found during these 25 years of research on context modeling and use, lead to a robust CxG formalism (defined with only four item, action, activity, contextual element and ESIA) that is implemented in a piece of software easy to use for modeling a large number of very different types of activity in a large spectrum of applications (subway, power systems, management, medicine, psychology, etc.), thanks to making explicit the contextual element and instantiation with knowledge and reasoning. A contextual element is implemented as a pair of contextual and recombination nodes, with the return effect that a contextual element is a reasoning step with various expressions depending on the instantiation, although mental representation has a uniform description of all corresponding mental models. Another finding concerns the sense that it is possible to give now to contextual reasoning that intervenes in different types of activities such as decision-making, problem solving and task realization that can all be assimilated to contextual reasoning. It looks like a pleonasm, because all reasoning can qualify as contextual, but, we wish to insist on the fact that context, or at least a part of it, is explicitly modeled and used with knowledge and reasoning in these types of activities.

Some attempts at modeling problems in a bottom-up way from data propose a unified view of their problem where context modeling was not central. Four different applications are presented, namely the breast cancer diagnosis, the hierarchical task analysis, the ACA project and the chronic inflammatory bowel diagnosis. Breast cancer diagnosis has been the object of a summary view on all the methods and techniques used for realizing this task, based on best practices, not an explicit modeling of context. A change of representation of the flowchart was possible in a contextual graph with the 400 items described initially in 13 figures. It was easy to identify contextual elements as questions guiding practitioner reasoning. The use of activities in the contextual graph allows the separation of expertise of different natures and different granularities such as ductography and ultrasound. As a consequence, the representation is lightened. Hierarchical task analysis did not focus on behavior modeling. Plans have been added for understanding task contexts to represent system goals, sub-goals and plans, with feedback loops in a nested hierarchy. However, plans only were associated with the tree representation of objects for unscheduled or unexpected, rather than routine predictable events. The CxG formalism provides a uniform representation of all the elements with experts' experience as a complex combination of contextual elements, not limited to binary choices, considered in the initial approach, a way to make context explicit, but controlled by a branching tree of responses and estimates probability and utility of the different possible future states. In the ACA project, mental models are captured in a bottom-up approach of the "good" and "bad" behaviors of drivers. Categories of "theoretical" drivers are assembled on the basis of contextual elements. A category corresponds to a level of expertise of its members. Changing driver's behavior consists of computation of the path across intermediate categories between starting and goal categories. Driver's behavior is analyzed in two spaces, a behavior space (a contextual graph of possible behaviors) and a situation space (with three types of situation, normal, critical and pre-critical). The analysis resulting in the two spaces allows us to determine if a behavior is normal or not, and the use of scenarios allows a driver to correct their behavior progressively by moving in categories. The contextualization of workflow for analyzing nonconformity during reception and registration steps in an Anatomical and Cytology Pathology (ACP) Department where actors have to deal implicitly or explicitly with many contextual elements to decide which actions must be done. Nonconformity is mandatory in a medical decision-making process that relies on a large number of heterogeneous contextual elements, to arrive at an action sequence. The modeling of the process by a contextual graph objectifies events influencing the ACP examination process and development of practices. The last application presented in this book concerns the approach of context in semiotics and the contribution that the CxG formalism with the notion of contextual elements could bring to semiotics as an extension of the model sign–signifier–signified. In terms of the CxG formalism, the instantiation (the *signifier*) is a qualifier of the contextual element (*signified*), and the instantiated contextual element (*sign*), a contextual element having thus a double role of signified and sign.

Finally, the CxG formalism is a passport for intelligent systems based on human experience. The "hard kernel" of our approach is the explicit modeling of context that leads to a homogeneous view on how a class of AI systems can become context-based intelligent systems. A discussion is presented on particular requirements for the special class of context-based intelligent systems that interested us, namely context-based intelligent assistant systems (CIASs). The goal is not a direct discovery such as for machine and deep learning, but a reuse and an extension of the human experience in the spirit of generative AI. For deep learning, the goal would not be to accumulate contextual knowledge (infinite dimension of context), but to be able to identify in the situation and environment contextual elements that can be relevant for a robot to accomplish its task and develop its mental representation in a kind of "modeling by acting". The CxG formalism provides powerful experience bases that can be served as a basis for deep learning in order to complete the known practices.

References

van der Aalst, W.M.P., ter Hofstede, A.H.M., Kiepuszewski, B., Barros, A.P. (2003). Workflow patterns. *Distributed and Parallel Databases*, 14(3), 5–51.

Agabra, J., Alvarez, I., Brézillon, P. (1997). Contextual knowledge-based system: A study and design in enology. In *First International and Interdisciplinary Conference on Modeling and Using Context (CONTEXT-97)*. Federal University of Rio de Janeiro, 351–362.

Andonovski, N. (2022). Episodic representation: A mental models account. *Frontiers in Psychology*, 13, 899371. doi: 10.3389/fpsyg.2022.899371.

Annett, J. and Duncan, D. (1967). Task analysis and training design. *Occupational Psychology*, 41, 211–221.

Ansoff, I. (1975). Managing strategic surprise by response to weak signals. *California Management Review*, XVIII(2), 21–33.

Arkin, A., Askary, S., Bloch, B., Curbera, F., Goland, Y., Kartha, N., Liu, C.K., Thatte, S., Yendluri, P., Yiu, A. (eds) (2005). Web services business process execution language Version 2.0. Working Draft, WS-BPEL TC OASIS [Online]. Available at: http://www.oasisopen.org/committees/download.php/12791/.

Arnaboldi, V., Conti, M., Delmastro, F. (2014). CAMEO: A novel context-aware middleware for opportunistic mobile social networks. *Pervasive and Mobile Computing*, 11, 148–167.

Attieh, E., Brézillon, P., Capron, F. (2013). Context-based modeling of an anatomo-cyto-pathology department workflow for quality control. In *Modeling and Using Context (CONTEXT-13)*. Springer, Berlin, Heidelberg, 235–247.

Babulak, E. and Wang, M. (2008). Discrete event simulation: State of the art. *International Journal of Online Engineering (iJOE)*, 4, 60–63 [Online]. Available at: https://www.researchgate.net/publication/220090348.

Bailly, B., Bellet, T., Goupil, C., Martin, R. (2003). Driver's mental representations: Experimental study and training perspectives. In *First International Conference on Driver Behavior and Training*, Stratford-on-Avon.

Bau, D.Y. and Brézillon, P. (1992). Model-based diagnosis of power station control systems: The SEPT experiment. *IEEE Expert*, 36–44.

Bedwell, W.L., Wildman, J.L., Diaz Granados, D., Salazar, M., Kramer, W.S. Salas, E. (2012). Collaboration at work: An integrative multilevel conceptualization. *Human Resource Management Review*, 22(2), 128–145.

Benitez-Guerrero, E., Mezura-Godoy, C., Montané-Jimenez, L.G. (2012). Context-aware mobile collaborative systems: Conceptual modeling and case study. *Sensors*, 12, 13491–13507.

Bernard, C. (1865). *Introduction à l'étude de la médecine expérimentale*, Republished in 1984. Flammarion, Paris.

Bikson, T.K. and Eveland, J.D. (1991). The interplay of work group structures and computer support. Rand Note N-34-29-MF, Rand Corporation.

Black, K.W. (1979). The small group—tightrope between sociology and personality. *Journal of Behavioral Science*, 15, 283–294.

Boland, R.J. Jr. (2008). Decision making and sensemaking. In *Handbook on Decision Support Systems 1: Basic Themes*, Burstein, F. and Holsapple, C.W. (eds). Springer, Berlin, 55–63.

Brannen, M.Y. (2004). When Mickey loses face: Recontextualization, semantic fit, and the semiotics of foreignness. *Academy of Management Review*, 29(4), 593–616.

Brézillon, P. (1983). Place et rôle du modèle en biologie : son intérêt et ses impératifs (Tome I) ; et son application à l'étude de la représentation compartimentée des métabolismes de la sérotonine et du calcium (Tome II). PhD Thesis, Université Paris VI, Paris.

Brézillon, P. (1999). Context in problem solving: A survey. *The Knowledge Engineering Review*, 14(1), 1–34.

Brézillon, P. (2003). Representation of procedures and practices in contextual graphs. *The Knowledge Engineering Review*, 18(2), 147–174.

Brézillon, P. (2005). Task-realization models in contextual graphs. In *Modeling and Using Context (CONTEXT-05)*. Springer, Berlin, Heidelberg, 55–68.

Brézillon, P. (2007). Context modeling: Task model and model of practices. In *Modeling and Using Context (CONTEXT-07)*. Springer, Berlin, Heidelberg, 122–135.

Brézillon, P. (2008). Explaining for contextualizing and contextualizing for explaining. In *EXACT'08: Proc. of 3rd International Workshop on Explanation-Aware Computing*, Patras, 21–22 July [Online]. Available at: https://CEUR-WS.org/Vol-391/00010001.pdf.

Brézillon, J. (2010a). Un système tutoriel intelligent pour l'auto-évaluation de comportements utilisateurs. Application à la sécurité routière. PhD Thesis, University Pierre and Marie Curie, Paris.

Brézillon, P. (2010b). A contextual methodology for modeling real-time decision-making support. In *Supporting Real-Time Decision Making: The Role of Context in Decision Support on the Move*, Burstein, F., Brézillon, P., Zaslavsky, A. (eds). Springer, New York, 65–88.

Brézillon, P. (2011). Contextualization of scientific workflows. In *Modeling and Using Context (CONTEXT-11)*. Springer, Berlin, Heidelberg, 40–53.

Brézillon, P. (2012). Modeling activity management instead of task realization. In *Fusing DSS into the Fabric of the Context*, Rescipio, A. and Burstein, F. (eds). IOS Press, Amsterdam, 51–62.

Brézillon, P. (2013a). Context-based development of experience bases. In *Modeling and Using Context (CONTEXT-13)*. Springer, Berlin, Heidelberg, 87–100.

Brézillon, P. (2013b). Contextual Graphs based management of large-scale expertise. In *18th Conference of the Association Information et Management (AIM 2013)*, Lyon, 22–24 May.

Brézillon, P. (2014). Context-centered tools for intelligent assistant systems. In *Context in Computing: A Cross-Disciplinary Approach for Modeling the Real World*, Brézillon, P and Gonzalez, A. (eds). Springer, New York, 97–110.

Brézillon, P. (2015). Modeling expert knowledge and reasoning in contextual graphs. In *Modeling and Using Context (CONTEXT-15)*. Springer, Cham, 18–31.

Brézillon, P. (2017). Contextual modeling of group activity. In *Modeling and Using Context (CONTEXT-17)*. Springer, Berlin, Heldeiberg, 113–126.

Brézillon, P. (2018). CxG-based simulation of group activity. *Modeling and Using Context, ISTE OpenScience*, Vol. 18-1. doi: 10.21494/ISTE.OP.2018.0231.

Brézillon, P. (2022). Modeling and using context: 25 years of lessons learned. In *Modeling and Use of Context in Action*, Brézillon, P. and Turner, R.M. (eds). ISTE Ltd, London and John Wiley and Sons, New York.

Brézillon, P. (ed.) (2023). *Research on Modeling and Using Context Over 25 Years*. Springer, Cham. doi: 10.1007/978-3-031-39338-9.

Brézillon, P. and Abu-Hakima, S. (1995). Using knowledge in its context: Report on the IJCAI-93 Workshop. *AI Magazine*, Spring, 16(1), 87–91.

Brézillon, J. and Brézillon, P. (2007). Context modeling: Context as a dressing of a focus. In *Modeling and Using Context (CONTEXT-07)*. Springer, Berlin, Heidelberg, 136–149.

Brézillon, P. and Brézillon, J. (2008). Contextualized task modeling. *Revue d'Intelligence Artificielle*, 22(5), 531–548.

Brézillon, P. and Pomerol, J.-Ch. (1996). User acceptance of interactive systems: Lessons from knowledge-based and decision systems. Research Report 96/16, June, LAFORIA, Université Paris 6.

Brézillon, P. and Pomerol, J.-Ch. (1999). Contextual knowledge sharing and cooperation in intelligent assistant systems. *Le Travail Humain*, 62(3), 223–246.

Brézillon, P. and Pomerol, J.-Ch. (2001). Is context a kind of collective tacit knowledge? In *European CSCW 2001 Workshop on Managing Tacit Knowledge*, Bonn, 23–29.

Brézillon, P. and Pomerol, J.-Ch. (2010). Framing decision making at two levels. In *Bridging the Socio-Technical Gap in Decision Support Systems. Challenges for the Next Decade*, Respicio, A., Adam, F., Phillips-Wren, G., Teixeira, C., Telhada, J. (eds). IOS Press, Amsterdam, 358–368.

Brézillon, P. and Turner, R.M. (2022). Pragmatic research on modeling and use of context. In *Modeling and Using Context in Action*, Brézillon, P. and Turner, R.M. (eds). ISTE Ltd, London and John Wiley and Sons, New York.

Brézillon, P., Gentile, C., Secron, M. (1997). SART: A system for supporting operators with contextual knowledge. In *Modeling and Using Context (CONTEXT-97)*. Federal University of Rio de Janeiro, 209-222.

Brézillon, P., Pasquier, L., Pomerol, J.-Ch. (2000). Representing operational knowledge by contextual graphs. In *Advances in Artificial Intelligence*. Springer, Berlin, 245–258.

Brézillon, P., Brézillon, J., Pomerol, J.-Ch. (2006a). Decision making at a crossroad: A negotiation of contexts. In *Proceedings of the Joint International Conference on Computing and Decision Making in Civil and Building Engineering*. Springer, Berlin, Heidelberg.

Brézillon, P., Drai-Zerbib, V., Baccino, T., Therouanne, T. (2006b). Modeling collaborative construction of an answer by contextual graphs. In *Proceedings of IPMU-2006*. Editions EDK, Paris, 11–26.

Brézillon, P., Brézillon J., Pomerol J.-C. (2009). Context-based methodology for decision making: Application for car driving. *International Journal of Decision System Technology*, 1(3), 1–20 [Online]. Available at: http://www.igi-global.com/JDSST.

Brézillon, P., Attieh, E., Capron, F. (2014). Modeling glocal search in a decision-making process. In *DSS 2.0 – Supporting Decision Making with New Technologies*, Phillips-Wren, G., Carlsson, S., Respício, A., Brézillon, P. (eds). IOS Press, Amsterdam, 80–91. doi: 10.3233/978161499399580.

Buyya, R., Yeo, C.S., Venugopal, S., Broberg, J., Brandic, I. (2009). Cloud computing and emerging IT platforms: Vision, hype, and reality for delivering computing as the 5th utility. *Future Generation Computer Systems*, 25(6), 599–616.

Clancey, W.J. (2002). Simulating activities: Relating motives, deliberation, and attentive coordination. *Cognitive System Research*, 3(3), 471–499.

Collins, A. and Gentner, D. (1987). How people construct mental models. In *Cultural Models in Language and Thought*, Holland, D. and Quinn, N. (eds). Cambridge University Press, Cambridge, 243–268.

Collins, A.J., Pour, F.S.A., Jordan, C.A. (2023). Past challenges and the future of discrete-event simulation. *The Journal of Defense and Simulation*, 20(3), 285–422. doi: 10.1177/15485129211067175.

Corvol, P. (2013). Claude Bernard et la médecine expérimentale au Collège de France. *La lettre du Collège de France*, December, 36. doi: 10.4000/lettre-cdf.1719.

Craik, K.J.W. (1943). *The Nature of Explanation*. Cambridge University Press, Cambridge.

Elmarzouqi, N., Garcia, E., Lapayre, J.C. (2007). CSCW from coordination to collaboration. In *11th International Conference on Computer Supported Cooperative Work in Design (CSCWD 2007)*. Springer, Berlin, Heidelberg, 87–98.

Endsley, M.R. (2000). Situation models: An avenue to the modeling of mental models. In *Proceedings of 14th Triennial Congress of the International Ergonomics Association and 44th Annual Meeting of the Human Factors and Ergonomics Society* [Online]. Available at: https://www.researchgate.net/publication/252843973_Situation_Models_An_Avenue_to_the_Modeling_of_Mental_Models#fullTextFileContent [Accessed 18 August 2022].

Endsley, M.R. and Jones, W.M. (1997). Situation awareness, information dominance, and information warfare (AL/CF-TR-1997-0156). United States Air Force Armstrong Laboratory, Wright-Patterson AFB, OH.

Eppstein, D. (1992). Parallel recognition of series-parallel graphs. *Information and Computation*, 98(1), 41–55.

Fan, X. (2011). Context-oriented scientific workflow and its application. PhD Thesis, University Pierre and Marie Curie, Paris.

Fan, X., Zhang, R., Li, L., Brézillon, P. (2011). A context-based framework for improving decision making in scientific workflow. In *ICCRD-2011: Proceedings of the 3rd International Conference on Computer Research and Development*, Shanghai.

Finta, L., Liu, Z., Mills, I., Bampis, E. (1996). Scheduling UET- UCT series-parallel graphs on two processors. *Theoretical Computer Science*, 162(2), 323–346.

Freig, S.A. (1996). Book review. *Journal of the National Cancer Institute*, 88(10), 683–684.

Furnas, G.W. (1986). Generalized fisheye views. In *CHI'86: Proceedings of Human Factors in Computing Systems Conference*, 16–23.

Ganet, L. (2006). Generation of explanations from the viewpoint of the contextual categorization. PhD Thesis, University Paris 8.

Garcia, K. and Brézillon, P. (2015). A contextual model of turns for group work. In *Modeling and Using Context (CONTEXT-15)*. Springer, Cham, 243–256.

Garcia, K. and Brézillon, P. (2018). Model vizualization: Combining context-based graph and tree representations. *Expert Systems with Applications*, 99(1), 103–114.

Giunchiglia, F. (1997). Contextual reasoning. *Epistemologia Special Issue on I Linguaggi e le Macchine*, 16, 345–364.

Gladstein, D.L. (1984). Groups in context: A model of task group effectiveness. *Administrative Science Quarterly*, 29(4), 499–517.

Goldbetter, A. and Lefever, R. (1972). Dissipative structures for an allosteric model. *Biophysical Journal*, 12, 1302–1315.

Gonzalez, A.J. (2014). Tactical reasoning through context-based reasoning. In *Context in Computing*, Brézillon, P. and Gonzalez, A.J. (eds). Springer, New York, 491–508. doi: 10.1007/978-1-4939-1887-4_30.

Gonzalez, A.J. and Ahlers, R. (1998). Context-based representation of intelligent behavior in training simulations. *Transactions of the Society of Computer Simulation*, 15(4), 153–166.

Gonzalez, A.J. and Brézillon, P. (2008). Comparing two context-driven approaches for representation of human tactical behavior. *Knowledge Engineering Review*, 23(2), 1–21.

Grimshaw, D.J., Mott, P.L., Roberts, S.A. (1997). The role of context in decision making: Some implications for database design. *European Journal of Information Systems*, 5(4), 113–122.

Gulati, R., Wohlgezogen, F., Zhelyazkov, P. (2012). The two facets of collaboration: Cooperation and coordination in strategic alliances. *Academy of Management Annalysis*, 6, 531–583.

Hatakka, M., Keskinen, E., Gregersen, N.P., Glad, A., Hernetkoski, K. (2002). From control of the vehicle to personal self-control; broadening the perspectives to driver education. *Transportation Research*, Part F, 201–215.

Hoffman, R.R. (1997). The cognitive psychology of expertise and the domain of interpreting. *Interpreting*, 2(1–2), 189–230.

Jacquez, J.A. (1972). *Compartmental Analysis in Biology and Medicine*. Elsevier, Amsterdam.

Johnson-Laird, P.N. (1983). *Mental Models*. Cambridge University Press, Cambridge.

Johnson-Laird, P.N. (2006). *How We Reason*. Oxford University Press, Oxford.

Johnson-Laird, P.N. (2010). Mental models and human reasoning. *Proceedings of the National Academy of Sciences*, 107(43), 18243–18250. doi: 10.1073/pnas.101293310.

Johnson-Laird, P.N. and Byrne, R.M.J. (1991). *Deduction*. Lawrence Erlbaum Associates, Inc, Hove and Hillsdale, NJ.

Johnson-Laird, P.N. and Savary, F. (1999). Illusory inferences: A novel class of erroneous deductions. *Cognition,* 71, 191–229.

Jones, N.A., Ross, H., Lynam, T., Perez, P., Leitch, A. (2011). Mental models: An interdisciplinary synthesis of theory and methods. *Ecology and Society*, 16(1), 46 [Online]. Available at: http://www.ecologyandsociety.org/vol16/iss1/art46/.

Kabil, A., Brézillon, P., Kubickki, S. (2015). Contextual interface for operator–simulator interaction. In *Modeling and Using Context (CONTEXT-15)*. Springer, Cham, 483–488.

Karsenty, L. and Brézillon, P. (1995). Cooperative problem solving and explanation. *International Journal of Expert Systems With Applications*, 4, 445–462.

Klein, G.A. and Calderwood, R. (1991). Decision models: Some lessons from the field. *IEEE Transactions on Systems, Man, and Cybernetics*, 21(5), 1018–1026.

Klein, G.A., Moon, B., Hoffman, R.R. (2006). Making sense of sensemaking 1: Alternative perspectives. *IEEE Intelligent Systems*, 21(4), 71–73.

Koenig, G. (1996). *Management stratégique: paradoxes, interactions et apprentissage*. Nathan, Paris.

Konopasky, A., Artino, A.R., Battista, A., Ohmer, M., Hemmer, P.A., Torre, D., Ramani, D., van Merrienboer, J., Teunissen, P.W., McBee, E., Ratcliffe, T., Durning, S.J. (2020). Understanding context specificity: The effect of contextual factors on clinical reasoning. *Diagnosis*, 7(3), 257–264. doi: 10.1515/dx-2020-0016.

Laird, J.E., Newell, A., Rosenbloom. P.S. (1987). Soar: An architecture for general intelligence. *Artificial Intelligence*, 33(1), 1–64.

Landauer, C. and Bellman, K. (1993). The role of self-referential logics in a software architecture using wrappings. In *ISS'93: Proceedings of 3rd Irvine Software Symposium*, Irvine, 1–12.

Law, A.M. and Kelton, W.D. (2000). *Simulation Modeling & Analysis*, 3rd edition. McGraw-Hill, New York.

Leplat, J. and Hoc, J.M. (1983). Tâche et activité dans l'analyse psychologique des situations. *Cahiers de Psychologie Cognitive*, 3, 49–63.

Lévine, P. and Pomerol, J.Ch. (1995). The role of the Decision Maker in DSSs and representation levels. In *Proceedings of the 28th Hawaï International Conference on System Science*, 42–51.

Logan, G.D. (1988). Automaticity, resources and memory: Theoretical controversies and practical implications. *Human Factors*, 30(5), 583–598.

Logan-Young, W. and Hoffman, N.Y. (1994). *Breast Cancer: A Practical Guide to Diagnosis*. Mt Hope, Rochester, NY.

Mansharamani, R. (1997). An overview of discrete event simulation methodologies and implementation. *Sadhana*, 22(Part 5), 611–627

McCarthy, J. (1993). Notes on formalizing context. *IJCAI*, 555–560.

McEwan, E.K. (1997). *Leading your Team to Excellence: How to Make Quality Decisions.* Thousand Oaks, CA.

Miller, G.A. (1956). The magic number seven plus or minus two: Some limits on our capacity for processing information. *Psychological Review*, 63, 91–97.

Miller, R.A., Pople, H.E., Myers, J.D. (1982). INTERNIST–1, an experimental computer-based diagnostic consultant for general internal medicine. *New England Journal of Medicine*, 307, 468–476.

Most, S.B., Scholl, B.J., Clifford, E.R., Simons, D.J. (2005). What you see is what you set: Sustained inattentional blindness and the capture of awareness. *Psychological Review*, 112, 217–242.

MUSTIL Team (1996). Sur la notion de modèle en Informatique. Internal report 96/12, LAFORIA, University Paris 6.

Nersessian, N.J. (2002). The cognitive basis of model-based reasoning in science. In *The Cognitive Basis of Science*, Carruthers, P., Stich, S., Siegal, M. (eds). Cambridge University Press, Cambridge, 133–153.

Pasquier, L. (2002). Modélisation de raisonnement tenus en contexte. Application à la gestion d'incidents sur une ligne de métro. Thesis, Université Paris 6.

Pasquier, L., Brézillon, P., Pomerol, J.-C. (2000). From representation of operational knowledge to practical decision making in operations. *Decision Support Through Knowledge Management*, 301–320.

Paterno, F., Mancini, C., Meniconi, S. (1997). ConcurTaskTrees: A diagrammatic notation for specifying task models. In *Human-Computer Interaction, INTERACT'97*, 362–369.

Peirce, C.S. (1931-1958). *Collected Writings* (8 Vols). Hartshorne, C., Weiss, P., Burks, A.W. (eds). Harvard University Press, Cambridge, MA.

Peräaho, M., Keskinen, E., Hatakka, M. (2003). Driver competence in a hierarchicalperspective; implication for driver education. Traffic Research, University of Turku, Turku.

Perault-Staub, A.M., Staub, J.F., Milhaud, G. (1975). Constancy and rhythmicity, a dual concept for homeostasis exemplified by 24 hours plasma calcium regulation in the rat. In *Calcium-Regulating Hormones*, Talmage, R.V., Owen, M., Parsons, J.A. (eds). Excerpta Medica, Amsterdam, 229–238.

Perera, C., Zaslavsky, A.B., Christen, P., Georgakopoulos, D. (2014). Context aware computing for the internet of things: A survey. *IEEE Communications Surveys and Tutorials*, 16(1), 414–454.

Pomerol, J.-Ch. and Brézillon, P. (1999). Dynamics between contextual knowledge and proceduralized context. In *Modeling and Using Context (CONTEXT-99)*. Springer, Berlin, Heidelberg, 284–295.

Pomerol, J.-Ch., Brézillon, P., Pasquier, L. (2002). Operational knowledge representation for practical decision making. *Journal of Management Information Systems (JMIS)*, 18(4), 101–116.

Pook, S., Lecolinet, E., Vaysseix, G., Barillot, E. (2000). Context and interaction in Zoomable User Interfaces. In *AVI 2000 Conference Proceedings*. ACM Press, 227–231.

Radjou, N., Prabhu, J., Ahuja, S. (2013). *L'innovation Jugaad*. Diateino Editions, Paris.

Richard, J.F. (1983). Logique du fonctionnement et logique de l'utilisation. INRIA Research Report No 202.

Richard, J.F. (1990). *Les activités mentales. Comprendre, raisonner, trouver des solutions*. Armand Colin, Paris.

Robertson, W.G. (1982). The solubility concept. In *Biological Mineralisation and Demineralisation*, Nancollas G.H. (ed.). Springer, Berlin, Heidelberg, 5–22.

Rosa, M.G.P., Borges, M.R.S., Santoro, F.M. (2006). A conceptual framework for analyzing the use of context in groupware. In *CSCWD 2006*. Springer, Berlin, Heidelberg, 300–313.

Russell, N., Hofstede, A.H.M., van der Aalst, W.M.P., Mulyar, N. (2006). Workflow control-flow patterns: A revised view. BPM Center Report BPM-06-22, BPMcenter.org.

Salber, D., Dey, A.K., Abowd, G.D. (1999). The context toolkit: Aiding the development of context-enabled applications. In *The SIGCHI Conference on Human Factors in Computing Systems (CHI '99)*. ACM, New York, 434–441.

Sarrazin, P., Biddle, S., Famose, J.-P., Cury, F., Fox, K., Durand, M. (1996). Goal orientations and conceptions of the nature of sport ability in children: A social cognitive approach. *British Journal of Social Psychology*, 35, 399–414.

Saussure, F. (1916). *Cours de linguistique générale* [General Course in Linguistics]. Payot, Paris.

Schank, R.C. (1982). *Dynamic Memory: A Theory of Learning in Computers and People*. Cambridge University Press, New York.

Schank, R.C. and Abelson, R.P. (1995). Knowledge and memory: The real story. In *Knowledge and Memory: The Real Story*, Wyer, R.S. Jr (ed.). Lawrence Erlbaum Associates, Inc, Hillsdale, NJ, 1–85.

Scott, W.A. (2011). Best practices? Practices are "best" only in context [Online]. Available at: https://www.ambysoft.com/essays/bestPractices.html [Accessed October 2025].

Shepherd, A. (2001). *Hierarchical Task Analysis*. CRC Press, London.

Sieck, W.R., Deborah, G.K., Peluso, A., Smith, J.L., Harris-Thompson, D. (2007). Focus: A model of sense making. Technical Report 1200, Research Institute for the Behavioral and Social Sciences.

Simons, D.J. (2000). Attentional capture and inattentional blindness. *Trends in Cognitive Sciences*, 4(4), 147–161.

SoftwareSim (2022). A gentle introduction to discrete event simulation [Online]. Available at: https://softwaresim.com/blog/a-gentle-introduction-to-discrete-event-simulation/ [Accessed 3 March 2025].

Sowa, J.F. (2000). *Knowledge Representation: Logical, Philosophical, and Computational Foundations*. Brooks Cole Publishing Co, Pacific Grove, CA.

Stanton, N.A. (2004). The psychology of task analysis today. In *The Handbook of Task Analysis for Human-Computer Interaction*, Diaper, D. and Stanton, N.A. (eds). Lawrence Erlbaum Associates, Mahwah, NJ, 569–584.

Swyngedouw, E. (2004). Globalisation or 'glocalisation'? Networks, territories and rescaling. *Cambridge Review of International Affairs*, 17(1).

Tahir, H. and Brézillon, P. (2013). Contextual graphs platform as a basis for designing a context-based intelligent assistant system. In *Modeling and Using Context (CONTEXT-13)*. Springer, Berlin, Heidelberg, 259–273.

Torres da Silva, V., Choren, R., Pereira de Lucena, C.J. (2005). Using the UML 2.0 activity diagram to model agent plans and actions. In *4th International Joint Conference on Autonomous Agents and Multiagent Systems (AAMAS'05)*. Springer, Berlin, Heidelberg, 594–600.

Turner, R.M. (1994). *Adaptive Reasoning for Real-World Problems: A Schema-Based Approach*. Lawrence Erlbaum Associates, Hillsdale, NJ.

Turner, R.M. (1998). Context-mediated behavior for intelligent agents. *International Journal of Human–Computer Studies*, 48(3), 307–330.

Turner, R.M. (2022). Pragmatic reasoning in context: Context-mediated behavior. In *Modeling and Using Context in Action*, Brézillon, P. and Turner, R.M. (eds). ISTE Ltd, London and John Wiley & Sons, New York.

Turner, R.M. and Brézillon, P. (2022). Toward pragmatic context-based systems. In *Modeling and Using Context in Action*, Brézillon, P. and Turner, R.M. (eds). ISTE Ltd, London and John Wiley & Sons, New York.

Valdes, J., Tarjan, R.E., Lawler, E.L. (1979). The recognition of series parallel digraphs. In *Proceedings of the Annual ACM Symposium on Theory of Computing*, 1–12. doi: 10.1145/800135.804393.

Van Elslande, P. (1992). Les erreurs d'interprétation en conduite automobile : mauvaise catégorisation ou activation erronée de schémas? *Intellectica*, 15(3), 125–149.

Vieira, V., Brézillon, P., Salgado, A.C., Tedesco, P. (2007). Towards a generic contextual elements model to support context management. In *Proceedings of the Fourth International Workshop on Modeling and Reasoning in Context* (MRC-2007), 49–59.

Watson, I. and Perera, S. (1998). A hierarchical case representation using context guided retrieval. *Knowledge Based Systems Journal*, 11(5–6), 285–292.

Weick, K.E. (1995). *Sensemaking in Organization*. Sage Publication, Thousand Oaks, CA.

Woods, D.D. (1985). Cognitive technologies: The design of joint human–machine cognitive systems. *AI Magazine,* 6(4), 86–92.

Wyer, R.S., Jr. (2007). Principles of mental representation. In *Social Psychology: Handbook of Basic Principles*, Van Lange, P.A.M., Higgins, E.T., Kruglanski, A.W. (eds). The Guilford Press, New York and London, 285–307.

Ziegler, B.P. (1976). *Theory of Modelling and Simulation.* John Wiley & Sons, New York.

Zwaan, R.A. and Radvansky, G.A. (1998). Situation models in language comprehension and memory. *Psychological Bulletin*, 123, 162–185.

Index

A, B

activity, 11, 54, 112, 162
  modeling, 161
actor/actor's
  activity, 165
  experience, 54, 163
  reasoning, 163
acyclic and directed graph, 8
base of experiences, 10
branches, 74
browsing, 209

C, D

CIAS's line of reasoning, 207
communication, 211
context
  knowledge and reasoning, 104
  of an activity, 217
context-based explanations, 208
    intelligent assistant systems, 207
contextual
  element, 60, 164
  graph, 21, 59, 72, 168
    and tree representations, 143
  knowledge, 55
  nodes, 33
  reasoning, 105, 164, 167, 168, 170
Contextualization, Decontextualization and Recontextualization (CDR), 42, 177
CxG (Contextual Graphs), 71
  _1.0 version, 71
  -based simulation/simulator, 118, 128, 131, 163, 166, 172, 211
  formalism, 71
  path, 21, 54
  software, 72, 211
decision making, 12, 70, 157

E, F

ESIA (Executive structure of Independent Activities), 77
experience base, 157
focus of attention, 55, 162
four sources of context, 27, 56

G, H

generic framework, 47
glocalization, 179
good and bad practices, 40
group
  activity, 113, 121, 165
  decision making, 153
  experience, 165
human reasoning, 11

I, K

incremental knowledge acquisition, 210
independent subtask, 124
instantiation, 68
  process, 163
Intelligent Assistant Systems (IASs), 206
interaction, 122
knowledge, 55

L, M

learning by
  accommodation, 170, 210
  assimilation, 170, 210
loops in a directed and acyclic graph, 127
mental model, 12, 58, 70
  development, 20
  tree view, 170
mental representation, 12, 20, 21, 56, 70
model, 2

N, O

nonlinear reasonings, 153
onion metaphor, 46, 61
operational knowledge, 63, 163
operator-simulator interaction, 148

P, R

pair of contextual and recombination nodes, 10, 75, 164
practical reasoning, 58
proceduralization, 56
proceduralized context, 21, 57, 80, 89, 163, 167
reasoning, 70, 164
reserved contextual element(s) (RCE), 125, 166

S, T

sense making, 16
shared context, 113, 128, 131, 165
simulation of a contextual reasoning, 22
situation, 162
task realization, 51
training, 211, 214
turn, 117
  management, 123
  sequence, 124

V, W

voting system, 35, 81
working context, 80

Other titles from

iSTE

in

Information Systems, Web and Pervasive Computing

2025

ABEL Marie-Hélène, MATTA Nada, KARRAY Hedi, SAAD Inès
Ethics and Digital Transition

BATTA Priya, KUMAR Abhishek, MANOJ S. Oswalt, CHINNATHAMBI Dhaya, RAVI Srivel
Sustainable Supply Chains and Carbon Footprint Reduction: The Blockchain Advantage

DJOUAD Anaïs
The Hypermodernity Factory: Working with Relational Technologies
Intellectual Technologies Set – Volume 10)

KUMAR Abhishek, BATTA Priya, MANOJ S. Oswalt, CHINNATHAMBI Dhaya, RAVI Srivel
Blockchain and the Water Supply Chain: Opportunities, Challenges and Innovations

STOCKINGER Peter
The Art of Communication: Semiotic Foundations and Strategic using Applications

2024

ALBAN Daniel, EYNAUD Philippe, RICHET Jean-Loup, VITARI Claudio
Information Systems Management: Governance, Urbanization and Alignment – 2nd edition

PINET François, BATTON-HUBERT Mireille, DESJARDIN Eric
Geographical Data Imperfection 2: Use Cases

SEDKAOUI Soraya
Automated Data Analytics: Combining Human Creativity and AI Power using ChatGPT

2023

POMEROL Jean-Charles
Action in Uncertainty: Expertise, Decision and Crisis Management

REVEST Valérie, LIOTARD Isabelle
Digital Transformation and Public Policies: Current Issues

2022

ACCART Jean-Philippe
Library Transformation Strategies

BEN REBAH Hassen, BOUKTHIR Hafedh, CHÉDEBOIS Antoine
Website Design and Development with HTML5 and CSS3

BOADA Martí, LAZARO Antonio, GIRBAU David, VILLARINO Ramón
Battery-less NFC Sensors for the Internet of Things

BRÉZILLON Patrick, TURNER Roy M.
Modeling and Use of Context in Action

CHAMOUX Jean-Pierre
The Digital Era 3: Customs and Practices

KARAM Elie
General Contractor Business Model for Smart Cities: Fundamentals and Techniques

LAURENT Sébastien-Yves
Conflicts, Crimes and Regulations in Cyberspace
(Cybersecurity Set – Volume 2)

2021

EL ASSAD Safwan, BARBA Dominique
Digital Communications 1: Fundamentals and Techniques
Digital Communications 2: Directed and Practical Work

GAUDIN Thierry, MAUREL Marie-Christine, POMEROL Jean-Charles
Chance, Calculation and Life

LE DEUFF Olivier
Hyperdocumentation
(Intellectual Technologies Set – Volume 9)

PÉLISSIER Maud
Cultural Commons in the Digital Ecosystem
(Intellectual Technologies Set – Volume 8)

2020

CLIQUET Gérard, with the collaboration of BARAY Jérôme
Location-Based Marketing: Geomarketing and Geolocation

DE FRÉMINVILLE Marie
Cybersecurity and Decision Makers: Data Security and Digital Trust

GEORGE Éric
Digitalization of Society and Socio-political Issues 2: Digital, Information and Research

HELALI Saida
Systems and Network Infrastructure Integration

LOISEAU Hugo, VENTRE Daniel, ADEN Hartmut
Cybersecurity in Humanities and Social Sciences: A Research Methods Approach (Cybersecurity Set – Volume 1)

SEDKAOUI Soraya, KHELFAOUI Mounia
Sharing Economy and Big Data Analytics

SCHMITT Églantine
Big Data: An Art of Decision Making
(Intellectual Technologies Set – Volume 7)

2019

ALBAN Daniel, EYNAUD Philippe, MALAURENT Julien, RICHET Jean-Loup, VITARI Claudio
Information Systems Management: Governance, Urbanization and Alignment

AUGEY Dominique, with the collaboration of ALCARAZ Marina
Digital Information Ecosystems: Smart Press

BATTON-HUBERT Mireille, DESJARDIN Eric, PINET François
Geographic Data Imperfection 1: From Theory to Applications

BRIQUET-DUHAZÉ Sophie, TURCOTTE Catherine
From Reading-Writing Research to Practice

BROCHARD Luigi, KAMATH Vinod, CORBALAN Julita, HOLLAND Scott, MITTELBACH Walter, OTT Michael
Energy-Efficient Computing and Data Centers

CHAMOUX Jean-Pierre
The Digital Era 2: Political Economy Revisited

COCHARD Gérard-Michel
Introduction to Stochastic Processes and Simulation

DUONG Véronique
SEO Management: Methods and Techniques to Achieve Success

GAUCHEREL Cédric, GOUYON Pierre-Henri, DESSALLES Jean-Louis
Information, The Hidden Side of Life

GEORGE Éric
Digitalization of Society and Socio-political Issues 1: Digital, Communication and Culture

GHLALA Riadh
Analytic SQL in SQL Server 2014/2016

JANIER Mathilde, SAINT-DIZIER Patrick
Argument Mining: Linguistic Foundations

SOURIS Marc
Epidemiology and Geography: Principles, Methods and Tools of Spatial Analysis

TOUNSI Wiem
Cyber-Vigilance and Digital Trust: Cyber Security in the Era of Cloud Computing and IoT

2018

ARDUIN Pierre-Emmanuel
Insider Threats
(Advances in Information Systems Set – Volume 10)

CARMÈS Maryse
Digital Organizations Manufacturing: Scripts, Performativity and Semiopolitics
(Intellectual Technologies Set – Volume 5)

CARRÉ Dominique, VIDAL Geneviève
Hyperconnectivity: Economical, Social and Environmental Challenges
(Computing and Connected Society Set – Volume 3)

CHAMOUX Jean-Pierre
The Digital Era 1: Big Data Stakes

DOUAY Nicolas
Urban Planning in the Digital Age
(Intellectual Technologies Set – Volume 6)

FABRE Renaud, BENSOUSSAN Alain
The Digital Factory for Knowledge: Production and Validation of Scientific Results

GAUDIN Thierry, LACROIX Dominique, MAUREL Marie-Christine, POMEROL Jean-Charles
Life Sciences, Information Sciences

GAYARD Laurent
Darknet: Geopolitics and Uses
(Computing and Connected Society Set – Volume 2)

IAFRATE Fernando
Artificial Intelligence and Big Data: The Birth of a New Intelligence
(Advances in Information Systems Set – Volume 8)

LE DEUFF Olivier
Digital Humanities: History and Development
(Intellectual Technologies Set – Volume 4)

MANDRAN Nadine
Traceable Human Experiment Design Research: Theoretical Model and Practical Guide
(Advances in Information Systems Set – Volume 9)

PIVERT Olivier
NoSQL Data Models: Trends and Challenges

ROCHET Claude
Smart Cities: Reality or Fiction

SALEH Imad, AMMI, Mehdi, SZONIECKY Samuel
Challenges of the Internet of Things: Technology, Use, Ethics
(Digital Tools and Uses Set – Volume 7)

SAUVAGNARGUES Sophie
Decision-making in Crisis Situations: Research and Innovation for Optimal Training

SEDKAOUI Soraya
Data Analytics and Big Data

SZONIECKY Samuel
Ecosystems Knowledge: Modeling and Analysis Method for Information and Communication
(Digital Tools and Uses Set – Volume 6)

2017

BOUHAÏ Nasreddine, SALEH Imad
Internet of Things: Evolutions and Innovations
(Digital Tools and Uses Set – Volume 4)

DUONG Véronique
Baidu SEO: Challenges and Intricacies of Marketing in China

LESAS Anne-Marie, MIRANDA Serge
The Art and Science of NFC Programming
(Intellectual Technologies Set – Volume 3)

LIEM André
Prospective Ergonomics
(Human-Machine Interaction Set – Volume 4)

MARSAULT Xavier
Eco-generative Design for Early Stages of Architecture
(Architecture and Computer Science Set – Volume 1)

REYES-GARCIA Everardo
The Image-Interface: Graphical Supports for Visual Information
(Digital Tools and Uses Set – Volume 3)

REYES-GARCIA Everardo, BOUHAÏ Nasreddine
Designing Interactive Hypermedia Systems
(Digital Tools and Uses Set – Volume 2)

SAÏD Karim, BAHRI KORBI Fadia
Asymmetric Alliances and Information Systems:Issues and Prospects
(Advances in Information Systems Set – Volume 7)

SZONIECKY Samuel, BOUHAÏ Nasreddine
Collective Intelligence and Digital Archives: Towards Knowledge Ecosystems
(Digital Tools and Uses Set – Volume 1)

2016

BEN CHOUIKHA Mona
Organizational Design for Knowledge Management

BERTOLO David
Interactions on Digital Tablets in the Context of 3D Geometry Learning
(Human-Machine Interaction Set – Volume 2)

BOUVARD Patricia, SUZANNE Hervé
Collective Intelligence Development in Business

EL FALLAH SEGHROUCHNI Amal, ISHIKAWA Fuyuki, HÉRAULT Laurent, TOKUDA Hideyuki
Enablers for Smart Cities

FABRE Renaud, in collaboration with MESSERSCHMIDT-MARIET Quentin, HOLVOET Margot
New Challenges for Knowledge

GAUDIELLO Ilaria, ZIBETTI Elisabetta
Learning Robotics, with Robotics, by Robotics
(Human-Machine Interaction Set – Volume 3)

HENROTIN Joseph
The Art of War in the Network Age
(Intellectual Technologies Set – Volume 1)

KITAJIMA Munéo
Memory and Action Selection in Human–Machine Interaction
(Human–Machine Interaction Set – Volume 1)

LAGRAÑA Fernando
E-mail and Behavioral Changes: Uses and Misuses of Electronic Communications

LEIGNEL Jean-Louis, UNGARO Thierry, STAAR Adrien
Digital Transformation
(Advances in Information Systems Set – Volume 6)

MONINO Jean-Louis, SEDKAOUI Soraya
Big Data, Open Data and Data Development
(Smart Innovation Set – Volume 3)

NOYER Jean-Max
Transformation of Collective Intelligences
(Intellectual Technologies Set – Volume 2)

VENTRE Daniel
Information Warfare – 2nd edition

VITALIS André
The Uncertain Digital Revolution
(Computing and Connected Society Set – Volume 1)

2015

ARDUIN Pierre-Emmanuel, GRUNDSTEIN Michel, ROSENTHAL-SABROUX Camille
Information and Knowledge System
(Advances in Information Systems Set – Volume 2)

BÉRANGER Jérôme
Medical Information Systems Ethics

BRONNER Gérald
Belief and Misbelief Asymmetry on the Internet

IAFRATE Fernando
From Big Data to Smart Data
(Advances in Information Systems Set – Volume 1)

KRICHEN Saoussen, BEN JOUIDA Sihem
Supply Chain Management and its Applications in Computer Science

NEGRE Elsa
Information and Recommender Systems
(Advances in Information Systems Set – Volume 4)

POMEROL Jean-Charles, EPELBOIN Yves, THOURY Claire
MOOCs

SAAD Inès, ROSENTHAL-SABROUX Camille, GARGOURI Faïez
Information Systems for Knowledge Management

SALLES Maryse
Decision-Making and the Information System
(Advances in Information Systems Set – Volume 3)

SAMARA Tarek
ERP and Information Systems: Integration or Disintegration
(Advances in Information Systems Set – Volume 5)

2014

DINET Jérôme
Information Retrieval in Digital Environments

DUBÉ Jean, LEGROS Diègo
Spatial Econometrics Using Microdata

HÉNO Raphaële, CHANDELIER Laure
3D Modeling of Buildings: Outstanding Sites

KEMBELLEC Gérald, CHARTRON Ghislaine, SALEH Imad
Recommender Systems

MATHIAN Hélène, SANDERS Lena
Spatio-temporal Approaches: Geographic Objects and Change Process

PLANTIN Jean-Christophe
Participatory Mapping

RIGO Michel
Formal Languages, Automata and Numeration Systems 1: Introduction to Combinatorics on Words
Formal Languages, Automata and Numeration Systems 2: Applications to Recognizability and Decidability

TORRES-MORENO Juan-Manuel
Automatic Text Summarization

VENTRE Daniel
Chinese Cybersecurity and Defense

2013

BERNIK Igor
Cybercrime and Cyberwarfare

CAPET Philippe, DELAVALLADE Thomas
Information Evaluation

LEBRATY Jean-Fabrice, LOBRE-LEBRATY Katia
Crowdsourcing: One Step Beyond

SALLABERRY Christian
Geographical Information Retrieval in Textual Corpora

TURENNE Nicolas
Knowledge Needs and Information Extraction: Towards an Artificial Consciousness

2012

BUCHER Bénédicte, LE BER Florence
Innovative Software Development in GIS

GAUSSIER Eric, YVON François
Textual Information Access

STOCKINGER Peter
Audiovisual Archives: Digital Text and Discourse Analysis

VENTRE Daniel
Cyber Conflict

2011

BANOS Arnaud, THÉVENIN Thomas
Geographical Information and Urban Transport Systems

DAUPHINÉ André
Fractal Geography

LEMBERGER Pirmin, MOREL Mederic
Managing Complexity of Information Systems

STOCKINGER Peter
Introduction to Audiovisual Archives

STOCKINGER Peter
Digital Audiovisual Archives

VENTRE Daniel
Cyberwar and Information Warfare

2010

BONNET Pierre
Enterprise Data Governance

BRUNET Roger
Sustainable Geography

BUFFET Olivier, SIGAUD Olivier
Markov Decision Processes in Artificial Intelligence

CARREGA Pierre
Geographical Information and Climatology

CAUVIN Colette, ESCOBAR Francisco, SERRADJ Aziz
Thematic Cartography – 3-volume series
Thematic Cartography and Transformations – Volume 1
Cartography and the Impact of the Quantitative Revolution – Volume 2
New Approaches in Thematic Cartography – Volume 3

LANGLOIS Patrice
Simulation of Complex Systems in GIS

MATHIS Philippe
Graphs and Networks – 2nd edition

THERIAULT Marius, DES ROSIERS François
Modeling Urban Dynamics

2009

BONNET Pierre, DETAVERNIER Jean-Michel, VAUQUIER Dominique
Sustainable IT Architecture: the Progressive Way of Overhauling Information Systems with SOA

PAPY Fabrice
Information Science

RIVARD François, ABOU HARB Georges, MERET Philippe
The Transverse Information System

ROCHE Stéphane, CARON Claude
Organizational Facets of GIS

VENTRE Daniel
Information Warfare

2008

BRUGNOT Gérard
Spatial Management of Risks

FINKE Gerd
Operations Research and Networks

GUERMOND Yves
Modeling Process in Geography

KANEVSKI Michael
Advanced Mapping of Environmental Data

MANOUVRIER Bernard, LAURENT Ménard
Application Integration: EAI, B2B, BPM and SOA

PAPY Fabrice
Digital Libraries

2007

DOBESCH Hartwig, DUMOLARD Pierre, DYRAS Izabela
Spatial Interpolation for Climate Data

SANDERS Lena
Models in Spatial Analysis

2006

CLIQUET Gérard
Geomarketing

CORNIOU Jean-Pierre
Looking Back and Going Forward in IT

DEVILLERS Rodolphe, JEANSOULIN Robert
Fundamentals of Spatial Data Quality

Printed and bound by CPI Group (UK) Ltd, Croydon, CR0 4YY

13/09/2026

14961014-0006